A Clash of Heroes

STUDIES IN JEWISH HISTORY
Jehuda Reinharz, General Editor

A Clash of Heroes

BRANDEIS, WEIZMANN, AND AMERICAN ZIONISM

Ben Halpern

New York   Oxford
OXFORD UNIVERSITY PRESS
1987

Oxford University Press

Oxford   New York   Toronto
Delhi   Bombay   Calcutta   Madras   Karachi
Petaling Jaya   Singapore   Hong Kong   Tokyo
Nairobi   Dar es Salaam   Cape Town
Melbourne   Auckland

and associated companies in
Beirut   Berlin   Ibadan   Nicosia

Library of Congress Cataloging-in-Publication Data
Halpern, Ben.
A clash of heroes—Brandeis, Weizmann,
and American Zionism.
(Studies in Jewish history)
Includes index.
1. Zionism—United States.   2. Brandeis, Louis
Dembitz, 1856–1941.   3. Weizmann, Chaim, 1874–1952.
4. Zionist Commission.   5. Zionists—Biography.
I. Title.   II. Series.
DS149.H338   1987   956.94′001′0922   86-23543
ISBN 0-19-504062-7

2 4 6 8 9 7 5 3 1

Printed in the United States of America
on acid-free paper

In Memoriam

HAYIM GREENBERG
1889–1953

Preface

This study was stimulated by a birthday celebration for the late Zalman Shazar (1889–1974, third president of Israel) held at the Zionist Congress in Jerusalem in 1968. On that occasion Shazar suggested that a comprehensive history of Zionism should be prepared as an appropriate birthday present for
him. A committee set up to consider the matter decided that such a history
would require a program of preliminary studies, which was duly initiated
with the support of the World Zionist Organization (WZO). The late Emanuel Neumann (1893–1980) gave steady and enthusiastic support to the project and was particularly concerned to see a proper study made of the American Zionist movement. This was a task I undertook as a member of the
committee and, especially, as a former aide to each of the men during my
years on the WZO staff.

For a number of years, accordingly, annual WZO research grants to Brandeis University enabled me to support doctoral studies by students interested
in Zionist, particularly American Zionist, history. The dissertations and subsequent publications that resulted, many of them cited hereafter, were a
major resource that made possible the present work. I was also generously
assisted in years past by the John Simon Guggenheim Foundation (1961–62),
the Social Science Research Council (summer 1965), and the National
Endowment for the Humanities (1970–71). The research developed during
the periods of leisure they made possible was most directly applied in training
and guiding students. The present volume is a welcome opportunity to
express my gratitude for the aid that contributed so much to this as well as
to my other labors over many years. During the composition of the study, I
was privileged to take part in Professor Shmuel Ettinger's seminar on nationalism at the Hebrew University's Institute for Advanced Studies in 1981–82;
in the final stages I was able to work closely with Professor Jehuda Reinharz
as an associate of the Tauber Institute for the Study of European Jewry,

headed by him, at Brandeis University. I am deeply indebted to both and to the institutions for the stimulating, collegial exchange of ideas I had the good fortune to share.

This, then, is a book to which friends, students, and colleagues—too many to be adequately acknowledged—have contributed by their conversation and their writing. It started as an act of piety and friendship, simply as a straight-forward narrative account of a part of American Zionist history. It was quickly diverted into the channel dug by previous work of my own in the field of sociologically oriented history, in particular into the problem of the relations between leaders and followers. Such a problem-oriented inquiry has only been possible because of the extensive documentary research of others, much of it completed in recent years. Rather than seeking to establish with accuracy the sequence of events, I have been able to rely heavily on the crit-ical studies that have recently appeared and to devote my main effort to anal-ysis and explanation and the methodological complexities of combining biog-raphy and history in a single study.

I have, accordingly, drawn heavily on published materials, documentary collections, and expository literature, except where the analysis required resorting to archival sources or in controversial cases. The voluminous pub-lication of Weizmann letters and papers makes virtually all significant cor-respondence in the Weizmann archives available to the general reader, and the extensive annotation provided is a convenient store of pertinent materials drawn from other archives that have been preserved. The published Brandeis papers are less comprehensive but still serve to document a major part of the argument. These circumstances have, I hope, enabled me to pose an explicit problem at the outset and deal with it by citing critically edited materials readily available to general readers. I trust that scholars will bear with the idiosyncrasies of a generalist with patience—for example, in the matter of the roughly phonetic and popular transcriptions of Hebrew expressions that I use—and will find something of interest in the concrete application attempted here of a problem-oriented historical-sociological approach.

Brookline, Massachusetts   B.H.
May 1986

Contents

A Clash of Heroes

Introduction:
Heroes and Their Public

Isaiah Berlin has spoken of Chaim Weizmann as a historic hero in a well-defined sense: one who altered his people's history in a way that would have been impossible but for his extraordinary gifts and achievements.[1] Weizmann's gifts were amply attested by many who did not share Berlin's personal regard for him. They regarded the British commitment to Zionism as a major error by statesmen who were fascinated by Weizmann's exotic oriental charm. As for achievement, if the restoration of a Jewish state could not have happened without Weizmann's efforts, he would certainly deserve to be called a hero in Berlin's sense for having brought it off.

But such a judgment can never be made conclusively. Toward the end of Weizmann's career, others, like David Ben-Gurion, made the decisions by which the Jewish state was proclaimed; in the sequel Weizmann was relegated to a purely ornamental office, president of Israel. Later, when the Begin government came to power, Weizmann's old rival Vladimir Jabotinsky was officially celebrated as the true hero of the period when Weizmann dominated Zionist history; Weizmann's role was revised to something between irrelevancy and villainy. The issue, in fact, is essentially polemical and not suitable for serious analysis.

A hero, in another sense, is one who is felt to embody the ideals of a people, to enact their values with exemplary character and talent. Such a man is a hero for his times, whether he leads on to glorious victory or to tragic defeat—and a hero for all times that appreciate the meaning of his life. This is a matter of history that is verifiable and may be analyzed with reasonable objectivity.

For American Jews Louis D. Brandeis is a hero universally revered, almost a patron saint. He made history by his contributions to American law. Modern America bears the imprint of legal doctrines enunciated by Justices Holmes and Brandeis and brought to fruition in the reform administrations

3

of Woodrow Wilson and Franklin D. Roosevelt. Both presidents esteemed
Brandeis' Puritan rigor—the biblical quality that made FDR habitually refer
to him as "Isaiah"—no less than his intellectual power.

All this was certainly enough to make Brandeis an object of pride for
American Jews. But they also felt sure of him as truly one of their own: a
great man not estranged from them, as so many eminent Jews were, but one
they could count on, who undertook, indeed, to lead them. This particular
eminence is one Brandeis enjoyed because of his role in the history of American Zionism.

A hero embodies the values and virtues esteemed by his admirers. A
leader is often chosen on other grounds. The leader of a subordinated group
may well be selected from its "periphery," as the psychologist Kurt Lewin
remarked: that is, he is qualified to lead the group because he masters the
skills and values required for dealing with the outsiders on whose goodwill
or tolerance the in-group depends.[2] Both Brandeis and Weizmann rose to
Zionist leadership in this way: Brandeis because of his prominence in American progressive politics; Weizmann because he enjoyed the confidence of the
British War Cabinet.

At the close of World War I, Brandeis and Weizmann came into sharp
conflict over the future direction of the Zionist work in Palestine. The differences, which seem fairly technical and rather minor in perspective, were said
by both antagonists to rest upon fundamental values. It was a conflict
between Washington and Pinsk, to use the imagery of the time: between the
personal styles of the two leaders, each exemplifying the characteristic values
of his following and his local background and each deprecating the style and
values of the other. Brandeisists disparaged their opponents as undisciplined,
incompetent, hysterical East Europeans; Weizmannites condemned the Brandeis coterie as American assimilationists.

The clash began at an international Zionist meeting in London in 1919
when Weizmann had to yield unwillingly to Brandeis' terms. It ended, to all
appearances, in Cleveland in 1921 at the convention of the Zionist Organization of America (ZOA) when Weizmann's American adherents defeated the
incumbent administration, controlled by the Brandeis group. American Zionism, it would appear, had decided in favor of Pinsk over Washington. But
appearances were not reliable, as soon became clear.

The crux of the dispute, the fault line from which other lines of cleavage
branched off, was the issue of an appropriate structure that would facilitate
non-Zionist cooperation in building the Jewish national home. Weizmann's
subsequent success in achieving this through an expanded Jewish Agency for
Palestine has been viewed as an adoption of Brandeis' conceptions. How
much of this contention is myth and how much reality is a matter for discussion. But it is clear that the American Zionist mainstream movement eventually developed into something much closer to the Brandeis than the Weizmann formula in their debate. With the rise of Israel, according to the current
clichés, all American Jewry has become "Zionist"—and precisely in the sense

that Brandeis hoped to achieve this goal. But here, too, one must examine what part is myth and what part reality.

These matters are the subject of the chapters that will follow. Here, by way of introduction, they will be examined in general terms.

Self-conscious Zionism regards itself as a revolutionary nationalist movement: that is, a movement radically altering the status of Jews by revising their traditional values, particularly those concerning their proper role in history. The Zionist revolution claims to change radically both the collective history and individual biographies of those who experience it. It arose out of a succession of crises that touched off major shifts in Jewish social structure—population movements, occupational change, new forms of organization—together with radical revisions in attitudes, most clearly expressed (and, many agree, originated) by exceptional individuals, the intellectual elite. This is the accepted doctrine. But we may ask: How far does the implied connection of history and biography go?[3]

The pogrom wave of 1881–82 in Russia clearly was a crisis that raised the flow of Jewish emigration from Eastern Europe to the level of an alarming problem. At the same time it was a traumatic shock for some Russified or semi-Russified young intellectuals with whom Zionism entered history. The tolerance of Russian progressives for anti-Jewish mob violence appalled such young Jews and made them seek reunion with the community from which they sprang. They perceived hostility to the Jews to be ingrained, a permanent condition in Gentile lands; no longer believing in emancipation by others, however liberal and enlightened, they now dedicated themselves to autoemancipation.

As they sought to return to their fathers' house, so the older, traditionalist community welcomed the prodigal sons returning. Thus the common crisis led some in both generations to combine in forming the Zionist movement. It was a movement composed in part of pious Jews, committed even earlier to aid the small Jewish community in Palestine and help immigrants to settle there. For such traditionalists pogroms were not a traumatic, disillusioning event that required a reevaluation of insecurely held values. They had a firmly fixed pattern of responses to what for them was a familiar aspect of the Jewish Exile, part of the anchorage of their well-established identity.

The movement (especially in its extensions in Western Europe and in cooperating bodies) also comprised some whose commitment to aid the Jews in Palestine was not conceived as an alternative to the liberal creed of emancipation and enlightenment, but as a direct expression of it. They were attached less to the new nationalist activism (though many were liberals of a particularly militant, activist kind) than to an older project of humanitarian philanthropy.

Thus the Zionist movement itself, from its earliest days, was an organization sustained by a variety of disparate impulses not related systematically to a single, consistent ideology. Frustrated in action by unfavorable conditions, early Zionism had a vigorous history of ideological debate. Disputes between pious and secularist Zionists and strains between nationalist and philanthropic tendencies in the movement were reflected in major new trends in Hebrew literature and the Yiddish and Russian-Jewish press. Young Zionists like Weizmann, who had to form their identity in the 1890s, were presented with more specific options than were the first generation, who responded to the pure, unqualified ethos of autoemancipation.

The identity a man achieves is tied to his relations to others and to values mutually held. A historic trauma experienced by a susceptible subject at a time when his identity is still unformed produces at the least a clear demand to choose. In the case of Zionism, what was clear initially were details of the situation involving values that were emotionally rejected: exile—the permanent hostility of Jewish-Gentile relations—and passive redemption—whether by emancipation or the Messiah. What Zionism proposed to do positively instead was much less definite, since anything at all that was intrinsically opposed to the rejected conditions was emotionally satisfying to the original, Zionist, activist impulse. For the generation whose identity was fixed in the trauma of the pogroms, the emotional core of Zionism—autoemancipation by any and all means—could serve as a sufficient biographic defining principle that imposed systematic order on values. Those maturing later, like Weizmann, were heirs to a different situation: collective history had closed off alternative Zionist options from one another, forcing choices among positive programs of action.

With Theodor Herzl's advent, the horizons of Zionism were expanded for both collective history and individual biography. In Western Europe and from Western perspectives, Zionism could show itself in emphatically political colors, raising its concentration on politics to the level of an ideological principle with other aspects of Jewish nationalism subordinated, if not ruled out. In Herzl's organization ideological divisions that had already developed in early Zionism, and new ones as well, emerged as Zionist parties. Also, the new West European recruits whom Herzl attracted to the movement came with different personal experiences of the "Jewish problem" than the Easterners.

Western Zionists in the fin de siècle did not face the disillusioning realization that emancipation would not be won, as did Russian Jews; nor did they experience its reversal, like their future descendants under Hitler. But their experience did encompass other anomalies and frustrations inherent in the Jewish problem after emancipation had been won. They saw the rise of racist, political antisemitism in Central Europe; and even after its (temporary) decline at the polls, they were exposed to continual slights by the antisemitic dueling fraternities and other students at the universities. For many, as for Herzl himself, this was the source of a resentful, wounded pride that eventually expressed itself in Zionism. What also contributed to that development were the expulsions of Russian Jews in 1891, many of whom made their way westward through Germany to seek new havens. German Jews generally, like Western Jews in other affected countries, were sensitive to the problem of antisemitism that the influx might raise for them, and they recognized a responsibility to seek a solution. Some, whose pride and sympathy led them to identify with the Russian refugees, found a solution and a Jewish focus for their own lives in Zionism.

An underlying anomaly persistently confronted the emancipated Jewries, applying with particular force to those detached from the synagogue. To be emancipated in a secular nation-state meant that Judaism was free to practice its separate cult but that a separate Jewish ethnicity should not persist. This posed certain problems even for Jewish religion; while a Reform movement arose that more or less fully accepted the consequences, more conservative Western Jews retained an attachment to the ethnicity still persisting in Eastern Europe and manifested for some in a new, attractive, modern way by the Zionists.

Synagogue-goers in one way or another found plausible adjustments to their emancipated status. The problem was far more troublesome, in principle, for Jews detached from religion, like Herzl or Max Nordau or like Brandeis in America. A Jewishness based on freedom of religion that left them still Jews, though irreligious, was a problematic status for which individualistic liberalism offered neither a reasonable explanation nor an excuse. One way of dealing with the matter was to dismiss it as of minor importance. But when personal or collective crises precluded such an escape, there were only two ways to go: the way of Jewish self-denial or the way of Jewish pride. Pride led Brandeis and others like him to Zionism.

The old quarrel over the hero in history—whether the genius and virtue of individuals or the statistical laws of mass action determine events—can be made to seem trivial under the cold eye of common sense. A movement like Zionism is made up of small groups of leaders who decide matters and (large or small) masses of members to whom they are (periodically or irregularly, immediately or remotely) accountable. In a small executive group, the personal backgrounds, values, and relationships of a few leaders are obviously highly significant in shaping decisions. In the response of the mass following, it is the impersonal statistical balance of the diverse impulses swaying popular moods—as in price movements in mass markets or fluctuating ratings in opinion polls—that has to be considered.

The objective nature of the issues to be decided, of course, also determines the course of any movement's history. The best outcome, from the perspective of the dominant leaders or popular opinion, may or may not be the one that objective conditions compel. The factors decisive in one case are often unrelated to those that apply to others; but sometimes they may converge to produce the same, or similar, effects.

A time when the hero, the mass, and the objective occasion came together in a single dynamic impulsion would clearly be one of high historic significance. Just such a conjunction is the model on which Erik Erikson's psychohistorical studies of Luther and Gandhi purport to be based. This has become something of a cliché in recent studies of history from the vantage point of the hero. Both Brandeis and Weizmann have been described as heroes of a generation. They are pictured as having addressed themselves to the central objective need of a community: Brandeis to that of American Jewry; Weizmann to that of prenatal Israel. They are said to have embodied the crucial experiences and offered a personal resolution of a generational crisis.

It in no way depreciates the value of such a model if one notes that whether, or how far, it applies in any particular case is a matter for empirical investigation. The following chapters attempt this for the case of Brandeis, Weizmann, and American Zionism.

1

Weizmann

Childhood in Russia

Chaim Weizmann was a natural Zionist from childhood. He was seven years old when the Russian pogroms of 1881–82 precipitated a tide of emigration and set off the Zionist movement.[1] The shock of these events reached into the far corners of Russian Jewry, and the boy's native village of Motol with its two hundred Jewish families, although untouched by violence, provided its share of emigrants. When he was eleven Weizmann was sent away by the family to Pinsk, some twenty-five miles distant, to study at the Russian secondary school, the *Realgymnasium*. He lived there for the first few years with his aunt and elder brother, then by himself until the age of eighteen. By the time he was fifteen, the town of Pinsk had turned him from a natural to an active Zionist.

The early Zionophile (Hibbat Zion) movement was an odd mixture of traditionalist and secularist Jews. The relationship proved difficult for both sides. The prodigal sons found the religious conformity demanded of them to be more than their conscience could bear. Orthodox Zionists were outraged by impieties committed by secularist comrades. Many on both sides left the movement as bitter opponents.

Those of more moderate temper who remained were under attack on either flank. The pious Zionists were loudly criticized in Orthodox circles for consorting with sinners who desecrated the sacred traditions and the Holy Land. The Zionist intelligentsia, at a time of increasing Russian-Jewish radicalism, were castigated by the class-conscious avant-garde for collaborating with clerical reactionaries and the bourgeoisie. The same issues, and others more intramural, were argued among the Zionists themselves; but, given the repeated frustrations of the movement under its legal and political handicaps in Palestine and Russia, these ideological polemics were distinguished for vigor and ingenuity more than for their practical bearing and effect.

9

It needed a specially favorable milieu to rear a natural Zionist in those years. Pinsk supplied a haven of loyalty and moderate conservatism in the contemporary Zionist wilderness. Weizmann attended the synagogue of Rabbi David Friedman, one of the few Orthodox luminaries sympathetic to Hibbat Zion. Zvi Hirsch Maslianski (in later years an immensely popular lecturer in the American Yiddish-speaking community) was then beginning his career in Pinsk. Weizmann's memoirs recall as local heroes the Eisenbergs and Shertoks (parents of Israel's first foreign minister, Moshe Sharett), pioneer families who went to farm the land of Palestine. He reports with pride that collections from the households assigned to him set records for small donations to the Zionist cause in Pinsk.

Weizmann's childhood situation was not precisely a standard one for "normal" development, but neither was it unprecedented in the Jewish Pale of Settlement. His parents both appear in his memoirs as benign but not very decisive figures. His father, a lumber merchant, was frequently absent, as his work kept him away in the marshes or on the river or canals, overseeing the felling, hauling, and floating of timber to the market in Danzig. His mother, Weizmann says, was the family's central figure, but she too was "always either pregnant, or nursing an infant, so that she had little strength left for her growing brood."[2] He himself was sent to live with his grandparents when the next sibling in succession was expected.

If the children were "left pretty much to [them]selves," there was the compensation that Weizmann recalled neither parent as a harsh, or even strong, authoritarian person. He remembers his father as a mild, somewhat melancholy man, who "on the whole . . . did not dislike" his work and who "seldom preached at us." His mother, in later years after Weizmann had left home, became a more "vital" participant in the freewheeling—even child-dominated—Weizmann ménage; but her role is pictured as one of undiscriminating support for grownup offspring whose ideas and activities she could only tolerate, but not share. While Weizmann was a child at home, discipline was maintained by a "maid-of-all-work, adviser, family retainer—and family tyrant. She bossed all the children, and occasionally mother, too."[3]

Clearly, these recollections in Weizmann's old age greatly underrate both the strength of his parents and his own ties to them. His sister Haya's memoirs depict a far more impressive father and mother; the regular contributions of funds Weizmann supplied for his siblings' professional education (as well as his constant reminders to his fiancée that she must visit his parents) betray a powerful filial dependency and devotion well into his mature years. It remains true that in his autobiography Weizmann shows us a mother he loved, but found amusing, and a father he loved, but also pitied: in both cases his parents were not recalled as a strong presence in his childhood. Such memories could be read as suggesting lingering feelings of neglect—and Weizmann might have felt they revealed a bit too much. For he adds, "It is perhaps an exaggeration to say that we were often left to ourselves. In father's absences, the *Rebbi* [his teacher] stood in *loco parentis*. And then there were uncles and aunts without number."[4]

Like other shtetl children, the Weizmann brood were well supplied with parental surrogates in their extended family and village milieu. But Weizmann does appear exceptional in the intensity of his bonds with substitute parents. For two or three years in early childhood, he was sent to live in his grandparents' big house, which adjoined his family's home. When the old man was widowed, he moved with his beloved grandson into the Weizmann home, where his special relation with the child continued. The youngster was also the particular favorite of his Rebbi and of his uncle, a childless man who formally adopted Chaim as his son—probably to afford him protection from conscription. When he was living alone in Pinsk in his teens, Weizmann would spend summers with his uncle, floating down the Polish streams part of the way to Danzig on a raft of logs. His vacation visits home during that time were gala events, rejoiced in by the family and friends near and far, as his sister Haya recalls.[5]

Weizmann's family stood relatively high in the class and economic scale of the Pale of Settlement. His father, descended from a distinguished Hassidic lineage, was looked up to in the Motol community and synagogue, and his mother's kin were well-to-do local merchants. Yet young Weizmann was always made aware of the uncertainty of his status and the need to make it secure. Weizmann noted that his father was more scholar than businessman. Not until Chaim Lubzhinsky, a son-in-law, took a more active part in their business association was the elder Weizmann able to provide such luxuries as vacations abroad for his family. Chaim Weizmann began to support himself partially from the age of fourteen; and although his position as a tutor in a wealthy industrialist's home allowed him to live among the Pinsk upper class, it hardly gave him independent security. In his first year in a German university in Darmstadt, he covered his expenses by teaching Hebrew and Russian at a Jewish boarding school in another town, Pfungstadt, where he now resided. It was an adolescence that left him well trained for competition and success: imbued with a strong will to fulfill the expectations of his proud and loving family and thoroughly aware that he would have to work hard in order to do so.

The example and precepts of his father could serve him as a warning and a guide. Weizmann's understated observation that his father "did not dislike his work" is more adequately elaborated in his sister Haya's memoirs. She tells us that the elder Weizmann wanted his children to study an academic profession or learn an artisan craft rather than fall back on some characteristically Jewish commercial trade like his own. By this comment she meant to call attention to the modernizing bent shown in her father's willingness, unusual in his generation and milieu, to train one's offspring to be artisans. But it also reveals his sharp distaste for the risks and uncertainties, and clearly also for the indignities, of the life of a Jewish middleman in the Pale of Settlement. For all the powerful attachment to his roots that he acquired, Chaim Weizmann was brought up by his parents to strive to outgrow his origins.[6]

Chaim, the second son, was the third among fifteen children; but he was clearly the one in whom were placed the special hopes and expectations held for an eldest son among the East European Jews of that time. His older brother, Feivel, showed small interest or special ability in book learning, though he excelled in drawing and all manual skills. He was sent to Pinsk as an apprentice lithographer at the same time that Chaim went there to study at the *Realgymnasium.* Later, when his father needed help in his business at home, Feivel returned to Motol and remained with the family business and the family home thereafter. The decision to teach his son a trade was, of course, in accord with his father's "modern" views; but clearly, even from this viewpoint, it was a second-best option. The best hopes of the family surely rested on Chaim, who opened up a path to the university and the professions later followed by his younger siblings—with financial as well as moral support from Chaim. From the time he was left on his own, at an early age, to train for his future, young Weizmann must have had the sense of succeeding to a firstborn's birthright and obligations.

Weizmann was aware that, like his father, he, too, was a man in transition. He notes that he was one of the last to be admitted to a Russian secondary school before restrictive quotas were set for Jewish students. This did not mean that his academic course was free of other obstacles—in addition to a shortage of funds. Young Weizmann was driven not only by the inner pressure to excel, but by outer demands to catch up. Before he could follow the courses at the Pinsk *Gymnasium,* he had to master Russian, for his mother tongue was Yiddish and his early studies, of classic Hebrew and Judaic texts, had all been conducted in that language. On entering a German university, he found that Yiddish was not an adequate basis for effective communication with Germans and German culture and that the science he had learned in Pinsk left him well below the level of other beginning students. But if Weizmann had reason to complain of real handicaps in the struggle to excel (and complaints on many scores were a constant feature of his lifelong correspondence), his experience justified a growing confidence that he could work hard and well enough, at anything he tried, to fulfill the high expectations placed upon him.

Confidence and pride became rooted in his character in the face of other challenges as well, challenges that called into question his identity as a Jewish, nationalist intellectual. Like other young men, especially those of transitional generations, Weizmann and his friends defined their social position and political views—in short, their cultural identity—in the school they attended. Weizmann's memoirs echo the standard denigration of the traditional Jewish elementary school, the *heder,* regularly decried by modern writers as a bleak, authoritarian, harsh system of rote memory drill without emotional stimulation or imagination. But it appears that he was allowed to choose his own teacher from his indulged childhood, and he developed warm, affectionate relations with more than one. In any case he did not turn from his Jewish schooling in such revulsion that Russian and German schools provided alternative models able to win his total identification and utterly neutralize his Jewish loyalties.

He recalls the Pinsk *Gymnasium* with a hostility not uncommon among

Russian students of his time. He notes its narrow bureaucratic spirit and remembers the staff as generally incompetent. His favorite Russian authors were the dissident writers of the period, and he recommended this literature to the younger pupils he was tutoring. The rebellion his schoolmasters provoked had a specifically Jewish cast as well. He recalls with relish how the Jewish students made a point of excelling in the class on ancient Slavonic in order to annoy their instructor, who was believed to feel that the subject was beyond the grasp of Jewish minds. This was a victory for Judaism as well as a demonstration that young Jews like himself, who had no native knowledge of Russia or of Russian culture, could not only learn the elements of a modern, new civilization, but come to excel in it.[7]

His first studies at a German university were taken at Darmstadt, which he would reach by train from his residence in Pfungstadt. The time at university was dominated by his intense dislike for the German-Jewish Orthodoxy of the boarding school where he lived and taught. Overworked, underfed, and unhappy, he broke down with nervous exhaustion and retreated to the intimacy of his Russian-Jewish home as a haven from the pious pomposity of Pfungstadt.

In 1893 Weizmann returned to Germany, this time to Berlin. Here and in Swiss universities until 1904, he defined himself and his intended role more fully. In his early years he had acquired habits of work and a confidence in his powers that, as a tutor, he tried to impart to pupils of his own. He preached diligence and persistence, in the spirit of the *Haskalah* (the Hebrew enlightenment he had imbibed from childhood), and preached Zionism as a way to master the modern scientific culture from which Jews had been detached for centuries. He urged his pupils to excel in these for their own careers' sake and for the future of their people. In Germany and Switzerland he was to broaden these still narrowly pedagogical perspectives into a vision of the political leadership he felt called to as his destined role.

The Student Zionists

German university life presented Weizmann with new goals to reach as well as new handicaps to overcome, and it revealed broad, new intellectual horizons.[8] The opera and concert halls, the garrulous conviviality of the cafés, and the new world of Nietzsche and other current German literary idols exerted their fascination on him, as they did on his friends among the Russian-Jewish students. He also fixed on a specific professional objective through his studies in chemistry, moving swiftly into laboratory research under outstanding pioneers in the growing field of chemical dyestuffs. But he did not find, in German Jewry or in general German society, a new milieu he might wish to enter with full identification. Instead, as in the Pinsk *Gymnasium* and the Pfungstadt-Darmstadt years, his self-image as a Russian-Jewish intellectual took on a clearer, sharper definition.

In metropolitan Berlin, as in Pfungstadt, he again lived apart from the resident Germans, but not now in isolation. He entered into the vibrant life of the Russian-Jewish student and the émigré colony as one of a small, embattled group of Zionists. It was with these comrades that he fully identified; their habits and attitudes became decisive, as a model or a foil, in forming the individual shape of his own commitments. The destiny that shaped itself for him was one of political leadership—but a leadership strenuously achieved, grudgingly acknowledged, and confined to the restricted sphere of a small, oppositional minority in the student colony and the Zionist movement.

Pre-Herzlian Zionism occupied a peculiar place among the emerging activist parties of Eastern European Jewry in the 1890s.[9] In the beginning, the Zionist slogan of autoemancipation—constituting in principle a claim to political autonomy and a demand for immediate political action—had been a sharp ideological challenge to others in the community. Traditionalists and modern-minded Western Jewish philanthropists had, indeed, promoted resettlement in the Holy Land on lines foreshadowing later Zionist projects, but they clearly had no intention to seek Jewish political autonomy. This unstated difference turned into open opposition following the emergence of Zionism.

Early Zionism was severely hampered by conditions it encountered in both major areas of its operation. Official hostility to minority nationalism effectively ruled out any organization for political action in Russia or an avowed goal of political autonomy in Palestine. The movement had to suppress its basic political impulse, resort to evasions and half measures in Russia and Palestine, and accommodate itself to the eleemosynary, apolitical methods of earlier supporters of Jewish settlement in the Holy Land. Cooperation among Russian-Jewish Hibbat Zion, Western non-Zionist philanthropists, and an admixture of Western Jews in the philo-Zionist clubs created by Eastern immigrants in Western countries dulled the ideological edge and militant image of the newborn Jewish nationalism.

Conditions in Russia permitted open manifestations of Zionism only through local clubs and public exhortation in the synagogues. A formal international Zionist conclave had to take place across the Russian border—in Kattowitz (Silesia)—in 1884. In Russia itself philo-Zionists could concert their action only through correspondence or meetings in private homes—always aware that they might be under police surveillance and must not overstep the bounds of tacitly extended official tolerance. By the 1890s, Russian Hibbat Zion was a faltering, stagnant organization, disdained by most of the intelligentsia as an irrelevant combine of bourgeois and clerical conservatism. This view was fortified by the general agreement among Zionists that they could not concern themselves (at least collectively) with the issues of social reform or revolution in Russia since the "Jewish problem" was to be solved only by resettlement in Palestine.

At that very time the crisis of Russian society was mounting to its climax, and growing numbers of young Jews and Jewish workers were attracted to the revolutionary movements. In 1897 (the very year that Herzl convened the

First Zionist Congress) an energetic, devoted group of social democratic agitators organized the Bund, a Jewish socialist labor movement committed both to revolutionary action in Russia, in concert with other Russian workers, and to the securing and protection of Jewish civil rights and the interests of Jewish workers. To the chagrin of young Zionists, these Jewish socialists appropriated to themselves the slogan of autoemancipation. They argued that only the revolutionary Jewish proletariat would fight for the civil rights of Jews, since the Zionists along with the rabbis had sold out to the czarist regime. The quietism of the Zionists in Russian affairs and their frustration in the Palestine project, their own chosen field, made the movement indeed appear inactive and impotent—an image antithetical to that which had aroused nationalist enthusiasm in the 1880s. Thus it was no small undertaking to defend Jewish nationalism, in its then-current shape, against polemicists like G. V. Plekhanov, Parvus, or L. Martov in the German and Swiss universities.[10]

In Berlin Weizmann joined the Russian-Jewish Academic [Wissenschaftlicher] Society, an active center of such polemics. He came as a new recruit to an already well-established company of young Zionist leaders. Founded in 1889, five years before Weizmann's arrival, the society counted among its members Leo Motzkin, its president; Nachman Syrkin, who emerged as the first theoretician of socialist Zionism; Victor Jacobson, who became a lifelong diplomatic representative of Jewish and Zionist interests in stations from Constantinople to Geneva; and Shmarya Levin, who went from a post as Crown Rabbi in Ekaterinoslav to the Duma and then became perhaps the most beloved of the traveling spokesmen of Zionism, especially in America. These were men six to seven years older than the barely twenty-year-old Weizmann, a major difference at that age, and he looked up to them with deference. Leo Motzkin in particular became Weizmann's mentor and chief and instructed him in the characteristic views and Zionist attitudes that prevailed among the group.

Motzkin's early background was strikingly similar to that of Weizmann.[11] His father, too, was a timber merchant—an observant, traditional Jew who was open to the new trends. Regarded as a mathematical prodigy, young Motzkin was sent to Berlin at the age of fourteen to study in German schools. He was placed as a resident pupil in the home of David Cassel, a teacher of history at a liberal rabbinical seminary, the Hochschule fuer Juedische Wissenschaft; he then gained admission to the Humboldt Gymnasium in 1885 and two years later to the university. Motzkin thus became fully involved in the life of German Jewry and the German style of Western culture, but in a way that strengthened his self-awareness and commitment as a modern Russian Jew. He was exposed to the whole range of then-current scholarship and sectarian debate among German Jews, including leading liberal and Reform figures, many of whom could be met in Cassel's home. Together with his own early background, this introduction to current German-Jewish ideological discussion laid Motzkin open to all those influences that fed into the prehistory of German and Central European Zionism.

The position he arrived at was one clearly detached from Orthodox traditionalism, but equally far removed from a rationalism that would sever the historic roots of his Jewish identity. What most attracted Motzkin was the work of the historian Heinrich Graetz, who wrote of the Jewish past as a chronicle of heroism and high culture. He thus offered young intellectuals a basis for Jewish survival as a historic people still relevant to their own time. For Motzkin, Graetz was—together with another German Jew, Moses Hess—an immediate forebear of his own Zionism; the Zionist attitude he developed was, in this respect, one closely tied to the identity problems of a modern Jew in a Western society.

Another source of influence was the Viennese circle around the Hebrew litterateur and journalist Peretz Smolenskin.[12] Graetz could restore the pride of a Westernized Jew in his people's past and Hess could project a glorious destiny in the future for the nation. Smolenskin set up the staunch ethnic loyalty of Eastern Europe as a model opposed to the renegadism of which he accused Western Jewry since the days of Moses Mendelssohn. This revisionist view of modern Jewish history had a particular appeal to young students in Vienna whose roots were still deeply embedded in the traditions of the Eastern provinces where they were born. They found a leader in Nathan Birnbaum, who published a journal, *Selbst-Emancipation,* that sparked the activities of the Zionophile student societies in Vienna and beyond. Motzkin's Russian-Jewish society in Berlin maintained close ties with Birnbaum. They shared a nationalist awakening, echoing the response of Russian-Jewish intellectuals to the 1881–82 pogroms, but adding a specifically Western nuance to the doctrine of autoemancipation. Rather than securing civic equality for (already-emancipated) Western Jews by political action, Zionism as a cultural nationalism was to free them of the psychological subservience and assimilationism they had succumbed to under pressure of a hostile majority.

Another source of early German Zionism, also reflected in Motzkin's circle, arose directly from the plight of Russian Jewry. The refugee streams that flowed westwards after the pogroms of 1881–82 and the expulsion of Jews from Moscow in 1891 aroused German Jews to organize relief committees seeking to solve the persistent problem. Among these was the Esra society in Berlin, led by Hirsch Hildesheimer and Willy Bambus—an organization of, primarily, neo-Orthodox German-Jewish cast that attached itself to Hibbat Zion. A young German Jew, Heinrich Loewe, organized Jung Israel, a Zionist group in Berlin. The Russian-Jewish Academic Society maintained relations with Bambus and Loewe and shared in their activities; they were especially useful in helping to deal with the mass of refugees who daily clogged the Berlin railway station at Charlottenburg in 1891.[13]

The contemporary rise of political antisemitism was another factor that drew the small group of German-born Zionists to the movement. The first wave of the antisemitic assault had receded in German elections late in the 1880s, but Jewish students at the university still felt keenly the slights and humiliations offered by the aristocratic dueling corps and the exclusive fraternities. The response of ardent spirits like Herzl—and not only among those who became Zionists—was to repay antisemitic assailants in their own coin: Jews challenged them directly, by word or deed, rather than resort to back-door intercession or rely on friendly Gentile spokesmen, as had been the practice. This proud stance found a natural expression in the doctrine of auto-emancipation, which was the Zionist idea that appealed most effectively to Russian-Jewish intellectuals as well.[14]

But there was a further feature that could easily divide Western and Eastern Zionists across this common ground. In Eastern Zionism autoemancipation initially meant opting out of Russian politics and society. Western Zionists (though not Herzl) tended to avoid this conclusion and interpreted their Zionist autoemancipation personally: as liberation from individual (not corporate) subservience, from coerced assimilationism; they contended that a moral stiffening of spines through Zionism would make Jews all the better citizens where they now lived. Western Zionists might agree that the basic modern situation for Jews was best exemplified in Russia and that emigration to the Jewish homeland was its radical solution. But, they added, emancipated Western Jews, living in an exceptionally benign situation, need not share in the exodus. Nevertheless, even though they did not intend to move to the Jewish homeland, now or ever, Zionism had a direct, personal significance for them: it would solve their special problem of pride and personal identity.[15]

The East-West split on such issues was neither universal nor uniform. Certainly, men like Birnbaum or Motzkin, primarily identifying with Eastern Jews but fully acculturated in the West, could not well divorce themselves from their Western milieu and its concerns. Even in East European Zionism, initially focused on migration, the frustrated efforts of colonization in Palestine shifted the focus of the movement toward essentially local activity.

In 1889 when the Russian-Jewish Academic Society was founded, the new star on the horizon of Hebrew literature was Asher Ginzberg, a young businessman in his thirties who emerged in Odessa under the nom de plume of Ahad Ha'am (One of the People).[16] An incisive critic of both the "enlightened" and traditionalist camps in Hibbat Zion, he became the storm center of lively ideological debate. From the start he attacked the subsidized colonization in Palestine not only as economically unsound, but as morally corrupted by the paternalistic philanthropy of Baron Edmond de Rothschild and other (minor) supporters. Such charges of parasitism and dependency found a quick response among young men imbued with the ethos of autoemancipation. An elite Zionist secret order, the Bnei Moshe, with Ahad Ha'am as its grand master and guide, attracted a wide range of activists to its ranks. Motzkin became a member, and in 1895 he brought Weizmann in as well.

Bnei Moshe and Ahad Ha'am personally very soon provoked sharp conflicts on issues of secular Hebrew culture and religion that sharply divided Hibbat Zion. Convinced that the necessary preliminary (and ultimate aim) of all other Zionist action was the renewal and activation of a national consensus (a national will) Ahad Ha'amists devoted themselves to Hebrew education, the rebirth of spoken Hebrew, and the promotion of a secular Hebrew literature and culture in the Diaspora as well as in Palestine. This program provoked fierce protests from traditionalists, who viewed it as one more modernist assault on all they held most sacred; Ahad Ha'am and the Bnei Moshe came under their attack both within the Zionist movement and outside it. It was not a result Ahad Ha'am himself desired, but it only enhanced his aura in the eyes of young Russian-Jewish intellectuals. It found an equally responsive audience in Central Europe among men like Birnbaum and Motzkin, who saw in the Ahad Ha'amist approach a natural succession to the cultural nationalism of Smolenskin, which they had espoused.

In other ways, however, Ahad Ha'am's way of thinking was less inviting. A Motzkin might welcome the scathing Ahad Ha'amist critique of the colonization in Palestine, but if new settlement and political action were deferred to the indefinite future, promoting Hebrew alone was not enough to satisfy him. Ahad Ha'am bluntly denied that Zionists should concern themselves at all with the immediate, concrete problems of suffering Jews, such as poverty, emigration, and political oppression—a stance that led anti-Zionist radicals to single him out as one of the striking symbols of bourgeois Zionist irrelevancy. Motzkin's group had to defend fellow Zionists against such attacks by the revolutionary cosmopolitans, but they, too, shared activist conceptions and attitudes. For a while Motzkin and Weizmann cooperated with a Bundist-oriented group of writers in preparing Yiddish literature for mass distribution; they tried to alleviate the problems of Russian-Jewish would-be students, increasingly hampered by barriers in Western schools as well as in Russia; and, unhappy with the stagnation of Hibbat Zion, they joined in abortive efforts to convene the philo-Zionist societies and reorganize for more effective action.

For all their close connection with Ahad Ha'am, the Berlin group was ready for the electric impulse of Theodor Herzl's appearance. Motzkin took a notably active part in the First Zionist Congress, seeking to hold Herzl to a more forthright statement of his goal, a Jewish state. Afterwards, in spite of Ahad Ha'am's outspoken criticism of the congress and his refusal of membership in the new Zionist organization, his Berlin disciples remained enthusiastic supporters. Yet, their prior commitments to ideological positions that were without meaning for Herzl predisposed them to become, eventually, an element of opposition in the new organization.

Weizmann began his studies in Berlin at the Charlottenburg Polytechnic Institute in 1893, just short of nineteen years old; soon after, he became associated with a group of student Zionists who, more than anyone, helped define his goals. Notwithstanding Motzkin's extensive ties with German Jewry and the Academic Society's occasional participation in local activities, attention was almost entirely fixed on East European Jews, particularly on the Russian-Jewish student colony. These young Russians were largely oblivious of the German-Jewish community—certainly, this was the case with young Weizmann. He found his place at once in the tight little student group of Russian

Zionists. With them he fought ideological battles against the revolutionary cosmopolitans of the Russian-Jewish student colony, becoming thoroughly immersed in the style and themes of their Russian progressivism while passionately resisting their radical, assimilationist or Bundist, antinationalism. In this milieu, his involvement in German or German-Jewish matters needed be no more than minimal, just as his special concerns were of little interest to the larger, outside communities. In the company of others of his own kind, Weizmann's condition as a Russian-Jewish outsider was shaped into a positively affirmed identity.

Yet when he had to return to Pinsk (where his family was now settled) after two or three semesters in Berlin, it was like a remand into exile. He sent a stream of beseeching, veritably anguished letters to his Berlin friends—to Motzkin, above all—imploring them to pass on regularly the full news of the doings of their Academic Society. He reported the scene in Pinsk in terms verging on disgust, deriding its intellectual life, decrying its moral deficiencies, and mentioning efforts to effect improvements by himself and his Zionist friends in alternating outbursts of pride and despair. The fact that his return to Pinsk had been forced, not chosen (since his father's difficulties in supporting him in Berlin had compelled it), no doubt contributed to Weizmann's besetting gloom. But it is equally clear from his letters that he now saw himself as a Russian-Jewish intellectual, shaped in the mold of his Berlin friends; this ideal made him take a very contemptuous view of the common run of Russian Jews—of their plutocratic leaders as well as their toiling (or wheeling-dealing) masses, of their traditionalists as well as their assimilationists.

But there was another side to his complex attitude toward the Berlin group. The pressure of need that forced Weizmann to interrupt his studies must have reinforced his horror of future insecurity and redoubled his drive to make his mark in his profession. He returned to Berlin in 1896 with aid from his father and his brother-in-law, Chaim Lubzhinsky, whose business association had now prospered enough to assure the young man regular support. This, no doubt, is the basis for Weizmann's recollection that he was, in a small way, able to help out his impecunious friends—he had a coat available for pawning and sometimes considered a friend entitled to share his funds temporarily, or even indefinitely. But the position they were in was one he utterly rejected (and somewhat feared) for himself. About one of them, Zvi Aberson, Weizmann wrote words applicable to a good many others:

> This man with the sharp analytical mind and the huge fund of knowledge had fallen, through lack of discipline and consistency, perhaps through hunger and privation, into complete unproductiveness. His daily life was one long fever of activity without purpose; and it was filled with all the dodges of poverty.[17]

Weizmann himself was no model of careful fiscal management. He tended all his life to need loans from others, living as he did at the outer edge of, or well beyond, his current means; but he could not go on, as some of his friends did, without at least the prospect of an income that would justify his rate of expenditure (or one substantially higher) in the future. He could, temporarily, lean on others, just as he was ready to lend them support—but he could not bear a position of fixed dependency, personal or institutional. For all his deep identification with his comrades, to whom he was initially so deferential, these were specific differences, well understood by himself, that set him apart.

Weaknesses he found in them were to be feared all the more in that he found them so appealing and was determined to overcome them in himself as prime obstacles to achieving professional success and personal independence. Their bohemianism responded to his own bent for sociability and endless discussion. Their passion for talk even had political virtue among East Europeans given to three- or four-hour orations and day-long debates extending through the night; even more compelling was the example of their noble dedication to public causes at the expense of private interest. But the young Weizmann was already profoundly averse to the besetting dilettantism of those eternal students who, like his own particular leader, Motzkin, might never earn their professional degree or might forever dissipate their talents in profitless activities. Returning to Berlin in 1896, he plunged again into the thick of the social and political life of the student Zionist circle. But he combined this with a fierce dedication to his studies and laboratory work, sustained with a consistent energy and determination that were soon noticed by his instructors.

The chemists at Berlin-Charlottenburg were prominently involved in research that contributed largely to the dyestuffs industry. Weizmann was inducted into this area and quickly achieved results his instructor thought likely to have significant practical applications. This was done by dint of strenuous labors. For about three weeks during this period, the family in Pinsk was seriously alarmed (as his sister's memoirs recall) by a sudden cessation of the regular flow of letters from Chaim. The suspense was relieved—and the mystery resolved—by Chaim's triumphant announcement of his success in experiments he had been pursuing: sometimes he had spent his nights sleeping in the laboratory in a feverish determination to bring the search to a conclusion. The family celebrated the victory with a joyful conviviality worthy of a wedding. Chaim himself came home that summer armed with an invitation to visit in Moscow a Russian friend of his Berlin professors. The exact purpose of the trip is variously described—by Chaim, as an attempt to sell his invention for industrial use and so ease the financial burdens of his father; by his sister, as a chance to deliver an academic lecture in the capital—but in any case seems to reflect hopes for swift professional advancement and economic security.[18]

There is a remarkable, almost evasive, vagueness in Weizmann's account of his summer visit to Moscow, which contributed largely to his failure to attend the First Zionist Congress. His memoirs have been severely criticized for the errors in recollection that abound, but in the case at hand Weizmann seems more embarrassed than forgetful. He tells us that he "threw himself into Zionist work" during the 1897 summer vacation, that is, he agitated the cause of Herzl's forthcoming congress and was named a delegate for Pinsk. This activity, he recalls, delayed his visit to Moscow, where, in turn, he had to stay an additional day and so missed the congress opening—without having managed to market his chemical discovery. In Brest-Litovsk he then met his father, who offered him the funds to get to the congress before it ended; but in his personal disappointment and his reluctance to burden the family further, as he explains, he did not accept. There is much obscurity about this explanation; at any rate, this was one of repeated occasions when Weizmann's private goals and public commitments forced a choice—one that, in this case, left what he later regretted as a "gap in the record."

In September Weizmann returned not to Berlin, but to the Swiss University of Fribourg, where his mentor had taken up an appointment. Here he completed his studies and was granted his doctorate after submitting his dissertation in January 1899—two studies on the electrolytic production of chemicals for the dyestuffs industry. During this year and a half of concentrated study and research, he also found a new field for Zionist work near Fribourg in the university town of Berne—where there was a colony of Jewish students—while sharing fully in the heightened activity of his old circle of friends in Berlin. The emergence of Herzl led the Russian-Jewish Academic Society to add a new, unmistakably Zionist name, Kadimah, to its title, henceforth Russischer Juedischer Wissenschaftlicher Verein-Kadimah. Weizmann plunged fully into the affairs of the new Herzlian organization, taking on administrative duties as joint-secretary together with its leader, Motzkin. The latter followed up his noteworthy role at the First Zionist Congress by consenting to visit Palestine at Herzl's request and present a report at the Second Congress in 1898—all this, of course, at the expense of his dissertation in economics, to which field he had turned from his mathematical studies. Weizmann, for his part, added to his term-time Zionist labors in Berne-Berlin an expanded tour of propaganda in Russia during the summer recess. He was again chosen as delegate to the Zionist Congress by Pinsk (and increasingly by other constituents as well) and from the Second Congress in 1898 played his part with growing confidence in the World Zionist Organization's (WZO's) public assemblies.

In 1899 Dr. Weizmann, fresh from his doctoral studies, was appointed privatdocent and assistant to Karl Graebe, the professor of chemistry at the University of Geneva. This professional elevation also marked a significant, if subtle, change in his Zionist status. In Geneva, where an important colony of Jewish students was gathered, he figured as a senior member of the Zionist circle, no longer as in Berlin a junior adjutant. A new phase of growth, fostered as well by other circumstances, had begun.

When Theodor Herzl issued his call for a Zionist congress, the young activists found the occasion they had been seeking to reinvigorate the movement. Others did not share such ready enthusiasm; their welcome of the new recruit was shaded with wariness of his leadership and alarm at his polemical stance.

For Herzl, the resort to mass agitation (or, as he put it, stirring up Acheron) was his fallback position after failing to win over the Rothschilds and Baron Maurice de Hirsch, the powerful sponsors of other Jewish colonization schemes.[19] His congress threatened the leadership of notables in the Jewish community. He attacked their method of resettlement in Palestine by infiltration, through semicovert loopholes, instead of seeking a clear basis in Turkish public law. Veteran leaders of Hibbat Zion dreaded such tactics, for they had acquired a vested interest in the undisturbed progress of small projects based on similar methods of infiltration.

Although Herzl's forthright pronouncements won the approval of the student Zionists, they retained strong sympathies for the pre-Herzlian leaders who were critical of his tactics. Old ties and personal affinities could be set aside in the revival of an activist mood, which Herzl so splendidly symbolized, but they did not fade into oblivion. As years passed with no brilliant success and no prospect of action that could be shared by Herzl's followers, some of his policies proved increasingly distasteful. The alliances Herzl seemed to prefer and his methods of leadership were felt to hamper efforts to recruit young, intellectual Zionists. Weizmann and his friends moved into a position of ever-more open opposition.

Herzl's pamphlet, *Der Judenstaat,* made its primary appeal to Zionists by its clear-cut nationalist analysis and solution of the Jewish problem and by its bracing, imaginative description of the process through which it would be accomplished. It also contained a strategy for gaining Ottoman consent and the support of the Great Powers by combining the Turkish need to finance their national debt with the interest of the European nations in a rational plan to move Jews out of some countries without adding excessively to their number in others. He hoped to achieve this goal by publicly proclaiming it on behalf of the Jewish people as their national aim and by setting up a "Society of Jews" and a "Jewish Company" to authorize and execute the plan. When he failed to conquer the notables who normally provided Jewish leadership and disposed of adequate funds, Herzl turned to the masses, expecting them to fulfill the same functions.

The First Zionist Congress was not made up of regularly chosen delegates, for no organized body, but the will of one man convoked it and set up its procedures. Some existing philo-Zionist clubs sent elected delegates or representatives who found it convenient to be in Basle; some individuals responded to Herzl's personal request to participate; and some just chanced to be in the area and came out of a sympathetic interest. Among those who did not come were the leaders of Hibbat Zion in Odessa, Berlin, and London—not necessarily because of outright opposition, but reserving judgment. Journalists like Ahad Ha'am or the young populist thinker and social revolutionary, Chaim Zhitlovsky, came to observe and later to criticize the clearly historic development. The Russian-Jewish student Zionists of Berlin came and played an active part.

The Second Zionist Congress, held a year later, in 1898, was more formally organized. The delegates were chosen by constituent societies in the several "territories" under rules and voting qualifications set down by the WZO. The Russian Zionists now sent a major delegation and held a preliminary conference in Warsaw on the way to the congress.

They brought with them the old ideological issues that had flourished in Hibbat Zion. Advocates of continuous resettlement in Palestine came to the congress ready to defend their enterprise against the neglect that an exclusively diplomatic strategy might entail. A contingent of rabbis and Orthodox-Zionists came to fight for rabbinical control of Zionist propaganda—or alternatively, a ban on all Zionist cultural and educational projects.

Herzl rejected the Orthodox demand, but he pledged that the WZO would never do anything offensive to religion. The opposing position, adopted by the Russian Zionist majority at their preliminary meeting, was embodied in a congress resolution that proposed Zionist support for the cultivation of (secular) Hebraist culture. This provoked some initially supportive Orthodox circles into vociferous opposition and left those who remained in the Zionist ranks weakened and dissatisfied. It was hardly what Herzl needed; in subsequent congresses, he tried to win back Orthodox supporters by blocking debate on issues of culture. By barring cultural activities unacceptable to traditionalists, Herzl occasioned the formation of an internal Zionist opposition among Weizmann's circle of friends.

Earlier, in Russia, where the legal scope for activity was severely limited, such issues were fought out in the press or as a traditional intracommunal dispute. The structure of the WZO—a quasi-parliamentary representation of the Jewish national will—laid the groundwork for a new level of contention and eventually turned the diffuse ideological quarrels of Hibbat Zion into organized party struggles. It was part of Herzl's historic achievement to have made this possible, but it was far from being his intention. He needed the congress to legitimize him as the diplomatic agent of a nation and to provide financial and technical facilities to implement his proposals should his mission succeed. He did not need disruptive ideological squabbles and general attacks on the very authorities whom he wished to approach. During his brief remaining lifetime, he succeeded in suppressing or restricting such expressions at the congresses. But his methods of stemming the rising tide of partisanship contributed to the birth of an opposition that turned to party organization. Motzkin, Weizmann, and their associates were the first to adopt this course effectively.

The move to open opposition did not occur at once, nor with decisive impact when it eventually happened. In the first years the student Zionist circles were anxious to bridge the gaps threatening to open between Herzl and his Zionist critics. They did not lose their sympathy with the Hibbat Zion agenda of continued settlement support or with Ahad Ha'am's cultural strategy when they committed themselves to Herzl's more daring program of political action. But they hoped that the Russian veterans would accept Herzl's leadership and the primacy of the WZO—even though they often sided with them against Herzl on particular matters. Such matters included not only ideological issues but questions of organization and personal differences.

The structure set up for the WZO at the First Congress provided for a regular congress elected by the territorial Zionist federations in proportion, roughly, to the enrolled membership of their constituent local societies.[20] The qualified membership would consist of those who signified their adherence to the Basle program adopted by the First Congress by purchasing a shekel (at a more or less nominal fee set by each country in its own currency). Between congresses Zionist policy was to be governed by the Action Committee, selected (in principle) at the congress from among its members and divided for effectiveness into the Greater and the Smaller Action Committee. At the First Congress the Greater Action Committee was fixed as a body of twenty-three members. Of these, five residents of Vienna were chosen directly by the congress, constituting the Smaller Action Committee that was to serve as Herzl's executive cabinet or auxiliary and advisory board. The remaining members were to be chosen by the various Zionist territorial federations in ratios more or less corresponding to the relative size of the Jewish population in the major countries. (In later years, both parts of the Action Committee were expected to be chosen by the congress, though sometimes this could not be completely achieved before the sessions ended and other arrangements had to be agreed on.)

How to use this structure in making Zionist policy was a bone of contention from the beginning. Herzl, who quite clearly recognized the historic (not to say, mythic) quality of his achievement in convening the congress, nevertheless, treated it as the mere platform for his personal lobbying and diplomacy. He did say in his diary notes on the First Congress, "At Basle I founded the Jewish State. . . . [In] fifty years [1947!] everyone will perceive it." He had "worked the people up into the atmosphere of a State and made them feel that they were its National Assembly"; and since the "essence of a State lies in the will of the people for a State," the First Zionist Congress had, in essence, created the organ of Jewish national sovereignty. But he also said, in the immediate context, that "the will of one powerful enough individual" was itself a sufficient ground for exercising national sovereignty, and he had a clear sense of his own emergence as a popular idol, a quasi-messianic figure. One might almost judge that Herzl himself, not the congress, claimed sovereignty.[21]

He ran the organization he called into being on principles of strongly presidential government, virtually as his personal instrument. He himself conducted its main activity, the approaches to the Ottoman and major European courts. The WZO's periodical publication, *Die Welt,* was launched and financed in good part at Herzl's own expense and with his father's generous support. He got meager help and advice—he asked for little—from his Vienna group of close associates who formed the Smaller Action Committee. The Greater Action Committee was hardly used by Herzl as a body that functioned collectively to advise or determine policies. He preferred to treat its members as correspondents abroad, through whom, more or less individually, he expected to rally popular support, seek communal backing, and raise subscriptions for the Jewish Colonial Trust, the financial instrument that the WZO was to create as an accessory to Herzl's diplomacy. This had some justification owing to the restrictive policy of the Russian and Habsburg regimes, and it continued the tradition of Hibbat Zion's discreet organizational practice. But some of the Russians considered themselves entitled to exercise greater authority between congresses, both locally and in the affairs of the world organization, and friction developed repeatedly on this score.

There were, as always, personal considerations that led to dissension.[22] Those who joined Herzl with a background of Zionist work older than his own naturally looked on him as a leader who, though invaluable for the access he gave them to the Western political world and political style, was still a tyro in Jewish and Zionist affairs. They often expected to guide him from the wings, if not to use him simply as a front. It was disturbing to such veterans, including the Berlin student Zionists, when the claims of a man like Nathan Birnbaum to a leading place were coolly ignored by Herzl. They held Herzl partly to blame when Dr. Birnbaum drifted away from the movement into an increasingly remote oppositional position. Another group of discontented Zionists were Western radicals notably represented by Bernard Lazare (the French anarchist writer who had emerged as a leading Dreyfusard). Disquiet over Herzl's one-man rule of the organization, his reliance on a bank (the projected Jewish Colonial Trust) as the instrument of Zionist policy, and the suppression of social protest and cultivation of conservative elements required by his diplomacy, led Lazare, too, to desert the WZO. The Berlin group saw these developments not simply with regret, but with growing uneasiness about Herzl's leadership. Yet they still hoped to win over disaffected elements to an organization and policy line basically committed to their new leader, Herzl.

They soon found that they themselves were hampered in working among young, progressive potential Zionists by Herzl's stand on issues particularly significant for them and the clientele they hoped to reach. The critical issues were those of the place of (secular) cultural activity in the WZO agenda and the kind of coalition of bourgeois-clerical forces that they perceived to be increasingly favored by Herzl within the WZO.

In Germany, Switzerland, and France, where Weizmann's circle regularly conducted Zionist agitation among Jewish students, the main opposition that had to be dealt with were the socialists: the Bundist protagonists of revolution, Yiddishism, and the pressing immediate claims to life and liberty of the East European Jewish mass as well as the Russian Social Democratic and Social Revolutionary parties. The same opponents challenged those Zionists in Russia who were in close touch with Weizmann's comrades. Here, too, the image of Zionism among young radicals (as of Hibbat Zion earlier) continued to be that of an irrelevant, reactionary force—unconcerned with the immediate problems facing Russian Jewry, committed to a utopian illusion that precluded any realistic immediate action, and dominated by a cabal of bourgeois and clerical conservatives.

At the Fourth Zionist Congress in 1900, a resolution calling for a concrete WZO commitment to the cause of Hebraic culture, proposed by Martin Buber, was prevented from receiving appropriate congress consideration through Herzl's parliamentary maneuvers. Herzl's ban on activity the young Zionists found vital for their work among progressive Jews was felt as a blow suffered directly, and it challenged an oppositional response. When, soon after, Weizmann, Motzkin, and their circles in Berlin and Geneva began to talk of organizing a Zionist youth conference and possibly an autonomous youth organization in the WZO, the issue was one directly between them and the leader. The beginning of party factionalism in the WZO was at hand.[23]

The Democratic Faction

In the 1899–1900 academic year, Weizmann began work in Geneva as a faculty member. Continuing the line of research he had developed in his dissertation, he produced a series of publications and patent applications jointly with Dr. Christian Deichler, an old Berlin colleague, who was able to interest the Bayer works in their results. Weizmann in those years received an annual retainer in order to develop his discoveries into a commercially exploitable process.

He also found time for fairly heavy participation in student activities. His memoirs claim six hours daily devoted to Zionist work, including, no doubt, attendance at favorite cafés, occasional concerts and theaters, and interminable political rallies. His summer vacations in Russia to visit his family were used for propaganda tours, now extended beyond the neighborhood of Pinsk to the far reaches of southern Russia. Each summer was rounded out by his participation in the Zionist Congress (held annually until after the Fifth Congress in 1901). Contacts made on these occasions enabled him to be an effective fund-raiser for causes he favored.

In Geneva Weizmann was a senior member of Russian student society: teacher, tutor, and laboratory supervisor to aspiring scientists and young women studying medicine. Now past twenty-five years of age, he was the chief of the Geneva organization of student Zionists and had students (particularly young women) as his adjutants. To his contemporary and boon companion, Zvi Aberson, he gave occasional material support, and he made regular contributions for the higher education of his younger siblings. At the same time he maintained old ties with his Zionist friends in Berne and Berlin.

His special relationship to Leo Motzkin, as of lieutenant to commander, was one he cultivated with loving care. "Our dear good Leo," he wrote to a friend in 1901, "even he is not spared by fate all kinds of petty worries that prevent him from giving himself up completely to the cause." At Zionist congresses, Weizmann stood together with Motzkin, echoing themes sounded by

his acknowledged leader. As they grew steadily more critical of Herzl's policies and began to consider forming a youth faction, Weizmann thought of
himself as the man in the field carrying out the strategies Motzkin would plan.
"I may be a good recording machine," he wrote to Motzkin, "I even have my
own views on things, but you, my friend, you are the head." But these ful-
some compliments, however sincerely meant, were delivered during a period
when Weizmann, deeply involved in preparing a youth conference (with the
prospect of a youth faction in view), was trying desperately to regain the confidence and cooperation of a strangely recalcitrant Motzkin.[24]

The idea of a youth organization had been raised early at Zionist congresses; following a disappointing Third Congress, the student Zionists
tended to envisage such an organization as a progressive, ideological opposition party in Zionism. Motzkin was one of the most articulate spokesmen
of this conception. After the rebuff suffered at Herzl's hands at the Fourth
Congress, concrete suggestions for a conference to plan the project came from
a student Zionist group in Munich. Weizmann at once responded and began
to organize a preliminary conference. He sought Motzkin's participation with
special insistence; but to his dismay, when Motzkin finally replied after
repeated entreaties, it was to say he could not attend. He cited as reasons
personal problems that beset him and also his doubts whether a "homogeneous" group would be available to bring such a meeting to a successful
conclusion.

The issue of homogeneous participation at the meeting was a policy difference between the two men, arising less from opposing conceptions than
from diverging personal situations. Weizmann, taking up the organization of
a youth conference from his base in Geneva, extended his range to cover
Zionist youth groups in Russia as well as the Western universities, whereas
Motzkin was absorbed in a battle then being fought by his Berlin society. In
February 1901 Kadimah ran a rally to condemn the Bund for failing to have
the Jews mentioned in a resolution against the oppression of subject nationalities, which had been adopted by the Second International. Weizmann
wanted to cast a wide net in organizing his conference and questioned the
wisdom of prosecuting a feud with Jewish radicals at that time. This attitude
did not add to Motzkin's confidence in his younger comrade; hence, his concern about homogeneity at the planning session for the Zionist youth conference. Later, Weizmann proved even less enamored with Jewish radicalism
than was Motzkin. The difference between them was fundamentally tactical.
There was also a growing personal friction.

If, as Weizmann averred, Motzkin was the presiding genius and Weizmann his executive officer in the field, it made relations difficult when Weizmann took the initiative and Motzkin's influence was limited to belated hints
of disapproval from a distance. In 1901 apparent insubordination and even
more serious offenses by Weizmann led to public reprisals on Motzkin's part
and a decisive breach in their friendship. Apart from the difficulties of their
new relative physical and social location, one clear and painful reason for
their division was a romantic complication in Weizmann's life.

During his final doctoral studies at Fribourg, when Weizmann was close to the student colony in nearby Berne, he became attached to Sophia Getzova, a leading student Zionist. They were understood to be engaged not only by the student circles, but by Weizmann's family in Pinsk where Getzova was a welcome guest. She was also the close friend of Paula Rosenblum, who became Motzkin's wife. On moving to Geneva, Weizmann met a new circle of young students and developed his customary warm relations with them, notably with the women. He found particularly attractive those who came from southern Russia. Fresh and eager, they seemed free from the complexities and constricted Jewishness of students like Getzova, who came from his own part of the Pale of Settlement. One girl, Vera Khatzman, soon captured his affections completely and they became lovers.

The dilemma this presented for Weizmann was intense. He faced the dread prospect of explaining his betrayal not only to his fiancée, but to his parents, and he put off the ordeal as long as possible. After many months, he brought himself to tell "the whole truth" to Sophia Getzova, yet managed to maintain a continuing comradely relation with her in spite of the lasting hurt he evidently inflicted. For over a year more he hid the facts from his parents; he required Vera Khatzman to do the same on her vacations at home in Rostov-on-Don, even while sending her a revealing stream of letters and postcards. But he could not effectively hide from the "unwanted eyes" of the students in Geneva. The news, titillating and outrageous, called down a storm of indignant gossip in Berne and Berlin, and it appears that Weizmann was obliged to account for his behavior before a comrades' court. These developments (by which the Motzkins were personally touched because of their friendship with Getzova) signaled a break between Motzkin and Weizmann—and speeded Weizmann's casting off on an independent course of his own.[25]

In April 1901, with Motzkin absent, Weizmann chaired the preliminary planning conference in Munich to organize the Zionist youth conference later that year. He presented proposals common in his circle for activities supplementing what was lacking in the agenda of the WZO and especially appropriate for intellectuals and progressives. The proposals were largely adopted in a resolution contemplating the following program: examining ideological issues and confronting ideological opponents in a campaign to win over Jewish youth and intellectual forces; promoting cultural and social advancement in the Diaspora; and conducting studies of Palestinian conditions, with a view to facilitating Jewish settlement there. The meeting also set up a bureau, under Weizmann's direction, to organize the Zionist Youth Conference, and named student representatives from Munich and Geneva together with Jacob Bernstein-Kohan and Leo Motzkin as members. Weizmann then launched into a strenuous effort to carry out the task; he soon found himself, as a public figure, forced to define new positions not only in relation to Motzkin, but to other, more senior Jewish and Zionist leaders.

Weizmann now faced the question of a homogeneous composition of the conference, which had been raised by Motzkin earlier. The issue arose sharply in the case of Nachman Syrkin, who had staked out an independent ideological position at the Zionist congresses, in provocative lectures in Zurich and Berne, and in his manifesto, *The Socialist Jewish State* (first published in 1898). Syrkin wished to combine a Zionist-socialist cooperativist program in Palestine (or another territory, if Palestine proved unattainable) with social-democratic agitation à la Bund in Russia and other Diaspora lands. He now organized a socialist-Zionist group and wished to attend the Zionist Youth Conference—after having announced his withdrawal from the WZO. Weizmann, concurring with Motzkin's view—notwithstanding his desire for the broadest possible representation—ruled out Syrkin's personal participation. So too, although he was gravely disappointed when Bernard Lazare retracted a promise to present a paper at the conference, he found it far easier to part company with Lazare than to renounce the WZO and its Basle program, as Lazare did.

It was a more difficult problem to maneuver between conflicting pressures from Herzl and Ahad Ha'am, far more important figures for Weizmann. On July 2, 1901, Herzl wrote to him in strict confidence, asking Weizmann to cancel the Youth Conference, as it might harm negotiations he was then secretly conducting—but without explanation. Weizmann parried by requesting permission to disclose the letter to his responsible colleagues, who alone could authorize such an action. Meanwhile, he was making a serious effort to pin down Ahad Ha'am for a paper to be presented to the conference. Knowing that Ahad Ha'am favored a separate organization to conduct cultural work, Weizmann took pains to assure the revered veteran that—in practice, if not formally—the proposed body would be largely independent of the WZO. He could not follow Ahad Ha'am's line implicitly because his Zionist scale of values at the time gave priority to political aims—if not immediate political activities. Besides, he was not sanguine of success in a revolt against Herzl: "If only we knew that there was already a group of responsible men of action," he wrote to a friend in regard to Herzl's demand to cancel the conference, "we could declare war on H with a light heart. As it is, . . . everything . . . may crumble." In any case he was relieved of any pressure from Ahad Ha'am when the latter announced that he was retiring from public affairs for a period of self-examination and therefore could not participate. In the following months Herzl and Weizmann's young Zionists made their peace, and the conference was held in conjunction with the WZO Congress in December 1901. Motzkin attended, but did not offer a paper.[26]

In the months before the Zionist Youth Conference, Weizmann had still been striving to soothe the irritated, recalcitrant Motzkin. But instead of achieving appeasement, the Zionist conclaves in Basle widened the breach. At the Youth Conference Weizmann leveled unaccustomed sharp criticism at Motzkin. He then appeared at the congress with Vera Khatzman on his arm, greatly distressing Getzova and scandalizing her friends. At this point of mutual resentment, another quarrel arose between the two men. Nachman Syrkin, whose socialist-Zionists chose to meet at the same time in Basle, initiated discussions in which Weizmann and others joined privately, without formal approval of their group. Syrkin's proposal—to apply pressure on non-Zionist Jewish philanthropic agencies and compel them to conduct their work of aiding emigrants in conformity with a nationalist strategy—was extreme. But still it was an example of the democracy in action Motzkin had always advocated; it even enjoyed a measure of Herzl's sympathy, though not support. However, Motzkin branded any association with the subversive Syrkin as no less than treasonable, ignoring Weizmann's pleas that his actions were purely private and that no parallel organization had come out of the talks. The Berliners, dismissing objections that public airing of the dispute would harm their new young party, insisted on formal action. The matter was thrashed out in painful meetings in Berlin in March 1902, and the groups continued to work together. But the friendship and leader-follower relation with Motzkin was broken; Weizmann was now cast loose on his own course.

The Zionist Youth Conference, conducted with restraint under an agreement with Herzl, had not set up a separatist organization. Instead, it resolved to organize the Democratic Faction within the WZO. The Faction would try to influence policy through the whole range of Zionist activities and also promote independent efforts in areas neglected by the Herzlian administration: particularly the promotion of Jewish national culture, the study of Palestine as a potential field for practical development projects, the elaboration and defense of Zionist ideology in a new journal, and the advancement of the interests of Jewish students, workers, and emigrants. At the immediately following Fifth Zionist Congress, the young democrats secured a resolution declaring that "the education of the Jewish people in a national spirit [is] an essential part of the Zionist program" as well as the formation of a cultural commission, with Ahad Ha'am, Bernstein-Kohan, and Weizmann among its members. In the independent activities that the young Zionists would conduct after the congress, Weizmann and Motzkin were to assume their accustomed roles: Motzkin would devote himself to formulating the program of the new Faction and other tasks of intellectual leadership, while Weizmann, through an information bureau he would set up in Geneva, would be responsible for the detailed administrative conduct of the new group's affairs.[27]

In June 1902 a program for the new organization was adopted by the committee named by the Youth Conference and awaited only Motzkin's revision; but within a few weeks Weizmann was fuming, "True to himself, Motzkin has written nothing yet." Later, he wrote concerning plans for an annual conference of the Faction, "Mr. Motz[kin] 'wants to take the lead in the convening of the Conference, if Geneva [i.e., Weizmann and his aides] agrees to carry out a considerable portion of the work.' How do you like that?" He no longer welcomed such a relationship with Motzkin. "I shall take the convening of the Conference on myself, on condition that I get no direction from anywhere."[28]

Freed from tutelage to senior comrades and an established academic in his twenty-eighth year, Weizmann commanded a group of younger comrades who worked under *his* directives in Geneva. His other collaborators included two young men, Berthold Feiwel and Martin Buber, who served successively as editors of Herzl's journal, *Die Welt.* Until each broke with Herzl and left Vienna, they provided liaison with the WZO administration. For Feiwel and Buber, products of Slavic provinces in Austria-Hungary, Weizmann was a respected veteran Zionist colleague and an important contact with Russian Jewry. At the Youth Conference Weizmann met Samuel Shriro, a Baku oil magnate who was impressed by the conference and Weizmann's role in it. Thus there was now the prospect that Weizmann's vacation tours in Russia could be turned to practical advantage in the Faction's projects. Though other senior Russian leaders looked askance at an autonomous youth group in their midst, Weizmann developed close ties to Bernstein-Kohan, whose special role in the Zionist federation made him particularly congenial. This association was remarked by the Russian police, who kept a close watch on all unauthorized activities; one police report referred to Weizmann's role as "agitator" for Zionist elements led by the notorious Dr. Bernstein-Kohan, a man with a police file going back to his expulsion from the university in Petrograd in 1881. Such a reputation, whether deserved or not, could hardly sit well with Herzl—nor could Weizmann's association with Bernstein-Kohan, who was an opponent of Herzl's partisans in Russian Zionism. However, neither side was interested in provoking a break. Despite their disagreements, the WZO and the leaders of the Democratic Faction were able to support each other's projects—and for Weizmann, the workhorse as well as leader of the Faction, practical undertakings counted more than doctrinal disputes.

If his efforts all too often ended in disappointment during the Geneva years, it was the idleness of his comrades rather than the activity of official opponents that proved most frustrating. Meanwhile, the success of the Democratic Faction at the 1901 Zionist Congress led Orthodox Zionists in Russia to organize their own Zionist faction, Mizrachi. Owing to a new Russian policy (seeking to undercut the appeal of revolutionaries by sponsoring government-authorized reformism), a legal Zionist conference was allowed to be held in Minsk in 1902, preceding the WZO Congress of that year. The Mizrachi turned up in force at that meeting, whereas the Democratic Faction was weakly represented. The future looked dim for Weizmann's party. When a new wave of progressive young Zionists arose, they organized separately as socialists.

For half a year Weizmann tried to use his Geneva office as an information bureau, a nerve center for the activities of the Democratic Faction, only to give up in disgust when little if anything came in from the field to report. He then turned to a campaign to create a new Jewish university or institute of advanced education for the benefit of Russian-Jewish students, whom German universities were beginning to block from entry. He organized a census of Russian-Jewish students abroad, wrote a pamphlet (with Buber and Feiwel) outlining a project for the Jewish university, raised funds in Russia for the effort, and with Buber's help secured support from the WZO. At the same time he tried to promote other projects that originated in the Democratic Faction, in particular, the Juedischer Verlag, a publishing venture initiated by

Buber, Feiwel, the artist Ephraim Lilien, and an older Zionist friend, Davis Trietsch. His association with these writers and artists evidently had a special value for Weizmann. His rather submissive attitude to Motzkin and his other Berlin comrades in the past was not simply an acknowledgment of their seniority; it betrayed a feeling that his training and professional future lay in inferior areas, applied science and industry, whereas they had classical humanistic training as students of philosophy, political economy, and literature. His new friends were likely to make more of a mark in German culture than his old friends could ever expect to do, and they looked to him not only for backing and sponsorship among Russian Zionists but also for decisions on Zionist policy.

Weizmann took up the challenge of leadership with great self-confidence but without a clear objective and under singularly unpromising conditions. His opposition to Herzl was not, at that time, based on a well-defined alternative doctrine, like that of Ahad Ha'am's; it was dictated by distaste for Herzl's Zionist associates, his authoritarian style, and the doctrinaire concentration on the single—at the moment, clearly unpromising—tactic of backstairs and platform diplomacy. Moreover, Weizmann was far from sanguine about the outcome of any frontal challenge to Herzl's authority; he hoped to work within a framework of autonomy that would enjoy WZO support. But the relationship to Herzl, always uneasy, soon ended in a rupture, which arose not over an issue of substance but over questions of personal loyalty.

In 1902 Herzl's utopian Zionist novel *Altneuland* was published and was promptly attacked by Ahad Ha'am as blatantly un-Jewish. Max Nordau replied in *Die Welt* on March 3, 1903 with a scathing, derisive, and deliberately insulting assault upon Ahad Ha'am: he undertook to deny him any right to be called a Zionist. Buber, Feiwel, and Weizmann felt "honour-bound to protest most vigorously, in the name of many Western European Jewish authors" Nordau's "defamations and degradations [of] this genuine and perfect Jew who, long before the advent of political Zionism, appeared as the most radical combatant on behalf of the national movement." Yet, as Weizmann explained to a young critic, Kalman Marmor, although he and his friends "considered Nordau's conduct reprehensible," they remained "opposed to Ahad Ha'am because he [was] not a political Zionist."[29]

Such distinctions could not affect the chilly reserve that marked Herzl's subsequent correspondence with the Weizmann group. In May 1903, shortly after the Kishinev pogrom shook all Jewry, Weizmann, in his own and Feiwel's name, wrote a lengthy appeal to Herzl for "united effort," detailing the contributions the "young Zionists" were making and could make if not driven into the opposition. The modern-minded youth they represented were uniquely fitted to accomplish the central immediate task: to implant in the growing communities of the West the spirit of East European Jewish nationalism. Herzl drily replied that he did not think "the divisiveness which the conduct of the Faction reveals can serve this common purpose." Weizmann himself he dismissively judged to be "a person who has been misled, but nevertheless a useful force who will once more find his way back and proceed along the right road together with all of us." Buber, who had similar correspondence with Herzl at the time, left his editorial post at *Die Welt*. Weizmann, too, found himself increasingly identified with Herzl's antagonists with whom he was emotionally aligned but not necessarily joined by conviction.[30]

Weizmann's Zionist views at the time bespoke an urge for practical, effective action wherever an immediate possibility existed rather than any long-range theory. The Jewish university-institute that he proposed was conceived as a response to the pressing need of the general Russian-Jewish student population. Although Zionists were to initiate the project, Weizmann hoped to attract "all sections of Jewish students," to arouse "Jewish public opinion in Russia, Rumania, Germany, Austria, and America, etc.," and to press the non-Zionist Jewish Colonization Association (ICA) to support it. He therefore did not share the position of most Zionists, including Motzkin and other Russians, that a Jewish academy should be established *only* in Palestine, even if this meant delay and offered no immediate relief.[31]

So, too, his opposition to Herzl's single-mindedly *political* Zionism did not make him, like Ahad Ha'am, an equally single-minded *cultural* Zionist or an apolitical supporter of small-scale colonization along the old lines. Weizmann and his friends watched with keen hope Herzl's mysterious negotiations in 1902 concerning a charter for colonization in Palestine or Mesopotamia and in 1903 concerning the Sinai area of El-Arish. When Herzl's failures had to be publicly conceded, their disappointment was real—but so was their anger at the show of optimism that they felt had concealed the actual situation from the world and from active Zionists. The Weizmann reaction was to seek any available immediate action in which Zionists could immerse themselves while retaining the ultimate goal. Thus, he took up an old idea current among nationalists and suggested that Zionists seek to assist the emigration then in progress to havens other than Palestine in order to regulate it in accordance with nationalist aims. He also began to press more insistently for a program of research regarding settlement possibilities in Palestine itself, even if no immediate prospect of large-scale projects under a charter then existed.

Weizmann responded at first in the same pragmatic way when the British proposal to settle Jews in East Africa—the so-called Uganda project—was announced by Herzl in August 1903 on the eve of the Sixth Zionist Congress. Under the shattering impact of the Kishinev pogrom, Weizmann felt, like Herzl, that the Zionists could not reject any opportunity to alleviate the dire need of refugees from Russia; at the caucus of the Russian delegates to the congress, Weizmann was one of the speakers in favor of the Uganda proposal. He offered a resolution that read:

> Congress does not conceive the action in Africa as the ultimate aim of the Zionists, but deems it necessary to regulate emigration, and consequently finds that the Zionists must unify all colonization societies or convene a con-

gress in order to decide on East Africa. Zionist funds will not be expended
for this purpose. The Congress proposes that the A[ction] C[ommittee] shall
not desist from action in Wadi El-Arish.

Weizmann's proposal was ignored at the Russian caucus, and he played a
minor role in the proceedings of the congress itself. Indeed, after briefly
declaring his support of the Uganda project, he voted in the end against it.
Nevertheless, he was one of those named by the congress to investigate further the British proposal; having declared his opposition, he was able to use
his membership on the study commission to advance the fight against the
Ugandists.[32]

The Sixth Congress forced a sharp change in Weizmann's Zionist attitude,
for which he was less than fully prepared. He explained his switch, in a rather
brief and vague formula, at a meeting of the anti-Uganda opposition in Basle
shortly after the congress:

> Before the import of the project had been made clear to me I supported it;
> but in the course of the debate I discovered [in the statements of its
> supporters] that it meant that Zionism was to be transformed . . . The truth
> is that Herzl is not a nationalist, but a promoter of projects . . . He only takes
> external conditions into account, whereas the power on which we rely is the
> . . . people and its living desires . . . It is the people's consciousness that has
> to be bolstered . . . Cultural work must be put before all else.

Weizmann was not in the habit of putting one element in a complex social
or political equation "before all else"; but as he now showed, when circumstances compelled a clear choice, he could make it decisively and adhere to
it with his characteristic determination.[33]

He now elevated into an ideology views generally current in his circle but
held as matters of principle only by the more abstract thinkers among them.
A clear and sharp distinction between the attitudes of Eastern and Western
Jews had been made by Ahad Ha'am, contrasting the spiritual freedom of the
subjugated Easterners with the spiritual slavery he saw in the emancipated
Westerners. Buber's mystical subjectivism of that period, arising from a
movement of Western self-criticism and self-deprecation, saw in the rooted
piety and ethnic loyalty of Eastern Jews a source of redemption for Jews in
the West. Weizmann now began to sound similar notes in the heat of battle.

Weizmann's analysis described the Zionist movement as divided in principle between the opposed attitudes of Eastern and Western Europeans. The
Easterners like himself understood Zionism as a "life-giving force," broadly
concerned with the "free development of the nation." The "idea of statehood" was its "highest expression," but by no means the sum total of its content. Westerners, on the other hand, conceived of Zionism as a "mechanism."
Like their Orthodox allies (who also were "partly detached from living Judaism" because they were "confined within their rigid formulae") they were
"unable to perceive the connection [of Zionism] with the soul of the people."

Zionism remained for them a "cliché, completely devoid of Jewish content" and narrowly focused on "so-called diplomacy" and a "'Jewish Statism' that smells of philanthropy." The Zionist movement had been formed originally by a compact in which the East was to supply the content (as well as the mass following) and the West was to supply the political forms, which the Easterners could not create for themselves given the abnormal condition of their life. Although the East carried out its responsibility and even "shaped [the political forms] into an organic force as a result of [their] Jewish content," the Western leaders failed to become true Jewish nationalists. The crisis that had broken out was therefore an inevitable one that accurately reflected the "abnormal situation of the Jews."[34]

For all his claiming to speak for the spirit of the people, Weizmann knew very well that the people's actual desires and preferences did not run with his own—hence the need for "bolstering" their consciousness. Nothing could have demonstrated this more clearly than the contrasting reactions to contemporary events. When Herzl went to negotiate with V. K. Plehve, the minister whom Jewish opinion held responsible for the Kishinev pogrom, the intelligentsia was scandalized. The Democratic Faction sensed that one of the terms of an agreement that Herzl might strike could be the suppression of their own group's special activities in Russia. But the popular masses, who greeted Herzl as a messianic hero at the Vilna train station, gave him unwavering devotion in spite of his overture to the enemy. Then at the Sixth Zionist Congress, the opposition to Herzl's East African project comprised, indeed, the majority of the veteran Russian leadership as well as Weizmann's close friends; but the opposition could hardly feel that they truly represented the desires of the people. Not only Mizrachi, the group that spoke for the mass of traditionalist Jews, but also most of the socialist-Zionists, the strongest growing force among Zionist-minded youth, joined Herzl's regular staunch supporters on this issue. Weizmann's own kin, both the young radicals and the bourgeois elders, opposed his stand, as did Shriro, his main financial supporter. Even within the Democratic Faction, a leader as prominent as Motzkin continued to waver between yea and nay on the East Africa project.

Having taken his stand in opposition at the Sixth Congress, Weizmann together with Buber and Feiwel began working to align the Democratic Faction with the Nay-Sayers. He hoped to get financial support from the leaders of the Russian Zionist federation for the journal *Der Jude,* as a fighting organ of the cause of ancestral Zion, and for other cultural and research activities of the Faction. At the same time the structure a.id functional plan of the Faction were to be altered along lines favored particularly by Buber. The loose, ineffectual youth organization was to be converted into a trimmed-down working group of academic activists, assigned specific tasks of theoretical elucidation and practical research that were immediately necessary and practicable and best suited to their professional skills. Buber, who declared himself to be opposed in principle both to "democracy" and to "factional" political organization, favored the change as a point of ideology. Weizmann, a working scientist, appreciated the superiority of expert management by a single hand over management by committees: in his own practice, he usually contrived to use the preferred method. But he now favored a cadre system of committed activists for lack of another option, that is, because of the failure of a better alternative—mass organization.[35]

In October 1903, within two months after the close of the Sixth Zionist Congress, Weizmann took advantage of his position on the East Africa Commission and went to London by way of Paris to check the Uganda proposal. His plans for active Zionist work included a trip to Palestine in the spring to study the prospects for the university there. After that he thought of placing himself at the disposal of the Nay-Sayers for additional Zionist labors. During his London stay (the only significant part of the program to be carried out), he was aided by Major William Evans-Gordon to reach British political and civil service figures. Evans-Gordon was one of those somewhat antisemitic Englishmen who were later helpful to Weizmann, as to Herzl earlier. Weizmann had met him in Pinsk over a year earlier when, in order to ease England of an unwelcome burden of Russian Jews, the Major was investigating the causes of the influx of Jewish migrants to his country. With Evans-Gordon's help, Weizmann spent a good deal of time on private diplomacy, interviewing such qualified persons as he could reach on the East African matter—without at that time being able to converse in English. He was elated on learning that the British were regretting their East African offer; some informants also indicated support for Zionist aims in or near Palestine. In letters to his close friends, Weizmann showed how he felt about this venture into diplomacy: "Herzl," he exulted, "would already be talking of 'gigantische Erfolge'." He prepared detailed memoranda for the Russian Nay-Sayers.[36]

But this period of euphoric activity did not last long. Weizmann, on becoming a Nay-Sayer, took an increasingly militant line, allying himself to Menahem Mendel Ussishkin's intractable leadership. But the Nay-Sayers seemed weak and divided, unable to stand up to Herzl. Worse still, their strong man, Ussishkin, the only one who lifted Weizmann's spirits, *did not* give his young ally the kind of acceptance he sought. On returning to Geneva from London, Weizmann sent Ussishkin proposals for the future organization of the Nay-Sayers, including the plan for using his academic working group as their intelligence and propaganda staff. But Ussishkin saw no point in maintaining a separate academic unit and continued to urge that they merge with the general Russian Zionist body. Although he shared Weizmann's views on the appropriate form and policies of a reorganized WZO, he had his own plan to lay before the Nay-Sayers and did not need to refer to Weizmann's draft. Indeed, when the Russian Zionist leaders met in Kharkov on Ussishkin's initiative, the proceedings and final resolutions were held in secret and Weizmann was not kept informed.

Weizmann's own projects, meanwhile, were successively frustrated. Yielding to the pressure of older Zionists, he had agreed that the proposed university must be created only in Palestine, which meant an indefinite deferment. He therefore proposed to organize an Institute of Summer Vacation

Courses in Europe as a preliminary step and launched a strenuous campaign together with Buber on behalf of that plan; but here, too, support and cooperation lagged badly. Another major project, the new journal *Der Jude,* bogged down for lack of funds and because of personal difficulties between the editors, Buber and Feiwel. Finally, until the end of 1903, Weizmann worked to reconvene a youth conference for the Democratic Faction, growing steadily more embittered at the indolence and unresponsiveness of his comrades in Russia. "Russian incapacity," he once said, "ruins the finest people, turning most of them into minor Hamlets."[37] In January 1904 shortly before the youth conference was to open, he was asked to postpone it because the Nay-Sayers were about to confront Herzl with their "ultimatum" (the demands adopted by the conference of Russian leaders convened by Ussishkin at Kharkov) at a meeting of the top Zionist leaders in Vienna. That effort ended in a fiasco for the Nay-Sayers and also in the final collapse of the youth conference as well as the Democratic Faction.

Throughout this time of feverish activity and growing malaise, Weizmann's personal situation grew increasingly difficult. In the last months of 1903, he began to spit blood and complained of "shattered nerves," and he had to give up work for a while under his doctor's orders. By then, Vera Khatzman was known and accepted by his family and friends as his intended wife, and Weizmann had to consider, as he turned twenty-nine, how his financial and professional future could be better secured. His laboratory discoveries had not been taken up for production by the Bayer works, and his retainer from them was no longer available. Another retainer offered by Shriro for research he might do in petroleum chemistry was withdrawn after the Sixth Zionist Congress, where the two adopted opposing stands. He was painfully aware that his scientific research had been interrupted recently by his immersion in Zionist labors; and he saw no assured future in the German-Swiss university world. His visit to Russia in April 1904 left him deeply depressed about the bleak prospect for Jews in the Pale of Settlement. Under these pressures, his inclination to find a home in a new country matured to a decision.[38]

Weizmann's personal and professional ambitions and his evolving Zionist views played into such a decision in a complicated and perplexing pattern of uncertainties. At one point, when he talked of devoting full time to Zionist work, Vera Khatzman sharply brought him back to his senses by asking whether he wished to turn into another Bernstein-Kohan, a man whose neglect of his medical practice for Zionist activity had only served to bring him into contempt among Zionists. Weizmann hoped that his university project might eventually provide an appropriate post for him in Palestine; after all, he was a *melamed* (a schoolteacher) by trade, as he once remarked. But this was a remote prospect. Moving to America, if possible, or to England, might serve two purposes: he could gain status and experience as a chemist, which would later be useful in Palestine, and he could also carry out his Zionist mission to bring Western methods to Eastern Jews in their new centers of mass settlement.[39]

During his October 1903 visit to England, Weizmann had made initial inquiries about opportunities that might be open to him as a chemist. He solicited the aid of the Sephardic rabbi in London, Haham Moses Gaster, a leading British Zionist and a strong Nay-Sayer, who might regard Weizmann's settlement in England as a powerful reinforcement for his own cause. He was also referred by his academic sponsors in Germany and Switzerland to Manchester, where the university had set up new modern laboratories. Weizmann made an initial friendly contact with Professor William Perkin, Jr., a famous Manchester chemist, and in March 1904 Perkin wrote suggesting that Weizmann could break into British academic life by working for a time in his laboratory. When this proposal developed further, after Weizmann's return from his parting visit to Russia, and it appeared to hold out promise of an eventual appointment, his course began to seem set. To some comrades he wrote sadly that he would be forced by this move to drop out of active Zionist work for a while; to others he wrote hopefully that he would now come to Palestine, by way of England, strengthened both as a chemist and as a Zionist leader.[40]

Suddenly, in May, an opportunity appeared that might let him go to Palestine immediately. His correspondent in Palestine, Chaim Bograchov, wrote him that a suitable position was available in the new teachers' college founded by German philanthropists in Jerusalem. Weizmann immediately submitted his application and wrote to friends asking their support; but his application was rejected. Soon thereafter, with the aid of a loan from his brother-in-law, Chaim Lubzhinsky, he set out for England.[41]

On July 3, 1904 as Weizmann was preparing to leave Geneva, Theodor Herzl died. Weizmann, sharing the shock and grief of all Zionists and of the whole Jewish world, eulogized the hero at a public ceremony conducted by his group in Geneva and mourned him in letters to his friends. On July 6 as he left Geneva, he wrote to Vera Khatzman that Herzl's death had "left us a frightening legacy." He spoke of "a great weight on my heart," and he felt that in the face of the "difficult times that await me . . . a heavy burden has fallen on my shoulders, and the shoulders are weak and tired."

So, having reached a dead end in Geneva and with his Jewish and Zionist worlds lying in shambles about him, Weizmann set out to the West, hoping to build both worlds and his personal life anew.

Retreat to Manchester

Weizmann's memoirs describe his "flight to England" as a "deliberate and desperate" step, taken to ensure his endangered future. He implies that he had resolved to suspend his Zionist activities in order to devote undivided attention to science and his academic career. Yet, his letters from Paris and London in July 1904 were filled with accounts of political activity. He secured interviews in the Foreign Office with Lord Percy, the undersecretary of state, and Sir Clement Hill, superintendent of African protectorates, and managed to get their confirmation of a summary of the talks he composed—a coup that powerfully reinforced his belief in his gift for diplomacy. He felt he had conclusive proof that the Uganda plan was dead, that its proponents were pulling the wool over the Zionist public's eyes. He sent back a confidential report, which he hoped would be published for the impending Zionist Annual Conference, a major meeting fully empowered to set policy between the biennial congresses; but his friends decided to make no use of Weizmann's report. The long-awaited encounter at the conference ended without a clear victory for either side in the Uganda dispute.

This proved to be more than a momentary setback for Weizmann. It ushered in a long, dreary period when he was removed from the mainstream of Zionist affairs. When he wrote that Herzl's death had placed a great burden upon *his* shoulders, he betrayed a remarkably developed sense of his vocation for the top leadership. He pointedly noted that on his visit to Nordau, the old man had said pleasant things about Weizmann's qualifications to succeed Herzl; but he had also said, "Sie sind aber zu jung" ("But you are too young.") Weizmann may have graduated from youth leader to senior activist, but he was still too young for any role greater than follower or aide of whatever older leader he might attach himself to. England was the wrong base for such a position in the crucial years after 1904.[42]

The Kishinev pogrom, Herzl's East African project, and the upheavals arising out of the calamitous Russo-Japanese War had evoked a radical, activist, highly ideological awakening among young Russian Zionists.[43] The movement was hugely expanded, and historic changes were initiated in Eastern Europe and in Palestine. Many young leaders began their careers in that period: among them, Weizmann's future antagonist, Vladimir Jabotinsky, and the socialist-Zionists who went to Palestine as laborers and eventually became Weizmann's chief allies—and his supplanters. Weizmann, in England, could have no personal involvement in the crucial developments of the time.

As the Democratic Faction was sinking into total dissolution, the role it had sought for itself as an ideological party was being taken up by others. The quest for autoemancipation by the new generation was focused neither on cultural nor political issues, but on solutions for the "abnormal" Jewish social-economic structure. One party, opposed by Weizmann because it rejected Zion (as impracticable, unavailable, or encumbered with prohibitive burdens of traditionalism and sentimentality), sought a territorialist solution by concentrating Jewish emigrants in some other country. Another party— led by the brilliant dialectician Ber Borochov—shared Weizmann's commitment to Zion, but he held it in suspicion because it used Marxist analysis to argue the Zionist case and was committed to social revolution. Thus, not only his age and his residence, but ideological differences—on his side, rather an avoidance of ideology—separated Weizmann from the innovations of the new generation of Zionists.

A third trend had fewer positively disturbing features for Weizmann. Some radicals were ready to defer all Zionist or territorialist resettlement and concentrate on *Gegenwartsarbeit* (a minimum program of immediate local activity leading to the *Endziel* [ultimate aim]). Their program included securing civil rights, national autonomy, and cultural, social, and economic reconstruction in Russia by local political action in alliance with other Russian progressives. Similar ideas were current among bourgeois Zionists. A meeting of Jewish journalists, including Vladimir Jabotinsky and Yitzhak Gruenbaum, initiated a move for a general Russian Zionist conference, which took place in Helsingfors (Helsinki) in December 1906. Motzkin was in attendance and took an active part, but neither Ussishkin nor the Russian Herzlian leaders were there. Led by Yehiel Tschlenow, the more moderate rival of Ussishkin among the Russian Nay-Sayers, the conference endorsed the "practical Zionist" program for immediate settlement planning in Palestine parallel with political work. Its most significant contribution was a program for *Gegenwartsarbeit* drafted by Jabotinsky. It called for democratic reform of the Russian state, full and equal rights for Jews, fair representation of minorities in elections, and the recognition of Russian Jewry as a national minority, with autonomous rights exercised through a democratically elected Jewish national assembly. Individually, Jews were to have the right to use Hebrew and Yiddish in public institutions and to observe a legal day of rest on Saturday rather than Sunday. Thus, the Russian Zionists broke sharply with their previous avoidance of domestic politics. They now participated directly in electoral and parliamentary Russian politics through their own parties and in blocs, and they adopted an agenda rivaling that of the Bund in its appeal to the immediately pressing concerns of Russian Jewry.

Such an agenda could well have appealed to Weizmann in his earlier days. An eclectic attack on the whole range of practical hardships confronting Russian Jewry was precisely the approach congenial to his unideological spirit. But he had committed himself ideologically in the Uganda debate to those who demanded a policy narrowly focused on the goal of Zion. In the Nay-Sayer camp he aligned himself with Ussishkin, the hard-liner who aimed to purge territorialist deviationists from the WZO at the first opportunity; accordingly, like Ussishkin, Weizmann opposed involving Zionist parties in the domestic politics of Diaspora countries. If he had been in Russia, he might have followed Ussishkin's example of avoiding the Helsingfors conference deliberately. Living in England, he was able to view the local political activities of Russian Zionists without indicating opposition, but with a cool neutrality.

The English Zionist movement had begun as a response to the plight of Rumanian Jews in the late 1870s and Russian Jews in the 1880s.[44] The refugee streams of those critical times presented opportunities as well as problems to British Jewry. The exaggerated reaction to the imagined threat of a flood of immigrants had overtones of Jew-hatred. On the other hand, there was a long-sustained tradition of extending protection to Jews in Palestine within the sphere of influence Britain was building in the Near East. In this context British Jewry had a special interest in aiding fellow Jews in Palestine: religious sentiment, humanitarian reform, and a desire to support British policy and be associated with the seats of power were all involved.

A political approach to Zionism was thus native to the English movement, which attracted prominent leaders of the Anglo-Jewish establishment as well as East End immigrants. But political efforts, whether through an approach to the Sublime Porte or a popular petition in London, seemed to harden Ottoman opposition to Jewish immigration and land acquisition in Palestine. Shortly before Herzl emerged on the scene, the English philo-Zionists had abandoned political action and confined themselves to minor projects of resettlement unobtrusively pursued. The warm welcome the leaders gave Herzl on his first visit to London became chilly when he returned after his diplomatic campaign in Constantinople; this made him respond eagerly to the offer of a young journalist, Jacob de Haas, to recruit support for him in London's immigrant quarter. Herzl's invitations to the First Zionist Congress were rejected on practical grounds by the West End Zionophile leaders; among the East European immigrants, both the congress and the organizing effort that followed found a more positive response.

The British Zionist movement, reorganized after the congress, was strongly identified with Herzl's political approach but largely made up of immigrants open to the appeals and influences of their old-country background. As the years passed without a signal success of Herzlian policy, East End Zionists drifted away from their West End leaders and Zionist clubs in provincial cities began to chafe under the dominance of the London center. The East African project precipitated a cleavage that turned old rivalries into something like feuds. Initially, the prospect of a "Zionist" project in East Africa that would find its place in British foreign policy revived the old British Zionist tradition of political activism; Herzl's prime agents and supporters in the affair were the Zionist leaders Leopold Greenberg, Joseph Cowen, and Israel Zangwill. When the project collapsed and Herzl died, Zangwill left the WZO (under Ussishkin's pressure) to found the Jewish Territorial Organization (ITO). Greenberg and Cowen, the leaders of the English Zionist Federation (EZF), remained essentially faithful to their old ideas and did not fully accept the taboo the Seventh Zionist Congress in 1905 laid on the territorialists. But the movement, which had steadily declined during these trials, was now hopelessly conflict ridden. The new ideological conflict brought to the surface all the tensions among disparate parts of the EZF. It was in this environment that Weizmann had to find a role for himself in the painfully emerging post-Herzlian era.[45]

Weizmann in those years lived under the pressures common to a whole generation of Jewish emigrants, though, of course, he enjoyed advantages available to few. He "fled" from Switzerland at a time when his own roots and those of his native community were being torn up. He came to England with no contract of employment, though—unlike most other immigrants—with excellent references and contacts and some resources of his own. He was compelled to give immediate priority to finding a livelihood for himself and his intended bride. Beyond this, he faced a period of anxious and strenuous labor to achieve his goal of professional eminence and independent wealth.

During the few weeks that Weizmann spent in London in July 1904, he combined politics with a job search. He wrote to Ussishkin that a post in London would offer better opportunities for his political work than elsewhere in England; at that point, his dealings with Professor Perkin with regard to Manchester had not led to conclusive results. Soon after, Perkin met him in London and they arrived at an agreement, as he wrote to Vera Khatzman, that would relieve him of the burden of "chasing aimlessly all over London. I have lost the habit of living in such an enormous city, and it gets on my nerves." To Zvi Aberson in Geneva he wrote the next day that although Professor William Ramsay in London had promised him about the same as Professor Perkin in Manchester, though "in a less positive way,. . . I prefer Manchester, the more so as the University is brand new there and very well appointed. It has an excellent laboratory and library, the climate is better, the town cheaper, and one can always move to London if the opportunity arises, *reculer pour mieux sauter!*" As always, he was able to phrase the bare facts with delicacy, in a way that suited the sensibility of his correspondent and presented his own case in the best light.[46]

Weizmann settled in Manchester, relying on Professor Perkin's indefinite and contingent promise that he might get Weizmann a research fellowship in his college by Christmas if he did good work in the laboratory before then. Such a fellowship provided payment for assisting in the professor's research and instruction; it would allow the research fellow to give a course—without pay. Perkin suggested that his prospective assistant begin work in the laboratory immediately while he, Perkin, was away on vacation. Thus Weizmann undertook at his own risk and expense to complete enough research within a few months to justify a Christmas appointment, and—as he proposed to teach a course—to master fluent English speech within that period.

His success in these undertakings was remarkable and required extraordinary efforts. Before going to the Zionist Annual Conference in August, he had set himself up in the laboratory and within a month after his return he completed two technical articles in collaboration with Perkin's assistant, William Pickles. These were the first of a series that "Charles" Weizmann began to publish in British scientific journals in rapid succession, together with Perkin's research group. After Christmas he was duly appointed a research fellow and made the supervisor of Perkin's new organic chemistry laboratory, but at a salary that was far from meeting his anticipated expenses. He supplemented his income by working for Charles Dreyfus of the Clayton Aniline Company, a chemist who was also a community leader and active Zionist. His research for this firm was begun, like his fellowship, under Perkin's sponsorship. It was based on experiments on camphor initiated by Perkin and, apart from work at the Clayton Aniline factory during the academic recess, it was carried out at the university with the aid of Perkin's students. But this additional income did not suffice for Weizmann's needs; in later years he read examination papers for other universities. Even then, he had to borrow regularly from friends to carry him until his salary and fees were paid.

Not only hard work, but oppressive loneliness made Weizmann's first years in England a time of stress and depression. He had thought that Vera Khatzman might be able to complete her medical studies in England, but this turned out to be an illusion. His fiancée, in fact, stayed behind in Switzerland for two years before they could marry and be united in Manchester; during that interval personal and family troubles put a strain on their relations. These circumstances did not help make England, nor Manchester in particular, a happy place for Weizmann. His letters frequently complain of the dullness and grayness of life there, of the vain complacency of the assimilated wealthy Jews, and of the vulgarity and ignorance of the new immigrants; he writes with yearning of the life he had left behind in the Geneva student colony. Some of his bitterest complaints are reserved for the Zionists of provincial Manchester as well as the Zionists in the capital.[47]

His disparagement of English Zionists was directed at all their contending varieties. The West End leaders could stand as a model of Western philanthropic-cum-political, exclusively state-oriented and diplomatic, vicarious Zionism, which (to his mind) was not truly nationalist. His identification with the East End immigrant Zionists and with the provincial clubs, largely manned by the same type, was strengthened by practical considerations. His natural audience for Zionist agitation, especially in the beginning, was the Yiddish-speaking group for whom his folksy humor and sharp wit were a familiar, highly appreciated evocation of the old country. But he also responded to the immigrants with the same impatient aversion that he had for their like in the Russian Pale of Settlement. As soon as possible he left the immigrant neighborhood and made his home in a more acculturated middle-class quarter among other academics.

On his arrival in England, Weizmann was sufficiently prominent in world-Zionist affairs to be of concern to British leaders caught up in the Zionists' internal quarrels. The chief antagonists were the Haham, Dr. Moses Gaster, the Sephardic rabbi who was the leading Nay-Sayer, abetted (for reasons of their own) by provincial leaders in towns like Manchester and Leeds as well as by the largely immigrant fraternal society, the Order of Ancient Maccabeans. On the other side, the Herzlian political Zionists, Joseph Cowen and Leopold Greenberg, publisher of the *Jewish Chronicle,* dominated the national leadership and the London Zionist societies. Weizmann was courteously welcomed and even mildly courted by both sides; but it was clear that his sympathies lay with the Gaster camp, and he developed personal ties with the Haham rather than the incumbent leadership.

Gaster became Weizmann's initial guide on the ways of English life and gave him advice and assistance, including personal loans. Weizmann, for his part, lent his weight to Gaster's campaign to control the British Zionist organization. But his commitment to Gaster was limited by his view of himself as primarily attached to the Russian movement. He wished, therefore, as he reported to his Russian friends, to keep a certain distance from the local quarrels. In addition, Weizmann was not convinced, as Gaster was, of the Haham's vocation to succeed Herzl.[48]

Notwithstanding his reserved attitude toward the British Zionists, Weiz-

mann attended the EZF Conference in Leeds in January 1905 and was elected
to the Executive Committee as a vice president on Greenberg's nomination.
Together with Gaster he campaigned during the spring of 1905 for anti-
Ugandist delegates to the Seventh Zionist Congress; but in the period following the congress, he acted in concert with the WZO coalition leadership that
was established, particularly with Ussishkin and Nahum Sokolow during
their visit to England, to seek a harmonious accommodation between the
contending British leaders.

The struggle over Herzl's succession was not cleanly and decisively resolved
at an early occasion but continued fitfully, with compromise solutions satisfactory to neither side. During Herzl's lifetime, he carried out the main Zionist labors personally, as chairman of the Action Committee. The small group
of Action Committee members who resided in Vienna, most of whom were
personally attached to Herzl, were expected to assist him, but he frequently
was moved to complain in his diary of their inactivity. With Herzl's death
this structure of responsibility urgently required revision, for it depended
entirely on Herzl's indispensable authority and talents. This situation set the
terms of the immediate struggle over the succession during the first years of
Weizmann's emigration to Britain.[49]

The Vienna group of Herzl's aides felt they had the best claim to succeed,
but they were not regarded by the rest of the movement as having the requisite ability or legal title. The only one who enjoyed the prestige for succession in the eyes of all was Max Nordau; repeated efforts were made to persuade him to accept, but in vain. The Russians, given the conditions in their
country and their inner division, could not seek the top leadership; but they
could give decisive support to contending Western Zionists in Vienna, Paris,
Berlin, or London—all of whom were more or less closely aligned with
Herzlian policies. In the event they, like the majority of other Zionists, turned
to David Wolffsohn, a Russian-born timber merchant from Cologne, who
was one of Herzl's closest friends and advisers—but not an ardent supporter
of the East African colonization proposal. The Seventh Zionist Congress
directly elected an executive group, the Smaller Action Committee, in which
Wolffsohn balanced, and by implication led, a coalition of three Herzlian
Westerners and three "practical" Zionists, including Ussishkin and Bernstein-Kohan along with the Berlin botanist, Dr. Otto Warburg. This confirmed the essential compromise that had been worked out and put into effect
during the year that had passed since Herzl's death.

Weizmann, as a member of the congress' Standing Committee, shared in
the general control of the proceedings and in the nominations' procedures
that produced this result. He was also named an English member of the
Greater Action Committee. Although some of the stormiest scenes at the congress attended the election of English members of the Action Committee, particularly in the case of Joseph Cowen (who was supported by Zangwill), Weizmann was not a controversial candidate.

The faction Weizmann supported could not be said to have dominated the reorganization of the WZO at the Seventh Congress, in spite of their considerable success in electing delegates. But they could congratulate themselves on substantial victories in defining policies. The hard-liners led by Ussishkin had the satisfaction of seeing the territorialists leave the congress when a resolution was passed confining the Zionist movement to work in and for Palestine and adjoining lands. They were hopeful that the WZO would now be directed from Berlin, where Professor Warburg resided. But this arrangement depended on Bernstein-Kohan, perhaps also Ussishkin, becoming salaried officials of the WZO. This was a status to which, not long before, they had tried to reduce Herzl, with the clear intent of controlling him; certainly, Ussishkin understood the implications for himself. He took over the helm of the Odessa Committee of Hibbat Zion and dropped out of direct competition. Wolffsohn's dominance was assured, and the executive functions of the WZO were transferred to Cologne, where Wolffsohn resided. Ussishkin had retreated to his regional base and Bernstein-Kohan, after living for a time in Palestine, withdrew into saddened and frustrated obscurity in Russia.[50]

Yet, the WZO—with Professor Warburg guiding the work and under Wolffsohn's tight fiscal control—now initiated a new era of small-scale resettlement in Palestine, expanded its cultural activity, and took a new line on political work in Palestine, without the Herzlian prerequisite of an enabling charter. After the Young Turk Revolution in 1908, the whole WZO leadership, with Nordau in the van, explicitly avowed that it no longer held a charter to be essential now that Turkey had a democratic regime. Increasing weight was laid on what could be done practically under existing political conditions. Meanwhile, men of roughly the same persuasion as Weizmann moved into responsible posts in the WZO. The veteran Hebrew journalist, Nahum Sokolow, came to assist Wolffsohn in Cologne; Victor Jacobson was posted in Constantinople, where Jabotinsky came to join him in lobbying the Ottoman parliament and cultivating public opinion through the press; and the young Zionist technician, Dr. Arthur Ruppin, conducted the field offices of the WZO in Jaffa and began a new epoch of Zionist resettlement.

Nevertheless, the dominant voice in the WZO was that of Wolffsohn, Herzl's epigone. Issues continually arose that rankled the Easterners, in Russia and abroad, as well as their Western sympathizers. In Germany itself the originally dominant Herzlian leaders were challenged by younger recruits who sought a bridge to East European Jewry under the guidance of Kurt Blumenfeld, a new man, and Martin Buber. Weizmann in England watched this from a distance and was drawn into parallel efforts at home.

Recovery

In August 1906 on the eve of a WZO Annual Conference, Weizmann married Vera Khatzman in Zoppot, near Danzig. She had just completed her doctorate and hoped to practice medicine in England. Chaim had been reappointed for two years at a slightly increased salary of one hundred twenty-five pounds per annum; he was assured that the university wished to retain him and that there were prospects of a professorship soon. After the wedding, the young couple attended the Zionist Annual Conference, spent a few days in Switzerland, and then set out for their new life together in Manchester.

The loneliness of the preceding period was ended, but their years of struggle were not over. Vera Weizmann, compelled to prepare for British medical qualifying examinations and soon to become a young mother, did not begin her practice until 1913. Chaim continued his steady, determined advance in his profession, but he could not outrun the growing load of expenses and responsibilities that continually seemed to overtake him.

In a renewed contract with the Clayton Aniline Company, Weizmann was released from the irksome obligation of working in the factory during the academic recess. He was able to use his vacations for Zionist meetings and for new research interests that he was developing. In 1909 he began to work with Professor Auguste Fernbach at the Pasteur Institute in Paris. He plunged into the study of microbiology and took up the researches that led to his major discoveries of fermentation processes for the production of acetone and butyl alcohol, later applied in the manufacture of synthetic rubber.[51]

Weizmann's circle of acquaintance and influence grew steadily, both among scientists and persons active in public affairs. At a Zionist meeting, he gained the friendship of Samuel Alexander, the eminent Manchester philosopher. A close bond developed between both Weizmanns and the family of the physicist and mathematician, Arthur Schuster. Schuster, a Frankfurt Jew converted to Christianity, was a strong professional support for Weizmann in university politics; Schuster's wife, Caroline, and daughter, Norah, combined personal friendship (expressed in a decidedly erotic vein by Weizmann at times) with a strong interest in Jewish concerns. Schuster's wife, whom Weizmann referred to in his correspondence as "Mother," was the daughter of a minister and had a markedly philosemitic attitude. She saw Weizmann as an ally in conveying to her children their father's Jewish heritage.

His contacts and influence in the Jewish community also widened in a somewhat similar pattern.[52] His first friends in Manchester were found in the immigrant, Yiddish-speaking quarter of Cheatham, but this was not the circle in which he moved in later years. In 1904 in London, Kalman Marmor, Uriah Moonitz, and Dov Aberson (the brother of Zvi, Weizmann's Geneva comrade) might have filled the place of the friends of his student years, but all three emigrated to America, leaving Chaim to bemoan the spiritual desert into which life had cast his lot. In 1908 Ahad Ha'am, who fully shared Weizmann's background and intimate values, settled in London as director of the English branch of the Wissotzky Tea Company. Weizmann became deeply and permanently bound to his old mentor and new friend. He stayed in Ahad Ha'am's house when he was in London, used it as a mail drop, borrowed money from him, shared in Ahad Ha'am's personal griefs, and consulted him as an oracle on Weizmann's own personal and Zionist affairs. This new intimacy, maintained during Weizmann's subsequent rise in the Zionist movement, undoubtedly affected the style and substance of Weizmann's formulations and positions on current issues. Around Ahad Ha'am there collected a group of younger men like Leon Simon and Norman Bentwich, university-trained professionals who adopted the cautious rationality and realism of his approach and echoed the themes of his cultural Zionism. For them and for young men of similar background in Manchester (especially the journalist, Harry Sacher, and his two brothers-in-law, Simon Marks and Israel Sieff, of the Marks and Spencer stores), Weizmann, along with Ahad Ha'am, became the leader of a new force in English Zionism.

Before Ahad Ha'am's arrival, Weizmann's Jewish associates were mainly bourgeois leaders of British Zionism and the general Jewish community, with whom, as he often complained, he had little in common beyond communal work.[53] Nevertheless, they became useful allies when conflicts arose between rival factions in Zionism and Anglo-Jewry. They also widened Weizmann's horizon for work among British Gentiles—politicians, in particular. Weizmann's employer, Dr. Charles Dreyfus, was not only the head of the Manchester Zionist Society, but also local chairman of the Conservative party. Such a man must have found Weizmann useful for access to the Yiddish-speaking voting public (and to European Zionist leaders) as well as to academic circles. Dreyfus arranged a meeting between the young man and Arthur Balfour, the Tory leader, during the 1905–6 general election. The local Jewish Liberal leaders (among them Nathan Laski, the father of Harold and Neville Laski) brought him together with Winston Churchill, their candidate for Cheatham. Though Weizmann was able to make no use of these contacts for many years (by which time they hardly retained great potency), he valued the meetings highly and kept well in mind the openings he believed they afforded him.

After David Wolffsohn took over WZO leadership, Weizmann evidently believed that he could continue some activities started in Geneva within the limits of a Manchester base. He was heartened by the plans of the WZO Commission for the Investigation of Palestine, headed by Professor Otto Warburg. The commission proposed to set up summer courses in Europe—Weizmann saw this as a continuation of his own aborted institute—and also intended to establish an agricultural experiment station in Palestine. Weizmann hoped to participate in both projects personally. He welcomed the effort, during the visit of Ussishkin and Sokolow to England in 1906, to seek non-Zionist participation in a committee for Palestinian affairs and hoped to see prominent Gentiles, like Balfour and Churchill, included on the committee. There were personal elaborations, extending the leaders' programs beyond their capacity, and little came of Weizmann's private dreams: the summer courses were not held; the agricultural experiment station was, indeed, set up (under the direction of the Palestinian agronomist, Aaron Aaronsohn), but Weizmann had no hand in it; and the Palestine Committee functioned on a more modest scale than Weizmann envisioned.[54]

Weizmann became actively involved in WZO efforts to resolve the differences between the British Zionist factions. The Seventh Zionist Congress had created a working agreement among WZO leaders, but it had not conciliated the hostile British factions. In fact, two closely related issues on which Wolff-sohn and his opponents had come to an understanding—the attitude toward territorialism and the policies of the Zionist financial instrument, the Jewish Colonial Trust—were precisely those that stirred up new quarrels between the British rivals. The Zionist Congress, in confining its resettlement plans to Palestine and adjoining areas, had received Wolffsohn's assurance that the Jewish Colonial Trust would amend its bylaws to include a similar restriction of its operations—operations that had until then remained a pious wish, but were not limited to the Palestine area under its charter as a British corporation. Precisely the latter point was raised by Zangwill at the congress—he insisted that the exclusion of extra-Palestinian colonization was unconstitutional; Greenberg argued that any change in the Colonial Trust's bylaws would make possible a reversal of policy by a future majority of stockholders; Cowen contended that such a change could only be effected by court order—he persisted in this stand effectively, forcing the later court decision on the matter. On returning to England, Zangwill built his non-Zionist ITO in opposition to the EZF; the latter was effectively crippled by the battles of its leaders, Cowen and Greenberg, with their rival, Gaster.

The British dissension remained an urgent problem for the new leaders; Weizmann, as a relative newcomer and an associate of the Russians in the new WZO executive committee, helped mediate an agreement. The EZF Conference in February 1907 elected a new administration, with Dr. Gaster as president; Joseph Cowen as vice president for the London region; and Weizmann as vice president for the provinces. The new arrangement failed to bring peace or renewed vitality to English Zionism. Weizmann grew increasingly detached from Gaster's leadership and avoided meetings of the executive committee, where the differences between the British Zionists were fought out. In 1908 when Gaster secured an EZF administration entirely to his taste, Weismann withdrew as vice president for the provinces and was replaced by another practical Zionist. A year later the EZF Conference restored a balance, over Gaster's objections, giving him Greenberg as his London vice president. Gaster then resigned, not being able to work with Greenberg on any terms, and all his group, including Weizmann, withdrew from the executive committee.

Weizmann viewed all these proceedings with growing distaste and with a degree of neutrality: as he saw it (and accordingly advised WZO President Wolffsohn), there could be a London-based regime only if it were "homogeneous"—either all Gaster's as before or all Greenberg's—since the London Zionists would never work together. His preferred alternative was to shift the center to Manchester; this would entail his own more active (though, as he claimed, reluctant) involvement. In his impatience with the EZF, Weizmann became interested in alternative frameworks for practical work. At an early stage Weizmann had felt that the federation could be left to its own devices while he and Gaster devoted their time to the Palestine Committee, in which Zionists and others would work to develop Palestine for Jewish settlement; unlike Gaster, he continued to favor the Palestine Committee as a parallel enterprise even after the practical Zionists won control of the EZF. Following the 1908 defeat, Weizmann joined other Gaster supporters in devoting his local efforts to the Order of Ancient Maccabeans, though he did not become a member. The British practical Zionists won recognition of the order as a separate Zionist organization in the WZO, not subject to the EZF—initially at the Ninth Zionist Congress in 1909, then fully at the WZO Annual Conference of 1910. In that year Weizmann helped forge a compromise to reunite British Zionism and accepted an EZF vice presidency again under the new, political Zionist president, Joseph Cowen. This meant an irreparable break with Gaster, but not with the Order of Ancient Maccabeans; Weizmann's Zionist work in England remained concentrated in the sphere of the order, and not the federation.[55]

The changing course of Weizmann's Zionist activity in England was closely tied to his involvement in WZO affairs. His role in this arena grew steadily more prominent as well as more partisan and controversial; yet he remained somewhat an outsider. After 1907 Weitzmann could not manage to attend all WZO Annual Conferences or Greater Action Committee meetings, although he was eligible (and was also urged) to attend them; at the congresses, which he did attend, his manner seemed detached, ironic, and almost bored. Nevertheless, his faction regularly elected him chairman of the congress' steering committee, beginning with the Ninth Zionist Congress in 1909. In that capacity he played a central part in major conflicts of the movement.[56]

The Eighth Zionist Congress in 1907 saw the formal acknowledgement of Wolffsohn's ascendancy and the control of the movement by his headquarters in Cologne. The executive group consisted of Wolffsohn, president of the WZO; Dr. Otto Warburg in Berlin, again in charge of Palestine activities; and the banker Jacobus Kann of The Hague, a staunch supporter of the Herzlian line Wolffsohn inherited. Moreover, the financial institutions of the WZO were firmly controlled by the political Zionists. The Jewish National Fund, created for land purchase and development, was headed by Wolffsohn's old friend, the Cologne lawyer, Dr. Max Bodenheimer. Wolffsohn himself headed the board of the Jewish Colonial Trust and, with board members like Greenberg, dominated the bank's decisions. In Herzl's day, the practical Zionists had attacked the strategy of holding the trust's funds available for the opportunity of a diplomatic coup in Turkey and demanded that they be used for immediate constructive work in Palestine. Wolffsohn, on the other hand, had opposed his revered leader's attempted political dictation of the bank's policy. Now, as head of the trust and the WZO alike, he could maintain a nominally independent, prudent fiscal management with control of the political institution.

The underlying strains produced clashes at the congresses between executive and opposition and recurrent frictions between Wolffsohn and some of his officers, who were practical Zionists. A major source of opposition was the independent action of Ussishkin, from his new vantage point as head of the Hibbat Zion Odessa Committee.

The rise of the Young Turks in Constantinople forced reconsideration of Zionist strategies. The Russian Zionists boldly proposed a status of national autonomy for the Jews in Palestine. The Odessa Committee initiated an expanded Zionist propaganda campaign in Constantinople; strengthened by their aid, Jacobson was able to win over Wolffsohn for a new approach that was aimed, through a subsidized press, at the Ottoman reading public and the newly installed legislature. Wolffsohn and Nordau adjusted to the new situation by publicly discarding the aim of a colonial charter for Palestine and renounced attempts to put pressure on Constantinople by soliciting support from interested powers in other capitals. They remained fixed on lobbying through bureaucratic channels and were wary of a general attack on Ottoman public opinion; this led the practical Zionists to charge them with deficient political activism. As for the demand for national autonomy in Palestine published by the Russian Zionists, this could only seem like an unnecessary provocation to those still applying quiet diplomacy to persuade the Turks to open up Palestine for Jewish immigration. Ironically, the political Zionists produced a provocation of their own when Jacobus Kann published a book that proclaimed the goal of Palestine as a Jewish state. This time it was the team of Jacobson and Jabotinsky (the latter in sharp contrast to his later stance) who protested against the open declaration of a maximal Zionist aim.

There was also contention over matters of practical Zionism. Ussishkin's demand—raised at the 1906 WZO Annual Conference—to use Jewish National Fund income to set up an agricultural mortgage and loan bank, touched off a sharp debate. The work of Otto Warburg, aided in the field by the new Jaffa office headed by Dr. Arthur Ruppin, was the target of continual criticism by political Zionists. Wolffsohn's support for practical Zionist projects not only was limited by his fiscal caution, but was increasingly tied to the recrudescent ideological dispute.[57]

The practical Zionists came to the Ninth Congress in 1909 determined to oust Wolffsohn from the presidency. Weizmann was again chairman of the Standing Committee, which was dominated by his faction. He thus played a major part in negotiating a committee proposal, assented to by Wolffsohn, to expand the Smaller Action Committee and make Wolffsohn an *ex officio* member as chairman of the Jewish Colonial Trust. The president of the WZO was not to be chosen by the congress, but by the Smaller Action Committee from among its members. But when the latter proposal was brought to the plenary session, the leaders of the German federation led a revolt and defeated it. This caused those intended for the additional Smaller Action Committee posts to withdraw. The previous administration remained unchanged and continued for two more years to manage the WZO from Cologne.

The Ninth Congress sharpened the divisions in the Zionist movement decisively and involved Weizmann in quarrels that committed him to an increasingly well-defined ideological position. Weizmann's role at the congress was severely criticized by his opponents, while Weizmann attacked Wolffsohn's inconsistency and imputed ill faith to the German delegation.

Later, during a visit to England, Wolffsohn publicly implied that Weizmann had frittered away, if not misappropriated, Zionist funds entrusted to him for the university project or for industrial development in Palestine. Weizmann's threat to resign his Zionist positions produced a clarification, but not an apology that could have restored friendly relations. Others among Weizmann's friends—in particular Sokolow, who left his post in Cologne—joined in an active oppositional campaign, which now acquired a sharp ideological edge, especially in the German movement.[58]

Shortly after the congress, the sociologist Franz Oppenheimer published an article in *Die Welt,* posing the issue of Western versus Eastern Zionism.[59] Although East Europeans, denied "liberty, equality and fraternity" in their birthplace, naturally regarded themselves as a separate nation, he argued that Western Jews (in spite of German antisemitism) were free and fully identified with their country. Their Zionism, as in his own case, was a matter of ethnic pride, of fraternal concern for their Eastern brethren, who must be resettled in Palestine; in no way did their Zionism imply separation from the German nation or a need for German Jews to seek a new homeland elsewhere. This article, in the wake of the conflict at the congress, aroused the opposition of a new generation of German Zionists. Buber, after a considerable period of detachment, emerged again as a Zionist figure and became their mentor. Feiwel, too, renewed activity and tried to build an *Ost und West* movement in Central Europe. Like the rising young activist, Kurt Blumenfeld, they declared, in opposition to Oppenheimer's thesis, that Western Jews should solve their problems in unity with the East and in essentially the same way, even though their hardships might be psychological rather than political or economic.

As in other cases, when driven to an ultimate position, Weizmann identified himself emphatically as an Easterner; and since he was an Easterner who wished to absorb the best Western civilization, he responded enthusiastically to the new German East and West movement. Returning from the Ninth Congress, he tried to organize an English counterpart for the German group, basing it chiefly on the Order of the Ancient Maccabeans. The new activists were to try to reform the WZO, but they were not limited to that context. He contemplated a separate organization that would develop practical colonization projects in Palestine, and collaborate with the Russian Odessa Committee and similar agencies in Berlin and Vienna. He also had in mind recruiting non-Zionist notables, especially among London financial circles who, he was informed, were not impressed with the success of the Jewish Colonial Trust and could perhaps be induced to support a new policy of practical Zionism. Little came of these efforts, but Weizmann's involvement in disputes that polarized the positions of political and practical Zionism led him to define an emerging ideological position, later generally named *Weizmannism.*

Weizmann's emergence as the embodiment of an ideological position in Zionism was a slow—one might even say reluctant—transformation. It did not fully appear until he became the acknowledged leader of world Zionism; but its beginnings may be traced to the conflicts with Wolffsohn, in which he was a minor figure.

As a diagnostic and prescriptive ideology, concerned with long-run, basic conditions, Zionism, like other ideologies, often found itself unable to respond to the short-run necessities of its constituency. At its very inception the movement opted for Zion rather than America as the proper goal for Russian Jewish emigrants, placing the long-run national interest of Jews above short-run individual needs. But throughout its history Zionism also responded repeatedly to its basic impulse of practical activism and pursued short-run solutions of pressing problems at the expense of ideological purism. Both territorialism and Russian Zionist *Gegenwartsarbeit* were such a shift in Zionist policy in the early 1900s—at least for the general run of Zionists, though many elevated their choice to the level of an ideological doctrine.

Until the Sixth Congress in 1903, Weizmann had been exceptionally open to the appeal of short-run tasks. His commitment to the Nay-Sayers, made in the heat of the debate, initiated a sea change whose effects became slowly apparent in the long conflict that divided the Zionist movement after Herzl's death. The associates Weizmann chose (rather than the logic of a theoretical insight) led him into an ideological corner, where he eventually took up his self-conscious position. The early years gave stray hints of ultimate Weizmannism, with its clear preference for long-run gradualist solutions. He opposed the territorialists, as Wolffsohn did, after 1905. He also was cool to Wolffsohn's 1906 attempt to convene Jewish organizations for consideration of ways to aid the mass of Jewish emigrants—an initiative that would have enjoyed his warm support previously. He opposed EZF involvement in a battle against British immigration restrictions as being outside the scope of Zionism and better left to other Jewish organizations. He was herded by circumstances into the role of a single-issue Zionist, concerning himself increasingly with the primary question of practical Zionism: how Palestine might be developed gradually for Jewish resettlement.

The change can be traced in semantic usages that became characteristically Weizmann's. He had often described Eastern Zionism as "organic," meaning no more than a historically deep-rooted and popular movement, as opposed to the "mechanical," or shallow modernist quality of Western Zionism. In his mature years, Weizmann's approach is also termed *organic*—in the more specific sense of slow evolutionary development—as opposed to opportunistic reliance on political action alone.

Using another term not unknown among his circle, Weizmann adopted the designation of *synthetic Zionism* as peculiarly his own. He meant by this the continuous effort to build up the Zionist position in Palestine by settlement and cultural development under whatever political conditions prevailed, so that the strength gradually accumulated could support Zionist diplomacy at the point when decisive steps became possible. Weizmann first spoke of synthetic Zionism at the Eighth Zionist Congress in 1907, meaning at that time to propose a basis on which Wolffsohn and the practical Zionists could cooperate: practical work in Palestine as complementary, not an alternative, to Zionist political action. And, indeed, Wolffsohn could well have used the same term to describe his own current Zionist approach. As relations deteriorated, Weizmann's side tended to argue for practical Zionism as the prerequisite condition for political success; the political Zionists, of course, took the inverse position.[60]

The Tenth Zionist Congress in August 1911 finally saw the victory of the practical Zionists. Wolffsohn, tired and ill, withdrew from the battle, content to influence Zionist affairs from the sidelines through his control of the Jewish Colonial Trust. Weizmann was now no longer a member of the opposition, but an old and influential friend of the policy-making circle. In the next year the German Zionist movement—the local support of the Zionist headquarters staff, which was now concentrated in Berlin—was also taken over by partisans of a radical, cultural/practical Zionist doctrine. These changes led to broader, deeper involvement by Weizmann in major WZO policy matters, even though, located in England, he was still a remote, rather secondary associate of the main leaders.

Weizmann's relative detachment from the current affairs of English Zionism together with his relative prominence in the WZO was a significant advantage. The Zionist movement in Western countries, including England, consisted of closed groups that were not strongly attractive to outsiders. The membership was recruited in large measure from the immigrant community; Zionist societies, apart from their ideological appeal, offered newcomers a congenial milieu that eased their transition into a strange new Western way of life. But precisely the old-country atmosphere that attracted immigrants made such Zionist clubs foreign to long-settled Western Jews as well as to the younger Zionists who were native-born or acculturated to Western ways from childhood. Western-born Zionist veterans in England, as elsewhere, formed their own groups and took on the leadership of the movement, at first as their natural right. Younger Zionist recruits, even though thoroughly Western in their culture, were hardly more at home in the EZF's Anglo-Jewish establishment than in the cozy ghetto of the immigrant societies. The quarrels between the two veteran cliques bored them. The maverick image of the lonely Weizmann, the Manchester intellectual with his broad Continental contacts, offered a welcome alternative for many in a wide circle of acquaintances. Although he did not build a coterie quite like that of Geneva, he became the friend and mentor of a new group of able young Zionists.[61]

Weizmann's scope as a Zionist leader was extended by his growing familiarity with the work in Palestine. He had a hand in the attempts initiated by Ussishkin—during the latter's 1906 visit to England—to organize a Palestine Committee and investment syndicates outside the political movement, and he corresponded with Professor Warburg in this connection. The latter recruited Weizmann in 1908 to the board of directors of the major Zionist agency for land purchase, the Palestine Land Development Company. (Weizmann at first demurred, for lack of funds to buy the twenty-five-pound share in the company required of each director, but Warburg solved the problem by transferring the necessary share to Weizmann from his own holdings.) A year earlier Weizmann had made his first trip to Palestine. This arose out of his remarks at the Zionist Annual Conference of 1906 that provoked a direct challenge in the official journal, *Die Welt,* by Johann Kremenetzky, an electrical engineer and industrialist who had been one of Herzl's inner circle in Vienna: "Dr. Weizmann complains that he has nothing on which to base effective propaganda for Palestine. . . . Were he to go to Palestine and establish a small chemical industry . . . I should be willing to assist him." Weizmann promptly took up the challenge. After some discussion and correspondence, Kremenetzky agreed to fund a trip, first to the European centers of the essential oils and perfumery industry, then to Palestine to study the possibility of developing a similar agriculture-based industry there.[62]

Weizmann's Palestine voyage gave him a chance to know more closely the young labor Zionist activists who were bent on forming a Jewish farmer-worker class in the country. When he returned to England he delivered a buoyant report on the progress of the Palestine settlement, stressing the significance of the socialist Paolei Zion and particularly Hapoel Hatzaïr, the more nationalist, populist-oriented workers' group. The Palestinian socialist Zionists eventually became primary allies in the years of his Zionist presidency, but the initial meeting with them led to no immediate forging of closer bonds. Weizmann's Palestine trip proved an interlude from which he returned to a life still centered in England.

His friendship with Ahad Ha'am occasioned a renewed, more concrete connection with Palestine as the possible base for his own future life. The founder of the firm that employed Ahad Ha'am was an old pre-Herzlian religious Zionist, Kalonymus Wissotzky. At his death in 1904, Wissotzky's will was found to provide for a number of benefactions to Palestinian Jewish institutions; Ahad Ha'am was named one of the trustees of the considerable residual estate, with a hundred thousand rubles to be dispensed annually over the next five years. The idea was suggested that the Wissotzky estate together with the Hilfsverein der deutschen Juden, a German-Jewish philanthropic agency organized in 1901, should build a school for advanced technical studies in Palestine. In 1909 Shmarya Levin returned from a trip to America with news that the banker Jacob Schiff had been drawn into this enterprise, which now became a triple partnership: the Wissotzky estate (with cultural Zionists largely represented) and German and American philanthropists. This development revived Weizmann's old hopes; over the next few years he worked and planned to advance the idea of a department of chemistry or agricultural industry that he could head in the proposed Technion—or Technicum, as it was then called. However, the *Curatorium* (Board of Trustees) of the proposed college failed to give a high priority to the studies Weizmann proposed. In 1912 he sought the help of Judah Magnes to persuade Nathan Straus, the venerable American philanthropist, to convert the "health station" he and his wife were planning in Palestine into part of the broader scientific institute Weizmann still hoped to head in the proposed technical college. Meanwhile, as these future prospects were delayed, he continued to advance his standing as a British scientist and advised Vera to go ahead with her qualifying examinations, since their removal from cold, gray Manchester to sunny Palestine might take some time.

Weizmann's career plan required him to become reasonably wealthy so that he could serve Zionism without depending on it for a living as well as reasonably eminent in science so that he could deal with men of eminence on a plane of equality. He patented discoveries with promising industrial applications, and he extended his work in industry from the Manchester dyeworks to every area open to his varied contacts. His research in dyes, aromatics, and fermentation products gained him access not only to manufacturers and pharmaceutical houses, but to the laboratories of top scientists. He planned to attain membership in the Royal Society and a professorship in organic chemistry at Manchester in a matter of years. But he was fated to suffer sharp disappointment in spite of the talent and labor he devoted to these efforts. In November 1909 he became a naturalized British citizen (with Gaster's aid); a month later, being now qualified in that respect, he was nominated by Manchester colleagues for membership in the Royal Society. However, this honor was one he did not attain then, or later. Disappointed as he was at this failure, he had even greater cause to be chagrined at the circumstances under which his other aim, to become a professor of organic chemistry at Manchester, was denied to him.

In February 1910 Professor Perkin contracted with Weizmann to employ him at a salary of one hundred pounds per annum and one third of royalties to carry out experiments on the manufacture of synthetic rubber that Perkin had undertaken for the firm of Strange and Graham.[63] Weizmann had been doing work in this field together with Fernbach at the Pasteur Institute, where fermentation research was more advanced than in Manchester. Therefore, he proposed that Fernbach's team, too, should be involved, and an agreement was arrived at to this end at the close of the year. By December 1911 Weizmann had perfected a process for rubber synthesis to be patented by him and Fernbach, with the expectation that the company would undertake its manufacture. In the event, Strange and Graham did not venture to manufacture rubber according to the new method, but in 1912–13 they built a plant for the production of intermediate products discovered in the course of the experimentation. Meanwhile, Weizmann sought to have a new set of agreements drawn up that would secure his rights, both directly and in the firm's contracts with Fernbach and Perkin. This led to a dispute with Perkin that ended in a decisive estrangement between the two chemists.

In the meantime it was announced that Perkin was to leave for a position at Oxford and his professorship of organic chemistry had to be filled. Weizmann's friends, Arthur Schuster and Samuel Alexander, asked about his intentions regarding Palestine, and he assured them that he would surely remain in Manchester for four or five years. But his appointment, he heard, was being opposed, especially by Perkin himself; soon he had even more cause for his growing irritation and anger. It turned out that the chair in organic chemistry would go to a man whose previous work had been in another field, whereas he, who had worked specifically in organic chemistry and biochemistry, was to be offered a subordinate post as reader. His immediate reaction (which he later checked with Schuster) was to say that his circumstances did not permit him to reject what the university might choose to offer him; but he felt he had been "materially and morally" wronged by Perkin, that the administration was now condoning those wrongs, and that he would "try to get out of [Manchester]" as soon as possible. To his wife, resting in Cannes, he wrote in January 1913, "Verunya, it will soon be time for us to get out of this swamp and go to Palestine. There at least the swamp will be our own."[64]

At the moment, however—as Weizmann wrote to Harry Sacher—although he had been ready for Palestine for years past, "Palestine is not ready for me." Instead, the WZO offered other possibilities. It appears that Weizmann was approached to take Victor Jacobson's place in Constantinople as the Zionist agent there. This offered a way to leave Manchester, to be sure, but clearly meant giving up the academic and professional standing he had achieved for the life of a Zionist functionary. With his wife away on a long rest cure in Cannes, Weizmann turned to the Schusters, mother and daughter, as his confidantes in a matter of intimate personal values. He presented the issue in terms of the highest, disinterested motives, as one to be decided solely according to what would serve the Zionist cause. At the same time he confessed, "I am frightened. Fascinating as the work is . . . it will kill me positively in three or four years. . . . I have promised mother [Caroline Schuster] not to bind myself and ask for leave to consider the matter until May." When Weizmann came to Berlin for a meeting to plan for the coming Zionist Congress, another suggestion was made: that Weizmann move to Berlin as a member of the Smaller Action Committee and become a full-time professional activist. Such an avenue of escape from his humiliating position in Manchester did not tempt Weizmann to abandon chemistry and the academy; he still aimed, under increased tension, to keep his Zionist and professional careers on separate, converging courses.[65]

There were other developments in Berlin, however, that sent him home in a state of elation. It was decided to revive the project of a Jewish university in Palestine, to which Weizmann had given so much devotion in his Geneva days. Weizmann together with Berthold Feiwel and Leo Motzkin were named a committee to plan the project and empowered to co-opt others; a presentation of the subject was to be delivered by Weizmann at the next congress. Buoyed up by this new task, he was able to accept new arrangements for his future work in Manchester and for his continuing research. The university offered him an appointment as Reader in Biochemistry and Lecturer in Colouring Matters, with an increased salary, funds for an assistant, and a light teaching load. His independent research was also provided for by a consortium formed by his close friend and Zionist ally, Julius Simon, who undertook to finance it on a regular basis. Vera Weizmann, too, established herself in her profession as a public health physician. The Weizmanns were finally able to take up again a position in public affairs and society like that of their Geneva days but from a firmer base as a mature, reasonably secure couple.

The renewed university project intensified Weizmann's cooperation with many old friends and led him into a swiftly expanding network of important new connections.[66] He did his work from the Manchester center, but he was in continuing contact with the office in Berlin. Ussishkin wished to be part of the project and Jabotinsky enlisted, hoping to conduct propaganda and data collection along the same lines as Weizmann's own early efforts in Geneva. The university committee reunited Weizmann with Feiwel in a common task, reinforced his friendship and collaboration with Julius Simon, and tightened his relations with Judah Magnes, through whom he now first encountered the American-Jewish elite.

The latter two were friends made by Weizmann at Zionist meetings during the Uganda debates where they joined in common opposition to the Herzlian policy. Simon, a well-to-do Mannheim businessman with strong intellectual interests, had been attracted to the Ahad Ha'amist principles and the Russian-Jewish culture of the student colony in nearby Heidelberg, where Magnes also studied for a time. When Feiwel found himself without employment after Wolffsohn gained control of the WZO, he became the director of Simon's office in Strasbourg, where the firm was negotiating a large slum-clearance project; to the surprise of all, the bohemian Jewish poet turned out to be a shrewd and efficient manager. With Weizmann, the Simon household developed a close personal bond. Weizmann's ties to Magnes, formed at the 1905 Zionist congress, remained intact after the latter returned home to America and the former went to England. Weizmann's efforts on behalf of the Technical Institute in Haifa had brought about heightened cooperation with both Simon and Magnes. This was raised to a new level by the revived project of a Jewish university in Palestine.

One of Weizmann's first acts on being appointed to the university committee was to visit Paul Ehrlich, the famous discoverer of an antisyphilitic drug. To his unbounded delight, the great man proved willing to endorse and cooperate in the university project. Weizmann was also able later to do some work in Ehrlich's laboratory, combining the professional and Zionist aspects of a new relationship in his characteristic way. Ehrlich's support proved crucial in extending the circle of influence to which Weizmann reached out.

His most important new contact was with the veteran patron of the Palestine settlement, Baron Edmond de Rothschild. This was a relationship that required the eager Weizmann to temper his urgency with patience, to learn to listen more than to urge, and to bend his own preference to suit another— all in the name of the greater and future goal. His first impulse on taking up the task of the university was to press for action with all urgency along the same lines as he had followed years before: collecting evidence of the need for the university by surveying the situation of Russian students; demonstrating potential support by a tour of Russia and by enlisting student organizations; and collecting curricula and budgets of similar institutions in order to have a concrete plan to present to the congress. To these methods he now added the request that Jacobson, who had returned to his post in Constantinople, try to obtain legal clearance for the project from the Turks. As in years past Weizmann found his collaborators lacking in energy and inclined to leave too much of the burden on his shoulders; but his complaints were milder and more patient than in the past, and he did have help allotted to him both in Manchester and in Berlin by the WZO. He heard with more attention than before the objections of some comrades to the enterprise; but neither Ahad Ha'am's scruples about alarming the Turks by announcing a major new Jewish cultural activity in Jerusalem nor the opposition of others to diversion of funds from economic to cultural investments greatly affected him. What did give him pause was the chance that Baron Rothschild might become interested and would be put off by too public and premature propaganda.

Weizmann learned at the special conference of Zionist leaders in Berlin in March 1913 that the baron might be induced to invest in the Zionist effort by buying land through the PLDC. The renewed activity of the practical Zionists and their readiness to stress gradual economic methods rather than political display, it was said, had made him begin to take the WZO more seriously as a positive factor. In June Jacobson, who had been urging delay in publicity regarding the university project until prospects of successful fund-raising were better, reported from his visit to Paris that Baron Rothschild had indicated that he might support the idea materially. Weizmann by now was awaiting a decision (at a Greater Action Committee meeting his academic obligations did not permit him to attend) on the procedures regarding the university project that the leaders would support at the congress some months later. He was ready to accept a more moderate pace than his own enthusiasm would require; for, as he wrote to an old friend, "the spirit of 4, rue Lombard [his former Geneva address] is now gone. One doesn't live in Manchester for 9 years without penalty."[67]

All he asked was that the congress not merely hear his presentation concerning a Jewish university in Jerusalem, but adopt preliminary measures to accomplish the aim. Impatient with the divided authority of the past, he expressed to Julius Simon his willingness to take charge of the effort if the committee named would be concentrated in England and constituted of his own circle of advisers:

> On the understanding that the Congress adopts my resolution and sets up a predominantly "English" Commission (Ahad Ha'am, Sacher, [Leon] Simon, myself) which together with you and the S[maller]. A[ction]. C[ommittee]. would definitely prepare the plan for the Annual Conference, and would also prepare the propaganda and the committee, my personal plan would be as follows: In the spring I would go to Palestine, perhaps also to Constantinople. After completing the plan, let us say in June, to go with Jacobson to the Baron in Paris; and after the Annual Conference, from the end of September to mid-November, I would be able to work in America.[68]

The congress in August met Weizmann's requests in its resolution and the committee it set up, but events took a course thereafter that called into play all Weizmann's growing skill as a diplomat and conflict manager.

Soon after the congress a dispute began to rage between the Zionists and the German sponsors of the Haifa technical institute over the language of instruction to be used at the new institution.[69] The zeal of Russian Hebraists, shown in Ussishkin's demand at the congress in August to make Hebrew the language of instruction in all departments of the new Jewish University, was manifested on the board of the Technicum by Shmarya Levin, who made similar demands. The Hilfsverein resisted this proposal on the grounds that Hebrew was not adequately developed for teaching technical and scientific subjects. Of course, it was also their mission to spread German cultural influence in the Near East, as the Alliance Israélite Universelle was doing on behalf of France. As a consequence all the Russians on the board, including the moderate Ahad Ha'am (who did not share the confidence of other Hebraists that Hebrew could indeed serve as a language of instruction in all fields) submitted their resignations. The dispute swiftly escalated. The trustees of the Wissotzky estate withheld the next annual installment of the bequest to the Technicum. The Hilfsverein threatened to have the institution declared bankrupt, to buy up its assets, and proceed to run it as a German project. The teachers in Israel then went on strike against the Hilfsverein; the German agency, in reply, proposed to abandon its teachers' seminary in Jerusalem; and the WZO was propelled into assuming responsibility for the whole Hebrew educational enterprise in Palestine in spite of the cost. The turmoil caused the American supporters of the Technicum to withdraw into neutrality—in disgust with both parties to the dispute.

Throughout the quarrel Weizmann held loyally to the position of his Russian comrades, even though like Ahad Ha'am he did not share their zeal and had even more reason for dismay at the effects of their bellicosity. In his later recollections, he came to identify more fully with the Hebraist militants of the dispute, one of the cardinal conflicts in the heroic revival of spoken Hebrew; but at the time he was acutely aware of the complications it introduced into his primary problem, that of securing wide support and harmony in the campaign for the Jewish University. It turned out that in the final analysis a Zionist quarrel with the German Jews made them more acceptable rather than less as potential associates for Baron Rothschild, whose loyalties, of course, were French. Weizmann had greater reason to be concerned about the Americans, with whom he had created some contact through Magnes.

Weizmann began to court Magnes' cooperation from the moment he was involved in the revived university project—a natural continuation of their correspondence about the Technicum. Through Magnes he sought the support of leading academics, rabbis, and Jewish philanthropists in America. Ahad Ha'am strongly urged such a policy, and at his insistence Weizmann proposed to convert the English working committee that the congress had granted him (on which Ahad Ha'am proved unwilling to serve) into an Anglo-American committee, for which he solicited Magnes' membership.

From the start it became apparent that Weizmann and Magnes held rather different conceptions of the proper structure and functions of the Jewish University. For Weizmann, the needs of Jewish students and of the Palestine settlement project were primary, and he wished to initiate the project with a law school and a research and teaching institute in basic and applied, particularly medical and agricultural, science. Magnes, on the other hand, gave first priority to Judaic studies and wished to concentrate fully on building first an Ahad Ha'mist, but theologically tinted, center for Jewish humanistic culture. Weizmann was ready to revise his plan to accommodate Magnes' preference by proposing an initial commitment to build faculties both in medical science and in Judaica as the beginning of the University. But he soon took another tack after he finally succeeded in meeting the baron and hearing what the old philanthropist and patron of the Palestine settlement was inclined to support.[70]

Following preliminary contacts in Paris with the Rothschild entourage, Weizmann met the baron in January 1914 and wrote in triumph to his wife:

> So it has happened! I saw the Baron, spoke to him for 3/4 of an hour. He is *for the University* and for reasons similar to yours and mine, namely the Jewish national ones, and this is why he is against a medical school at the beginning, but for an *Institut de Recherches* similar to Pasteur's. *J'y contribuerai*, he told me. He is a good Jew.[71]

It was a great advantage to Weizmann that he not only worked at the research institutes of Pasteur and Paul Ehrlich, but had been able to secure Ehrlich's cooperation in his project. So, too, Rothschild's decided preference for scientific research as the start of the enterprise was a powerful influence in swaying Judah Magnes to give up his insistence on a teaching and research center in Jewish culture as the first priority in deference to the baron's fears of the political implications of stressing teaching and Jewishness too prominently. Weizmann was able, while enjoying the baron's support for his own special interest in scientific research, to appear as the friend of Magnes' interest in the humanities and in Jewish subjects for which he included some provisional facilities in his plan. So, too, under attack from those like Jabotinsky who undertook to raise funds and do propaganda for the project among the Jewish public, Weizmann was able to persuade Rothschild to make some concessions and relax his opposition to public agitation.

The baron soon made clear one particular concern that he sought to promote in his new relations with the Zionists. He planned for his son, James de Rothschild, to succeed him in the leadership of Jewish communal affairs and saw in the project of educational institutions in Palestine an occasion to initiate the young man into his destined role. Weizmann gained an important new collaborator by lending his willing aid to the baron's plan and dealt regularly with James—or Jimmy, as he soon became known among Zionists— through the coming years. So, too, he consolidated the support Magnes had won from Nathan Straus and others in the United States and brought into the orbit of his scheme groups of physicians and philanthropic organizers in Germany, England, and Russia, where projects were floated that could either compete or contribute to his own.

In August 1914 a meeting to bring together all the strands Weizmann had woven with such energy and finesse was to take place under Rothschild's aegis. Then the war intervened, abruptly ending all such projects of peace and setting the scene for Weizmann's full emergence as a leader.

2

Brandeis

The Family

Weizmann won his place in the central WZO policy-making circles, after long and devoted labors, when the practical Zionists rose to power shortly before World War I. He was then in his late thirties, a veteran in the movement. At about the same time, Louis D. Brandeis, eighteen years senior to Weizmann, first joined a Zionist society. He was regarded from the start as meant for first rank if only he would accept the task. Yet, authorized biographers found no more than dubious rumors of an early interest in Zionism and little of anything Jewish in his background.[1] Relying on interviews with Brandeis himself, the biographers reflect his judgment that his turn to Zionism in his mid-fifties was something totally new, for which his past life had not prepared him. This was an overstatement, expressing Brandeis' feeling that he ought to have had much more knowledge of the movement he was suddenly called upon to lead. Brandeis' Jewish background, unusual or even peculiar as it was, nonetheless had significant effects long before Zionism gave him a style of Jewishness he could adopt as a positive commitment.

Brandeis' grandfather and great-grandfather in Prague had been leaders in the Frankist cult that swept Central Europe in the late eighteenth century. The adoration of Jacob Frank as the Messiah and the other antinomian beliefs and practices of the cult no longer attracted the descendants of its votaries a century later; indeed, they were inclined to suppress its tradition. Yet, a certain elitist, liberal self-consciousness continued to be preserved into Louis Brandeis' generation. His mother's uncle, Gottlieb Wehle, left a testament in 1867 that exhorted his children to revere their sectarian forefathers, who sought the "true spirit" of Judaism. But Josephine Goldmark, Wehle's granddaughter, claims that although he was an active Frankist in his youth, he retained no more than a belief in immortality in his older years. She herself deplores the mystical enthusiasm and sexual excesses of her ancestors' cult, even though they expressed a justifiable revolt against Talmudic Judaism and the desperate straits of the Jews in earlier, less enlightened times. Brandeis' mother, Frederika Dembitz Brandeis, speaks in much harsher terms of the "crazy beliefs" of her family circle and praises her own mother for not being "drawn into the general religious exaltation." Yet, clearly, she shared the family pride in "the fact that some of the noblest men and women belonged to their group, and there reigned a kind of freemasonry among the members." Frederika Brandeis meant by "noble" a reference to the social status as well as the character of those she mentioned. Little as she could share their religious enthusiasm, she wholeheartedly shared their reverence for their kinsmen, the Von Honigsbergs and Klarenbergs, aristocratic heroes of the movement.[2]

Frankist noblemen were often converts to Christianity, conducting in the Christian church the same kind of clandestine cultism that other members of their subversive freemasonry carried on in the Jewish community. The Wehle and Brandeis Frankist families lived as Jews in the Jewish community. They were among the founders of the Prague Reform Congregation in the 1830s and, as pillars of liberal Judaism, a legitimate, respected part of the community. Yet, the former Frankists continued (as did Louis Brandeis) to maintain close, even endogamous, ties with one another. Given the history of Frankism, such ties extended beyond the Jewish into the Christian community, where they were proud to count aristocrats among their old associates and relatives. This produced a marginal subcommunity capable of impressing a powerful elitist identity among its young members while not binding them to specific beliefs or practices appropriate to their sense of vocation.

Frederika Brandeis' reminiscences (written in the letters to Louis at his request after he left home to settle in Boston) strikingly reflect the spirit of this family. She speaks of Prague and the Wehle clan as a "Jerusalem or Mecca" that even in her childhood—spent in Polish towns in Prussia—was referred to "with love and longing." The women of the family, lovely and cultivated romantic heroines, often lived lives shaded with tragedy because of the impractical, impulsive, brilliant men they married. Her own father, Dr. Siegmund Dembitz, who was one of the last converts to Frankism and spent some years in a noble household in Warsaw in the service of the cult, was "handsome, tall and stately, as Hungarians are," but also "impractical and inconsiderate." He "looked like a prince" and "was of Portuguese descent" by way of a grandfather from Amsterdam. Until the age of eleven, Frederika shared schools and tutors and close companionship with the daughters of the Polish petty nobility in the Prussian border towns where her father served as physician.

But the primary memory she had of life with her father was one of deprivation, particularly the loss of the warmth and intimacy of the extended family circle. After his medical studies and marriage, her father never saw his own parents again, although they survived for a few years. Their daughter-in-law, Frederika's mother, who "mentioned them occasionally with great tenderness and filial love" in her letters to Prague, indicated that they were "very deeply grieved by the parting from their youngest child"—a hint that could not have gone unnoticed in this letter from Frederika to her own youngest child in far-off Boston. The greatest deprivation caused by Dr. Siegmund Dembitz's "impracticality"—that is, by the circumstance that having qualified to practice in Prussia, he had to live there and not in Bohemia near the Wehle clan—was the separation of the family from the clan center in Prague. This, Frederika reports, was "very hard" on her mother, Fannie Wehle Dembitz. To think of her mother's story made her heart bleed. "It was a story almost as sad, even if different from the 'head of the Medusa'"—an image of her father, she said, that came to her often, though it wronged him.

Such a harsh conclusion is hardly justified by her detailed account of life in the provinces where her father practiced. She remembers herself as a happy child, and she responded so fully to the Christian society around her that, she believed, the Prague clan once brought her home to live with them in order to protect her from overexposure and give her a firmer Jewish background. If her memories were overcast with a retrospective gloom, she says, it was because "I know the end of the tale and my heart bleeds when I read of the beginning." Her father could not stay more than two or three years in the same place, and frequent uprooting undermined the family's prosperity. Each time they moved Frederika was sent to live with Aunt Amalia or Uncle Moritz in Prague for extended periods, sometimes with her mother and brothers, sometimes alone. On two of those visits infant brothers died, leaving only her brother Ludwig (Lewis), four years younger than herself. When she was twelve, her mother also died. Frederika had to become her father's housekeeper at a time when the family budget increasingly depended on support extended by their kin in Prague. Eventually, she was brought back again to the clan's bosom while her father sought a new position.

The haven in Prague provided more than the safe refuge of an extended parental group. Frederika found in the Prague cult circle young kinsmen and friends who were the closest companions of her youth and remained intimate friends of the Brandeis clan later, in their several new homes in America. The children of the Brandeis, Mauthner, and Taussig families shared with her dancing and music lessons, joined in dramatic readings, and sometimes exchanged romantic confidences. The girls gossiped together about the young men much admired in their circle, like Moritz Hartmann, the young revolutionary poet who was their tutor, Wilhelm (William) Taussig, and Adolph Brandeis, who became engaged to Frederika not long before the associated families emigrated to America.[3]

In reading Louis Brandeis' early correspondence, there can be little doubt that his mother's emotional intensity exerted the most pressing influence on the young man. Letters to other correspondents, like his father or his brother—although frequent and affectionate—are written in a far easier and freer tone than those to her. Her intent to educate her children in the spirit of her own convictions was always evident. Strongly averse to religious enthusiasm, she had a deep respect for the (by now, rather abstract and attenuated) religious idealism the Wehle clan cherished. Their example made her tolerant of the Jewish and Christian ceremonials of her environment—a tolerance tinged with conspicuously more warmth toward Protestant than toward Jewish rites. But her purpose was to train her children in "the spirit not the form of religion," and they were not exposed to "any definite religious belief" at home. Louis Brandeis grew up to share his mother's distaste for formal religion; and, as she affirmed with tender pride, he fulfilled her hopes for a character formed by a "pure spirit and the highest ideals."[4]

Frederika Brandeis must have been less pleased with her son's deep identification with her brother, Lewis Dembitz. Young Brandeis, originally named Louis *David,* indicated where he was seeking his identity by changing his name to Louis *Dembitz* Brandeis. However flattering a mother might find this sign of attachment to her family, she could not have approved wholeheartedly if she thought her son was following in the footsteps of her muchloved but (to her mind) sadly erratic brother, who shared too much of what she deplored in her father. The painful circumstances of the family after her mother's death, she felt, had tragic consequences for her brilliant young brother. "Ludwig, then thirteen years old, left to himself, suddenly became an ardent orthodox Jew, unfortunately of such intensity of belief that it affected his whole life."[5]

When young Louis Dembitz Brandeis adopted not only his uncle's name, but his career, one is tempted to see this as his bid for liberation from his strongest parental bond. But it was Lewis Dembitz, the eminent abolitionist, rather than Lewis Dembitz, the Orthodox Jew, who was to be emulated. Dembitz's commitment to liberal and humanitarian causes was characteristic of the clan as a whole. Josephine Goldmark's story of her parents and kinsmen, *Pilgrims of '48,* indentifies them with the German émigré movement to America in the wake of the failed revolutions of 1848. The title best fits her father, Dr. Joseph Goldmark, one of the student leaders of the Vienna revolution, who fled from Europe under politically motivated charges of treason and murder. Her mother's family, the Wehles, were less active politically in Europe but were also strongly committed to liberalism. Adolph Brandeis and the impulsive Dr. Siegmund Dembitz had apparently sought to be active in the revolutionary movements, and the latter had to flee to Prague after volunteering his services as a surgeon in the ill-fated Polish 1848 uprising.

Other economic and political motives for the clan migration were more typically Jewish than revolutionary. The Wehle and Brandeis families' textile print business had been steadily declining, and Adolph Brandeis, soon to become a bridegroom, had to leave Prague to seek training in farm management or merchandising. Another factor was sensitivity to the perennial menace of antisemitism. In her memoirs Frederika complains that the family had to move on one occasion because her father had "persuaded himself that because of the Polish Revolution of 1832 the Poles and the Germans were not friendly and both parties might be hostile to him." Gottlieb Wehle's testament refers to anti-Jewish outbreaks that accompanied the 1848 Revolution in Prague as one reason for the clan's emigration.[6]

The move to America was undertaken in a spirit congenial to the Frankist
tradition and attuned to a current enthusiasm among progressive Germans.
The plan was to establish a farm colony where the clan could settle together
and live as a community close to nature. Such a project evokes echoes of early
Frankist leanings to forms of primitive communism. It reflects more directly
a fashion among Germans imbued with the Forty-Eighter spirit, which led a
group of progressive German aristocrats in the late forties to found farm settlements on the Texas frontier. This movement inspired a community of German liberals (among them the parents of Charles Nagel, who later married
Louis Brandeis' eldest sister, Fannie) who stood out as abolitionists in the
South and had to flee north during the Civil War. In a far milder way, the
Brandeises, who settled in Louisville, Kentucky, occupied a similar position
amid the Southern sympathizers there.[7]

Before the main body of the clan moved, Adolph Brandeis was sent ahead
in the summer of 1848 as an advance agent. He accompanied a friend who
was commissioned by the Rothschild firm to investigate the American investment market. This enabled Adolph to study at close hand the social and economic as well as the political traits of the New World. He quickly became an
ardent admirer of American institutions, and his letters to Prague overflowed
with praise of the freedom and friendliness of their future home. On the other
hand, he soon arrived at a sober, far from optimistic estimate of their prospects of success as farmers on the frontier. He advised his elders to acquaint
themselves with starch manufacture or another suitable business instead of
seeking to play the role of pioneer farmers and frontiersmen. He urged them,
in any case, to hasten their departure from Europe and decide their future
course on the spot upon arrival. On April 8, 1849, the clan embarked from
Europe.

At Cincinnati, where the family settled down provisionally—twenty-six
in all came to join Adolph Brandeis—they decided to follow the young man's
plan and build their future on the thriving commerce of the Ohio-Mississippi
river system. The Wehles—Aunt Amalia, Uncle Gottlieb, and Uncle Moritz
with their households and the two Brandeis bridegrooms (a third bridegroom
had returned to Prague with one of Gottlieb's nubile daughters)—moved to
Madison, Indiana, on the Ohio River, midway between Cincinnati and
Louisville. There, the firm of G. and M. Wehle, Brandeis and Company set
up a grocery and built a cornstarch factory. Dr. Siegmund Dembitz stayed
behind in Cincinnati with Lewis: the father to practice medicine, the son to
become a law clerk preparing for the bar. The clan dispersed further when the
two Brandeis bridegrooms, the brothers Adolph and Dr. Semmi, moved their
young families downriver to Louisville, where Dr. Semmi practiced medicine
and Adolph founded the wholesale grain and produce business that eventually made him one of the leading citizens of that boomtown. Two years later
in 1853, the Moritz Wehles left Madison for New York and after ten years
there returned to Prague; but during their stay in New York, a permanent
branch of the clan was established in the eastern metropolis. Regina, one of
Gottlieb Wehle's twelve children, went to New York with her Uncle Moritz's

family and met and married Dr. Joseph Goldmark, an old schoolmate of Dr. Semmi Brandeis; their daughter Alice in later years became Louis Brandeis' wife. After nine years in Indiana, the Gottlieb Wehle household also moved to New York. Another extension of the scope of the clan reached to St. Louis: the Taussigs who settled there were part of the Prague circle and Jennie Taussig, Wilhelm's daughter, became the wife of Louis Brandeis' brother Alfred. His elder sister, Fannie, also lived in St. Louis after she married Charles Nagel, a young German-American lawyer.

The clan transplanted to the New World maintained its old ties in spite of a dispersion stretching from Missouri to New York. Beyond these family connections, the clan had a variety of options for integration into their new environment, exceeding those of other German-Jewish immigrants. If they had come without the funds that built the Wehle-Brandeis company so soon after their arrival, they might have been forced to take the road of others among their contemporaries.[8] A typical course of the penniless German Jew was to take up the peddler's pack, hoping to move up to a country store in a small town and then to Cincinnati as a jobber or wholesale merchant. The capital to finance such a career would come from longer-settled Jews, since no other credit was readily available to such an immigrant. His business ties would be largely based on Cincinnati, the regional center of the German-Jewish community, the fountainhead of its religious and communal authority. Only through this mediating structure did many Jews find their place in the general American social and economic milieu. The Wehles and Brandeises were able to integrate not only through the Cincinnati-based Jewish and non-Jewish German immigrant community, but also directly through their access to American Society at large.

Only Lewis Dembitz chose an integration that included all three options—Jewish, German, and American—at once. His "Orthodox" Judaism, which so distressed his sister, was open to the "modern" Americanizing influences characteristic of the German-Jewish immigrant community of the time. He was a leading figure in the synagogue not only in Louisville, where he joined the Brandeises and set up his law practice after he married. He became a nationally recognized scholarly authority on Jewish law, a prominent figure among the conservatively oriented party in American Judaism, and an early leader in American Zionism. At the same time he became prominent in local and national politics. He was one of those who moved the nomination of Abraham Lincoln at the Republican party convention in 1860 and one of the midwestern German progressives who gave the Forty-Eighters the reputation for liberal activism associated with the name of Carl Schurz.

The women of the first generation, including Louis Brandeis' mother, Frederika, found adjustment to American ways a more difficult problem and were inclined to cling to old-country ties and habits. Since their Jewish roots were not extensive, this meant a strong attachment to the Central European German culture, heavily loaded with the heritage of the Enlightenment, which they brought with them from Prague. They had packed for the voyage considerable household effects, including two grand pianos and a cheval glass

as well as the hope chests of three brides, and they made every effort to repro-
duce in the New World the life style and *Gemuetlichkeit* of the Old. German
remained, under their influence, the language in which one conversed and
corresponded with one's elders in the family circle; Louis Brandeis in his
mature years was not simply jesting when he wrote to his brother Alfred that
their mother would be shocked to hear of him reading a German book in
translation. Living in the area of dense German settlement along the Ohio,
the family found a relatively supportive environment for their tradition of
European culture. Young Louis was sent to the German day school in Louisville for his education.[9]

The men, more exposed to the American marketplace, entered the life and
public affairs of their new home with little inhibition. This was not true of
all, for some re-emigrated with their families to Europe; it was true more
fully, and in a different way, for the young men than for their elders. Adolph
Brandeis' initial enthusiasm for things American ripened into a political
alignment with the antislavery, Free-Soil, and free trade factions in American
politics, as did Lewis Dembitz's and the other younger men's sympathies.
Uncle Gottlieb, on the other hand, fell into the pattern of the longer-settled
German Americans. He preferred the Democratic party since the abolitionists appeared tainted with anti-immigrant nativism and demanded abstention from beer, skittles, and traditional German Sunday festivity under the
coercive pressure of Sabbath blue laws.

The divided responses to America cultivated among the German immigrants also reflected divisions in the native-American community in a town
like Louisville.[10] The railroad and the steamship facilitated the transport of
Southern farm products up the Mississippi from New Orleans, and made
Louisville a thriving "cosmopolitan" center of trade. Upon this base the
upper class of native-born Anglo-Saxon and Scotch-Irish promoters, bankers,
lawyers, merchants, and politicians built an opulent, exclusive, and elite Society on the model of eastern metropolises like Philadelphia and New York,
complete with horse shows and debutante balls at Galt House, to which German immigrants were not admitted. The political leanings of this ruling class,
from which the town at large took its bearings, were strongly Southern in
sympathy—although, denied the preferred refuge of a neutral stance, their
business interests made the Kentucky leaders stay in the Union during the
Civil War.

The dominant attitudes were not unchallenged among the native-born,
Anglo-Saxon citizenry. There was a significant opposition, based on both economic interest and political leanings. Antislavery and Free-Soil sentiments
prevailed among a dissenting minority before the Civil War. These sentiments were reinforced by growing agrarian opposition among local farmers
and shippers to the ruling clique of railroad men and bankers. Although these
dissidents were also native-born Anglo-Saxons for the most part, they did not
practice such tight exclusion of immigrants as did more conservative Ken-
tuckians. Both before and after the Civil War, it was possible for the German
Forty-Eighters in Louisville to associate with congenial old-stock Americans

with whom they shared political and cultural interests. The Brandeis brothers, Adolph and Semmi, together with close friends in their inner community were among the founders of a library and reading circle, of which Lewis Dembitz was the leading figure; the *Nation* was regularly read and debated, and the young liberal intellectuals of the town were educated there as in a folk university. The achievements of Adolph Brandeis and Lewis Dembitz in business and the law and their service in voluntary and official public capacities made them figures of local eminence beyond the German-Jewish community. The young legal luminary Dembitz, through reports of his political action and writings, became a nationally known name in liberal as well as Jewish circles.

The immigrant experience of the Brandeises and their kinsmen must be judged as eminently successful. Once settled in Louisville, the Brandeis home and business prospered. Adolph Brandeis founded the firm of Brandeis and Crawford, which played a major part in marketing the rich agricultural produce of the South. The firm expanded rapidly, acquiring a tobacco factory, a flour mill, a large farm, and a river freighter named the *Fanny Brandeis*. When the Southern sources of Brandeis and Crawford's commerce were cut off by the Civil War, the firm entered into profitable contracts with the U.S. government. Having built up what his wife in later, less fortunate, years ruefully described as a considerable fortune and having gained local fame as the man who opened up eastern markets for Kentucky wheat, Adolph Brandeis was a citizen of consequence, a leader in the Chamber of Commerce.

Conditions changed drastically for the family business after the Civil War, and it was Adolph Brandeis upon whom the turn of the tide had the severest impact. There were no more government contracts to rely on and the prewar Southern connections of the firm were under harsh pressures of the Reconstruction era. By 1872, shortly before the crisis of 1873, Adolph Brandeis decided to wind up the partnership and go out of business. He was able to do this, as Frederika's memoirs tell us, while saving his honor—that is, the creditors were eventually satisfied—but lost his fortune and, even more, his earlier enthusiasm and sanguine outlook. Frederika's memoirs speak of her husband in this period with the same gloomy tone as her references to the feckless males that the sorely tried women of the clan had to bear with in the past; in later years, Louis Brandeis' letters to his father are filled with the kind of cheerful small talk a thoughtful son works up for the special benefit of an elder who has too little of importance to fill his mind and needs to be lifted out of chronic depression. The financial stress of the family never became desperate, and in the 1880s the family firm began to prosper once more. Now it was not Adolph, a silent senior partner, but his son Alfred who won recognition and self-esteem as the one responsible for restoring the family fortunes.

In May 1872, shortly after the affairs of Brandeis and Crawford were wound up, Adolph was persuaded by Lewis Dembitz to take the family for a trip to Europe. The party—parents, daughters Fannie (aged twenty-one) and

Amy (aged twenty), and sons Alfred (aged eighteen) and Louis (not yet six-teen)—planned to spend fifteen months on tour, but they stayed for three years because of an illness to which Amy and then Fannie succumbed. Alfred alone returned at the scheduled time. For the year 1872–73, Alfred and Louis joined their mother and sisters in visits to museums and concerts, all the way from London to Venice, and their father in walking tours in the forests and mountains of Austria and Italy. It was a glowing experience that Louis fre-quently recalled in his continuous, almost daily, correspondence with his brother in later years. The *Wanderjahr* became possible when the original plan to enroll Louis in a renowned secondary school, the classical humanistic *Gymnasium* in Vienna, fell through because his preparation in Louisville did not suffice for passing the entrance examination. In the fall of 1873, as Alfred returned to America and the rest of the family stayed behind to care for the ailing Fannie, Louis went to Dresden by himself to apply to the *Annen-Real-schule* there, a school with a curriculum adapted to middle-class professionals rather than to the classical tradition. He was able to persuade the administra-tion to exempt him from entrance examinations and for the next two years studied French, Latin and German literature, physics, chemistry, mineralogy, and mathematics, completing the course with distinction.

The rigorous training he received in a German *Gymnasium* made a deep impression on the young Brandeis. He used to tell his law clerks that he had learned to think there. He also said, to an interviewer, that the German pater-nalism and authoritarian, formal discipline of the Dresden school "got on my nerves," for "I was a terrible little individualist in those days." The family, including Louis' father, whose enthusiasm for everything American had evi-dently waned in the depression that befell him after his severe financial losses, came to believe that a scholarly profession in the old country was best suited for their younger son. But Louis, who clearly knew his own mind, had no intention of continuing his education in Europe and making his career there. Instead, in the fall of 1875, having spent the summer reading a standard law text in Louisville, he entered Harvard Law School at somewhat less than nineteen years of age. He aimed to follow in the footsteps of that eminent American lawyer, his uncle Lewis Dembitz of Louisville.[11]

If one compares the family backgrounds that shaped the identities of our two protagonists, Brandeis and Weizmann, there are striking resemblances. Both had fathers who, by frequent absence on business trips, exercised something less than rigorous, authoritarian discipline on their sons, and who evoked, by their personal reverses, a shade of commiseration as well as the submissive respect owed to a mid-nineteenth-century paterfamilias. Brandeis, like Weiz-mann, was sheltered and bolstered in his self-image by deep ties to a warm, protective extended family. The differences in their childhood circumstances were more subtle matters. The most obvious was that Brandeis' mother, unlike Weizmann's, was a strong, profoundly emotional presence in her child's life, almost overwhelming in her solicitude. Also, when his father lost financial security and self-confidence in the crisis of 1873, Brandeis did not succeed to the role of the responsible son in the same way that Weizmann (in his own estimation) did, through the default of his elder brother. Alfred Brandeis proved more than adequate to the demands that the family situation placed upon the senior son; when Louis left for Harvard, Alfred lent him the initial sum he needed. The task required of Louis was not to harness himself to responsibilities for others, but to make the most of his own unusual talents. He went to Harvard on this highly personal quest.

One cannot read the record of Brandeis family reminiscences and correspondence, preserved with much care and piety, without feeling that Louis Dembitz Brandeis' identification with Uncle Lewis, whose name he adopted, played some role in the liberation of the young man from his highly charged relationship with his mother and father. It proclaimed and established the profound attachment he felt to his parents and all they stood for, while, by adopting as a model one whose independence and individuality went beyond such norms as even this highly tolerant clan culture might impose, it declared young Louis' intention to be his own man. That such a liberation was necessary seems clear.

Lawyer and Public Advocate

Brandeis, like Weizmann, was one of those young men who form well-defined attitudes, habits of work and thought, and strong personal attachments at school. Weizmann, we noted, owed much to Russian and German culture, but fortified his Jewish identity in conscious detachment from the broader milieu. One could say something like this about Brandeis only in his years at the Dresden *Realschule;* he defined himself there as an American, not a Central European. But the Harvard milieu shaped his self-image directly; he came to feel the Pilgrim Fathers to be the true ancestors of his spirit, and he developed the habits and attitudes that made others perceive him as a Puritan. Also—unlike Weizmann, who was closely bound to a small Jewish group of Zionist fellow students—Brandeis at no time had a close, let alone exclusive, circle of Jewish friends at Harvard Law School; nor did he belong to any other clique of like-minded associates there. He shaped himself as a strong individual within a loose network of congenial friends and institutional connections. Harvard and the Pilgrim Fathers gave him ideals, not an exclusive bond with their current heirs. As for his Jewishness, it remained open, but decidedly nebulous and inchoate.

Brandeis' academic record at the law school became a local legend. He was noted for an extraordinary memory, acuteness and lucidity, persistent industry, and courage in the face of handicaps. Long hours of study in poor light caused eye strain severe enough to make doctors advise him to drop his law course. Seeking further advice, he was told to restrict his hours of work and take regular exercise in the open in order to build up a frail physique. He adopted a regimen of rigid self-discipline, followed for the rest of his life, and budgeted his time and effort to yield maximum output at the least possible cost. Also, he arranged for fellow students—like his future law partner Sam Warren—to read to him and was able to achieve a record of unmatched excellence by relying on his memory.

Finances were also a matter requiring close care. He had entered Harvard on the strength of a two-hundred-dollar loan from his brother and with a Boston Jewish philanthropist, Jacob Hecht, standing as surety for his tuition payments. In the second year he applied for scholarship aid, but on the advice of Professor Charles Saunders Bradley did not take it up when it was granted. Instead, he earned his expenses by tutoring, beginning with Bradley's own son. After two years he completed the degree requirements and, since baccalaureates were normally granted only to adults over twenty-one, was awarded his degree by special action of the Harvard Corporation. Returning for an additional year of study in 1877–78, he was appointed a proctor in Harvard College by President Eliot. He earned enough from this and other sources to pay off his debts and save a sum for investment in the kind of safe and conservative bonds he favored for the rest of his life.

Brandeis was a somewhat exotic figure at the law school. One friend wrote home about him: "Hails from Louisville, is not a college graduate, but has spent some years in Europe, has a rather foreign look and is currently believed to have some Jew blood in him, though you would not suppose it from his appearance."[12] In spite of the young man's outstanding scholarship and the respect for German education at Harvard in those days, this background quite sharply distinguished Brandeis from proper Bostonian students who had gone to Harvard College and joined all the right clubs. Notwithstanding young Louis' deep attachment to Harvard and Yankee culture and in spite of the exceptional recognition and influential friends that his academic prowess gained him, he did not move as smoothly into a Boston career on graduation as did his classmates who conformed to local standards. After completing a year of postgraduate studies and having become officially adult, Brandeis had to seek an entry into his chosen profession somewhere other than in Boston. He returned to the haven of the family in Louisville.

There followed a year in which the direction of Louis' future was a matter of intense concern, earnestly discussed by the extended family. The clan in Louisville had been augmented in 1867 by the arrival of Otto Wehle, a younger cousin of Brandeis' mother, who came from Prague to become a lawyer and later married Louis' sister Amy. Louis had spent his summers reading law in Otto Wehle's office in 1876 and 1877 and could have gone into practice with him, close to the bosom of the family. But, with much soul-searching, he decided against settling in Louisville and went off on his own to St. Louis.

There, too, the family offered a haven, for the lawyer Charles Nagel had recently married Fannie, the sister with whom Louis Brandeis had a powerful affinity. Nagel strongly urged Brandeis to join him in his office; but like the rest of the family, he was acutely sensitive to the young man's need for independence and a free field to develop his remarkable potentialities. Rather than press Brandeis against his inclination, Nagel helped him find a position with the law firm of James Taussig, a prominent St. Louis attorney. Taussig, too, had family ties with the clan, for he was the brother of that William Taussig who had been part of the Prague social circle of the Wehles and Brandeises, and whose daughter Jennie had recently married Louis' brother Alfred. Thus, the new position signified that the fledgling had left the nest, indeed, but not yet reached independence, his true destination.

Brandeis found the work in Taussig's office fairly dull and trivial, and he was homesick for his old life and associations in Boston. The Louisville family tended to feel that the true field for their young scholar was not in the arena of active law practice at all, but in the scholarly environment of a center of culture. The way back to Boston was opened for Louis Brandeis when his classmate, Sam Warren, second-ranking student in his year after Brandeis, proposed that the two should set up their own law firm.

On graduation Warren had gone into the firm of Shattuck, Holmes, and Monroe, where one of the principals was the brilliant legal scholar, Oliver Wendell Holmes, Jr. Warren, like Brandeis, was a young man with exalted ambitions, not satisfied with a life of routine legal business or, on the other hand, of gentlemanly idleness. He felt strongly the obligation to make the most of his talents in some field of public service, perferably of scholarly attainment. He now saw an opportunity to take over the publication of a law journal, combining this with an independent law practice, for which he could rely on the business of his father's papermill and his other New England connections. He urged Brandeis to join him in the venture, which would allow them to combine personal independence with a significant role in legal scholarship and public life.

Brandeis exercised great caution before taking up this extremely interesting proposal. He was concerned about his financial security and independence, not wishing to rely on Warren's connections alone. Warren carefully checked the market, citing the experience of another new firm set up by a young Boston attorney with a young Western (Jewish) partner where the combination had worked out well. These reports coupled with his own strong inclination induced Brandeis to make the venture, and in the fall of 1879 the firm of Warren and Brandeis was created. Even though the projected editorship of a law journal fell through, Brandeis found another outlet for his talents. He served for two years as law clerk to Horace Gray, chief justice of the Massachusetts Superior Court, until the judge was appointed to the U.S. Supreme Court. Such an assignment gave him the desired opportunity for a broad concern with legal issues beyond the scope of his own growing personal practice.[13]

His ties to Harvard provided an additional option—to combine the scholarship his clan valued with the active practice he wanted. It was gratifying to be invited to give the course on evidence at Harvard Law School; later, the whole family shared his pride when he was offered an assistant professorship, although he professed himself unready to accept since his needed more time in active practice. His commitment to the law school led him to shoulder the duties of secretary of the projected alumni association—one of the rare occasions when Brandeis took on a workhorse role such as was regularly assumed by the young Weizmann. Brandeis' service to the law school gained him an honorary master's degree from the university, a recognition not of professional attainments but of the kind of layman's service the grateful academy honors in its most loyal sons. The Harvard connection was one Brandeis sustained with dedication all his life, and it was his letter of credence as an adopted son of the best Boston society.

Young Brandeis, who followed a careful course of self-improvement, kept a record of the eminent and interesting Bostonians he met, in the same spirit that he copied memorable passages and wrote abstracts of significant literature in his notebooks. His social acceptance in Boston circles was something that came naturally with his intellectual achievements in the relatively open academic world of that time and place; but it was also something he actively pursued. Harvard, not to speak of Boston, was already a complex community and rapidly grew more so in the closing decades of the century. The Harvard Brandeis cherished, then and for the rest of his life, was not the whole range of Harvard society. His temperament and circumstances gave his Harvard identification a particular bias.

Brandeis found highly congenial the empirical bent and scholarly, Germanic professionalism fostered by President Charles W. Eliot, a chemist by training. But the highest values of Harvard culture still remained the genteel philosophical humanism cultivated by the eminent men of letters of the college faculty. Brandeis, never having studied at the college, had relatively remote contact with these luminaries. As a law student and young lawyer, his closest associates and patrons were law professors and professional colleagues. Moreover, unlike Weizmann, who acknowledged the superior claims of the humanities over his own field of applied science, Brandeis admitted no higher study than the law. He was distinctly averse to abstract theorizing, especially theological or metaphysical. Glendower Evans—a lawyer and close friend of Brandeis, but also an intimate of William James, who shared his mentor's fascination with mysticism and spiritualism—met with a brusque, irritated rejection when he once tried to argue these matters with Brandeis. The young Kentuckian's cast of mind made him find his most congenial associates among practical men, men of affairs and Boston reformers, rather than in the innermost circle of old New England culture. He might visit Brander Matthews' home and go to hear Emerson discourse, but he was unlikely to enter into the spirit of their concerns as a participant and not simply an observer.[14]

Apart from the law school, Brandeis found close companions at Harvard among men who shared his own slightly exotic image in Boston. He was drawn to the naturalist and geographer, Professor Nathaniel Shaler, a Kentuckian like himself; he was profoundly attracted by Shaler's Jeffersonian advocacy of small social units and regional variation against the tide of big city cosmopolitanism. On the other hand, as a product of German education, he represented a type of European cosmopolitan culture that President Eliot was trying to implant in the growing, broadening university. Thus he found congenial friends among young faculty members like Philippe Marcou and Ephraim Emerton who, like himself, had studied in Europe. Young Brandeis together with others of the family in Louisville joined the society that supported the Harvard Germanic Museum. His later membership in the *Turnverein* in Boston, a meeting place for the local German community, had a more prosaic background that arose from the simple need for exercise and his interest in finding clients among the German and German-Jewish businessmen in Boston.

As a pillar of the Law School's alumni association and one who supported the creation of the *Harvard Law Review,* Brandeis won the appreciation of influential men in the Harvard community. A particular bond between President Eliot and Bandeis was the young economist, Frank W. Taussig. This kinsman, the brother of Alfred Brandeis' wife Jennie, was not only a close friend, but remained Louis' authority and guide on economic issues for years. Before his appointment as professor of economics, Taussig had served as President Eliot's administrative assistant. Together with Brandeis' own merit, such multiple affinities left a sufficiently powerful impression on the Harvard president, so that many years later, when his retirement from office became imminent, he was prepared to propose Brandeis' name as his successor.[15]

Though Brandeis did not accept a law professorship at Harvard, he continued to maintain his interest in teaching. He wanted to develop legal education along practical lines, urging Harvard to give instruction in Massachusetts law; he himself initiated a famous course in business law at the Massachusetts Institute of Technology. His firm quickly became a desirable place for law professors to send their promising young graduates. Warren and Brandeis expanded their staff by taking on recent graduates personally recommended by—and in some cases related to—teachers at Harvard Law School; a practice which, of course, Brandeis continued in his days as Supreme Court justice. When he took over the leadership of American Zionism, the movement was enriched by first- and second-rank leaders drawn from Brandeis' multitudinous contacts with topflight Harvard Law graduates and *Harvard Law Review* editors.

Law practice channeled Brandeis' social contacts into new spheres of interest. Owing to the special conception he developed of his role as a lawyer, he moved from defending private litigants to advocacy of public causes. The kind of clients he represented privately had an effect on his evolving public concerns, directing his attention to significant issues and helping to form the principles on which he acted.[16]

Harvard and Boston connections provided most of the initial clientele available to Warren and Brandeis. Harvard professors would recommend the firm to those who sought advice in securing topflight counsel. The Warren family's papermills provided a significant part of their business; years later, Brandeis still had his office in the same building as the Warren enterprises.

Such connections gave the firm an important base in the Boston legal profession—but not at first the kind of practice characteristic of the leading local law firms.

The recognized elite among Boston lawyers were part and parcel of Brahmin high society; their law practice as well as their political leanings reflected the interests of their clients and social peers. Such a firm would be largely engaged in administering trusts and estates for old Boston families. Corporate enterprise grew increasingly important in their clientele, as in the practice of successful lawyers generally in the late nineteenth century. In Boston their clients were drawn from the textile industry, banking, and other areas in which the wealthiest, most influential Bostonians were engaged. These interests fostered a high-tariff Republicanism, favorable to the trusts and financial syndicates that grew dominant in national politics. The Warren papermills, which depended on imported raw materials, required a different approach, one akin to that of the farmer and shipper interests of Brandeis' Louisville connections.

Brandeis' contribution to the clientele of the partnership was expected to be drawn, in addition to Harvard sources, from Louisville and St. Louis and the German, particularly the German-Jewish, businesss community in Boston. Although he would join the *Turnverein* as a likely place to pick up some law business, under no conditions would he attend a synagogue, the most likely place to become a close associate of potential German-Jewish clients. During his Harvard days Brandeis' contacts with the local Jewry were evidently minimal; they amounted, perhaps, to little more than occasional attendance at the Sunday open house held by the Jacob Hechts. The first case Brandeis took to court in Boston was a suit to recover a payment owed to the Jewish United Charities headed by Jacob Hecht; Brandeis also served as attorney for the Hechts' extensive business and personal affairs. The Hecht connection extended through this active citizen's broad network of kinship and his commercial and communal contacts, thus making accessible a major part of the Boston's Jewish communal and mercantile leadership. Together with the paper trade and the boot and shoe industry reached through the Warrens and other Harvard sources (as well as the Hechts), the most prominent feature of Brandeis' clientele were members of the Boston mercantile community, a significant part of them Jews.

Like other leading lawyers, Brandeis derived a growing part of his practice from corporations. The complexity of their affairs led corporate clients to retain lawyers not simply to represent them in litigation, but to advise them on policies, especially on the legal implications of proposed policies, before they were implemented. However, such counsel was usually sought on special problems, like corporate law, taxation, or other well-defined fields of legal expertise. In Brandeis' case, owing to his conception of his duty as a lawyer, the role of general counsel developed into rather more than that, especially when he found congenial spirits among his clients. He had the habit of praising such clients as "loyal" to him; some, he acclaimed as industrial heroes.[17]

The Boston lawyers most congenial to Brandeis, men like Warren and

Holmes, were concerned with questions of the ethics and social function of the legal profession. Holmes had made a major contribution toward understanding the historical rather than dogmatic sources of jurisprudence. Brandeis developed his own clear and firmly held notions on these subjects and guided himself by them through his entire distinguished career. He conceived his role as a counselor not to be one limited to defending the interests of his client as perceived and defined by the client himself; he claimed the right to make an independent appraisal of the situation. To this task he applied more than his extraordinary legal skills; he also prided himself on his highly competent command of accountancy and his flair for facts and figures. Moreover, he developed special sensitivity to labor relations in any industrial dispute. Applying these approaches to problems referred to him as counsel, he aimed to propose solutions (not necessarily those first contemplated by the client) that would best serve the client's true interest as well as that of the others concerned in the case. Accordingly, he refused to work for subordinate officers of the corporations by whom he might be retained. He insisted on direct liaison with those able to make ultimate policy decisions or alter them in line with Brandeis' suggestions, made after a thorough study of the entire complex of problems involved in the case.[18]

It was an attitude other lawyers sometimes found it hard to comprehend; in later years when he became a target for the hostility of the Boston legal establishment, he was accused of misconduct when, for example, he applied such principles in his settlement of the Warren estate. He carried over this approach into his career as an advocate for the public interest, a role for which his favored procedure best fitted him and led him increasingly to seek out.

Brandeis' political views, which developed from moderate liberalism of the Manchester free-trade variety to militant progressivism, did not derive from clearly defined theoretical principles. He had certain fixed predilections—in favor of small and against large social and economic units; in favor of primary producers and against financiers and speculators; in favor of shippers and against carriers and railroad tycoons—rooted in the family's tradition and their interests as purveyors of regional produce to the market. The clients he served in Boston had similar views and interests, and, in the case of his German-Jewish clientele, a background of similar political traditions. He found, in the Old Bostonian community, associates who reinforced them. The marked, if gradual, shifts in his political positions did not abandon such values, but carried them forward (with notable leaps and bounds) in a sweeping, continuing progression. Two elements seem to have determined the course of his political growth: his own methods of work and thought and the associates he was thrown in with or sought out.[19]

Brandeis moved easily at first into the current trend among Harvard liberals, which fitted well the Forty-Eighter attitudes he had absorbed in Louisville. He was a sound-money, free-trade liberal like his uncle, strongly committed to civil service reform; this made it easy for him to join the Boston mugwumps who bolted the Republican party and supported Grover Cleveland in 1884. Brandeis thereafter assumed the posture of a political independent, generally associated with Young Democrats, but not fully committed to any party. On occasion he was approached to run for political office, but refused. He found his true political vocation in another role, as an attorney for public causes brought to his attention and capable of arousing his interest.

Public affairs, like teaching, represented a field in which Brandeis, in the tradition of his family and the Boston elite, felt himself called to serve. His drive to make himself financially independent would ultimately allow him to undertake public service as a free agent, not subject to pressure or material inducements from any side. He explained his views in 1891 to his fiancée, his cousin Alice Goldmark, whom at the age of thirty-five, after a long bachelorhood, he was about to marry. With her strong support, he was able to arrange his affairs so that a good part of his time was regularly available for unremunerated public activity.

Brandeis was surrounded by friends devoted to good works, many of them women active in charities or labor unions (including his own Goldmark cousins) and by clients (notably the Filenes) impelled, both by public spirit and their business interests, to sponsor public-interest lobbies or launch experimental social projects.[20] With German social thought and legislation as their model, some of Brandeis' German-Jewish clients set up a cooperative credit union. The Filene Department Store developed a self-governing cooperative association for their employees, with Brandeis' active assistance: a project that he was later to hold up as a model reform in industrial relations (as personnel policies were then called). Such clients and Brandeis' Harvard associates in the political reform clubs of Boston enlisted his aid in major reform efforts such as his battle against a private takeover of the Boston street railways. Friends in the labor unions and in social work proposed causes like the protection of working women and child labor. As he chose, one after another, specific practical issues among those for which his aid was solicited, his range of political interests broadened from case to case; it began to extend well beyond the limits of political reform approved in Boston society.

Reform activites and public spirit were generally approved in the Yankee milieu; other qualities Brandeis showed sharply deviated from the norm and ultimately drove him beyond the pale. Many Boston lawyers gave time as volunteers for public causes, but rarely on such a regular basis with such a substantial commitment of energy as Brandeis did—certainly not, as was his regular practice, by serving as counsel without remuneration in complex, time-consuming cases and issues. Another fixed habit, his practice of resisting a role of narrow advocacy and seeking solutions that would benefit all parties in conflict, was likely to carry him beyond the specific goals of some who initially approached him. Elite Boston may have been ready to regard excessive zeal for a particular philanthropic hobby—prison reform, settlement houses, or the like—as understandable and even laudable, but Brandeis began to be seen as deviant on a scale dangerous to social order.

This reputation was probably enhanced by the effect Brandeis' new political interests and his methods of work had on his changing circle of associates. Old acquaintances were estranged, and the new friends he made were increasingly drawn from persons active in the same causes. Moreover, his commitments to public issues far exceeded what could be done by a lay leader personally, and Brandeis recruited suitable paid executives, capable of sharing his vision and carrying out his designs. His savings bank insurance project was assigned to Alice Grady, his office secretary, as her immediate responsibility, and it became her lifetime career. For the Public Franchise League—started by Brandeis with Edward A. Filene and the psychologist Morton Prince to fight a proposed streetcar monopoly—Robert A. Woods sent him Joseph Eastman from the staff of his South End House Community Center; Eastman went on, with Brandeis' sponsorship, to become the leading member of the Interstate Commerce Commission. The circle of Brandeis associates who worked for him directly, or as professionals aligned with his policies, or simply as partisans of the same causes began to include some who were radicals by contemporary standards: social workers, trade unionists, and muckraking journalists. The relationship was never casual, though rarely intimate. Although Brandeis was far from being an approachable man, his style of leadership required such close rapport with his aides, not only on political but on moral issues, that he could work only with those he respected and liked. The political complexion of such associates naturally colored the public perception of Brandeis himself.[21]

Brandeis, who was anything but changeable in his basic attitudes, got his name as a radical only in part because his views were ahead of the times. It was no less a consequence of the fact that he did not keep up with the times as others in his professional and social position did in Boston. In 1905 Brandeis started his study of life insurance at the invitation of a group of concerned Boston policyholders. The solution he arrived at for the reform of the industry, low-cost savings bank life insurance, gained only the most meager support from Boston investors. Brandeis' attitude to this problem arose from the same kind of concern for the exploited poor—in this case, the working class, whose problems aroused his anxiety ever since the violent Homestead strike of 1890—that had made abolitionists of so many leading Bostonians in their day. But men of this sort, Brandeis' supporters in earlier reforms, did not extend the same sympathy and interest to free laborers. Moreover, they went along with the current trend, which favored the growth of large, monopolistic corporations, because they had so large a stake as bankers and investors in the burgeoning capital market. This involved relaxing the laws regulating corporations on which Massachusetts had prided itself. Thus, when Brandeis took up the battle in 1907 against the New Haven Railroad's attempt to absorb the Boston and Maine system, seeing this as a defense of Boston traditions against foreign interests, he found to his dismay that leading Bostonians like Henry Lee Higginson, staunch allies in the past, now bitterly opposed him.[22]

Brandeis must always have been aware that, as a Jew, his acceptance in Boston society was subject to some limitations. In spite of the liberalism of the elite and their marked interest in, and sympathy for, freethinking or liberal Jews, Boston was exclusive in its private precincts; with the rising feeling against immigrants, social exclusion became harder to breach. His sense of this reality clearly became far more distinct after his marriage. He remarked in later years that he had good friends among his Yankee clients, but his wife was not on their guest list for social occasions. Brandeis could have made the same observation in a much more painful connection. His law partner, Sam Warren, was one of his closest personal friends, and he remained so after leaving law practice following his father's death in order to run the family papermills. Yet, beginning with Warren's marriage to Mabel Bayard, daughter of Senator Thomas Bayard of Philadelphia (an occasion to which Brandeis was not invited), the social barrier became very marked; no visiting relationship developed between the two families. The close friends Brandeis made among upper-class Bostonians—the Holmes, the Delands, Elizabeth Glendower Evans, and others—tended to perceive themselves as deviants in the straitlaced community. But it was only after Brandeis was marked out as a radical that he was the target of open hostility. The attack against him, financed by adversary railroad interests, was launched by a news sheet—set up for the purpose—that resorted to openly antisemitic motifs.[23]

Brandeis found himself swimming against the Boston tide in the New Haven merger battle, and he was defeated in the first onset in 1909 by the bankers and their "lawyer minions." His annoyance, he wrote in jest to his brother, was such that he was "rapidly becoming a Socialist." The hostility he encountered grew much stronger and more public from that time, and his isolation increased. He became acutely aware of a change in moral atmosphere, which, like other Bostonians, he traced to a breakdown in the values of a once-homogeneous society. Testifying in 1915 before a New York factory regulation commission, he said, "We in Massachusetts in the past have been a community differing radically from most."; homogeneous, imbued with "the old puritanic sense," the Bay State had until recently been able to dispense with compulsory regulation of factories, trusts, and utilities, since a moral consensus enforced the merely recommendatory findings of its industrial commissions. The same sense of a breakdown of consensus had been traced by other Bostonians to the mass of Irish-Catholic and South and East European immigrants, which led them to press for immigration restrictions. Brandeis, reacting against the pressure of lobbying by financiers and special interests, drew other conclusions. He leaned increasingly to the new Progressive party line of state intervention in economic matters—and despairing of the survival of Puritan virtues in old-line Boston society, he began to see them exemplified in other quarters. He found a new fellowship with the Irish labor leaders and journalists and with the social workers, professionals and young businessmen among the Jews he encountered in his private and public law practice; and emerging from the confines of Boston, he made new friends across the country and overseas among the leaders of progressive causes.[24]

Brandeis' participation in national affairs began in a characteristic way in 1897 when he appeared as a spokesman for consumers' interests at a tariff hearing before a congressional committee. Although this early Washington appearance won little more than ridicule, in 1907 Brandeis persuaded the Supreme Court to reverse its previous opposition to wages and hours legislation with his famous brief in the case of *Muller v. Oregon*. He entered the case, characteristically, at the request of friends: his sister-in-law Josephine Goldmark, research director of the National Consumers' League, and Mrs. Florence Kelley, then the chief factory inspector of Illinois. Just as characteristically, his way of winning the case was to overcome the Court's opposition by seeking to absorb it rather than contest its legal grounds. Until Brandeis introduced his landmark "Brandeis brief," cases seeking to establish the right of legislators to regulate conditions of employment had sought to defend such action on legal grounds: as an exercise of the police power not subject to judicial review. Brandeis emphasized, instead, facts bearing on the case, assiduously gathered for him by Josephine Goldmark and her associates. Thus he directly met the requirements of the Supreme Court itself when it had ruled in previous cases that it had not been shown that labor laws in question had a "reasonable" connection with stated objectives, such as public health, comprised under the states' police power. As usual with him, Brandeis took up a specific issue proposed by friends and then sought to appear as a nonpartisan "counsel for the situation."[25]

But the hostility against him had by this time forced him into the role of general adversary of the Boston establishment. He was openly committed to serving the public by providing free legal counsel at the same level of competence that the wealthy corporate interests were able to hire. Having chosen sides to this extent, he became increasingly interested in advocates of progressive causes beyond his immediate circle, and he made deliberate efforts to acquaint himself with them. His own family, especially on the Goldmark side, was a rich source of suitable contacts. Dr. Felix Adler, his brother-in-law (married to his wife's eldest sister), was the famous founder of the Ethical Culture Society and was probably the first minister to commit his flock to serious social action in America.[26] His wife's other sisters, Pauline and Josephine, were active suffragettes and social-work activists, with direct access to centers of urban progressivism in Illinois and Wisconsin. His friends, the trade unionists John and Mary Kenny O'Sullivan, were hosts to visiting Irish nationalist and British socialist leaders whom he met in their Boston home. He followed the political and social conceptions of such men and women with increasing interest, stimulated as well by the writings of American radicals like Henry George and Henry Demarest Lloyd.

Elizabeth Glendower Evans, perhaps the closest friend of the Brandeis family, was one whom he both led and followed in the progress toward radical causes. In 1908 she went to England at his suggestion to study and meet the Fabians, and on her return he suggested she attend the conference of the Women's Trade Union League, being held at Jane Addams' Hull House in Chicago, From there Mrs. Evans went on to Wisconsin and the LaFollettes

and also visited the socialist mayor of Milwaukee. She came back with glowing reports of mid-western progressivism. She was particularly enraptured by
the LaFollettes, whom she was determined that Brandeis must meet. The
meeting of Brandeis and Robert LaFollette took place in Washington, D.C.,
in 1910 during Brandeis' appearances before the joint congressional committee that was set up to hear charges against Secretary of the Interior Ballinger.
The rapport between the two men was immediate, and a friendship and political alliance arose, joining them and their families and friends as closely as
Elizabeth Evans could possibly have desired.

The Ballinger case proejcted Brandeis into political involvement and public prominence on a new plane. In the 1908 elections, when the Democrats
had once more chosen the cheap-money champion, William Jennings Bryan,
as their candidate, Brandeis had voted for Taft, the Republican successor to
the trust-busting Teddy Roosevelt. In the Ballinger affair the Republican
administration was entangled in an alleged sellout of public lands to private
corporations; Brandeis was largely responsible for discrediting not only the
secretary of the interior, who later resigned, but also President Taft for his
maneuvers to cover up irregularities. In a merciless prosecution of the case,
he went so far as to track the movements of his own brother-in-law, Charles
Nagel, Taft's secretary of commerce, at the risk of permanently chilling the
relations between them. He was now anathema to political foes not only in
Boston, but in the country at large.

Not only his foes, but the friends and allies he now made, imposed new
roles and new demands of partisanship upon him in a broader range of issues
than he had previously selected in his desire to be "counsel for the situation,"
trusted by all parties. He was among those who in 1912 founded the National
Progressive Republican League, aiming to push LaFollette as the Republican
nominee for the presidency in the 1912 election. A commitment of this sort
involved endorsing not only the man, but a party and a whole range of progressive positions such as proposals to increase the direct participation of the
voting public in government—a policy that only mildly interested Brandeis
and in which he did not really believe. He was not the man to give blanket
approval to a party or a party program; in the same campaign that saw him
seek the Republican nomination for LaFollette, he also came out for the
Democratic candidate for governor in the Massachusetts state elections.
Brandeis took on an unfamiliar assignment when he went out on a speaking
tour for LaFollette in the Midwest at the beginning of the 1912 campaign. By
June the LaFollette boom had collapsed, much to Brandeis' sorrow as a friend
and admirer, but not to his surprise. He then committed himself to a new
man, Woodrow Wilson, the Democratic candidate, and involved himself in
still greater and wider responsibilities. He was brought into the councils of
the candidate on a wide range of domestic political and economic issues, and
he became one of Wilson's chief advisers. It was during those years of
enhanced and expanded political activity that Brandeis also became more
deeply interested in Jewish causes and declared himself to be a Zionist.

American Jewry and Early Zionism

When Brandeis became active in Jewish affairs, he found a divided community: religiously, between different versions of Judaism; socially, between new
immigrants and old settlers; economically and politically, between workers
and employers, radicals and conservatives. The main cleavage was between
established German Jews and East European immigrants. Many of the issues
were foreign to Brandeis, and he remained unconcerned with them. He was
drawn into others by his new role.

The upheaval of migration (especially into the still incompletely shaped
American milieu) was enough to unsettle traditional values among German
and Russian Jews alike.[27] The former, many of whom began as peddlers in
the back country, moved rather freely among other Americans and had to
learn their ways; when in time they prospered and grew wealthy, they even
more consciously sought acceptance and respectability. Just as upper- or middle-class Gentiles opted for the decorous formalism of Episcopalian or Presbyterian churches against the unrestrained enthusiasm of revivalist sects,
Jews in equivalent positions voted for ritual reforms in Judaism. Both the
Russian and the Rumanian Jews took a different route: they settled in dense
ethnic concentrations in metropolitan "ghettoes," where their encounters
with others were often hostile. They drew defensively on the familiar warmth
of one another, preserving old-country ties. When they built synagogues, their
rites were traditional, Orthodox. Some were atheistic or agnostic radicals, in
the style they had learned in Europe. In neither case did the Reform Judaism
of settled American Jewry appeal to them.

The German Jews (but not the Russian Jews) were joined some twenty
years after the first arrivals by rabbis, in many cases committed to Reform.
As religious prefessionals and full-time communal workers, some rabbis
desired a more formal, comprehensive organization of American Jewry not
limited by the local perspective of lay-dominated synagogues. This aim was
pursued with most success by Isaac Mayer Wise, an immigrant rabbi who
settled in Cincinnati. He built a rabbinical seminary there; helped in forming
a (laymen's) Union of Hebrew Congregations and the Central Conference of
American Rabbis; and tried to provide his scattered constituents with a standard, Americanized prayerbook and ritual. With this, he supplied the
fundamental requirements that, it was thought, would make the future of
American Jewry secure.

Wise hoped to unite American Jewry; the reforms he urged were consequently moderate and specifically colored by American conditions. But the
ideological commitments other rabbis had brought over with them from Germany caused his program to be realized in ways he had not always initially
projected. Under pressure from more radical reformers, Wise's institutional
creations—the Hebrew Union College and the Union Prayer Book—were
given a more markedly partisan ideological cast. This led conservative rabbis
and sympathetic laymen to build a rival college, the Jewish Theological Sem-

inary in New York. This was a rather feeble institution at first; in the early decades of East European immigration, the Cincinnati-based Reform movement remained the undisputed religious establishment of long-settled, Americanized German Jews.

However, Cincinnati was being shunted into a backwater of the American economy by the 1880s. The wealthiest, most powerful Jewish leaders gathered in New York, where the wealth and power of the nation were concentrated. Here and in the other metropolitan centers was also where the Russian and Rumanian slum dwellers had settled. The influx of the new immigrants gave rise to a nativist reaction, particularly noted among those liberal, East Coast Protestant circles most respected by leaders of the German-Jewish American community. The first task of the time, they concluded, was the speedy Americanization of the immigrants in order to head off the menace of rising antisemitism. For this work it was not Cincinnati, but the rising Jewish upper-middle class of the metropolitan centers who were most strategically placed.[28]

Like other immigrant communities in America, Jews had long maintained charitable societies to aid incoming members of their group. Such societies, traditional among Jews everywhere, were generally recognized ladders to the respectability and prestige that the wider American community granted to leaders in good works. The ramifications of this work, especially in the case of Jews, required leaders with broad national, even international, connections; traditionally, such work had involved ransom of captives, aid to transients, and intercession at imperial and feudal courts on behalf of fellow Jews threatened with official oppression or mob violence. In America such activities (including assistance to the Jewish community in Palestine) were at first subordinate to the local synagogue; but the charitable societies soon detached themselves and became parallel institutions. Action on a national and international scale was undertaken by the Board of Delegates of American Israelites. The board was originally intended to serve as the general representative of the entire religious community but ended as a function of the (Reform) Union of American Hebrew Congregations.

Other agencies, organized outside any congregational framework, entered the field and soon dominated it. The B'nai B'rith (a fraternal order organized by German-Jewish immigrants in 1843 in America and extended to other continents some fifty years later) was represented in Washington, D.C., by Simon Wolf, a lawyer and lobbyist who also represented the Board of Delegates. The B'nai B'rith was (until the twentieth century) a largely German-Jewish association centered in the Midwest. Finally, in 1906 the American Jewish Committee (AJC) was founded and swiftly emerged as the most powerful "representative" of American Jewry. From the beginning, this New York-based committee of notables was deeply involved with the problems of East European Jews, both in their countries of origin and in the immigrant quarters of American cities.

The new Jewish immigrants from Eastern Europe formed a sharply different social structure from that of the earlier Americans, including Jews.[29] The new immigrants did not typically become rural peddlers in the Midwest or the South; their most striking type was "proletarian," and they clustered in the large northeastern cities. Like their predecessors, they, too, depended on a relatively distinct American-Jewish economy. The peddler had relied on his credit with other German Jews for the capital to get started, but the new immigrants met them as worker against employer in the clothing, tobacco, and other consumer-goods industries where Jews became prominent. Class anatagonisms were added to the other frictions between the two parts of the Jewish community.

The newcomers responded in different ways to the strain of their move from the old country to the New World. The synagogue most nearly repro-duced for the older generation the characteristic environment of life in East-ern Europe. Traditionally Orthodox, the synagogue covered a wide range of social functions in the accustomed way; but it lacked the structure of family and community life that had supported it in the old country. It arose from the local initiative of laymen without the guidance that highly regarded rab-binical authorities had given in Europe. Nor did orthodoxy achieve the nationwide united organization that Reform Jews had built for themselves. Nevertheless, the immigrants' synagogue served as a major focus of much else in the community, including Zionist activity.

Other institutions were specifically adapted to ease the adjustment to a new milieu while preserving links to the past.[30] One was the *landsmanshaft,* an association of emigrants from the same town or province. It provided mutual aid in sickness and other times of need as well as a meeting place where old ties and familiar customs could shelter newcomers from the daily challenge of their strange new life. An extension of the same kind of services, not limited to European local ties and more advanced in American ways, was made available by the fraternal orders that soon flourished among the new immigrants. Both the fraternal order and the *landsmanshaft* were a charac-teristic form in which early Zionist socieities were organized.

For many immigrants the breakdown of older traditions had begun in Europe.[31] There were young people caught up in the currents of Russian populism, anarchism, and (in later years) the social democratic Bund and other revolutionary parties. In America they tried to organize the immigrant Jews as part of the trade union or the socialist or anarchist movements in order to overthrow, or reform, American capitalism. At first their success was sporadic; the Jewish immigrants were militant when aroused, but not easy to organize for a lasting commitment. But by the twentieth century the Jewish trade unions and labor movement had won a prominent place both in Amer-ican labor and in the Jewish community. The Jewish socialists came to dom-inate the Yiddish press, publishing the *Forverts,* the most widely read of the four major Yiddish daily newspapers.

The notables who felt responsible for their immigrant coreligionists nat-urally disliked such carryovers of European ways to America. They welcomed neither the traditionalism nor the radicalism that came from Eastern Europe. But soon they found cause to fear the ravages of too hasty and ruthless an

Americanization as well. Together with social workers and settlement-house volunteers active in the immigrant slums, they concluded that a policy of forced-draft Americanization had hastened the breakdown of respect for parents, sufficiently promoted by the difficulties the older generation faced in the strange new land. Consequently, a new policy of supporting traditional immigrant culture while teaching American ways began to gain favor.[32] This led to a certain appreciation for Zionism, among other moderating influences in the immigrant ghetto; for the Zionists, drawn from a broad spectrum of immigrant opinion on social and cultural issues, tended to be found among the more modern of the traditionalist Orthodox and the more Jewishly loyal of the radicals.

The early Zionist societies in America formed part of the network of institutions that gave the newcomers a sense of continuity with their old-country background.[33] Synagogues, *landsmanshaftn,* fraternal mutual-benefit societies, and workers' and young people's clubrooms were the forms in which many organized. Like the Zionist groups in Europe, they collected funds for the settlements in Palestine; some created pools of joint savings to purchase land in Palestine and settle their own members there; they conducted programs of self-education and general propaganda in the immigrant community; and, after the WZO was founded, they canvassed the community in order to sell the *shekel,* which qualified purchasers to vote in the elections of delegates to the Zionist Congress. Zionist clubs often had a short life span and transient membership, or they were diverted to activities other than directly Zionist ones. These clubs were a continual disappointment to the WZO central offices and were chronically oppressed by the disparity between their aims and their current activity. But they had a wider influence—particularly through the Yiddish press—than their permanently organized strength. This was shown when they were called on to arrange mass demonstrations, or assemble audiences for visiting Zionist leaders, or in street-corner or door-to-door canvassing.

Although most of the Zionists were new immigrants, many leaders were found in older-settled or more acculturated American-Jewish circles. The major Reform congregation in New York, Temple Emanu-El, supplied Rabbi Gustav Gottheil and his son, Professor Richard Gottheil, first president of the (post-Herzlian) Federation of American Zionists (FAZ). Dr. Stephen S. Wise, who was to be the acknowledged leader of American Jewry for many active years, was the Gottheils' friend and disciple. When Dr. Judah L. Magnes returned from his graduate studies in Europe, this alumnus of the Hebrew Union College soon made himself conspicuous as a Zionist leader.[34]

For some Reform rabbis, Zionism might offer an appropriate response to certain theoretical and practical problems of their own denomination. Reform doctrine considered Judaism a system of beliefs and ethical standards, corresponding exactly to the universal truths of philosophic rationalism, which were divinely revealed to Jews but accessible to all men as a rational necessity. The ritual practices of Judaism, however, were historically relative customs: those that were now outlived should be reformed in accordance with the standards of the time and place. But if Jewish doctrine was the same as deism or Kantian ethics and if Jewish ritual should be reformed in accordance with contemporary (i.e., non-Jewish) standards, what reason remained for Jewish separatism? Felix Adler, the son and intended successor of a senior rabbi at Temple Emanu-El, concluded that, indeed, there was no reason; he left Judaism for a more rigorous, universalist and humanist, non-theistic ministry that was combined with progressive social action. The attraction Adler's Ethical Culture Society had for young Jews gave loyal Reform leaders pause and made them appreciate the sources of Jewish loyalty in others.[35]

The standard Reform answer to these difficulties, on the theoretical plane, was a variant of the traditional doctrine of the Chosen People. The favorite nineteenth-century version of this doctrine attributed to the Jews a racial talent for religious and ethical insight. Non-Zionist Reform construed this to mean that Jews had to preserve their identity so that their racial gift, exercised in Dispersion, might benefit all mankind. Zionists (e.g., the venerable Reform rabbi, Bernard Felsenthal, or the secularist philosopher, Horace M. Kallen) held that the racial gift of the Jews could only be fully and freely expressed in a society largely constituted by Jews living in their own homeland.

Signs of a drift away from Jewishness, whether among the new immigrants or in Reform temples, concerned Zionists and non-Zionists alike. In 1902 the leading banker and Jewish notable, Jacob Schiff, helped bring Solomon Schechter, the Cambridge University Reader in Rabbinics, to revive the Jewish Theological Seminary in New York. A member of Temple Emanu-El and a supporter of the Reform Hebrew Union College, Schiff aided the conservative institution as an introduction to modern Western and American ways that the immigrants might find more acceptable than Reform. Schiff and his friends were also ready to support Yiddish lectures and other strongly ethnic (including Zionist) activities of the Educational Alliance in downtown New York. These were expedient measures intended for the benefit of others and did not necessarily express the principles of the philanthropists themselves. But Judah Magnes, serving in Temple Emanu-El at the time, tried (unsuccessfully) to bring back into the Reform service a more traditional ritual style, like that favored by the newcomers. His closest associates, both as a rabbi and a Zionist, were the scholars and intellectuals assembled at the Jewish Theological Seminary by Solomon Schechter. Nevertheless, the dominant official stand of Reform ideologists remained decisively hostile. Some Zionist practice might evoke sympathy, but Zionist theory was a direct challenge. A Reform rabbinical conference in 1885 declared Zionism incompatible with progressive Judaism, and in the heat of open conflict twenty-odd years later, Reform spokesmen declared Zionism incompatible with American citizenship as well.[36]

Notwithstanding the chronic antagonism and recurrent acute clashes, Zionism continued to draw support and leadership from establishment circles. Herzl's outspoken, highly public Zionist style provoked a sharp reassertion of Reform anti-Zionist doctrine; yet the Herzlian FAZ president, Richard Gottheil, actively recruited young immigrants in New York to train as rabbis in the Hebrew Union College. Even while accusing Zionists of dual loyalties in the public press, Jacob Schiff continued to support the Jewish Theological Seminary, which was becoming a Zionist stronghold with Schechter's implicit approval. The appearance of Zionists among students and on the faculty of the citadel of Reform, the Hebrew Union College, led to friction that caused Magnes to leave his post there voluntarily and three others on the faculty to leave under pressure amid charges of a breach of academic freedom. But later, even after Magnes left Temple Emanu-El upon the rejection of his ritual proposals and at the very height of his official Zionist activity, he developed a still stronger, more extensive connection with top establishment leaders. Stephen Wise, the most recalcitrant of mavericks, when offered the position of associate rabbi at Temple Emanu-El, produced a cause célèbre by rejecting the Temple board's right to check his sermons. He then went on to found his Free Synagogue, with substantial aid from uptown Jews.

Meanwhile, the establishment-related Zionist leaders carried on a running debate with anti-Zionists on theoretical issues. Judah Magnes took a prominent part in these arguments while still at Temple Emanu-El. In answer to the charge of Zionist dual loyalties, Magnes defended the legitimacy of multiple loyalties. He together with Israel Friedlaender and Horace Kallen developed the ideas of cultural pluralism, of a symphonic harmony of diverse ethnic themes in America, and of the inner affinity of Judaism and the American way of life—all of which Brandeis was to pick up and deploy in his own Zionist advocacy. They applied in the American context and in an American way doctrines familiar to the European Zionist movement and particularly close to those of Buber and others in Western Europe.[37]

The internal history of American Zionism mirrored the changes simultaneously occurring in the world movement, but here, too, with an American inflection Herzl's convocation of the First Zionist Congress led Professor Gottheil to found the FAZ, over which he presided in loyal support of his leader during Herzl's remaining years. In 1902 a still closer aide of Herzl's, Jacob de Haas, was more or less imposed on the American federation as its executive secretary and editor of its journal, the *Maccabaean*. After Herzl's death his American partisans left the leadership: Gottheil retired to his teaching at Columbia University, Stephen Wise moved to a rabbinical post in far-off Oregon, and de Haas left for Boston to become director of the YMHA and, later, editor of the *Boston* (subsequently, the *Jewish*) *Advocate*. They were replaced by a group associated with the Jewish Theological Seminary: Dr. Harry Friedenwald, an eminent Baltimore ophthalmologist, became FAZ's president, and Judah Magnes served (without salary) as secretary in place of de Haas. They stood for the cultural, practical Zionism that was gradually taking over control of the world movement from Herzlian political Zionism.

The ideological issues involved were raised in America as well, but selectively, and in a way that reflected local preoccupations. Much like the Western Europeans, acculturated American Zionists were chiefly concerned with the problems of their identity as both Jewish and American; the leaders from the seminary (somewhat like the German Zionists who looked for guidance to Martin Buber) were inclined to view these issues as issues of religion. This led to a certain extremism in the conclusions they drew from their European Zionist mentors.

Israel Friedlaender argued against stress on the hopeless or gloomy prospects of the Diaspora, an attitude common among immigrant (and Herzlian) Zionists. He contended that this analysis would not prove convincing to American Jews, with their special experience. Going further, he expected the national center in Zion to be paralleled, *permanently,* by healthy Diaspora communities, of which some at least—notably, American Jewry—would be vital centers of a creative Jewish culture. Thus, he took a position closer to the non-Zionist Simon Dubnow than to the Zionist outsider, Ahad Ha'am (both writers he had introduced to Western audiences by translation and interpretation).

Magnes took a radically partisan stand on another issue. In the debate that followed the Young Turk revolution of 1908, he provocatively declared himself a Hovev Zion—a pre-Herzlian Zionist. He not only denied—as many another Zionist might—that political guarantees were prerequisite to practical projects; he now stated explicitly that political autonomy was not even a necessary Zionist aim. Like the group as a whole, Magnes saw Zionism as an instrument subservient to a higher goal: the preservation and healthy development of the religious community. In the case of Schechter, support for Zionism was conditional—as he often hinted and sometimes said—on the movement's submitting to a religiously tinted, if not flatly religious, definition of its aim.[38]

Within the mainstream of Zionism, these were extreme positions, and they evoked expressions of partisan opposition. In 1911 a group of young academics associated with the Harvard Menorah Society, including Horace Kallen and Henry Hurwitz, issued a manifesto of protest against the anti-Herzlian trend they perceived the movement to be following. In 1913 a similar protest was signed by Jacob de Haas together with this group. Kallen tried to set up an American branch of the WZO opposition movement being formed by Max Nordau and others in Europe. Notwithstanding the personal partisanship of its leaders, issues that split or divided the WZO were elided in the official stand of the FAZ. The federation began with resolutions approving both the political stress Herzl had introduced and the projects of immediate resettlement begun before Herzl's day. The Americans felt (as had leaders of Hibbat Zion in Russia) that continuing practical work in Palestine was essential in order to supply current activity that would keep members involved with the organization, or they argued that practical projects were the surest way to gain support from non-Zionist circles that would not be attracted by Zionist theory. Whether political or practical Zionists led the FAZ, it was felt that current work in Palestine and the deferral of ideological issues were a tactical necessity in order to maintain the organization under American conditions—a factor repeatedly cited in self-justification.

Whether the FAZ's commitment to work in Palestine was, indeed, the effective way to maintain its organization is an open question. The American federation had no direct connection with a particular Palestine project—as did Hadassah, the women's organization—and FAZ membership ran an erratic, generally disappointing course, with sharp rises in times of Jewish crisis and deep declines between the crests.[39] However, it is quite clear that practical Zionist projects in Palestine could attract non-Zionist sympathy and support—though organized Zionism itself was not strengthened by it. Magnes was instrumental in gaining help for the technical institute and the Hebrew University through his friendship with the New York philanthropists. A particular favorite of the non-Zionists was the young Palestinian agronomist and paleobotanist, Aaron Aaronsohn, whom Otto Warburg had chosen to head the agricultural experiment station that was a centerpiece of his practical Zionist program. While exploring the Syrian and Palestinian hill country, Aaronsohn had discovered a species of wild wheat, thus achieving swift international renown. American university scientists and the U.S. Department of Agriculture invited Aaronsohn for a lecture tour, and he attracted the enthusiastic notice of Julius Rosenwald in Chicago and of the New York-Philadelphia-Baltimore circle of Jewish notables. He also gained the friendship of leading American Zionists like Judah Magnes and Henrietta Szold. But the FAZ had little or nothing to do with his work, either in America or in Palestine.

With such a gap between the diffuse sympathy Zionism could generate and its organized strength, FAZ leaders devoted increasing attention to questions of internal organization. The problem grew acute as the seminary leaders diverted their energies to new fields and left others to maintain the FAZ organization. Magnes became the central figure in forming the New York community, the Kehillah, and its liaison with the AJC. To work for the general Jewish community in this way, he explained, would be to serve Zionism most effectively. The FAZ stalwarts, however, complained pitiably that the American Zionist movement had been deserted by "prominence."

The Kehillah was an outgrowth of the ebullience aroused in New York Jewry by the Russian upheavals of 1903. The response of the American community was heightened by the immigrants of that time, who came, together with visiting agitators, directly from the scene. Social revolutionary heroes and members of the Duma—among them, Weizmann's old associate Shmarya Levin—toured the lecture circuit; writers and thinkers of the caliber of Chaim Zhitlovsky and Nachman Syrkin came to stay, enriching the Yiddish press and platform. New York's East Side became a center of Yiddish literature, dramatic performance, and radical politics observed with high interest by Gentile connoisseurs like Norman and Hutchins Hapgood and, with some trepidation, by Jewish conservatives. The trade unions and labor press, beginning to be solidly organized by earlier immigrant intellectuals, were infused with ideological partisanship by newly arrived Bundists. Young, freshly hatched socialist-Zionists fought with them—and among themselves—the same battles over Zionism, territorialism, and the socialist understanding of the Jewish economy that were raging in Europe, while contending for leadership in adjusting to American conditions. It was a milieu with which, among leading American Jews, the European student background of Magnes and Friedlaender made them peculiarly familiar.

The sporadic, disorganized protests and campaigns for relief and self-defense funds begun after the 1903 Kishinev pogrom culminated in 1905 in a major effort to unite the whole community not only for this emergency, but on a permanent basis.[40] Magnes and other Zionist activists, working with downtown socialist-Zionist leaders, had mounted a huge mass-protest rally and organized a defense fund, for which they secured the participation of Jacob Schiff and other uptown leaders. Magnes and his friends downtown used the occasion to propose a comprehensive American Jewish community organization: a democratically constituted body authorized to represent and act for American Jewry in future emergencies and on perennial current issues—by lobbying, mass presure, and other appropriate means— and chartered to defend Jewish rights at home and abroad and to promote the survival and health of American Jewry—by education and internal policing. It was, in effect, the Helsingfors program, transferred to America.

The established New York leaders felt they had to act to head off those who might preempt the issue of communal organization. A meeting was convened in 1906, to which the East Coast notables invited a group of "representative Jews" from across the country. Louis Marshall, Schiff's counsel and chief aide in communal affairs (and law partner with Samuel Untermyer in a firm of prominent progressive Republicans), proposed an executive committee to be chosen by the whole range of synagogues. This was offered as a reasonably "democratic" method of organization, but it could not satisfy either the nationalists or the radicals committed to a secular, ethnic Jewishness. It came under a different line of criticism from others at the founders' meeting. Established Jewish lobbying organizations and men like Oscar Straus, familiar with Washington politics, objected to mass participation in delicate affairs, which they thought were better handled by experts, through quiet diplomacy. Consequently, the AJC was created as a small, self-constituted committee; it then tried to co-opt a larger group of advisors and electors, representing the recognized existing Jewish organizations for the defense of Jewish rights, as well as other, newly emerging forces in the community.

The desire to be "representative" made the AJC sensitive to criticism in the Yiddish press and among Zionists, union leaders, and others. Such criticism soon followed. The tide was whipped to a peak in 1908 by Police Commissioner Thomas Bingham's statement that fifty percent of the crime in New York City was committed by Jewish immigrants. The Yiddish press, demanding mass protests to force Bingham's removal from office, launched a concerted attack against the AJC's attempt to deal with the matter quietly. They charged that the committee was neither willing nor able to act boldly against vilification of their community. Extending the issues of debate, they demanded recognition of leadership from their own, East European ranks, more responsive to the people's will and sensitive to its needs.

Action on these lines was initiated by a newly organized League of Young Zionists, led by the labor organizer, Joseph Barondess, who had recently joined the Zionist federation. Actively assisted by Judah Magnes, the initiators got together a wide selection of representatives of the immigrant community—leaders of *landsmanshaftn,* synagogues, unions—in support of their proposal for a New York *kehillah,* a comprehensive local community organization. With Magnes as their guide, they framed an arrangement that invited a close connection with the AJC. The executive body of the proposed *kehillah* would become the local (advisory and electoral) constituent body of the AJC, independently responsible for all New York matters but following the AJC line in national and international affairs.

This plan took a position satisfactory to the AJC in its statement of purpose, which pledged to promote the interests of "Judaism." The emphasis on the religious base of the community (which in any case was in accord with the implicit views of the seminary group) won the confidence of Orthodox circles as well. But it alienated the already-suspicious socialist radicals and figures like Henry Moskowitz of the downtown Ethical Culture Society, a social worker who had taken a prominent part in the preliminary labors that produced the New York Kehillah. A restriction against participation by not-yet naturalized immigrants kept out possibly troublesome elements like Nachman Syrkin, who also had been an active proponent of the *kehillah* idea. All this gave the Kehillah a certain conservative, vaguely middle-class bias; though it undoubtedly also represented a major advance in the recognition of the immigrants in communal affairs. Magnes hoped that the Kehillah bureaus would actively involve their mass clientele, maintain themselves in good part by fee payments, and feed popular influence into the conduct of the AJC itself. But these hopes were largely disappointed as the Kehillah bureaus became dependent on the largesse of a few wealthy donors.

Magnes' withdrawal from the FAZ administration left a gap not satisfactorily filled for years. President Harry Friedenwald was fully occupied in Baltimore with his medical practice and teaching; the salaried executive secretary he selected to aid him aroused opposition and had to leave after two years. Friedenwald, too, withdrew (to an honorary position), and a new setup was introduced to run FAZ affairs; the chairman of the executive committee (instead of a new president) ran the organization, as head of a three-member administrative committee. For a year Israel Friedlaender voluntarily assumed this responsibility, and Henrietta Szold, as volunteer secretary, was brought in to clean up the "Augean stables" of fiscal and organizational disorder that had accumulated. A year later, in 1911, Louis Lipsky, the editor of the FAZ journal, the *Maccabaean,* was elected chairman of the executive committee and head of the administrative committee, with a veteran Zionist, Senior Abel, and a Yiddish journalist, Abe Goldberg, as its other members.

Thus, after prominence deserted the FAZ leadership, the immigrant rank and file took up the reins.

For years the FAZ had been plagued with problems of internal organization; it was now the task of its new administration, sprung up from the ranks, to deal with them. By 1912 a second generation, reared in the immigrant community, had reached maturity and represented the Zionist hope for the future. One of their number, Bernard Rosenblatt, a lawyer recently out of Columbia University, became the (unpaid) FAZ executive secretary in the new administration and was soon added to the adminstrative committee. The problem was to attract more of his kind.

The structure of the clubs and lodges of the FAZ, so well adapted to exploit local ties stemming from the old country, could hardly integrate Zionists who lacked such European connections, and it erected barriers between immigrants of different European backgrounds as well. Also, the Zionist *landsmanshaftn,* lodges, and social clubs were not very responsive to central control by FAZ leaders. Their strength was in mobilizing broad support for short-range objectives of the central body, but they were remiss in transmitting dues to the federation, as they gave their own funding needs priority. This made the FAZ, in turn, delinquent, or ineffectual, in meeting its obligations to the WZO.

The remedy that naturally suggested itself to the FAZ leaders was to seek stronger, more direct ties of the members to the central leadership and stronger central control of the affiliated groups.[41] This desideratum was repeatedly blocked by constituent groups of the federation. In New York an Orthodox rabbi brought together a group of synagogue Zionists and downtown workers' clubs for a while in opposition to the FAZ's central control. In Chicago, where the first Zionist groups to align with the WZO were the Knights of Zion (KOZ), a fraternal society led by a Yiddish journalist, the FAZ's authority was even longer and more successfully contested.

The KOZ sought a direct connection to the WZO center, without going through the FAZ as its federal superior. The same status was claimed by the labor Zionist groups that began to be organized. The FAZ resisted such claims but ended by conceding to both the KOZ and the Poalei Zion the right to organize their special region or sector of Zionists recruitment autonomously, with a loose connection to the FAZ. In the case of the Poalei Zion, the right to deal with the WZO not through the American federation, but through its own "world union" of ideological party comrades was tacitly accepted.

In the case of its Orthodox-Zionist opposition, the FAZ took the initiative in organizing Mizrachi clubs under its own central authority. So, too, it applied a method of limited decentralization in organizing regional and local (especially New York) Zionist councils as intermediate bodies between the clubs and the central FAZ offices. In this way internal strains were reduced, but not eliminated, and a degree of central authority was preserved. Finally, the leaders resorted to the methods of the opposition in order to attract new types of members inaccessible to older societies. College youth, other young or Americanized types, and women were separately organized in forms thought likely to attract them. Individuals whom it was not easy to bring to any kind of Zionist club or regular meeting were offered membership "at large"—especially when they could be particularly useful accessions.

The new administration elected in 1911 addressed itself to these problems along the lines laid down by its predecessors. The long-standing quarrel with the KOZ (which in the meantime had also installed a new leadership) was resolved. Senior Abel and Louis Lipsky had been much involved in the efforts of earlier administrations to extend the FAZ's reach into new fields. They now faced the need to bring back "prominence" into the leadership as well. Both aims could be served by a new form of organization, the Zion Association.

The Zion associations were meant to offer a Zionist milieu for men who had risen in the class order of American society and were sufficiently acculturated to be beyond the reach of existing Zionist bodies. They would not only group such new members with others of their kind, but would spare them many of the minor duties that older Zionists thrived on. There would be few regular meetings or petty fund drives. Instead, one would seek members who could undertake major tasks of economic support and counseling and secure access to public opinion and government leaders beyond the reach of the FAZ.

A version of the plan designed for women even proposed to exempt them from the purchase of the shekel and from participation in the elections and governance of the FAZ and WZO. Hadassah, the women's organization that arose, assumed a far different shape than was planned by the men who suggested its formation. Henrietta Szold took this project in hand; she would have no part in a proposal to exempt women from voting or making policy in the movement at large. Also, she insisted on independent control of a major social task undertaken in Palestine by the women themselves, instead of an auxiliary role in projects the men might conceive and control.

Hadassah, of course, emerged as a major force in American Zionism—perhaps its most successful organized expression—and one closely tied to Brandeis. No such success attended the idea of forming Zion associations for men. The greatest achievement of the latter project may have been recruiting Louis D. Brandeis, who enrolled as a member of the Boston Zion Association on April 18, 1913.

Leader from the Outside

Brandeis' emergence as a Zionist leader signified no conversion to new beliefs radically different from his old ones.[42] The essential change was a shift in social attachments and emotional ties: a sharper sense of the American-Jewish terrain and his own place in it and a fatefully deepened personal commitment.

As a young man Brandeis evidently accepted the current stereotyped image of American Jews; particularly of the nouveaux riches German-Jewish settlers. Late nineteenth-century cartoonists and novelists pictured them as a crude, vulgar, materialistic lot, grasping and pushy (in contrast to the stereotypically refined, aristocratic Sephardic Jews, who were earlier settlers). Brandeis described his shipboard companions in 1875, on the return trip to America, as "on the whole rather unpleasant, very few interresting, very few fine, exceedingly many Jews." But the excessive Jews in question were not necessarily significant for his self-esteem (as they were, for example, for Walter Lippmann, who continued well into the twentieth century to imagine American Jews resentfully in terms of such nineteenth-century caricatures of his parents' generation). For Brandeis the vulgar, pushy Jewish stereotype applied to the others, not to Jews like his own circle.[43]

In letters to his father, Brandeis would refer to his clan as "Bohemian," unlike the "Bavarian" immigrants who came to America earlier. The contrast implied that his people, coming from Prague, were urban sophisticates, not backward rustics; they shared the militant liberalism of the Forty-Eighters, not the conservatism of the earlier wave of South German, tradition-bound emigrants. The ways in which some German-Jewish notables acquired their wealth, by financial manipulation rather than tangible production or service, heightened these distinctions in his mind. In the days when he was warring with the promoters of railroad stocks and insurance companies, he was severe in his judgment of Jacob Schiff, a leading competitor of J. P. Morgan in this field. Hearing that his brother had invested in stocks, he wrote him that such unnatural activities were not safe nor seemly for "one of us": ". . . I feel very sure that unser eins ought not to buy and sell stocks. . . . Prices of stock[s] are made. They don't grow; and their fluctuations are not due to natural causes."[44]

In later years a further differentiation begins to appear. In November 1905 Brandeis addressed a Jewish audience for the first time on a ceremonial occasion. He sent his speech to his father, writing in reference to his audience—a group of young professionals of the "Russian" immigrant community:

> There is more to hope for in the Russian Jews than from the Bavarian and other German. The Russians have idealism & reverence.

In so describing the Russian Jews, Brandeis ascribed to them qualities that stood high in his personal catalogue of values. Idealism (together with a tough-minded empiricism) and reverence (together with an unyielding independence of mind) were cardinal features of Brandeis' own character. Notwithstanding his clear perception of the historical relativity of law, Brandeis took a rigorous, absolutist, idealist view of basic moral values. His reverence, rooted in the family, attached itself in lifelong piety to the Pilgrim Fathers, his adopted patrimony. But by 1905 the current generation of New England Brahmins no longer seemed to him worthy sons of their ancestors. Among

the new associates who began to fill this role in Brandeis' mind were none
other than the immigrant Russian Jews.[45]

Brandeis' early Jewish contacts in Boston were chiefly his clients, among
whom the philanthropic leaders of the established community were well represented. They were mainly merchants, whose political leanings at first
meshed well with his own; they were interested in cheap transport and against
import restrictions, and they stood in the forward ranks of good government
reformers in the Republican party. Some—notably, Edward A. Filene—were
among Brandeis' outstanding allies in the progressive causes he later took up,
especially in the field of labor relations. But in the main, his Jewish merchant ·
clients confined themselves to a cautiously conservative loyalty to the Republican party. Accordingly, Brandeis' relations with them, other than professional, did not go beyond a rather distant friendliness. Since he did not live
among Jews and, of course, was never seen in a synagogue, his nonprofes-
sional Jewish contacts were largely restricted to the support he occasionally
lent to Jewish causes.

Other than local Jewish charities (to which Brandeis gave token contributions and occasional counsel), the causes American Jews publicly agitated,
then as now, concerned the difficulties of other Jews abroad—in those years
particularly in Russia. Foreign affairs were not a field where Brandeis felt his
skills and talent could be most effectively applied; although sympathetic to
the anti-imperialist criticism of American policy in the Philippines, he never
became deeply involved. So too, he fully sympathized with American-Jewish
protests against the pogroms and repression in Russia. At the request of his
aged friend, Jacob Hecht, he sought non-Jewish support and helped draft
appeals for the campaign Jews launched in 1902 against renewal of the Russo-
American trade treaty. Nor was this mere accommodation to the wishes of a
valued associate. In his correspondence with his father during the Russo-Japanese War (foreign topics evidently were thought likely to interest the old
man), Brandeis was no less enthusiastic about Japanese victories and Russian
defeats than, for example, was Weizmann at the same time in Geneva. Nevertheless, when another client asked him to speak at a fund-raising rally for
relief of victims of the Kishinev pogrom, Brandeis begged off.[46]

Soon, however, Brandeis began to notice Jews as a significant force supporting the domestic causes to which he himself was most committed.[47] Until
then, he had shared the general impression that while the wealthier German
Jews were staunchly Republican, Russian-Jewish voters, like other slum
dwellers, were sold to the Democratic political bosses. Immigrants under the
control of political machines were no less a bugaboo for him than for other
genteel reformers; he tended to understand the Boston Brahmins' campaign
to restrict the new immigration. In his speech in 1905 commemorating the
first Jewish settlers in New Amsterdam, he echoed Theodore Roosevelt's condemnation of "hyphenated Americanism"—a rather pointed warning against
corruption by the machine politicians' appeal for votes on grounds of ethnic
special interests. But in this case he could feel confident that he was addressing an audience responsive to his message.

The address was delivered to the New Century Club, founded by a group of young professionals and businessmen of the immigrant community who were making themselves felt as vociferous opponents of the local political bosses. Some years before Miriam Kallen (Horace M. Kallen's sister, a schoolteacher) and Robert Silverman (a young lawyer who was a member of the New Century Club and, like Kallen, an active Zionist) had launched a campaign against alleged corruption in the politically controlled school system, setting off a libel suit in which they had gained the legal aid of Brandeis' office. In 1905 the New Century Club leaders were campaigning in the Boston mayoralty elections against the machine candidate (John F. Fitzgerald, grandfather of President Kennedy) and for the reform candidate whom Brandeis supported.

Brandeis' appreciation for the Russian Jews was notably heightened and extended when he was asked to mediate the New York garment workers' strike in July 1910.[48] He found himself involved in a family quarrel, within a community united in its ethical norms, at the very time when the decline of the moral consensus of Puritan Boston, and his social exclusion there, had become painfully obvious. It clearly awoke echoes of his own family tradition, and fostered a deepening identification, to preside over a labor dispute in which labor officials and manufacturers could effectively invoke common values and rebuke one another with texts from Isaiah.

Greater familiarity, at the same time, produced a more nuanced view of the Russian Jews, foreshadowing the subtle, yet distinct, differences that were later to set him at odds with the Easterners in the Zionist movement. His pragmatic compromise, the "preferential shop," met with determined resistance from class-conscious, doctrinaire ideologists. The negotiations were rescued only after Brandeis' friends, Edward A. Filene and the communal workers Meyer Bloomfield and Henry Moskowitz, called in Jacob Schiff and Louis Marshall to help out. They were able eventually to secure a "Protocol of Peace" more or less on the lines Brandeis had proposed; thus, a board of arbitration was set up with Brandeis as chairman.

During his tenure of this position, the Russian intellectuals continued to complicate matters for Brandeis by insisting on arbitrating problems that he felt should be solved at the shop level. Brandeis complained to a fellow arbitrator, Walter Weyl (a young economist, soon to figure as an editor of a new liberal journal, the *New Republic*) that Dr. Isaac Hourwich, a persistent labor protagonist was "an inveterate trouble maker. . . . We shall have no peace with him in position."[49] In spite of such vexations, Brandeis took great pride in his mediation of the garment strike and in the procedures set up, in accordance with his plans, to preserve industrial peace in this largely Jewish trade.

Another situation impelled Brandeis in 1910 to issue public statements identifying himself as a Jew. At that time he had become a figure of national political prominence through his spectacular interrogation of government officials in the Ballinger hearings. His widening acquaintance with midwestern progressives brought him into new spheres of activity; in January 1911 he was among those who opened LaFollette's campaign for the Republic presidential nomination by forming the National Progressive Republican League.

In this context Brandeis' progressive friends felt the need to make him better known to a wide public in order to enhance his effectiveness. Toward the end of 1910 Brandeis gave a series of interviews to Ernest Poole, a young progressive writer who was Walter Weyl's brother-in-law and an admirer of LaFollette; in February 1911 *American Magazine* published an article by Poole sketching Brandeis' personal background and progressive views. Meanwhile, Brandeis, no mean connoisseur of the power of the press himself, agreed to enhance his political effectiveness in the same way in his own ethnic (Jewish) community. The instrument immediately available for this purpose was the *(Boston) Jewish Advocate,* the organ of the group of young acculturated, Russian-Jewish businessmen, professionals, and social workers associated with the YMHA and (in many cases) members of the New Century Club.[50]

Brandeis had long had a close working relationship with Max Mitchell, one of the backers of the *Advocate* who had served as superintendent of the local Federation of Jewish Charities and then, with Brandeis' encouragement and assistance, had founded a bank to serve the Jewish community. Mitchell was instrumental in gaining Brandeis' interest for the young activists of the New Century Club, and his journal, the *Advocate,* followed Brandeis' career with continuous interest. Many Brandeis causes such as savings bank life insurance and the public school system were of special concern to the small trader and working-class community the paper served; Brandeis' rising prominence was itself news especially gratifying to Boston Jewry. The editor of the *Advocate* in 1910 was Jacob de Haas; as an apostle of Theodor Herzl, he had a natural sympathy for anything that might shape the Jewish electorate as a consolidated political force. If Brandeis needed wider exposure among Jewish voters throughout the country as a national Progressive leader, the editors of the *Advocate* were ready and eager to do their part. De Haas sent a young Harvard student to interview the new Jewish luminary. The report, published in the *Advocate* with great éclat, was also sent to another Jewish journal, the *American Hebrew,* where it would reach the bulk of the country's committed and leading Jews.[51]

In order to establish Brandeis' credentials, the interview made a point of stressing that Brandeis was, indeed, a Jew—a matter that needed no proof in Boston but that was not at all evident to the rest of the country. Brandeis dealt with this question in a way that revealed his very lax, distinctly secular view of what being a Jew entailed: "There should be no doubt as to where I stand," he said, "Of course I am a Jew." Given the rumors cited by the interviewer that he had been "brought up in a Christian Unitarian family," he countered with an assurance that, "My early training was not Jewish in a religious sense, nor was it Christian." He referred with pride to his uncle, Lewis Dembitz, a well-known master of "certain phases of Jewish scholarship"; but he also cited in evidence—with no less assurance—his brother-in-law, Felix Adler, whom he did not hesitate to invoke as an exemplary Jew.

The interviewer, a member of the still strongly Zionist Harvard Menorah Society, made sure (perhaps on instructions from his Zionist editor, de Haas) to elicit a statement of sympathy for the Zionist movement, featured with prominence in the version of the interview that appeared in the *Advocate*. Sympathetic Brandeis may have been, but hardly on the basis of clearly worked out principles in 1910. In order to illustrate his views of the Jewish question, he gave his interviewer his 1905 address at the New Century Club in which he condemned "hyphenated Americanism." Clearly, he saw no contradiction between this stand and his Zionist sympathies; perhaps because (as Edward Filene once reported approvingly on this very point) his main concern was still to detach the immigrant voters from control by the political bosses, and he saw Zionism as a morale-building force that would raise the pride and self-respect of Russian Jews and immunize them against corruption by enticement or pressure.[52] Beginning with the perception that Zionism made independent, liberal voters of young Jews, he was later to develop the full-blown doctrine that a Jew had to be a Zionist in order to be a good American. But all this in 1910 was far from the foreground of his attention.

The press exposure Brandeis received in Jewish journals and in the *American Magazine* evoked an immediate response among leaders of appropriate Jewish organizations. The AJC was a natural claimant for a recruitment of Brandeis' demonstrated talents. But when this was suggested in April 1911 to Dr. Cyrus Adler, the advisor and scholarly authority for the AJC's leading figures, he replied that he knew "some of the members . . . [were] not fully in accord with the public policy of Mr. Brandeis." He conceded, however, that since Brandeis had "lately exhibited some Jewish sympathy and is undoubtedly a man of power who has the ear of the public . . . [it] might be worth while considering whether we could not in some way add him to our forces."[53]

Considerably more interest was shown by the Zionists; at that very time Brandeis was one of those whom Israel Friedlaender and Judah Magnes considered in their search for a new honorary president of the FAZ. That this was thought possible reflected earlier encouraging contacts with the Boston lawyer. On February 1, 1911, a letter had been sent inviting Brandeis to speak at the tenth anniversary dinner being planned for the *Maccabaean*. The editor, Bernard G. Richards, wrote that in his days as a reporter for Boston papers (and he might have added, as a man of socialist leanings antedating his Zionism) he had "watched with great interest and admiration, the work which you have done for the public good." Perhaps because of this indication of political affinity, Brandeis' response went beyond his usual perfunctory letter of regret. He declined the invitation and sent a token contribution but went on to restate his "sympathy with the Zionist movement." and "conviction that a great people, stirred by enthusiasm for such an ideal, must bear an important part in the betterment of the world." Over a year later, in April 1912, Richards wrote again, seeking Brandeis' participation at the FAZ Convention soon to be held in Cleveland. Since the invitation as sent in the name of the Convention Committee, Brandeis asked Richards to "express to the committee my appreciation ... and my profound regret that other plans made it impossible for me to accept." This was a courteous gesture but evidently not meaningless; for Brandeis offered no objection when the *Jewish Advocate* ran an article, announcing in advance of the FAZ Convention that the letter would be read publicly and, after the convention, headlined its report, "Louis D. Brandeis and Nathan Straus Join the Ranks."[54]

But this was premature, for Brandeis' formal affiliation had to wait until the next year. In March 1913 he appeared at a public meeting in Boston to welcome Nahum Sokolow, then a leading member of the WZO executive committee. He was sufficiently affected by Sokolow's address, according to report, to introduce his own brief remarks afterward by saying, "Thank you, Dr. Sokolow—you have brought me back to my people." Having lent his name and prestige to the movement by such gestures, he now was willing, through the Zion Association, to give it his expert counsel and guidance. He became the head of the American Palestine Committee (a body formed to encourage investment in constructive business enterprise in Palestine)—though, to be sure, he found that he could do very little in this capacity for lack of a suitable information base at the command of Zionists.[55]

Active identification as a Zionist came after a considerable period during which Brandeis found congenial Zionist figures, in Boston and elsewhere, who shared his progressive views and commitments. Stephen Wise, who had fought for progressive labor legislation from the pulpit and served as volunteer commissioner of child labor in Oregon, was one of the sources relied on by Brandeis' sister-in-law, Josephine Goldmark, in preparing material for his famous brief, In re *Muller v. Oregon.* Another Zionist, Bernard Rosenblatt, attracted attention by his book on cooperative work colonies for the unemployed. His ideas, including proposals for a guaranteed annual income and the nationalization of land rents, fell in with Brandeis' long-standing concern for regularity of employment and awakened echoes of the old agrarian utopianism dear to the Brandeis-Wehle clan. In 1912 when he came to Brandeis' notice, Rosenblatt was honorary secretary of the FAZ and a member of the committee who solicited Brandeis' participation at their convention.

In the same period Brandeis learned of another Zionist phenomenon that aroused him to positive enthusiasm. Returning from a Midwest campaign trip for LaFollette in January 1912, Brandeis was invited to a dinner in Washington where the merchant-philanthropist Julius Rosenwald spoke on behalf of the agricultural experimental station directed by Aaron Aaronsohn. Brandeis was so taken with the tale of this new young hero that in 1913, when Aaronsohn came on a visit to America, he ran a reception for him in Boston to which he invited President Eliot of Harvard and other local luminaries. "The guests were thrilled," as Brandeis evidently informed his biographer Alfred Lief, "and Brandeis beamed."[56]

In Boston itself Brandeis found new attractive Zionist-Jewish associations. Notable among them was the Harvard Menorah Society, a body of young men who appealed to many of his old, established values: they were Harvard men, enjoyed the support of President Eliot, and were committed to a slogan of Jewish noblesse oblige that matched Brandeis' own idea of an acceptable Jewish identity. Like others in Boston—for example, the settle-ment-house worker Robert A. Woods, the philosopher William James, and President Eliot himself—they were about a decade in advance of Brandeis in favoring cultural pluralism as the American way; one of their number Horace Kallen, was even then elaborating an explicit form of that doctrine that was later to be picked up, and adapted, by Brandeis. In 1910 Brandeis was asked to be the guest of honor at the society's annual banquet. He was constrained to refuse while expressing approval of Menorah's aims. In the next year, when he was again unable to speak, the society invited Judge Julian W. Mack of Chicago. Mack accepted but had to wire on the day before the banquet that he was prevented from appearing by his wife's sudden illness. In this emer-gency, Brandeis agreed to speak—or, as he put it:

> . . . less to speak to you than to testify to my appreciation and admiration of
> your Society and the work it is doing. My own education has been such that
> I could contribute little to that subject. But I have looked with the greatest
> of satisfaction to the development of this movement, as I have upon the
> development of Zionism—far as it was from me—as indicating that the
> spirit of idealism, that one product of Judaism which was surely survived, is
> as strong as ever, and in this America has much to hope for.

Following the banquet Brandeis arranged a meeting at his home, where he, in effect, offered his help. He served on a committee to promote the intercol-legiate Menorah Society, and in May 1913 he became a member of the Har-vard chapter. And in late 1914 when Brandeis took over the leadership of the American Zionist movement, he looked to his friends of the Harvard Men-orah group for help in recruiting the young talent he needed in his new tasks.[57]

In August 1912 Jacob de Haas came to see Brandeis in Cape Cod—with a letter of introduction from the Democratic National Committee—prepared to work with him for the Wilson campaign in the Jewish ethnic constitu-ency.[58] As they were about to part, the talk turned to Zionism, felicitously combined by de Haas with reminiscences of Lewis Dembitz, Brandeis' revered uncle, who had been an early American Zionist. Brandeis, prepared to be responsive to such topics, asked de Haas to take a later train back to Boston and continue their conversation at dinner with the family. This began a long, close relationship in which de Haas served Brandeis with the same devotion he had given to Herzl but in a far more privileged and confidential advisory position. Brandeis now began to study Zionist materials, with de Haas as his guide. When the war broke out and the Zionists planned their emergency reorganization, it was de Haas who wrote to Brandeis asking his permission to present his name for election as the head of the movement, and perhaps of world Jewry, at that time of crisis.

Brandeis became an active Zionist in somewhat the same way that he took up other causes. The new commitment was adopted not on his own initiative but, as usual, in response to an invitation from others. He was wanted, as he could hardly be unaware, not only for his expert counsel and skilled guidance—his prestige and authority were certainly no less important for those who wooed him. He was ready to lend both his name and his talents to Zionism as he grew steadily more convinced of the worthiness of the cause.

Until the progressive movement mobilized him for full-scale political agitation, Brandeis—notwithstanding his reputation as a dangerous rabble-rouser—had kept his political activity within well-defined bounds. He refused on several occasions to seek nomination for elected office, restricting himself to the role of advocate for the public interest on selected issues. These he took up one by one; all were immediate, tangible social concerns rather than basic problems with immeasurable, long-range, indirect consequences.

His entry into Progressive party politics meant undertaking tasks whose scope and effects could not so easily be delimited; but he was still able to preserve a considerable degree of detachment and independence. In the progressive movement, with its three wings—Midwest agrarian populists, Eastern Bull Moose stalwarts, and the newly progressive Wilsonians—it was easy for Brandeis to find tolerance in the ranks as well as agreement when he would dissent from one or another position of some progressives. For example, as an advocate of popular interests, Brandeis naturally mobilized popular pressure behind his lobbying efforts; but he was no believer in what we now call participatory democracy, and he did not favor the devices of referendum and recall advocated by his midwestern friends.[59] The public must be organized to claim its rights and defend its interests; but it should confine its exercise of ultimate political authority to electing the leaders in whom it had confidence and leave concrete policies and executive decisions to them and to competent experts—subject, of course, to the scrutiny and the comment of public opinion. Hence he strongly approved of another midwestern innovation, the device of administrative government by expert commissions, instituted by LaFollette in Wisconsin with the aid of university personnel; Brandeis later had a hand in creating and staffing such commissions on the level of federal government. As for the Bull Moose reformers, in addition to policies like conservation, which he fully approved, Brandeis accepted in part their demand for state intervention in economic affairs. But his disagreement with their doctrine of a New Nationalism (a program of domestic progressivism and benevolent economic imperialism made popular by Herbert Croly, who founded the *New Republic*) led Brandeis to an opposing political partisanship, more far-reaching than had been usual for him before.

After the collapse of LaFollette's campaign released Brandeis from that commitment, he joined Wilson's camp. He had to formulate for the campaign (and perhaps for the first time explicitly for himself) a broad-ranging, comprehensive socioeconomic doctrine as a progressive alternative to the Bull Moose platform. He now found it necessary to combine in a broad synthesis many themes of his past advocacy: the distrust of bigness, the suspicion of the money trust and its domination of the economy and corruption of politics, and his faith in regulation by expert commissions. Wilson's slogan, the

New Freedom (counterposed to the New Nationalism), adopted Brandeis' Jeffersonian idea of a competitive market regulated by the state in order to protect small enterprise and the interests of the consumer as an alternative to the Bull Moose Hamiltonian idea of corporate monopolies regulated in the national interest. After the election Wilson had to take a stand on the proposal of a Federal Reserve System framed by bankers and criticized by populist-minded progresssives, and he again sought Brandeis' advice. The draft of the project was revised to replace the banker-controlled Federal Reserve Board by one (nominally at least) set up as a public-controlled body.

Brandeis' identification with the Wilson administration might well have developed into an exclusive bond, tying him to association with a clearly marked-out group and closing him off from other progressives who might be more congenial to him in some respects. It was widely expected that he would be named to a Cabinet post such as secretary of commerce. Wilson, in fact, wanted him in the Cabinet as attorney general. But such opposition was aroused in circles close to Wilson, or able to influence his decisions, that he dropped the matter, continuing to use Brandeis as a detached advisor and consultant.

The uproar against the possible Brandeis appointment, voiced publicly and in Wilson's private councils, harped on two themes: his record as an agitator and his Jewishness. The Boston legal and business community, freshly bruised by Brandeis' attack on their railroad interests, mounted a vociferous, many-sided campaign in the press and by private lobbying. A channel particularly close to Wilson was employed when the prominent industrialist, churchman, and philanthropist, Cleveland Dodge—Wilson's old college schoolmate, political backer, and his chief supporter on the Board of Trustees at Princeton during the battles of his time there—urged the president to abandon his idea. Colonel Edward M. House, Wilson's confidential advisor on the composition of his team, also served as a channel for the opposition while carefully avoiding any direct clash with the president's will. He professed himself to be personally well disposed to Brandeis; but his private reservations were suggested in warnings that so controversial a lawyer "was not fit for that place [the attorney generalship]" or indeed for "anything of a legal nature." In a letter to Wilson he remarked on the "curious Hebrew traits of mind" that came to the surface now and then in Brandeis and made one "hold something in reserve" in one's approval of him. Guarded opposition also came from Jewish leaders. Jacob Schiff, responding to a pointed inquiry, stated that Brandeis might be a representative American (implying that only this should be properly considered) but, since he had no significant connection with the organized Jewish community, could not be considered representative of the American Jews (which, of course, was the politically pertinent point of the exchange).[60]

Brandeis remained scrupulously passive during this episode. He mounted no private campaign on his own behalf and said nothing publicly, to the point of refusing to speak on Jewish occasions that he might otherwise have found attractive. The outcome saved him from becoming bound to a bureaucracy

or to the conformity required in an official position. He was free to continue
as a confidential advisor for the president—and also to remain on terms of
close friendship, or alliance, with other progressives outside the administration and sometimes at odds with it. During Wilson's first term, (won by a
plurality, not a majority, of votes) the president realized the need to win over
the progressive Republicans, among others, to support his programs. When
in 1916, with new elections approaching, Wilson proposed Brandeis for a seat
on the Supreme Court, it was, of course, a recognition of the jurist's extraordinary qualifications and an expression of personal regard as well as token
compensation for the rebuff of 1913. But it was also intended to win over
progressives for whom Brandeis was a hero and, for many of the leaders, a
close personal friend. Brandeis might not have enjoyed broad acceptance of
this kind if he had entered the adminstration.

At first Brandeis joined the Zionists more in the spirit of his early, relatively
limited role as counsel for one or another public interest than in the spirit of
his role among progressives and in the Wilson entourage. It was a worthy
cause to which he was ready to contribute his economic and legal expertise
(and, of course, the prestige of his name) in well-defined, specific undertakings that might require his kind of competence. But Zionism was a broad,
essentially political and vaguely defined movement; its leadership was profoundly committed to indefinite, sweeping ultimate goals while being particularly hampered (at that time) in setting forth tangible, short-range objectives
for immediate action. Brandeis had to dismiss expectations that he would be
notably active in the responsibility he at first accepted, to head the Zion Association's committee for the economic development of Palestine. He found the
data made available to him on pertinent topics to be inadequate for planning
or action. He continued to study Zionist literature, but it concerned itself
chiefly with ideological issues and social, historical, and psychological anal-
yses of the Jewish situation. Then in 1914 when he took on the responsibility
of top leadership, he committed himself to an open-ended responsibility
made urgent by the manifold crises of war.

   The ideological issues Zionists debated among themselves and with others
had no direct, unequivocal relation to those Brandeis had worked out in his
version of progressivism. He could not apply his approach immediately to
current Zionist problems, but it remained a compass that guided many of the
positions he later adopted when he took up a leading responsibility. Many of
the partisan positions of the Zionist factions were without much significance
for him. The issue of the place of religious tradition in Zionism, as noted
earlier, was one he turned his back on even more firmly than did Herzl. It left
him completely cold; at most, he backed away when told that some proposal
he was thinking of, in all innocence, would offend the religious sensibilities
of some Zionists. Nevertheless, the core of his Zionist belief was the view that
Jewish tradition had left its traces in ethical values shared by even the most
unbelieving Jews and that this heritage deserved to be preserved—and Zionism was the way to preserve it. His affinity with the attitudes of the socialist-

Zionists, especially those wedded to a cooperativist-populist approach, was far greater; but here, too, he was indifferent to the ideological issues (e.g., concerning the nature of the Jewish economic problem) that divided them.

The only factional position in Zionism that he seemed at first to favor was that of the epigones of Herzl, like de Haas; but this was simply an accident of history, since his essentially eclectic attitude permitted him to avail himself without inhibition of other, factionally opposed, Zionist views, as he encountered them. At the July 1913 FAZ annual convention, Brandeis was appointed to the federation's executive committee on behalf of the Zion Association and was offered a mandate to attend the forthcoming World Zionist Congress. He accepted the first and declined, with regrets, the second position. However, in a letter to Sokolow, he submitted the following, as proposals to the congress:

First: . . . concentrate our efforts upon a few undertakings.

Second: . . . as pressure upon the Jews is increasing . . . , our efforts should be directed mainly toward opening up Palestine to the masses.

Third: . . . we need . . . possession of large tracts of land, coupled with such concessions from the Turkish government as will give to our people freedom of movement, control of our operations, and security for the investments necessary. . . .

Fourth: . . . at this juncture [of current Turkish difficulties] the offer of our movement to introduce . . . an intelligent and industrious population cannot fail to have great weight, . . . and the public offer to sell the Crown lands presents . . . a much sought opportunity. . . .

Fifth: . . . we need at the same time a large immigration . . .

Sixth: . . . we must have such conditions of settlement as will leave our people free from such entanglements as have arisen in the past, and must necessarily arise . . . if the Jews are not afforded an opportunity to act . . . with the . . . consent of the Turkish government.

Such proposals clearly reflect the Herzlian political Zionism of his friends (and almost sound as if they were drafted by de Haas, with barely suppressed antagonism to the incumbent leaders' practical Zionism). Yet in the speeches that Brandeis began making soon after, his favorite themes, stressing the high tradition of Jewish ethical commitment, sound like remote echoes of Herzl's eminent antagonist, Ahad Ha'am. Indeed, on reading what was available to him of Ahad Ha'am's writing, Brandeis expressed himself with unaffected admiration.[61]

In truth, however, Brandeis (or even Horace Kallen, the philosopher, whose formulations of Zionism Brandeis followed in their Ahad Ha'amist cultural emphasis but who, nevertheless, took a Herzlian line in intramural Zionist politics) could not be, and had no wish to be, a close student of the intricacies of Zionist ideological debate. He accepted readily, from any source, whatever echoed his own predilections. Of the six points in his letter to Sokolow, one is most characteristically Brandeisian: the first point, the injunction to "concentrate our efforts upon a few undertakings." The concentration on small, tangible tasks was natural enough when, at first, Brandeis treated his Zionism as one of the limited social welfare consultancies he took on in the public interest. It remained constant in his later years of overall leadership. The responsibility for dealing with the nebulous, protean aspects of a global problem and with sweeping ideological issues could not seduce Brandeis from his principled belief in work on a small scale, concentrated on tangible, compassable tasks.

Brandeis might approach Zionist work as a project of soberly defined dimensions, but it clearly had an emotional significance of quite a different order for him. Brandeis, a man not given to gratuitous outbursts of enthusiasm, was saying what was essentially true when he responded to Sokolow's address at the 1913 meeting with the avowal that the speaker had brought him back to his people. If not Sokolow that very night (nor, for that matter, merely the regular meetings with de Haas), certainly the whole encounter with Zionism and with the kind of people he believed he found among Zionists evoked a new sense of identity in Brandeis and created a lasting, profound attachment. His friend Elizabeth Evans, who knew him so well, was struck by the "glow" that shone in him at Zionist meetings. As he became fully active, he later drew around him a circle of close associates who revered him as their "Chief" and for whom he felt a personal responsibility (and sometimes personally aided with funds to free them for their public work). It was for Brandeis the kind of bond that paralleled, drew upon, and transformed the place he occupied in his family (turning the favored youngest child into the revered father figure); and it gave a bright new focus to the Puritan idealism learned—only to be shadowed with disillusionment—in Boston.

As noted earlier, Brandeis had always found commitment in others to his own goals a ready basis for personal approval; in turn, he was respected by his political associates for the quality of his commitment to their goals. In the years of his turn to Zionism, he had just made decisive partisan commitments to the progressive cause. Among progressives, of various leanings, he had also widened his circle of close personal friendships. His partisanship for Wilson did not limit his friendships to that particular circle; in fact, he seems to have had a more distant relationship with Wilson's close associates, official and personal, than with LaFollette's midwestern liberals and the Eastern New Nationalists, particularly the editors of the *New Republic*. These were the supporters Wilson hoped to win over in 1916 when he named Brandeis to the Supreme Court. In LaFollette's camp, Brandeis found Charles R. Crane as helpful a backer of causes Brandeis favored as Edward Filene had been— though not as close a friend. He also found Norman Hapgood, a journalist and editor who became as constant and devoted a friend as few others. His ties with the *New Republic* editors were warmly cordial, and their collaborator Felix Frankfurter was treated by Brandeis partly as his most trusted colleague, partly as a foster son. These were ties that set up a mutual devotion, with the reciprocal claims and obligations that arise from comradeship in a common cause.

Brandeis' Zionism, as noted, was continuous with his progressivism; and many of his Zionist friends, new as well as old, were allies in the progressive cause too. But his relations with Zionists were subtly different from those with his friends in the progressive camp. His loyalty to progressivism was not loyalty to a party, but to that more abstract entity, a cause. His relation to the Wilson coterie (especially after he remained outside the Cabinet) was that of an ally, not one of the family. His friendships among progressives were, indeed, strongly directed by political affinities, but not a party line. Affinities of other sorts decided which Progressive comrades he was particularly drawn to—and which were drawn to him. Among progressives, he was an intellectual leader rather than an organizational chieftain—even to the extent that such formal, institutional authority was feasible at all vis-à-vis the loosely connected congeries of independent voters who constituted progressivism. His friends owed him no institutional loyalty, but they freely offered it in personal affection and in the interests of a common cause. It is a mark of the free fellowship between them that among the persons whom Brandeis addressed by their given names in letters to them, these friends were prominently represented.

It is striking that he followed a different, more formal practice in his correspondence with most of his Zionist friends (apart from those who were progressive allies primarily). To be sure, the voluminous files of communications with Zionists in Brandeis' archives are very largely composed of directives, reports, and inquiries of an operational character. It is, nonetheless, clear that there was a strongly hierarchical quality in the relations of Brandeis with other Zionists, close and warm as their personal connection might be. When he took over the leadership, he drew around him a circle of devoted associates who revered him as their "Chief" and developed what we might call a cult of personality about him. They saw in him an embodiment of the values most highly prized by this group. What was demanded of Brandeis, then, was more than the expertise of a technical consultant, more than the acumen and insight of an intellectual; he had to live up to ideals his followers cherished for themselves in his every action. It was an obligation this latter-day Puritan performed very well for the inner circle of leaders he assembled in his Zionist labors.

Such a role was both traditional (since the days of Herzl) in the Zionist movement and essential to any effective central guidance of so diffuse a sentiment and so loosely organized and fragmented a body as American Zionism. The Zionists, especially in America at that time, resembled a demobilized army that could be made effective for action only by some influence that drew on their latent sentiment with compelling power. A crisis could activate them or an exciting occasion like the arrival of a notable visiting dignitary. If they were to be organized on a scale exceeding the parochial appeal of their local, limited, and selective traditional clubs, lodges, and *landsmanshaftn,* a leader who embodied *their* ideals in an exemplary way was the key element that had previously achieved this. The figure of a Brandeis (the people's advocate, successful professional man, eminent political figure and advisor of the president) was the kind of "prominence" that might do this—a "prominence" whose absence had so long been bewailed.

With the accession of "prominence," the American Zionists would gain leadership that embodied what might be called the sociological ideal of an immigrants' organization: to adjust to the standards of the host society that had (partially) admitted them. Beyond this, (and more essential in order to mobilize a movement of liberation), a leader was needed who could successfully embody the *historic* ideal of Zionism: to give practical political expression to the traditional myth of national redemption through secular activities that gave immediate promise of advancing toward that goal.

Brandeis' rise to the leadership of American Zionism at the onset of a world war gave his new clients, the inchoate mass of potential Zionists (especially the group of close associates who clustered about him), the hope that they, and all American Jewry and Jews the world over, had found such a leader—a man cast in the same mold as Herzl.

3

Wartime Leadership

Brandeis: Organizing in the Emergency

World War I not only caused suffering on a previously unimaginable scale, it also threw into confusion many assumptions concerning political issues. The Jews were directly affected individually as residents in war zones. As a collective body, they were especially liable to confusion, because the Jewish people had no control over the hostilities nor any well-established title to share in shaping the future peace. But their long tradition of international defense of Jewish rights and interests obliged them to act in the immediate emergency and plan for the uncharted postwar future.

On July 28, 1914 the Austrians declared war on Serbia; by August 4 Germany had crossed the Belgian border, bringing France and Britain into the battle. The densely Jewish regions of Poland became a battlefield by the end of August. Another zone of immediate concern was Palestine. The war cut the country's lines of supply, and European support for the community was severely impeded. By October the Turkish leaders had chosen to join the Central Powers in active hostilities, and all calculations based on the neutrality and continued integrity of the Ottoman Empire had to be reviewed.

The traditional aid Jews extended to one another across international borders was disrupted by the war. The relief campaigns organized by American Jewry a decade earlier had been disbanded, and it was necessary to make a fresh beginning. The AJC might feel entitled to initiate the necessary new organization, but it had to do so under the pressures of immigrant constituencies beginning to claim their place in the sun. Over a generation of East European settlement had yielded a crop of prospering immigrants—businessmen and professionals, contractors, realtors, manufacturers, lawyers, union organizers, and journalists—who provided leadership to an aroused community. Added pressure on the older establishment came from the influx of East European intelligentsia following the Russian upheavals of the 1905 era and joined during the war by active leaders driven from the war zones and from Palestine.

The Zionist movement was directly affected by the war. American Zionists had to assume responsibility for current WZO activities, since the Zionists in Russia and Western Europe were cut off from the Berlin headquarters and the community in Palestine. Considering the poor reputation and shaky state of the American movement, a daring program, indeed, was undertaken at an emergency Zionist conference on August 30, 1914. Convened by Louis Lipsky, as chairman of the FAZ executive committee, and Shmarya Levin, as a member of the WZO executive committee, the conference brought together all Zionist parties, including the socialists and the Orthodox religious Zionists. It established a Provisional Executive Committee for General Zionist Affairs (PZEC), with Brandeis as its chairman, and it undertook to raise an emergency fund of one hundred thousand dollars (eight times the previous year's FAZ budget) in support of international Zionist activities. Relying on the concurrence of Zionists abroad, the PZEC undertook "to act [as WZO headquarters] until such time when the Actions Comite shall reassemble"— which might mean until after the war.[1]

From the very start the PZEC understood that if it hoped to be an effective world Zionist force, it had to have the support of an American Jewry united as fully as possible during the war and in the peace settlement afterward. This meant, obviously, dealing with the AJC and its claims to authority. At the founding conference, an appeal from Arthur Ruppin, the WZO representative in Palestine, reached the American Zionists only through the channel of the AJC. Ruppin had applied for help to Henry Morgenthau, the American ambassador in Turkey, on August 12; on August 28 Morgenthau cabled a request for a minimum of fifty thousand dollars to Jacob Schiff to meet immediate needs. The AJC undertook to send half the sum, with Schiff personally adding an additional twelve thousand five hundred dollars; the Zionists' share was contributed by Nathan Straus. On the morrow of the conference, Brandeis wrote to the AJC chairman, Louis Marshall, announcing the formation of the PZEC and its planned functions: "To act on behalf of the [WZO] pending [its] reconstruction ... to maintain and strengthen [it] and to support ... Palestinian Institutions ... heretofore ... supported by [it]." In addition, the letter noted that in "any diplomatic negotiations on behalf of the Jews ... action should be taken by a united American Jewry"; and it gave notice that the PZEC considered itself authorized "to emphasize" the interests of world Jewry in Palestine "in any negotiations that may be entered upon by the Powers before or upon the conclusion of the war." The letter ended with an invitation to the AJC to help unite American Jewry and "cooperate with [the PZEC] in calling a conference of all the important Jewish organizations and groups in the country."[2]

Events soon clarified the feasible scope of PZEC activities, somewhat narrower than the sweeping early hopes of some American Zionists, but still ambitious enough.[3] A meeting of WZO leaders in Copenhagen in December

1914 left the Berlin center in charge of the WZO, with liaison offices in neutral countries—one in Copenhagen and another in The Hague for the Jewish National Fund (formerly managed from Cologne), which financed the Palestine work. The PZEC served as a liaison and center for a variety of extra-European Zionist federations. The movement as a whole was committed to a policy of neutrality in the issues between the belligerent nations.

As for the PZEC proposal to the AJC to join in convening a conference to unite American Jewry, an answer from Louis Marshall soon set clear bounds to what might be expected in that direction.[4] When Brandeis' letter was received at the end of August, the AJC was in session to consider calling its own conference of Jewish groups to organize for emergency relief. The Zionists were eventually included among others invited to join the AJC in forming a new overseas relief agency.

Overseas relief was to be one of the activities that enabled the PZEC, under Brandeis' guidance, to raise American Zionism to a new level of prominence and strength. But it was also a field in which the Zionists had to contend with, and ultimately submit to, the dominant position of the established AJC leaders. Brandeis' suggestion that the AJC join in organizing the community for still broader tasks after the war (with the Zionists conceded a leading position concerning Palestine) was simply ignored in Marshall's response to his letter. But this was to be the central issue in a fierce struggle between the AJC and the Zionists, led by Brandeis. Zionist success here, even more than the relief effort, mainly substantiated their title to represent American Jewish political interests in regard to Palestine during the war and in the peace settlement.

Once, in later years, Brandeis recalled for some old Zionist friends from Boston that he was assured that no more than a few months of his time were probably needed when he assumed the responsibility of leadership. If this recollection was correct, the Zionists who urged the task upon him could hardly have been entirely candid; it seems unlikely that he seriously harbored such expectations himself.

In 1911 those who had considered offering Brandeis the honorary presidency of the FAZ undoubtedly thought he might serve in a chiefly nominal capacity. But in 1914 the disarray of Zionist organization on the international plane placed different demands on his leadership. Brandeis could now offer not merely the prestige of his name, but the influence that a man close to the Wilson administration might bring to bear when issues of primary Jewish and Zionist concern came to be decided. As for Brandeis, he clearly came to the aid of Zionism in response to solicitation by trusted associates, not spontaneously, but he must have known that he was undertaking a commitment more nearly on the scale of his enlistment in the progressive cause or in counseling the Wilson administration than of his early lobbying on matters like mass transit in Massachusetts. Among the questions he began to study at once were the plans Herzl had projected for the structure of the charter he hoped to obtain from the Ottomans for building the Jewish "home" in Palestine; he

was making ready to assume wartime responsibility for the entire WZO operation and lead it in peace negotiations.[5]

Brandeis' accession lifted the hearts of Zionists in every camp, but in one
faction, or school, of American Zionism it was hailed with particular enthusiasm. Leading Zionists like Richard Gottheil, Stephen Wise, and Jacob de
Haas, who had become more or less inactive when the tide had turned against
Herzlian, political Zionism, saw Brandeis' rise as a call for their return to the
ranks, and perhaps to command. They saw in him a champion who might,
under their experienced guidance, restore the movement (in America first,
then the world over) to the Herzlian path. They also urged Brandeis to take
a militant line in American-Jewish affairs, challenging the anti-Zionist opposition in Cincinnati and the hegemonial claims of the New York-Philadelphia
AJC establishment.

Somewhat similar expectations were cherished by part of the official FAZ
leadership. Shmarya Levin, Judah Magnes, and Louis Lipsky actively pursued the prospect of transferring the WZO central control to America during
the war. Like de Haas, Lipsky and Levin urged Brandeis to act boldly in the
face of all opposition and to rally American Jewry in support of Zionist aims.
But Magnes had pinned his hopes for the reorganization of American Jewry
on the Kehillah already set up in New York and felt bound by the arrangement that recognized the AJC's prerogative to represent American Jewry in
matters beyond local bounds.

Brandeis took up his leadership with an extraordinary burst of activity,
but not precisely in a militant spirit. He approached the management of his
new Zionist clientele in much the same way as he had checked the budgeted
expenditures of his daughter's annual allowance when he sent her off to college: he required regular, frequent reports on membership and outlays from
each unit answerable to him, including very minor ones. He devoted himself
(and mobilized others) to an intensive campaign of speechmaking across the
country on behalf of Zionism. What he avoided doing, however, was to throw
down a gauntlet in the face of the anti-Zionist opposition or, certainly, less
antagonistic rivals like the AJC.[6]

Brandeis' long-established preference to mediate differences rather than
act as an *ex parte* advocate might seem to imply that all disputes can be
resolved in terms advantageous to both sides. Brandeis' liberalism was not
quite so optimistic. He was fiercely partisan when he felt he was dealing with
power-hungry corruption; but here, too, his methods relied on a democratic
consensus that could be attained by rational persuasion. His methods as a
partisan were those of lobbying and political pressure, both public and private, rather than of party organization and power-brokerage. As a Zionist
leader, he planned for the majority of American Jewry to accept his rational
exposition of the issues, compelling the recalcitrant minority to bow to a
clearly established consensus.

Given these assumptions and methods, it is understandable that Brandeis
was not eager to take up old quarrels in which the Zionists had involved
themselves before his time. He did not yield to Horace Kallen's urging to

challenge the Reform leaders by speaking to their students in Cincinnati, even though the administration refused to countenance his appearance as a Zionist. He did not hasten to support those who were eager to fight the AJC over the project of a democratically elected American-Jewish "congress." When convinced that the anti-Zionist opposition could not be swayed by his arguments, he hoped to outflank them rather than overwhelm them in a frontal attack. Consequently, he incessantly preached "Men! Money! Discipline!" to the Zionists as the most pressing need: he relied on a demonstration of overwhelming popular support to force a dwindling opposition to fall in line rather than be left out.

This approach implied that the existing array of organized forces did not reflect the true "general will" of American Jewry. The assumption might apply not only to the non-Zionist establishment, but to the existing Zionist organizations as well. When Brandeis said he could hardly imagine any self-respecting Jew's failing to welcome the restoration of the Jewish national home, he need not have had in mind a narrowly defined model such as those set forth in one Zionist party platform or another. His own conception was not specifically defined until later, in 1918; but if he expected to gain the assent of the overwhelming majority of American Jews, few of whom were enrolled or party-affiliated Zionists at the time, the possibility remained open that such a consensus defined by the community at large would not correspond to any existing Zionist ideology or be acceptable to self-conscious, veteran Zionists.

Although logically possible, such an outcome was hardly apparent at the time; other consequences were more immediate. Brandeis ran the PZEC with little consideration for the prerogatives of the Zionist bodies who created it. The provisional executive committee took charge of American Zionist policy in a decisive way, leaving the executive council of the FAZ, for example, with very little to do on its own. Moreover, Brandeis obviously interpreted the authority "democratically" granted him by the emergency conference as "presidential," in the America manner and in the tradition of Herzl. He took his own informed and rational, discretionary conclusions as decisive, without noticeable concern about the balance of opinion among the members. Also, he freely co-opted to the PZEC's controlling group, as his advisors and aides, those in whom he had confidence—naming them "associate" members elected by the provisional executive committee without consulting the basic constituency. Some were distinguished Harvard Law School alumni, like Felix Frankfurter and Judge Julian W. Mack; but they came into Zionist work without any previous connection. They represented, perhaps the kind of constituency Brandeis hoped to find among independent-minded, unaffiliated American Jews. But others, like the stock market operator, Eugene Meyer, who was more or less conscripted into leading a new Intercollegiate Zionist Society, mainly responded to Brandeis himself.[7]

Neither the encroachment on their authority nor doubts about some new associates caused more than restrained grumbling among the veterans. They were elated at the sudden lift in prestige that Brandeis gave them at once and at the steady increase in strength thereafter under his persistent and vigorous administration. Brandeis' unrelenting drive and tight supervision made the rapidly expanding Zionist machinery register and incorporate every source of new growth in its widening reach. What chiefly extended its reach were two fields of activity that mainly occupied American Zionists: the ramified over-seas relief effort and the struggle to organize an American Jewish Congress.

The first section of American Jewry to organize a relief agency was the Ortho-dox community, mainly consisting of immigrants with strong ties to the war-afflicted areas. Among those who set up a Central Committee for the Relief of War Sufferers on October 4, 1914, were representatives of the reinvigorated Mizrachi party, the Religious Zionists of America. Soon after, on October 25, the AJC in association with the PZEC and other invited bodies set up an agency called the American Jewish Relief Committee (AJRC), clearly signi-fying AJC dominance. Brandeis, who strongly objected to this name—having expected it to be called the *National* Jewish Relief Committee—nevertheless served as chairman of its New England campaign. American Zionists coun-trywide conducted their own emergency fund to finance WZO regular activ-ities and took part in the general Jewish relief campaign. Finally, almost a year later, in August 1915, the labor parties, Poalei Zion and the Socialist Territorialists, shared with the Jewish trade unions and non–Zionist socialists in creating a third agency, the People's Relief Committee. Thus Zionists were involved in all three overseas relief agencies created by American Jewry dur-ing the war as well as in their own special activities.[8]

The AJC, whose members and associates included the largest contribu-tors, was able to impose a certain (not always effective) control over the com-bined efforts of all three relief committees. Jacob Schiff had passed on the responsibility for direct management of this activity to his son-in-law, Felix Warburg—a man who had not until then taken part in the major Jewish activities of the AJC leadership.[9] He tried to regulate the several campaigns and apportion their total receipts in what he considered a fair, mutually acceptable manner. The meetings at Warburg's office of what his secretary called the "joint distribution committee" were eventually formalized as the American Jewish Joint Distribution Committee (JDC) and became the dom-inant operating agency for overseas relief, not merely a clearing house for the cooperating (and often openly competing) campaigns. It was at first an arena for sometimes sharp disputes between the partners, resolved in most cases by Warburg's gentlemanly mediation and the greatly preponderant weight of the wealthy donors he represented and on whom the others depended for supple-mentary support.

Thus the Central Relief Committee's campaign was accused by Brandeis' New England AJRC committee of diverting contributions from the general campaign; the Orthodox, for their part, objected to allocations to the Bundist schools in Poland, which were headed by Vladimir Medem, a man whom they would not accept as a legitimate Jew because he had been baptized as a child and brought up as a Christian. The Zionists objected to routing relief funds for the East European war zones through Warburg's brother Max in Hamburg, because the German banker's close ties with his government could expose Polish and Russian Jews to charges of consorting with the enemy. A persistent Zionist complaint was that funds they raised in the AJRC campaign from contributors who responded to the needs in Palestine were not earmarked, as they demanded, for Palestine. Brandeis discovered that neither the Zionists nor he personally could do other than bow to the ultimate control of the established philanthropic leaders in matters of relief: "our Zionists . . . [are] very active in [all] the Committees and in the relief work, . . . [but] they are generally outvoted on any questions along distinct Zionist lines."[10]

Nevertheless, Zionist involvement in the relief campaign contributed vastly to the rapid growth of Zionist influence in American Jewry. Apart from the special Zionist and general relief campaigns, which gave the PZEC access to greatly expanded lists of concerned Jews (all promptly registered for further cultivation), another new activity enlarged its direct contacts with potential supporters. American Jews with relatives and friends in the war zones and in Palestine were anxious to send them aid individually, not relying on the relief distributed by locally constituted communal bodies. By exploiting their worldwide network of movement contacts and offices, the Zionists became the main channel of this service for the community at large. Moreover, Brandeis' relations with the new U.S. administration easily rivaled those of the established older leadership, and the Zionists played a major role in obtaining government facilities essential to the relief and transfer operations. This added to the prestige of the American Zionist movement at home and abroad.

Under Brandeis' incessant pressure and spurred by his personal example, the movement pressed those who responded to its pleas for emergency aid to enroll in a Zionist society as well. The available forms of affiliation—in the FAZ or one of the connected ideological parties, youth organizations, women's clubs, fraternal orders, Zion associations, or simply through at-large membership—offered a wide range of options for more or less committed attachment, and the enrolled members increased at an accelerating rate. The large immigrant fraternal orders and *landsmanshaft* federations that were drawn into the general relief drives were urged to endorse the Zionist cause collectively and facilitate the mass enrollment of their members. In these ways the officially registered membership of the FAZ and its associated organizations rose from twelve thousand in 1914 to one hundred fifty thousand in 1918, and the reach of the PZEC was even wider.

The drive to organize an American-Jewish congress still further enhanced Zionist prestige and enrolled strength.[11] The most active protagonists of an elected Jewish congress were the Zionist-minded journalists of the Yiddish press. They proposed a Jewish congress not only to cope with the problems of war and the peace settlement, but to give the American Jewish community a new permanent form like that of the Helsingfors program. The socialist-Zionist parties were particularly active in this cause; on their motion, the

Zionist Emergency Conference instructed the newly formed PZEC to initiate action. Brandeis opened negotiations with the AJC in order to carry out this resolution, but without immediate effect. The PZEC attended the AJC-controlled conference that set up the relief campaign, allowing this activity unchallenged priority, while pursuing further discussions on organizing American Jewry for broader functions.

Meanwhile other agencies in which Zionists were involved—some newly formed, others already existing—took the issue in hand and in November 1914 began to force the pace of developments. Joseph Barondess, the popular labor organizer who had become a Zionist and headed the B'nai Zion fraternal order, organized his own Congress for Jewish Rights. His initiative attracted a wide circle of supporters among leaders of the immigrant community active in the New York Kehillah, Yiddish journalism, and socialist-Zionism. In March 1915 these elements founded a Jewish Congress Organizing Committee (JCOC), which became the prime force in the ensuing campaign for democracy in communal leadership.

The socialist-Zionists spurred parallel action in the American-Jewish labor movement. Largely made up of immigrants who came in the wake of the 1903–5 Russian turmoil, they were a minority force in this context, as in American Zionism, but one which here, too, posed effective challenges. Fellow immigrants of the 1905 wave who were Bundists met with much greater acceptance by the older leaders in the labor movement and the socialist Yiddish press. At the same time, socialist-Zionist leaders, Nachman Syrkin, Chaim Zhitlovksy, and the lately arrived Ber Borochov enjoyed immense respect as individual figures. They were joined during the war by men like Shlomo Kaplan-Kaplansky, despatched from The Hague to represent the Jewish National Fund; by the young Palestinian exiled leaders, David Ben-Gurion and Yitzhak Ben-Zvi; and by the Social Revolutionary party activist, newly turned Zionist, Pinhas Rutenberg.

In November 1914 Kaplan-Kaplansky induced Meyer London (a labor lawyer recently elected by New York's Lower East Side as its representative in the U.S. Congress) to call a meeting at his home in order to begin organizing for united action on general Jewish concerns. The meeting chose a Committee of Five—London himself; Nachman Syrkin; Chaim Zhitlovsky; the Yiddish poet, Abraham Liessin; and Joseph Schlossberg of the Amalgamated Clothing Workers. They published an appeal to convene the Jewish labor organizations in New York for action on a broad range of tasks—among them, joining with other Jewish bodies to secure representation at an eventual peace conference. After a period of jockeying, on April 18 a convention dominated by non-Zionist labor groups formed a National Workmen's Committee on Jewish Rights in the Belligerent Lands (NWC) and adopted a program largely restricted to the question of Jewish rights in Russia. The Poalei Zion and the Socialist Territorialists, who had demanded a broader program (including planned resettlement in concentrated, productive Jewish communities and immediate action through the Socialist International) as well as minority representation on the NWC's executive body, withdrew in protest.

They then mounted a campaign through the spring and summer of 1915 (with support in the Yiddish press and aid from the PZEC) denouncing the NWC leaders for betraying the cause of Jewish and labor unity.

In the same period a battle over the Jewish congress proposal was waged in the New York Kehillah. Judah Magnes and others in the leadership had favored a more "democratic" communal organization, with greater involvement of immigrant leaders; but at the same time, they were committed to the Kehillah's arrangement with the AJC. Magnes took part in the PZEC negotiations with the AJC on this question, and also in Barondess' early initiative—in both cases urging cooperation with the AJC. In February 1915 the Kehillah adopted a resolution calling on the AJC to convene the national Jewish organizations and consider a framework for united action. Magnes further proposed a meeting under the auspices of the Kehillah to be held in April on the broadest possible basis. The invitation was taken up by a broad spectrum of partisans, indeed, including secularist workers—among them, the Poalei Zion—who had previously abstained from participating in the New York community organization. The ardent Jewish congress partisans were able to push through (with Magnes' compliance, and against Marshall's vehement opposition) a resolution in favor of a congress. This opened a rift that the Kehillah leaders tried to patch up in subcommittee meetings with the AJC. At a second Kehillah meeting on May 23, a compromise was offered. The AJC would be asked to convene, not a "congress" (carrying disturbing implications of an *imperium in imperio*), but a "conference" of organizations. To balance this concession to the AJC, delegates were to be chosen democratically, that is, by vote of the members rather than appointment by the officers of the respective organizations. This resolution was passed against the opposition of the Poalei Zion, who wanted general elections by the community at large. But the Poalei Zion won another vote that sought to bind Kehillah representatives (meaning Marshall) to support the Kehillah position at the AJC. This simply angered Marshall, who took it as a personal insult; at an AJC meeting on June 20 the Kehillah's compromise was rejected and another AJC position was defined. The "conference" (to be held in October with an agenda strictly confined to the question of the rights to be claimed for Jews in "the belligerent lands") would be constituted of delegates chosen by each invited organization in the manner it preferred.

By this time the PZEC had finally taken a partisan position on the issues publicly. For months Brandeis had been feeling his way in the labyrinth of Jewish communal politics. Such irritations as the petty incident of his canceled address in Cincinnati or the more weighty matter of non-Zionist domination of the relief effort he bore with patience. If he avoided staking out final positions explicitly rejected by the AJC, he might yet emerge as a "counsel for the situation" acceptable to all parties. Moreover, not only Magnes but Judge Mack and others of his Zionists had close ties with the AJC. Brandeis vetoed a proposal Lipsky made to him in January 1915 to publish a Zionist statement proposing a Jewish congress. Yet the issues involved, unlike matters of relief, were too significantly related to his duties as a Zionist leader for him to continue standing aside should the AJC openly seek to deny the Zionists their claim to a hearing at the ultimate peace conference. When the April meeting of the Kehillah ended with Marshall's refusal to be bound by the compromise arrived at there, the PZEC soon committed itself to active support of the Jewish congress campaign. Thereafter, with Brandeis' strong backing, Zionists increasingly took over the direction of the JCOC; and when the socialist-Zionists mounted an intensified summer campaign among Jewish workers, they were given support by the PZEC's treasury.

Brandeis' reasons for getting actively into the fight over the congress included the judgment that the Zionists could sharply increase their chances to expand their influence and their enrolled membership by taking the lead in what was clearly a popular cause. His campaign for "Men! Money! Discipline!" was making significant progress, but not at a rate fast enough to assure success in demonstrating that an overwhelming consensus of American Jewry favored Zionist aims. A more militant approach was needed for this purpose. A week after the AJC laid down its own challenge by rejecting the Kehillah's compromise and announced that it would convene a conference on its own terms in October, the Annual FAZ convention was held in Boston. A PZEC session (against the vehement objection of Judah Magnes) resolved to "issue a joint call [together with other organizations] for an American Jewish Congress, which shall consider . . . steps . . . to obtain full civil status for the Jews in all lands and further development of a homeland for the Jewish people in Palestine."[12]

The summer of 1915 was marked by a furious campaign over the Jewish congress, with the PZEC and the AJC openly opposed to each other. The Zionists worked through the JCOC and the dissident labor forces, recruiting support for them and helping with funds and publicity. The latter bodies, the organizing instruments of the congress drive, adopted policies oriented to the constituency each addressed. The Zionists, generally recognized as the real antagonists of the AJC, had to follow a policy line determined by the primary concerns of the PZEC as Brandeis viewed them.

Although consciously inviting a confrontation, all parties involved hoped to avoid a final break—the aim, after all, was to achieve a united Jewry. Brandeis proposed to Dr. Cyrus Adler, the new AJC president, that the impasse be circumvented by a preliminary meeting of national Jewish organizations. The scope and procedures of a subsequent, substantive Jewish assembly would be agreed on at the preliminary meeting instead of being arbitrarily determined by the AJC as convener. Adler agreed to submit this proposal to the AJC executive committee but indicated that the executive was under instructions from the council, and would not undertake to overrule the larger body. It was not a response that appeased the Zionists.

An exchange of letters followed that was more a polemical exercise than an attempt at negotiation, and their contents were soon presented to the public in pamphlet form. Both sides during these private negotiations secured public statements favorable to their cause from friendly third-party organizations. The JCOC, under Zionist leadership, held mass meetings, organized local pro-congress societies everywhere, had articles and pamphlets published, and garnered declarations of sympathy from social organizations increasingly populated by prospering immigrants.[13]

Mounting pressure on the AJC through the summer was heightened by the attitude of some established, older organizations. The B'nai B'rith—which had never fully accepted the rise of the AJC to a dominance that overshadowed its own role—took a position of emphatic neutrality. It posed as mediator and invited the two parties to a carefully balanced conference of organization presidents in October—the very month of the AJC's planned conference. The meeting, held in the privacy of executive session, produced a crop of sharp disagreements that were promptly published in the newspapers. The attempted conciliation simply raised the intensity of the conflict and made the need for an understanding more obviously urgent.

There were parallel developments, meanwhile, among the working-class organizations.[14] The Bundist leaders of the NWC, who at first welcomed the withdrawal of the Poalei Zion and the Socialist Territorialists, came under severe criticism in the Yiddish press and trade unions for provoking a breach at a time of crisis. They were finally driven to reorganize, making room on the NWC executive for the unrepresented minority. One of the first actions of the expanded executive was to announce a new conference, to be held in September, that extended the New York-based NWC on a countrywide scale. That assembly was constituted in a way that gave the nationalist minority substantial representation, and it arrived at compromises acceptable to both sides. The essential agreement was on a program of Jewish demands for "full political, civil and national rights." "National rights," a red flag to the AJC-led establishment, of course, were part of the Bundist as well as the Zionist tradition. But it was a specific concession to the Zionists to name Palestine among other countries—"Russia, Galicia, Rumania, Palestine, etc."—with which the NWC was concerned.

A counterconcession demanded by the majority was that the nationalist workers abandon Brandeis' suggestion of a preliminary conference of Jewish organizations to plan the agenda of the projected Jewish congress. Instead, the program adopted by the NWC was to be offered as the predetermined agenda. Only on condition of its acceptance was the NWC committed to join a conference of organizations "which will call together a Jewish Congress to which the delegates will be elected democratically by local organizations." Another resolution (ensuring that the NWC would not be aligned unequivocally with the JCOC and the Zionists) instructed its negotiators to deal also with "certain important Jewish groups in America such as the American Jewish Committee and the organizations associated with it [who had] so far taken no part in the work." The NWC leadership chosen at the September meeting was dominated by the old majority, and the committee of seven chosen to negotiate with others was split between the factions in a way that portended internal friction.

The succession of conferences—from the FAZ convention in June to the

NWC assembly in September and the private consultation of leaders arranged by the B'nai B'rith in October—made it clear that there was no coalition in American Jewry strong enough to act on its own authority. The AJC and the "organizations associated with it" (essentially, the lay and rabbinical organizations of the Reform and newly created Conservative denominations) no longer represented a solid phalanx of the establishment after the B'nai B'rith demonstrated its neutrality in October. The AJC drew the necessary consequences and canceled its projected conference. The NWC's apparent unity, hailed so fervently after the September meeting, soon showed itself to be a hollow facade; it was shattered at the negotiating sessions with the AJC where the Bundist spokesman found AJC proposals to be acceptable that the Poalei Zion denounced as contrary to the NWC program. Finally, the incursion of the organized workers into general communal affairs robbed the Zionists of any claim to represent, exclusively and legitimately, the vast majority of American Jewry who were East European immigrants. Everyone now understood that a new base of agreement would have to be found.

Through Magnes' mediation, a nine-man tripartite negotiating team of AJC, JCOC, and NWC representatives was constituted and was able within a brief period to draft an agreed formula. This was approved by a majority of the AJC executive committee on October 10 (subject to approval by the annual meeting of its General Council in November) and by the New York Kehillah on October 12. However, when submitted to the JCOC, the draft was summarily rejected on October 12—to the great satisfaction of the Poalei Zion—and the congress advocates threatened to call their own preliminary conference of organizations.

Further negotiations yielded concessions—particularly by the AJC—that considerably narrowed the differences among the parties. A "treaty" based on JCOC acceptance of the September NWC formula (as summarized by Brandeis) was adopted in substance by the tripartite negotiating team. Debate now arose on the following proposal of the joint draft:

> That a Conference of national Jewish organizations be held for the purpose of considering the rights of Jews in belligerent lands and in Rumania, and that it call a Congress on a democratic basis at such time, and in such place and in such manner as it may deem best to secure such rights.

But now on November 14 the annual meeting of the AJC objected and demanded that the text be amended, substituting the following wording for the final clause: "and that it take steps to call a Congress on a democratic basis after the termination of hostilities." Thus, the AJC, like the JCOC earlier, repudiated the agreement accepted by its own negotiators, precipitating a new moment of crisis.[15]

Over the many months of argument and negotiation, the AJC had, nonetheless, gone far from its original insistence on a restricted meeting of preselected organizations, consulting privately. By agreeing to a conference agenda permitting discussion of the NWC-JCOC "national rights" plank and by conceding that the preliminary conference should determine independently the agenda for the subsequent "democratic" congress, the AJC had met major Zionist demands. The sticking point was the peremptory insistence that the congress be *explicitly* deferred until after the war. This was not only viewed as a piece of AJC arrogance that had to be repudiated, but there was also the well-founded fear that such an indefinite postponement would undermine Zionist success in organizing support for the congress idea and diminish their own ranks. It might easily be thought that the AJC's decision was taken with just such results in mind.

The atmosphere of mutual suspicion was further heightened when the NWC majority, at the end of December, abandoned its entente with the Zionists and announced that it would convene the three parties a month later to consider whether to defer the congress until after the war. Immediately thereafter the JCOC (in a move strongly disapproved by Brandeis) declared it would now put into effect its earlier decision to convene the preliminary conference to organize the congress elections. It invited the NWC and AJC to join as conveners by January 15, failing which action, the JCOC would proceed unilaterally. Then, on January 28, 1916, President Wilson nominated Brandeis to serve on the Supreme Court and the implicit rules of the contest over the congress issue were radically altered.

The nomination touched off a political war even more bitter and protracted than had been provoked by Wilson's attempt to include Brandeis in the Cabinet. This time Brandeis took an active part behind the scenes in the confirmation battle, abandoning the strict abstention he had practiced in 1913.[16] Assembling his records and proposing personages who might effectively support his case took much of his time, care, and effort. He was in constant touch with his law partner, Edward McClennen, and other friends who carried the public and private campaign on his behalf. The Supreme Court post was clearly one he strongly desired to win.

At the same time he was not certain how much it need compel him to sacrifice his active role in the political causes he had espoused. He was meticulous—almost picayune, indeed—in avoiding any personal gain from his position. On his appointment, he at once consulted with the chief justice about his personal investments in order to avoid any suggestion of a conflict of interest in cases that might arise before the Court. Also, on the chief justice's advice, he turned down the president's request, which came shortly after his Court appointment, to serve on a commission to settle border issues with Mexico. But this was justified on the grounds of the pressure of Court business and did not imply a ban in principle on political activity, that is, if pursued with due care not to taint the Supreme Court with impropriety. Thus, after his nomination and appointment, Brandeis felt free to continue his active Zionist leadership.

On March 26, 1916, the JCOC and an impressive group of cooperating organizations met in Philadelphia for a two-day conference.[17] They set up machinery to elect an American Jewish Congress to be convened between

September and December 1916. A congress executive committee of seventy was chosen, and there was provision for fourteen more members to be added if those organizations who had boycotted the Philadelphia conference should reconsider and apply to join. At the same time, however, the NWC (from which the Poalei Zion had again withdrawn) meeting in New York assembled its constituents from the eastern states in its own conference and pledged to continue the effort to unite all the major Jewish organizations in a democratic Jewish congress. This was an invitation the Philadelphia conferees had ruled out in advance by a resolution forbidding further negotiation. But the AJC, forestalled in its plans to convene a conference on the terms it originally proposed, now took up the NWC invitation, and the two newly allied committees undertook to convene a conference of national Jewish organizations to consider how a congress might be organized on generally acceptable terms.

There were now two blocs dividing American Jewish opinion between them and effectively preventing each other from achieving the goals either pursued. The Zionist-led coalition, having initiated the organization of a congress, had compelled the AJC-led coalition to adopt the same project as its own, abandoning its preferred alternative of a limited conference. But it was precisely this JCOC tactic, by precipitating the AJC's alliance with the workers, that ruled out the other, ultimate Zionist aim: to achieve a *united* American Jewish representation through organizing the congress. Not only did the AJC no longer seem likely to be isolated (especially with the evident slackening of energy among Zionist leaders because of Brandeis' preoccupation with the battle for the Supreme Court appointment), but the new dividing lines were drawn with previously unmatched sharpness and vociferation.

The immigrant community was split, with the Poalei Zion leaving the NWC to line up with the JCOC Zionists while their rivals formed an alliance with the AJC—leading to a furious battle of epithets in the Yiddish press. Jacob Schiff, in the heat of controversy, enraged the immigrant nationalists by suggesting that, in some part, they had brought their oppression in Eastern Europe upon themselves by their nationalist separatism. The storm of personal attacks he then endured made him threaten to withdraw his support and service for Jewish causes altogether in the future. The Zionists, too, experienced painful divisions. Magnes had submitted his resignation from the PZEC as early as June 30 of the previous year after the Zionists' decision to commit themselves to the congress project; it was accepted, after months of delay, in September 1915, with the contention that Magnes' views on matters of principle such as those implied in the Basle program had taken him completely out of the Zionist movement. Now in early spring 1916 other Zionists who were members of the AJC felt compelled to reconsider their position: Harry Friedenwald and Felix Frankfurter (but not Judge Mack) resigned their membership in the AJC; Israel Friedlaender detached himself from both antagonists, the AJC and the PZEC.[18]

It was in this atmosphere that the AJC, NWC, and associated organizations planned to meet (on July 16, 1916, in the Hotel Astor in New York) to work out their own version of a Jewish congress.[19] Nearly two months before that date, Brandeis' nomination to the Supreme Court had been approved by the Senate, and he immediately assumed his new judicial functions. He, nevertheless, continued to carry Zionist responsibilities, publicly as well as privately, though with the same relative restraint as in previous months. Thus he was one of those sent by the PZEC to the Hotel Astor meeting, ostensibly to explore what chances for conciliation might emerge from a gathering that presented itself as seeking a common ground on which American Jews could unite.

In its substantive conclusions, the Hotel Astor conclave did, in fact, approve a position that eventually led to an American Jewish Congress in which virtually all of American Jewry was able to participate. Meeting *in camera,* it adopted a resolution in favor of a congress, chosen on a democratic basis and not required to delay its session until after the war. On the other hand, it stipulated a restricted, predetermined agenda—not an open-ended one—for the congress, limiting its authority to the sole function of representing Jewish interests in the peace settlement. The congress would have to propose "suitable measures to secure full rights for Jews in all lands"—"full rights" being understood to cover civil, religious, political, and "group" rights (the last representing Marshall's euphemism for "national" rights). But it was not this propitiatory resolution that had an immediate impact on the public. Instead, an acrimonious clash involving Brandeis took place in the privacy of the deliberations, which was speedily made public and effected a sharp change in Brandeis' method of leadership.

Invited to present the PZEC's message to the conferees, Brandeis responded to a Magnes proposal that the two sides meet on terms of parity to iron out their differences. Brandeis replied that the way was open for the AJC and NWC to join the Congress executive committee, filling the fourteen seats provided for them as a supplement to the seventy already filled. A parity proposal would require altering this arrangement and could only be done by the same body, the delegates of the Philadelphia conference, who had created the Executive Committee. He then prepared to leave the conferees to their further deliberations, but Louis Marshall invited the guests to stay for the continuation of the discussions. Thereupon an outpouring of angry reproaches was vented upon the Zionists and Brandeis personally, particularly by Magnes and the NWC delegates. To compound Brandeis' embarrassment, the whole episode was made the subject of editorial comment in the *New York Times:*

> Justice Brandeis might with very great propriety have avoided taking part in such a controversy. . . . [W]e venture to express the hope that he will consider he is discharged of further obligation and will in future leave to others subjects of such controversial nature.

Justice Brandeis did not, of course, consider himself "discharged of further obligation," but he had to take seriously the imputation of impropriety. Within a week he resigned his temporary chairmanship of the Congress Executive Committee and other posts he held in Jewish organizations, including the PZEC. Nevertheless, he continued to guide them through the network of liaison personnel he put in place when he rose to the Supreme Court and now by calling on Stephen Wise to assume the public role of official leadership after the Astor fiasco.

As if sobered by the eruption of publicity in the general press, the two sides now came to a swift agreement.[20] The congress was to be authorized solely to formulate Jewish desiderata for the eventual peace conference, covering the claims for "full rights" previously agreed on. Its composition was to be chosen by "a democratic and universal suffrage," with further provision for "the selection of representatives by the various Jewish National Organizations." The existing executive committee of seventy was to be supplemented by an additional seventy (not fourteen) members chosen by the other negotiating partners, and the augmented committee would decide outstanding matters: what part of the congress would be directly elected and what part selected by the "National Organizations"; and at what time "before the cessation of the present European war" the congress would take place. The agreement, endorsed by the executive committee, then had to be submitted to the full roster of Philadelphia delegates (who, it will be recalled, had banned further negotiations) for their approval.

A wave of protest, led by the disgruntled Poalei Zion, forced the renegotiation of two points: the restricted competence allowed the congress and the provisions for the selection of delegates. A final agreement then provided that the question of postwar economic reconstruction could be added to the congress agenda (if the reconstituted executive committee agreed); and a formula for delegate selection instead of being left to the discretion of the new executive committee of 140, was fixed: seventy-five percent to be chosen by general election, twenty-five percent by the national organizations.

By the end of 1916 (not without further dissension) the union between the rival blocs was consummated. It was possible to go on to choose congress delegates and convene the congress sometime "before the cessation of the . . . war." But, while elections were finally held (on June 9–10, 1917), America's entry into the hostilities in April caused the congress session to be deferred until after the armistice.

It is instructive to consider the way in which Brandeis responded to the attack on him at the July 16, 1916, Hotel Astor meeting, followed by the *New York Times'* editorial—a combination of events that he took as evidence of a concerted plot by his foes in the Jewish community. On July 24 after Brandeis announced his resignation from his several Jewish posts, Louis Marshall sent him a letter of apology, both personal and official. He regretted "that in the course of the discussion . . . any one present permitted himself to make remarks which were out of place, offensive or in any way objectionable." The best that Brandeis could bring himself to say in response (on September 8) was the following:

Your letter . . . , which was acknowledged by my secretary, was later forwarded to me. I delayed replying because I felt doubt as to what the reply
should be. That doubt has not yet been resolved. Perhaps it will be on talking
matters when we meet.

He was even colder, and far more unbending, in regard to Magnes. Years
later, when an attempt was under way in 1919 to gain non-Zionists' support
for Zionist projects, Brandeis was invited to a conference with Jacob Schiff,
who had also asked Magnes as one of his party. Brandeis then wrote to Julian
Mack—the most genial of men, who was a friend of both sides and was trying
to bring about a conciliation of Brandeis and Magnes—and explained his
position:

> I fear you have entirely misunderstood my attitude. . . . I have no personal
> feeling toward [Magnes] whatsoever, I should have no objection to meeting
> him socially in private and discuss with him botany or Greek Genius; if I
> could be sure that no publicity would be given to the fact which might affect
> his relation to the Jewish cause. My belief in having all Zionists avoid him
> is purely a matter of judgment for the Cause. He has been tried and found
> wanting; and because he is able (within certain areas), attractive, has friends
> & has an important Jewish background, he cannot be inconspicuous; and it
> may be dangerous to put him into a position where his instability of char-
> acter may prove a disruptive force.

Brandeis was, of course, a hard polemical combatant and notably ruthless
in dealing with opponents. He could administer a dressing-down for errors
and omissions that kept associates in terror. At the same time he kept whatever emotion he suffered in an argument under firm control, conducting himself always with cool, rational courtesy. He has nothing but contempt (which
he did not hesitate to express) for a "crybaby" who would continue to complain after losing a political argument, and he had treated with cool equanim-
ity personal attacks he had suffered over a long, controversial career—most
recently (though with difficulty) in the battle over his nomination to the Court
in 1916. William Howard Taft had taken a leading role in opposing Brandeis'
nomination; but when the two met by chance on the street in Washington (in
December 1918) and the ex-president spoke to Brandeis in a friendly way, the
response was even friendlier, and the two repaired to the justice's home for a
long visit together.[21]

Brandeis, in short, did not bother to hold a grudge, as a rule, nor did he
let anger rule him in debate. This is not to say that he was without deep emotion. He was, in fact, a man of deep personal attachments—first of all to his
family and to a few intimate friends treated like family. If he ever incurred
the reproach of one of them, or felt he deserved it, or felt undeservedly
blamed—the reaction in such a case was far from indifference. When he and
his brother-in-law, Charles Nagel, broke over their respective relations to the
Taft administration, the two "did not 'see'" each other thereafter when they

chanced to meet. Brandeis as a youth disappointed both his parents and his sister, Fannie Nagel, when he refused to settle in Louisville or St. Louis and went off to Boston to practice law instead. He was relieved and thankful that they freely accepted his decision; but he felt constrained, nevertheless, to voice a kind of remorse at the pain his liberation would be causing them. At the time he went off to Harvard to become a lawyer, his brother Alfred, who helped finance the venture, had dropped studies he had begun in St. Louis and was helping out in the family business. Apart from the strong brotherly affection between the two, Louis considered himself specifically indebted to Alfred from that time and in later years insisted that he must repay by taking on himself the responsibility for aiding near and even remote kin when they were in need of funds.[22]

Something like this special sensitivity seems to be shown in Brandeis' reactions to Marshall and Magnes after the Hotel Astor episode. To be sure, there might be a tactical advantage in dealing with Marshall if one appeared as an aggrieved party; but both sides now were unfeignedly seeking a quick settlement, not holding out for victory. And even if Brandeis rather emphatically explains his attitude toward Magnes as a tactical expedient, it is the kind of tactic one employs to deal with a refractory kinsman—not a foreign irritant one can easily dispose of. Ostracism, not simple disregard and indifference, is what Brandeis proposed for his nearest Jewish antagonists—and this is far from his usual way with the opposition. The special complexion of his clash with Weizmann is here foreshadowed.

Weizmann: The Lobbyist as Diplomat

When Austria declared war on Serbia, Weizmann was about to leave for a vacation in Switzerland, to be followed by a meeting two weeks later in Paris on the university project. He went on his way on July 30, burdened with misgivings about the future of his work and hoping against hope that a peaceful settlement of international issues might avert the impending disaster. German troops invaded Belgium on August 4, bringing everything down in a general collapse, including any immediate prospects for further work on the university. Weizmann was stranded on the Continent for weeks, dreading what awaited the Jewish communities and his own family in the war zones. It was August 28 before he could return to England and try to orient himself anew.

Nearing the age of forty, Weizmann saw himself as one of the small, divided band of Jewish leaders who had to bear the responsibility in such an emergency. Those who undertook to do so were constrained by the conflicting interests of their respective countries during the war itself and regarding the kind of peace they desired.

In his initial agitation, Weizman thrashed about in random search of outlets for action. He turned to Ahad Ha'am regularly for counsel. Both understood that there was little that they could do in England to aid the war-sufferers. They did not expect that the British would protest the oppressive acts of their Russian ally in wartime, and aiding the Jews in Palestine meant sending supplies and funds across enemy lines. If anything were to be done, neutral Americans and German Jews would have to act.

Although both men recognized the facts, they were of very different temperaments and reacted differently. Ahad Ha'am's war years were profoundly shadowed by despair at the collapse of civilization that he perceived all about him. His dour conscience made him help wherever he could as opportunities arose, but his customary caution and disillusionment grew more profound in a calamity that loomed so much greater than any hopes. Weizmann, too, was one to accept the dictate of harsh realities. But he was basically inclined to action; when he found a feasible task, not only did his volatile humor turn from bilious to sanguine, but he put out of mind those griefs and anxieties that he could do nothing about.

The Turkish entry into the hostilities brought a statement from Prime Minister Herbert Asquith on November 9 suggesting the end of the Ottoman Empire not only in Europe but in Asia as well. Weizmann asked for Ahad Ha'am's views on this historic opportunity for Zionism and got the following response:

> I gave the Prime Minister's speech the attention it merits. . . . Every Jew in his senses must now be aware that a great historic hour has struck for Israel and for Palestine and something must be done. But when you begin to consider what's to be done, you can only be disheartened. . . . I do not mean to say . . . that I don't recognize the possibility of great changes in favor of our national cause. . . . But if [our] hopes are realized it will be by grace of fortune, not by anything we do to achieve it. . . .
>
> Nevertheless, I well understand your state of mind, (which is also mine . . .). We want to give ourselves the illusion that we are turning the wheel of our life. It is hard at a time like this to make peace with the idea of our total helplessness. And so—let's try to "move" things. Let us set up various talks with influential people and prepare public opinion (that same *Europaeisches Gewissen* which Nordau pictured so well [i.e., ironically] at the Tenth Congress). . . . We have spoken about the content of such propaganda before, and I still hold to my view that we must not make exaggerated demands.[23]

Weizmann, for all his generally hardheaded realism, did not approach his political work with this kind of self-doubt or simply out of a grim sense of obligation, but with zeal as enthusiastic as it was driven. At the same time he directed his energies to tasks that he thought feasible as well as necessary and urgent. At first the immediately possible and necessary tasks seemed to him to be those of reorganizing the WZO structure for effective wartime operation and the setting up of an impressive international (or inter-Allied) Jewish delegation to present the Jewish case at the eventual peace conference. As to the first matter, he (like other Zionists in England) strongly favored transferring the Zionist central headquarters to America, and he was prepared for a trip to the United States to help. He was full of plans to visit France and Italy and enroll a roster of eminent Jews—Henry Morgenthau, Luigi Luzzatti, and Edmond de Rothschild among them—to present the Jewish case at the eventual peace conference. But both projects were soon abandoned and Weizmann concentrated on what he could do personally in England.

The chronic disorganization of the English Zionist movement took its toll during the war. Weizmann had his connections with both feuding factions, the EZF and the Order of Ancient Maccabeans, but could hardly unite them. He could work additionally with the young Zionists grouped around Ahad Ha'am in London and a budding cadre in Manchester, which was partly an outgrowth of his own influence but quite capable of acting in ways not always to his liking. In 1915 Sokolow and Yehiel Tschlenow came as WZO emissaries and set up a framework for cooperation, with Sokolow remaining to give it authority and leadership; but this proved a far from certain cure for undisciplined individual initiatives. There appeared a number of free-lance agitators for a Jewish unit to join the Allied forces against the Turks in Palestine— Pinchas Rutenberg, Jabotinsky, Joseph Trumpeldor, and (later) Aaron Aaronsohn—with whom Weizmann had markedly equivocal relations. Thus, while acting on his own tack, as one of many Zionist spokesmen, he had to try to control the activities of others so that they supported, or at least did not disrupt, his plans.

In England, as elsewhere, Zionists had to contend with rivals whose claim to represent the Jewish community was no less bold than their own—and often had more general acceptance.[24] Moses Gaster and Leopold Greenberg, Jacob de Haas and Joseph Cowen had for years launched attacks on the Board of Deputies and the Anglo-Jewish Association while at the same time striving to gain more influence in those bodies. Younger men like Harry Sacher, Simon Marks, and Israel Sieff—who took a special interest in their local communal base, Manchester Jewry—tended to react in the same way. These Zionists were part of a broader, brewing rebellion of higher expectations that pitted provincial against London leaders, the newly rich and powerful against the dominant old elite: Rothschilds, Montefiores, Goldsmids, and Montagus. If Zionist aims were now to be presented to the Allies after the war, it might be necessary to show that there was an Anglo-Jewish consensus in favor of them. This required either successful negotiation with the communal establishment or an appeal over its head to the "masses"—or to other opposition leaders.

Efforts along these lines found Weizmann involved, though with much ambivalence. He preferred to project an image of himself as the spokesman of world Jewry, not of a British domestic lobby. For this purpose, organizing the local community to press demands on its government (as Brandeis did in America) would seem unessential—and involved unwelcome pressures to compromise, either with popular moods or the established oligarchy. Attempts to organize British Jewry on a broader base by a comprehensive union of synagogues were, in fact, made by the anti-Zionist, Lucien Wolf, and in his wake by Gaster; Weizmann maintained a cool distance from such efforts. He essentially agreed with the sentiments expressed in Ahad Ha'am's letter to him after Asquith's November 9 speech at the London Guildhall:

> Here, for example, someone proposes in the *J[ewish] Chronicle* calling a general Jewish meeting in London . . . with Lord Rothschild presiding. Can't we tell in advance what the results . . . would be? Those slavish souls could not even grasp what we are aiming at. It would all end in asking Grey [Foreign Secretary Edward Grey] to ask [his Russian counterpart] Sazonov to suggest in the right quarters that it would be proper to ease the oppression of the Jews in Russia a little. And if Grey should promise to do it, there would be such joy in Israel that it would bring men like us to despair in excess of shame and disgust.

In 1917 when Weizmann became president of the EZF, he blocked a proposal that the federation "organise and convene . . . a representative Congress of the Jews of the United Kingdom for the purpose of formulating the claims which the Jewish people should raise at the expected Peace Congress." In its place, he (and Sokolow) secured a resolution declaring "a publicly recognised, legally secured home for the Jewish people in Palestine to be the only solution of the Jewish question." As for winning "Jewish rights" for the Russian Jews, this was a matter for other bodies, if not simply a domestic issue for the Russians themselves to solve.[25]

Even if the Zionists should confine themselves to the issue of the national home in Palestine, they had to contend with the rival activities of other Jewish bodies. One of the first Jewish spokesmen to approach the Foreign Office soon after the war broke out was Israel Zangwill on behalf of his Territorialist organization. Both Weizmann and Ahad Ha'am were critical of this precipitate action, but Weizmann had to take it into account; unlike his old mentor, he was a party politician. Together with Cowen and Greenberg, Weizmann joined in negotiations with Zangwill for a common stand. As a base of compromise, he offered to commit Zionists to a program of regulating Jewish immigration not only to Palestine, but to other havens as well, justifying this in Zionist doctrinal terms as coming under the head of *Gegenwartsarbeit:* a position clearly labeled a concession from the Zionist side. Zangwill's response impressed a surprised Weizmann as fundamentally anti-Zionist and convinced him that there was nothing to hope for in this quarter. He also found it expedient to stress that he was more inclined than Ahad Ha'am to seek solutions for the material hardships, not merely the spiritual malaise, of Jewry—a tactic for which he then had to apologize to his younger associates, who felt he had misrepresented Ahad Ha'am's complex view. On discovering an antinationalist in Zangwill himself, Weizmann dropped any idea of outflanking the Anglo-Jewish oligarchy in this way and joined in discussions with the main establishment agency, the Conjoint Foreign Committee of the Board of Deputies and the Anglo-Jewish Association.[26]

This effort sprang from a meeting with provincial communal leaders in Manchester who were persuaded to include Zionist aims in their postwar program, which was mainly concerned with the emancipation of Jews in Russia. Harry Sacher (a Manchester man then living in London) with the aid of Leon Simon (another young man of Ahad Ha'am and Weizmann's circle) undertook to extend this understanding by an approach to Lucien Wolf, recently named to guide the Conjoint Foreign Committee's work on the pertinent problems. Sacher proposed a modest Ahad Ha'amism—virtually deferring Zionist political aims—as a basis on which all could unite. Wolf responded favorably, judging that a program of limited cultural and humanitarian practical Zionism would not alarm his principals. But he demanded a written formulation and an assurance that the Ahad Ha'am-Weizmann combine Sacher spoke for was authorized to represent the Zionists. On these conditions he indicated that the Conjoint Foreign Committee would invite Sacher's group to a conference—thus, of course, asserting his group's right to act for British Jewry and control access to the government.

Weizmann's riposte took the negotiation out of the context of local jurisdiction and posed it as a world Jewish issue, where the international WZO claimed superior competence. He said an answer to Wolf must be delayed until the arrival of Sokolow and Tschlenow, who alone could authorize him to speak officially. Such jockeying on both sides continued until the two Russians arrived and were able to bring the Conjoint Foreign Committee to a meeting in April 1915, neither side having defined its position in writing in advance.

This was in effect a final chapter in the dealings of Zionists with their Jewish opponents in Britain; it ended in the collapse of attempts to find a common ground. The Zionists refused to accept a formula that ignored their demands for a national status and special facilities for Jewish immigration and settlement in Palestine. The non-Zionists feared that the national status Zionists demanded would sustain antisemitic charges that Diaspora Jews were disloyal citizens and that a special favored status as immigrants and settlers in Palestine would undermine Jewish claims for equal rights in the Diaspora.

Efforts to unite English Jews for common action having ended for the moment, the Zionists and non-Zionists were left to lobby and agitate separately for their rival policies. On the Zionist side, moreover, a wide variety of activists were at work independently—and, often enough, at cross-purposes. They all tried to cultivate favorable public opinion through the press and pamphleteering or by direct contact in such circles as each could reach privately. Weizmann's diligent cultivation of influential British friends was aided by his young comrades, who prepared detailed memoranda to support his interviews and published pamphlets, books, and articles setting forth Zionist views. Sokolow not only acted in concert with these efforts, but lent Weizmann informal legitimation as a spokesman of the official movement. Above all, they tried to reach the policy-making leaders, whose personal leanings might prove decisive at a time when all traditions were being shaken and future political positions were open and uncertain.

A divided Jewish community and disunited Zionist movement were not the only complications that Weizmann had to face.[27] The British public and official circles were no less intricately divided in regard to the pertinent issues, which were many and tangled. There were Liberals and Conservatives, imperialists and Little Englanders in the voting public and the government as well as advocates of a Western Front strategy, opposed by those who favored opening up new fronts in the south and east to break the deadlock of trench warfare. The traditional British view that the Ottoman Empire had to be sustained as a barrier against Russian or French (as well as German) threats to Britain's lifeline to India had been shaken, but no alternative new policy had yet been agreed on. The India Office view of the Ottoman area, and particularly the Persian Gulf, as an extension of its domain (and a possible zone of colonization for India's excess population) differed sharply from that of the military and intelligence officers stationed in Cairo, who were tempted to think of themselves as future viceroys of a vast, new colonial domain of Arab principalities taken over from the Turks. Zionist agents who dealt with the British, with or without authority, had to take different lines according to the special concerns of those whom they approached.

Weizmann was one such agent among many; but as an officer of the EZF and a member of the WZO Greater Action Committee who was also a British academic and (soon after the war began) a British civil servant, he was in touch with an exceptionally wide range of potentially influential circles. This was an advantage of unusual significance, provided that Weizmann had the sensitivity and intelligence to learn the style in which each separate factor had to be addressed for the best effect.

His skill in this basic diplomatic art has been widely and justly praised, but he himself was struck by another, somewhat different advantage: the fact that he spoke to Britons (as he liked to point out to them) in a way quite unlike that of the Anglo-Jewish spokesmen they were used to meeting. He acted without qualification as the spokesman of Jewish national aims, not as a fellow Briton who implicitly challenged them to treat him as one of their own. This allowed him to speak out plainly and bluntly in a manner that had its attraction, not to say its somewhat exotic fascination, for many who were put off by the civil importunities of Anglo-Jews.[28]

It was precisely this difference in Weizmann that helped attract men like Balfour and C. P. Scott as well as Englishwomen who also appreciated the Continental gallantry of this unusual Jew. But it was an effective manner only when combined with understanding of the patterns of thought of those to whom he spoke. Weizmann was a man of sensitivity and always ready to take instruction in the proper style of discourse with others. As he had relied on Buber and Feiwel to style and draft materials in German, he now availed himself of the same service and tutelage from Simon, Sacher, and others in England. Even as late as the Paris Peace Conference, he let himself be instructed by Lewis Namier in the concise style expected in briefs and memoranda that British civil servants and statesmen could be expected to read.

Flexible adjustments in more substantive matters were effectively managed by his own intuition.[29]

The Rothschild family, from the time of the campaign for a university in Palestine, was a major source of Weizmann's political strength. He continued to nurture the connection with Baron Edmond and his son James through the good offices of James' wife Dorothy in London, after James was called up for service in the French army. She undertook to report Weizmann's plans and current activities to the old baron in Paris while keeping Weizmann in touch with the views of her husband and father-in-law. She also brought him into the social circle of her kin, the London Rothschilds, where he gained powerful support. The aging Lord Nathaniel Mayer Rothschild, who had defined his guarded attitude to Zionism in encounters with Herzl in earlier years, remained cool, but his sons, Charles and Lionel Walter (who in 1915 became the second Lord Rothschild), were won as firm supporters. Through the Rothschilds, Weizmann gained access to a wide range of the governing and business elite—among them, Lord Robert Crewe and Neil Primrose, highly placed, leading figures of British society and politics who were related by marriage ties to the Rothschilds.

Weizmann's academic position was another point of contact from which he was able to reach into leading intellectual and political circles. In order to renew his acquaintance with Balfour (who was now a member of the War Council in Asquith's government), Weizmann sought the help of Samuel Alexander, who arranged a meeting in December 1914. Sacher and Simon's circle of old college friends, writers, journalists, and civil servants was also open to Weizmann. He became in this way a known figure among the group who contributed to the new journal, *Round Table,* many of whom came from Lord Alfred Milner's famous "Kindergarten" of young administrators recruited to govern South Africa after the Boer War. They continued to influence opinion in the spirit of a reformed imperialism; Milner himself was eventually able to do so as minister for the colonies in Lloyd George's government.[30]

In Manchester at this time Weizmann met perhaps his most effective new ally, C. P. Scott, editor of the *Manchester Guardian.* Scott had close ties with Lloyd George, then chancellor of the exchequer, and used to meet him regularly at political breakfast conferences. Soon after Asquith's Guildhall speech, Scott was persuaded that the time might be ripe to explore a new status for the Zionists in Palestine, and he undertook to arrange a meeting between Weizmann and Lloyd George. Lloyd George managed to be late for that appointment on December 10, 1914, and asked Weizmann to meet first with another member of the Cabinet, Herbert Samuel. That meeting disclosed to Weizmann a new and surprising source of support, both in the government and the leading circles of Anglo-Jewry.

The meeting with Samuel had a powerful and lasting effect on Weizmann's further dealings with the British leadership. It had a less significant but, nevertheless, appreciable (and irritating) effect, for a period of about two years, in compelling Weizmann to include the irascible Dr. Gaster among the

Jewish leaders involved in his activities. This introduced an element of mutual suspicion and disagreement among the small group who ultimately had to deal with the Britons directly concerned with policy decisions. Gaster was viewed initially—not only by Herbert Samuel but by Sir Mark Sykes, two cardinally important figures for the Zionists—as the most natural Zionist representative to deal with. In fact, his long-standing feuds with other British Zionists and also his lack of confidence in a policy of unequivocal Zionist commitment to the Allies disqualified him for the role and complicated Weizmann's tactical problems in the years 1915–16.[31]

Much more telling was the instruction Weizmann received from Samuel on the mood and operative considerations of current discussions within the government. There were, of course, many matters that Samuel felt obliged to keep secret: information reserved for members of the government and its staff, including, for example, the whole subject of the Sykes-Picot agreement. But Weizmann learned from Samuel, even more than from C. P. Scott, how diverse and often unexpected could be the reactions to his Zionist preaching among critically important Britons. He was soon elaborating more nuanced formulations and differently directed arguments to support the Zionist case.

On one hand, he found that when non-Zionist Jews and previously detached English gentlemen were won over to Zionism, they frequently preferred a more radical definition of aims and a more direct and forthright tactical approach than his own Ahad Ha'amist moderation. Herbert Samuel, at their first meeting, surprised him by announcing not only that he had already discussed Palestine and would present a memorandum to the leading Cabinet officers, but that his formula had been more ambitious than Weizmann's. Supporters on the *Manchester Guardian* included not only Sacher and Scott, but the highly regarded military commentator, Herbert Sidebotham, who took a baldly strategic line and claimed that a British-protected Jewish state or dominion in Palestine was a simple necessity of imperial self-interest for England. The friends Weizmann made in the circle of the younger Rothschilds also tended to respond in this vein at times. But he also ran into contrary opinions in British circles, and in winning support he was sometimes expected to temper the propaganda of his more militant associates, a problem Weizmann continued to face for many years thereafter.

Thus he learned from Samuel that Grey, the foreign secretary, had listened to Samuel's argument with sympathy (though Asquith received it with sardonic amazement), but did not find it immediately practical, or readily accept the broad extension of imperial responsibility, or the clash with French claims that it probably entailed. Samuel himself had lowered his sights accordingly. Even the Tory Balfour tempered his philosophic responsiveness to the idea of a Jewish restoration with cautious awareness of the costs and complications Britain might incur. This made him prefer to involve others, particularly, the Americans, in sharing the burden. Finally, on the Liberal side, C. P. Scott alerted Weizmann to the anti-imperialist scruples that had to be respected, both in public opinion and in government circles.

The background of such varied inhibitions goes far back in the English military and diplomatic tradition. The fleet, not the land forces, served as Britain's first line of defense; throughout the nineteenth century, England had relied on a Continental balance of power, and, wherever possible, subsidized allies in Europe instead of sending troops to protect its interests. The empire, governed on similar principles, was protected by British naval dominance and ruled wherever possible by native potentates under proconsular supervision. Budgetary considerations contributed largely to this policy of colonial indirect rule.

These were lessons that Weizmann quickly learned.[32] He wrote to Scott:

> The British cabinet [Samuel had reported] is not only sympathetic towards the Palestinian aspirations of the Jews, but would like to see those aspirations realized. I understand Great Britain would be willing even to be the initiator of a proposal to that effect at the peace conference. But at the same time Great Britain would not like to be involved in any responsibilities.

The source of British hesitations was defined in what Samuel had told him of the foreign secretary's views:

> Sir E. Grey is in full sympathy . . . but would not like to commit himself . . . to . . . a British protectorate over Palestine. He thinks that such a step may lead to difficulties with France, and secondly, may go against the opinion of a certain school of liberals in this country.

Since Scott himself belonged to the school in question, it was necessary for Weizmann to frame suitable arguments in order to meet the scruples and reduce the burdens implied in a pro-Zionist policy for the Liberals.

He met the first problem by proposing that Britain install itself as protector, or trustee, on behalf of the Jewish national home rather than simply annexing Palestine as a crown colony. He further argued the strategic issue in calculatedly negative terms. Instead of stressing Britain's strategic interest in Palestine positively (and the utility of Jews as proxies), he urged, negatively, that it would be more costly and less effective to try to defend vital interests against another major power that would hold Palestine—the defensive hinterland of both the Suez Canal and the land route from the Mediterranean to Mesopotamia. This was an argument to which even a Liberal might respond now that Turkey could no longer serve Britain as a buffer. Finally, Weizmann formulated a position that remained his essential policy throughout his subsequent career:

> I therefore thought that the middle course could be adopted . . . viz., the Jews take over the country; the whole burden of organisation falls on them, but for the next ten or fifteen years they work under a temporary British protectorate.

With this rather bold proposal, Weizmann was in effect seeking to define a policy not yet defined in British quarters—one implicitly barred by the previous decision of the WZO in favor of neutrality. Levin and Magnes in America were not alone in their opposition to Weizmann's one-sided British orientation. An English Zionist like Gaster was also not prepared to stake Zionist hopes on England alone: he expected a negotiated peace that would leave Germany with at least partial influence on Palestine's future. Sokolow, who was assigned to work on the Allied side for Zionist aims during the war, and even Jabotinsky, who took on himself the same role as a free lance, were not as ready as Weizmann to declare a clear preference for Britain (rather than the Allies generally) as protector of the future Jewish national home. Jabotinsky's memoirs of this period report that he met Foreign Minister Théophile Delcassé in January 1915 at Weizmann's request and that the report of the cool reception he received decided Weizmann in favor of an exclusively British orientation—a decision Jabotinsky felt was regrettable. In this atmosphere it was politic for Weizmann to observe a certain restraint in publicly stating his views—at least until he could show more tangible prospects of eliciting a definite British pro-Zionist policy.[33]

Such a demonstration was still to seek in 1915–16. Weizmann had clearly achieved significant advances in presenting Zionist views to influential Britons. Nevertheless, he was still addressing himself to large, general issues, without direct application to the immediate policy decisions the government had to make. The latter were matters often restricted to the closed circle of government committees, bureaus, and staff- and line-command structures responsible for conducting the war. In September 1915 Weizmann himself became a part of the machine that was conducting the British war effort—but still without direct access to those who were making policy on the strategy of the war and related postwar political issues. The effect of his recruitment to the civil service was to place in question, and then to confirm, the confidence leading Britons could place in his loyalty and effectiveness—but not, for some considerable time, to acquaint him with important policy initiatives crucial to his campaign on behalf of Zionism.

Weizmann's war work arose out of his earlier research in organic chemistry.[34] The British navy found itself facing a shortage of cordite, smokeless gunpowder in whose manufacture the chemical acetone was used. Previous dependence on imports for this material now, it appeared, would have to be largely replaced by a domestic source if one could be found. Acetone had been one of the by-products of the fermentation experiments Weizmann's laboratory had carried out with a bacillus isolated by Fernbach. Weizmann's quarrel with Perkin had also occasioned a break with Fernbach; thereafter, further experiments were conducted by each team separately. The British and French governments were interested and commissioned pilot projects from the competing scientists. It was a competition in which the approach of Weizmann and his team proved decisively superior, the one best suited for production on an industrial scale.

Weizmann's patented process was first "sold" to the Admiralty—now headed by Balfour (after Churchill's withdrawal following the disastrous naval adventure at Gallipoli). This was a transaction that raised delicate issues for Weizmann. Hoping as he did to play a leading role as a Zionist negotiator with the British government, he could not easily accept the position of an ordinary civil service employee or treat his scientific contribution to the war effort as a simple commercial transaction. Although he certainly did not conceive it was a quid pro quo in relation to anticipated Zionist gains—and he emphatically discounted the myth to this effect propagated by Lloyd George's memoirs—his sense of the dignity he had to maintain did not permit him to deal with the matter in a routine manner. He therefore set no price on his patent, but transferred it to the government on the understanding that appropriate compensation would be awarded after the war, as the government saw fit. Meanwhile, he was granted the funds to develop his process for industrial production, which required taking a leave from the university to supervise this work for the Admiralty. Shortly afterward he was engaged (through the good offices once more of Scott) by the Ministry of Munitions, now headed by Lloyd George. The ministry took over breweries to produce acetone, and Weizmann's work was extended beyond directing a laboratory to supervising production on an industrial scale.

Weizmann's drive went beyond this special assignment, even without reference to his Zionist activities.[35] The Ministry of Munitions had appointed him to an advisory commission on dyestuffs chemistry and the general development of chemical technology in Britain in May, before he joined its ranks as a salaried officer. He entered the civil service with sweeping plans, which he spelled out at once, for advancing the competence of Britain and the Allies in applied chemistry during and after the war. He proposed himself for the task of a tour of Europe among Allied and neutral centers of chemical research in order to forward these aims. In all these endeavors, he had the warm support of Scott, who was in direct communication with Lloyd George. But such favor from high quarters, over the heads of his immediate superiors, could hardly endear him to the middle-level bureaucrats with whom he worked. Scott also suspected that hostility to a Jew and a foreigner caused the delays that held up Weizmann's European tour, the attempts to hand over control of acetone production to others, and similar obstructions that, Scott felt, would never have been tried against an Englishman of the in-group. His prompt support, and perhaps Lloyd George's interest in Weizmann's potential political usefulness, overcame such problems on occasion. But the general, long-range sympathy Weizmann's aims may have enjoyed did not at the moment tie in with an immediate tactical advantage for Britain that might have led to his being taken into account in discussions of policy-in-the-making.

Other Zionists who came into contact with official British circles closely connected with policy-making were those men, fairly marginal to the Zionist establishment, who tried to form a Jewish military force to fight on the side of the Allies: Rutenberg, Jabotinsky, Trumpeldor, and (later) Aaron Aaronsohn. Rutenberg, once an engineer at the Putilov munitions factory in Petrograd, was widely known for his part in the 1905 march of Putilov workers—

led by Father George Gapon—on the czar's Winter Palace and for having brought about the execution of the priest when he discovered him to be a police informer. Rutenberg's emergence as a Zionist activist in Italy at the very beginning of the war was unexpected and viewed with some suspicion by Weizmann—not to speak of Ahad Ha'am, who strongly opposed a militarist-diplomatic strategy and tactics adopted in emulation of Garibaldi and Cavour. Weizmann readily agreed that it was necessary to rein in Rutenberg's propaganda in France and Britain and thought that he could best do so directly, by himself staying in contact with the project in order to control it.[36]

A similar problem arose for Weizmann in regard to Jabotinsky, a Zionist of unquestioned credentials even when he took an independent line. Given his own pro-British leanings and without such inhibitions as applied to the case of Rutenberg, Weizmann found it a delicate task to balance his personal sympathy for Jabotinsky's project with the reserve he had to maintain in order to work with Ahad Ha'am and the officially neutral WZO spokesmen.

The onset of war threw Jabotinsky into the same state of excited uncertainty as other Zionists; as a journalist, he met the situation by securing a commission from a leading Moscow liberal journal to report on sentiment in Western Europe.[37] When Turkey joined in the hostilities, he responded decisively to the event, according to his memoirs, becoming a firm partisan of the postwar partition of the Ottoman Empire as the only hope for the future of Palestine and of Zionism. He also arranged to extend his assignment to include North Africa and so came to Alexandria in December 1914. There he found that some twelve thousand Jewish refugees, expelled from Palestine as non-Ottoman citizens or enemy aliens, had landed shortly before his arrival. He joined the committee organized to aid them and spent some time as a volunteer welfare worker in the barracks where they were housed. As early as November 1914 he had written friends about his idea of a Jewish unit to fight in Palestine for England or for England and France, and he now hoped to recruit support among the refugees. He found a crucial ally at once in Joseph Trumpeldor.

However, the two organizers soon learned that on the British side the current strategy was such that they could not hope for any offensive into Palestine that they might join. There were some British officers with Arab experience and contacts who had favored an armed descent on the Syrian coast at Alexandretta in the hope of raising an Arab revolt against the Turks, but mature consideration led to abandoning this idea. The Bunsen Committee, set up to consider policy toward the Ottomans in London, concluded that keeping the Turkish realm intact would be the best course; but if the Ottoman Empire were to be broken up, occupying Haifa rather than Alexandretta would better serve British interests. The military command at Cairo adopted a passive rather than forward policy, confining itself to building up a force in Egypt for defense against the Turks at the Suez Canal and for repelling attacks from Libya in the western desert.

But there were other factors unexpectedly favorable to the idea of recruiting a Jewish unit to serve with the British. The Russian consul in Cairo had begun pressing for the conscription of refugees who were Russian citizens into the czar's service—a prospect that was as repellent in Cairo as it was later to be for Russian immigrants in London. Service in a Jewish unit under British command could be an attractive alternative for the Jews and an escape hatch from embarrassment for the British. What was even more to the point, the Cairo command was being asked to supply land reinforcements for the Gallipoli campaign, which had been undertaken to relieve the Russians of Turkish pressure in the Caucasus, only to run into its own difficulties. The Cairo command was then recruiting Egyptians as a native labor force to back up combat units manned by Empire troops, and the same service was offered to the refugees in Alexandria. Specifically, they were given the prospect of forming a Jewish unit of mule drivers to bring supplies and ammunition to the frontline troops in Gallipoli.

This was not a proposal that suited the political designs of Jabotinsky—neither in its assignment to the Gallipoli front rather than Palestine nor in its demeaning shape of a labor corps, not a combat unit. Trumpeldor, who had won his medals and his commission—and lost an arm—as a Russian soldier at Port Arthur in the Russo-Japanese War, felt differently. In a war, any service anywhere that contributed significantly to victory was acceptable and honorable. (He later applied the same principle in civilian life as a leader among the socialist-Zionist pioneers who built the self-defense force and communal and cooperative settlements of the Jews in Palestine.) He agreed to the proposal and became the guiding spirit of the Zion Mule Corps that served in Gallipoli. Jabotinsky, having received a cable from Rutenberg asking for a meeting, returned to Europe to seek other ways of creating a Jewish military force to fight for Palestine with the Allies.

The propaganda that Rutenberg and Jabotinsky initiated in Italy, France, and England was disappointingly profitless for the immediate object—to create a Jewish armed force, although it won friends for the ultimate aim. However, in the Jewish community it stirred up active hostility. Rutenberg went to America, where he was persuaded to drop Jewish army agitation in view of America's neutrality; instead, he was drawn into the campaign for a Jewish congress. Jabotinsky encountered bitter frustration in continued work for his idea in France and England as well as on his return to Russia. In the summer of 1915 he attended a meeting of the WZO Greater Action Committee in Copenhagen, where his project and the service of Zionists in Gallipoli in the Zion Mule Corps were explicitly condemned. Jabotinsky responded by offering to withdraw from association with the Zionists in order to conduct his work without involving the WZO. He was able to get his editor to post him as a weekly correspondent in London, where he hoped to pursue this purpose. There he joined Weizmann in bachelor quarters, which they shared in the fall of 1915; Weizmann's government-commissioned chemical research and Zionist labors had temporarily separated him from his family, who stayed behind in Manchester until the next year.

Jabotinsky's account of that time notes with appreciation that Weizmann was one of the few Zionists in London who had any sympathy for his project and at a certain juncture lent it critical support. However, he notes a characteristic difference between his own and Weizmann's approach, which he seems to take as a matter of contrasting temperaments rather than of their respective styles and conceptions of leadership. He reports Weizmann as saying, regarding his caution in supporting the military strategy of his roommate:

> I cannot work like you, in an atmosphere where everybody is angry and can hardly stand me. Such daily friction would poison my life and kill any desire to work.[38]

Whether temperament or the different role that circumstances later prescribed for each is responsible, this is an apt description of the divergent Zionist careers of the two men. Even in 1915–16 Weizmann's Zionist activity, highly independent and individual as it was, already depended too much on being accepted as a recognized leader of the movement to permit him openly to back Jabotinsky's irregular and unpopular campaign.

Weizmann was even less connected with another Zionist project tied to the British military—indeed, for some considerable time he remained ignorant of its existence. Late in October 1916 Aaron Aaronsohn arrived secretly in London to reestablish ties for the espionage activity he and his friends had been conducting on behalf of the British for almost a year in Palestine. After two months of debriefing and discussions with British officers, he sailed to join the staff in Cairo for the invasion of Palestine, leaving the locally active Zionists barely aware of his presence in London—though he did write a lengthy "confession" to his American Zionist and non-Zionist friends and supporters of the agricultural research station, explaining the painful process of his turning to the repugnant role of a spy in revulsion against the Turks.[39]

In Cairo as an intelligence agent for the staff of a military force actively engaged on the Egyptian-Palestinian front, Aaronsohn was exceptionally close to the officers directly concerned with immediately significant strategic and tactical decisions. His detailed knowledge of the area—gained in scientific exploration and in the Turkish service over past years of combating locust incursions—was of directly applicable importance. Like Weizmann, he, too, was sensitive to the political effect of his own position in relation to his British superiors. He resisted their natural inclination to treat him as one more mercenary agent hired for his local expertise and contacts by refusing to be paid on this basis. Furthermore, he insisted on being the sole channel for issuing orders to his espionage group behind the enemy lines, against the British intention of having their own officer in direct control. (The British sensitivity to political-due bills that unwanted allies might present for postwar payment, after having taken part in the conquest of Palestine, was similarly shown toward the units the French and Italians sent to share in the offensive.) Yet, in spite of such an advantageous situation, Aaronsohn was able to exert no more apparent influence on major decisions important to the Zionist cause than the other Zionist activists of the moment.

What he, like the others, did achieve was to win over as friends, and gain the confidence of, a number of influential Britons with whom his military service brought him into close, confidential working relations. The same can be observed about all those who were able to serve in the immediately important military arena—where pressing decisions were to be made—while seeking to advance their Zionist aims. Their own nationalist political purposes were dismissed as an unwelcome, diversionary intrusion, or—in the case of Weizmann's top-level political contacts in particular—treated with the passive goodwill shown to untimely projects by sympathetic, but responsible, leaders. At the same time the respectful attention these men received because of their previous professional and personal status ripened into esteem and trust based on common effort. Thus, Weizmann's academic career, Jabotinsky's reputation as a journalist, Rutenberg's political and professional merits, and Aaronsohn's fame among agriculturists and paleologists opened doors for them to many men of influence: for Weizmann, it was C. P. Scott and for Jabotinsky it was Wickham Steed of *The Times* (London) who were accessible on this basis; and it was Rutenberg's revolutionary past and engineering work on publicly funded projects that made him welcome among Italian socialists as well as leading statesmen like Luigi Luzzatti. Other men who worked with Aaronsohn or Trumpeldor and became supporters of Zionism—like Colonel John Patterson (the commander of the Zion Mule Corps), Leopold Amery of the War Office, Josiah Wedgwood, and William Ormsby-Gore—developed the same kind of affection for their clients, half patronizing, half admiring, as in the better-known case of Britons who worked with the contemporary Arab revolt. In neither instance was a romantic, benevolent attraction directly convertible in political coin. It became effective politically only when the twists and turns of warfare made the Jews or the Arabs an immediately effective element in the world struggle—particularly when the British thought they had something to fear immediately from alienating one or the other. By 1916 such considerations were already affecting current decisions both in London and in the field of military and diplomatic battle.

Even before the war broke out, there had been gestures by the Arabs suggesting that they would welcome British aid in resisting Turkish pressure on them.[40] Not only Syrian refugee politicians in Cairo, but Abdullah, son of the Sherif Hussein in Mecca, had made advances; and (as noted earlier) there were officers in the Cairo staff who were attracted by the possibilities of this combination. The India Office, on the other hand, viewed such adventurism with dread because of the repercussions it might set off among Moslems in India. In the event, the pressure of Western Front warfare and the sober conclusions of the Bunsen Committee quickly suppressed thoughts of any offensive from Egypt, and the force assembled settled down to passive defense behind the Suez Canal.

What altered this policy was the Russian request to relieve it of Turkish pressure by an attack on the Dardanelles and, in the fall of 1915, the need to land troops in Salonica after the Bulgarians entered into an alliance with the Central Powers. These military engagements touched off a series of negotiations among the Allies and with others whom they hoped to bring over to their side. Given their long-standing policy of propping up Turkey as a buffer against more formidable rivals, the British were rather less prepared for the division of Turkish domains after the war than were other Allies. The Bunsen Committee, on the whole, advised against any partition of Turkey in Asia; but if other Allied demands had to be satisfied, it advocated basing British defense on the area adjacent to Egypt, through at least an international (rather than French) regime in Palestine and British control south of a line from Haifa to Mesopotamia and the Persian Gulf. Mark Sykes, who had been an aide to the Bunsen Committee, was assigned the task of negotiating with the French along these lines in December 1915.

By that time the British were already involved in tentative discussions with Arab spokesmen that had to be taken into account. Early in the war the British had learned that a posture of defense in Egypt from behind the Canal allowed the Turks to advance unhampered across the Sinai Desert and harass them seriously at the Suez line. If the Arabs of the peninsula supplied camels and other aid, the Turkish assault would enjoy significant advantages. To prevent this, it might be worthwhile to encourage the Sherif Hussein to lay claim to the caliphate (to which his family's descent from the Prophet's lineage established some title), thus rejecting the hegemony of Turkey and the holy war (*jihad*) that it had proclaimed against the Allies. But this modest beginning soon grew to larger proportions. Syrian nationalists based in Damascus and with ties to similar Arab opposition forces in Mesopotamia made contact with the Sherif and brought him into their compact. This meant that he expanded his claims on the English from simple protection of his position in the Hejaz to one for "independence" (which might in large areas be compatible with British "protection") over the whole extent of Arab-dominated lands. It also implied that, instead of the previously contemplated neutrality and repudiation of the *jihad,* the Arabs now committed themselves conditionally to an armed revolt against Turkey; that is, if their demands were accepted and if the military situation permitted.

When Hussein first proposed this bargain, in July–August 1915, the official British response was to take it as a ridiculously exaggerated claim, but one to be temporized with in order to avoid alienating the Arabs. Yet, for other Britons on the staff in Cairo and Khartoum, Hussein's initiative revived the vision of a "North African or Near Eastern viceroyalty including Egypt and the Sudan and across the way from Aden to Alexandretta [that] would surely compare . . . with India itself." Their inclination to respond favorably was soon reinforced by a more powerful incentive, that of an apprehended danger felt to be so imminent as to provoke hasty reactions verging on panic. An Arab defector from the Turkish force in Gallipoli reported in October that unless the Arab nationalists received "immediate assurance" of a satisfactory response to Hussein's demands, they were about to "throw themselves into the hands of Germany who he says had furnished them fulfillment of all their demands." The Foreign Office responded to the alarm that was sounded from Cairo with a vague, general instruction that indicated what was acceptable in the terms proposed by Hussein and suggesting that detailed boundary negotiations be undertaken, but—in view of the reported urgency—leaving the local officials to formulate the precise response in such a way as not to alienate the Arab chieftain. What emerged, without reference to London for approval, was the McMahon letter of October 24, 1915, which accepted without further ado the boundaries proposed—with the famous exception, modification, and reservation about whose interpretation controversy still rages.[41]

The cause of this precipitate action, as McMahon ruefully protested within the following year, was the urgent demand of the military command, hard-pressed in Gallipoli, to avert the added difficulties threatened by effective German propaganda among wavering Arabs in the Turkish forces. The price Britain paid was to become continually more involved in both military and political support for its faltering Arab allies; they not only fell short of the aid Britain expected of them, but required greater British efforts to rescue them from the difficulties that befell their eventual revolt.

What helped produce not merely greater British involvement, but sympathetic commitment—notwithstanding the increasingly apparent burdensomeness of the Arab connection—was a shift in the defense strategy of the command in Egypt.[42] In November 1915 Lord Horatio Kitchener, the minister for war, drew his conclusions from the early Turkish raids up to the Canal and ordered a new defense line to be set up ten kilometers east of it. A new commander, Sir Archibald Murray, sent to carry out a withdrawal from Gallipoli, also began a slow advance into the Sinai toward Palestine, laying a rail line and digging wells to supply his troops as they went. Meanwhile, the Sherif and his sons, who had been playing a double game with both the Turks and the British, finally threw off the mask and began the Arab revolt in June 1916 with attacks on Turkish positions in the Arabian Peninsula. They soon were checked, after initial successes, and had to appeal for British help, abandoning their previous reluctance to admit infidel soldiery onto the sacred precincts of the Prophet's native land. In this way they acquired the invaluable accession of Lawrence of Arabia, among others, Britons whose fascination with the desert Arabs was deepened by years of ensuing close cooperation with their protégés.

The Arab rebels also counted on a new British offensive against the Turks, whose beginnings might be discerned in Murray's slow advance into the Sinai. Late in November 1916 the offensive began. Soon after, in December, a new government headed by David Lloyd George came into power in London. This combination of factors initiated a new period, as the Jewish element in the strategic picture was brought into sharper focus. The relations of Zionists with the London British government now played out a scenario similar to that between the Cairo headquarters and the Hejazi leaders.

A romantic attraction to the Jews, nourished by a cult of the Bible in English tradition, had even deeper roots than the fascination with the mystical desert and the Bedouin, seen as the noble savage. So, too, the legendary menace of

the ubiquitous, eternally wandering Jew cropped up in new versions suggested by current history. All the leading Zionists who worked at influencing
British policy sought, each in his own way, to play on these strings. Sokolow
worked throughout the war on a history of Zionism, tracing its roots back to
Christian millenarianism, primarily in England, without neglecting France.
Weizmann found a romantic idealism, arising out of childhood familiarity
with the landscapes and epic characters of the Bible, more effective in opening
up British leaders to his arguments than considerations of military and political strategy. Jabotinsky, for his part, discovered that Europeans of the upper
strata had only the vaguest notion of Zionism and reacted to it in conversation with the kind of interest they might extend to talk of vegetarianism, but
they became attentive when he brought up the subject of a Jewish military
contribution to the war effort. The response each noted was characteristic of
the contacts each made at different times and places.[43]

At the outbreak of war and following Turkey's choice to side with the Central Powers, articles in the press and Samuel in private talks in Whitehall
proposed a pro-Zionist policy for Britain in positive humanitarian and political terms. Weizmann and other Zionist leaders had long been accustomed to
make their case on negative grounds as well, presenting Zionism as a way to
divert Jewish youth from the social radicalism so much disliked by many
Gentiles and to keep unwelcome Jewish immigrants away from England's
door. But such arguments, both positive and negative, were too general and
remote to have much effect on decisions taken during the war. By the beginning of 1916, however, the Jews were beginning to have a clearer, more present relation to matters of immediate concern for British policy—especially
so, as a perceived threat.

There were long-standing difficulties, both real and imaginary, that British
officers took note of in relation to Jews from the beginning of the war. Above
all, of course, the virtually universal hostility to Russia among Jews was a
nuisance even in dealing with Anglo-Jewry and a serious handicap in other,
neutral countries. As Britain became increasingly dependent on credit in
America, this grew to be a critical matter. Also, being allied with Russia had
led some Britons to give credence to the Russian apologetics and anti-Jewish
propaganda produced in rebuttal of protests against pogroms and legal
oppression. The suspicion and hostility to Jews engendered in this way
extended to the case of Jews in the Ottoman Empire after the Young Turk
revolution; the myth that a Jewish-Masonic conspiracy (backed by German
finance in one version, by the French in another) was the moving force in
that upheaval and in the subsequent disturbance of the British position and
interests was widely accepted among experts close to the Foreign Office.
Finally, when Britain was compelled to resort to conscription in January 1916
and immigrant Jews, exempted as aliens, seemed to be profiting by the war,
the pressure of rising popular antisemitism was felt by government circles.
These were developments that gradually forced the Jews upon the attention
of policymakers as a force that had to be dealt with urgently.[44]

The problem in America was complicated for the Allies by the fact that bankers of German origin were quite prominent in the Jewish community and in Wall Street, and had been able, for example, to bring about the abrogation of the Russo-American trade treaty as recently as 1913. Also, the Yiddish press was dominated by socialist journalists whose hostility to Russia was especially fierce and who tended to see the war as an imperialist imbroglio in which all sides were at fault. The French were the first to take action against the successful propaganda of Germany in the Jewish community, in which an old German Zionist associate of Weizmann's, Dr. Isaac Straus, worked closely with Ambassador Johann-Heinrich Bernstorff. In November 1915 they sent Professor Victor Basch (a socialist, historian, and Zionist sympathizer who had lent a hand to Weizmann's university campaign) to work among the American Jews, where he paid particular attention to the downtown proletariat and its socialist organizers and sent back reports documenting the difficult situation. He also offered a partial solution: although the Allies could do little to alter Russian policy, which was the main problem, there was another possibility—they might gain sympathy by satisfying Jewish aspirations in regard to Palestine. Underlying this proposal was an estimate of powerful pro-Zionist sentiment in American Jewry, recently demonstrated by the battle over convening the American Jewish Congress.

French Jews who joined a government-inspired committee for action among their coreligionists in neutral countries made sure that Lucien Wolf received reports of Basch's mission. He felt it his duty to pass on his evaluation to the Foreign Office, and in December 1915 he sent a memorandum endorsing Basch's analysis. He stressed the need to alter Russia's behavior toward the Jews if the dangerous pro-German leanings of some American Jews were to be checked; but also, speaking as a non-Zionist, he confirmed the strength of Zionist sentiments and agreed that an appropriate statement favoring Jewish interests in Palestine would be effective as a measure to gain sympathy.[45]

The British Foreign Office began getting other appraisals, solicited and unsolicited, that reinforced their concern about Jewish, particularly American Jewish, sentiment. Edgar Suarès, a leader of the Alexandrian Jewish community, warned of German activity seeking to win Jewish support, and as a non-Zionist closely connected with American Jewish relief efforts in his area independently confirmed the analysis and prescription advanced by Wolf. From America Horace Kallen sent a similar proposal to gain sympathy for the Allies by a pro-Zionist statement, which he framed in positive political terms. The responses from British personnel in the field and on the staff were often marked by a lively awareness and acceptance of then-current anti-Jewish clichés. Some, like the ambassador in Washington, discounted the Zionist strength among Jews. Ambassador Cecil Spring-Rice, in fact, suggested that American Jews be warned that their attitude would provoke antisemitic reactions against their brethren in England and other Allied lands. A different line was taken by Foreign Office staff experts with background in Eastern countries and their own special phobias about Jews. Commenting on the suggestion forwarded from Alexandria, Hugh J. O'Beirne wrote in late February

1916 that an appealing offer to the Jews on Palestine might cause them to
withdraw support from the Young Turk regime, "which would then auto-
matically collapse." He was aware, perhaps from talks with Samuel, of Zionist feelings against an international administration contemplated for Palestine in the Sykes-Picot talks and their leanings toward a British protectorate,
"which seems impracticable." He therefore proposed the following:

> While there would necessarily be an international administration of some
> kind in Jerusalem itself, it is conceivable that in the rest of Palestine the Jews
> could be given special colonizing facilities which in time would make them
> strong enough to cope with the Arab element, when the management of inter-
> nal affairs might be placed in their hands under America's protection.[46]

Meanwhile, Jabotinsky had gained access to the War Office through the
recommendation of Colonel Patterson and proposed an expedient of his own:
without committing themselves to a statement touching on Palestine's political future, the English might make their appeal to Jewish sentiment by simply taking up his proposal to create a Jewish brigade to fight the Turks there.
The War Office referred this matter to the Foreign Office as being fraught with
political implications, and the Foreign Office referred it back as a matter for
the military to decide.

In the meantime Lucien Wolf did not rest idle. When the Foreign Service
showed extreme reluctance to press Russia, notwithstanding Wolf's belief
that the French were now ready to do so, he fell back on the Palestine issue.
On March 3, 1916 he submitted a draft of a Conjoint Foreign Committee
statement on Palestine, which was essentially the one he had offered without
success as the basis for a united stand with the Zionists. He now intended to
propose it to the French committee and wanted government approval to present it to a mass meeting in London's East End in order "to impress, especially
upon the foreign element, the necessity of making every possible sacrifice for
the cause of the Allies, with which all Jewish hopes are bound up"—a reference to the current agitation about the exemption of foreign Jews from
conscription.[47]

Wolf's formula set off a discussion in the government: some doubted that
any action at all should be taken, since the Jews themselves were so divided;
others argued that a more positive pro-Zionist stand than Wolf's was needed
to sway the Jewish public. Instead of giving Wolf the approval he solicited, it
was decided to consult the Allies. Lord Crewe, acting for the ailing Grey, sent
a cable in the Foreign Secretary's name to Petrograd, where Sykes and Fran-
çois Georges-Picot were consulting the Russians on the agreement to partition the Turkish Empire. The text of Wolf's formula was included, with the
comment that it seemed "unobjectionable" but might be more effective if
O'Beirne's formula rather then Wolf's were used:

> [W]e consider that the scheme might be made far more attractive to the
> majority of Jews if it held out to them the prospect that when in course of

time the Jewish colonists in Palestine [have] grown strong enough to cope
with the Arab population, they may be allowed to take the management of
the internal affairs of Palestine (with the exception of Jerusalem and the Holy
Places) into their own hands.

The Russian response was favorable, consistent with their earlier assurances
to the Zionist spokesman, Tschlenow, and their concern that Catholic France
not gain sole dominion over Palestine and the Holy Places. It was just this
intimation that French traditional claims in the Holy Land might be again
reduced to no more than a share in an international enclave, limited essentially to Jerusalem, that no doubt produced a cool rejection in Paris.[48]
    After some time Wolf was informed that French objections, referring to
the divided opinion among Jews, precluded the approval he sought. He must
have become aware that the situation in America, which he himself had diag-
nosed for the government, suggested an even more chilling conclusion: if
Zionist sympathy was dominant among Jews, the Zionists might be the ones
to deal with, not the group Lucien Wolf spoke for. With this possibility in
mind, he visited Baron Edmond in France in July and gained his support for
a new effort to reach an agreement in the community. James de Rothschild,
back in London with a war wound, pressed the issue. He convened the parties
at his home on August 17, only to see a further sharpening of the differences
between them. Moreover, the fact emerged in correspondence with Wolf and
was made public that, while seeking agreement, he had already unilaterally
sent his own proposal to the Foreign Office. The result was that when his
effort to bring the parties together had failed, James de Rothschild found himself an aggrieved party aligned with the Zionists.[49]

In the meantime another dispute that involved some Zionists drew public
attention.[50] Jabotinsky seized the opportunity of the feeling aroused by conscription and the exemption enjoyed by alien immigrants to step up his advocacy of a Jewish military unit, both in a public campaign and in private interviews and written submissions. The result was to make him as well as the few
English Zionists like Cowen and Greenberg who supported the same
approach, publicly and privately, the objects of loud and furious popular
attack in the East End. The established Jewish notables, for their part, were
worried by the antisemitic reaction that immigrant Jews might arouse, and a
Rothschild-initiated recruiting committee was set up to deal with the problem—but to no avail. In the spring Wolf once more proposed a different expedient: to set up another committee made up of prominent East European
Jews, who might be better able to address the East End population in language
they understood. Weizmann was named to this committee, and Jabotinsky
also joined.
    By the spring consideration was being given to drastic measures, like com-
pelling Jews who claimed exemption from serving in the British forces to do
so in the Russian army. Herbert Samuel now returned to the Cabinet as home
secretary, and had to deal with this matter. He announced the intention to

apply the draconian alternative in the House of Commons on July 6, 1916, causing alarm both in the East End and the established Jewish community as well as no little disturbance in the Liberal and Labor public. Alternative ways of handling the problem were offered in Parliament, relying on persuasion and inducements like expedited citizenship instead of threats of deportation. Lucien Wolf, noting that Zionists like Sokolow and Weizmann veiled themselves in silence but could not oppose the government or share the East End's recalcitrance, suggested that they be brought into the new Russian-Jewish recruitment committee whose formation he proposed to Samuel. Weizmann and his colleagues were able to serve as a mediating force between the government and the East End, their own natural constituency. They obtained a delay in conscription in order to attempt a new recruitment of volunteers, and they suggested concessions in the procedures of conscription if it should be applied.

Weizmann in this way temporarily retained the confidence and good will of both the government and the Jewish public at a time when others were losing their hold on one or the other. Jabotinsky worked along with the Russian-Jewish committee and supported its proposals, but he also embarked on a renewed campaign of his own. He argued that recruitment would succeed best if alien immigrant Jews were allowed to form units of their own instead of merging in the general forces. Since, as he had learned, the army was unwilling to form "foreign legions," except for home defense, he proposed a Jewish legion as a combat force for "Home and Heim," that is, as a territorial militia in England and as an expeditionary force on the Egyptian-Palestinian front when needed. His active agitation for this aim, which he believed would now be welcomed as an honorable alternative to forced service with the Russians, only brought him under new attack. His meetings were broken up by organized hecklers and barrages of potatoes, and all sections of the community leadership united in repudiating him. The few who did not and actively and openly supported his drive—or even, like his main patron, Cowen, spoke out in support of the government's hard-line threat of deportation—suffered the same kind of hostility and rejection.

Through all this Weizmann did the work of a mediator, reasonably well trusted by all sides and known to be *persona grata* in government circles. When Lloyd George took over the War Office, Weizmann helped Jabotinsky get new consideration for his project by using his customary private channel—an approach through C. P. Scott—with, however, the same result as earlier, an eventual rejection. But in the summer that followed, Weizmann took no part in the public campaign for a Jewish legion that aroused such antagonism. Instead, he confined himself to the work of the Russian-Jewish committee, trying to moderate the government's harsh demands on the East End. So, too, he was able to appease the outraged Zionist clubs who threatened to abandon the EZF when its president, Cowen, publicly supported Herbert Samuel's proposed sanctions against alien immigrants who refused military service. In the aftermath of that squabble, Cowen withdrew his candidacy for reelection as president the next year, and in February 1917 Weizmann became the EZF president by common consent.

The year 1916 ended with a combination of developments that radically improved the conditions for Zionist activity, especially in approaching the government. Even the burden of Jabotinsky's long series of setbacks was lightened. His task of demonstrating success in recruiting the needed number for his proposed Jewish corps was greatly alleviated when veterans of the Zion Mule Corps, evacuated from Gallipoli, came to London and were reenlisted as a unit. More to the point was the preparation of an offensive into Palestine with an attack at El Arish. But the most critical change was the new Lloyd George government installed in December, headed by a prime minister known to favor breaking the Western deadlock by opening an eastern front, and also a man personally well disposed to the Zionist cause. With him a new Cabinet entered office in which the Zionists had a sudden accession of powerful friends, soon to include Balfour as foreign secretary. The long-considered option of dealing directly with Zionists in order to win the sympathy of Jews in neutral America and in the East now took on tangible form. Mark Sykes, a central operative in the whole range of British policy decisions on the Ottoman area during the war, now concerned himself more intensively with the Jewish factor and became the channel for negotiations with the Zionists.

The ground was prepared for the major developments of the year 1917. The critical events that marked that year—the Russian Revolution and America's entry into the war—found the Jewish involvement already in the foreground of attention.

The Critical Year

In 1917 the political fortunes of Zionism were enhanced and Weizmann gained general recognition as the paramount Zionist leader in England. The changes in the British government in late 1916 brought in friendly ministers and new assistants, Sir Mark Sykes and Leopold Amery, who gave powerful tactical support in forming a pro-Zionist policy. When Jabotinsky and Weizmann had approached the government in July 1916 on the question of a Jewish legion, Lloyd George simply referred the petitioners to Lord Edward Derby, the officer responsible for manpower in the War Office. Here the matter died, for the established second-rank officers saw no reason to alter their fixed policy. Now, in 1917, Amery piloted to a successful conclusion Jabotinsky's appeal not to disperse the reenlisted veterans of the Zion Mule Corps among units destined for the front in Flanders. Instead, they were posted together to train in a London territorial defense regiment and were available as the nucleus of a potential Jewish combat force for service in Egypt and Palestine.[51]

Meanwhile, the deadline for demonstrating that Jabotinsky could recruit successfully in Whitechapel had passed and the government was concerting plans with Russia to draft the immigrants for service in English or Russian units. In January Amery urged Jabotinsky to present a new memorandum to the government, as the proposal to form a Jewish regiment might evoke more willing cooperation under the new conditions. Under Amery's editorial eye, Jabotinsky framed his proposals in the narrow context of the recruitment problem, downplaying the wider Zionist implications. In spite of this caution, the War Office noted political difficulties, citing possible French objections. The Foreign Office (and the prime minister as well) realized that French opposition would have to be overcome in any case, as the developing invasion of Palestine was making the Sykes-Picot understanding seem too generous in its concessions to French claims. On the other hand, Balfour proved more sensitive than the military to another obstacle: the resistance Jabotinsky's activities were meeting in the Jewish community. Thus, Amery's urging, backed by Sykes, failed to move Jabotinsky's memorandum rapidly to Cabinet consideration, though preliminary discussions continued. Jabotinsky expressed his despair of immediate success by joining the Zion Mule Corps veterans in the territorial militia as a private soldier; Trumpeldor, barred as an officer from British military service, went on to Russia. Further progress in the cause of the Jewish legion depended (however indirectly) on the success of the Zionist political campaign—that is to say, on Weizmann's work. And Weizmann's political work depended on the community's trust in his leadership, which, in turn, depended on his keeping a safe distance between his official Zionist actions and the Jewish legion campaign—even while he privately aided Jabotinsky's efforts.

By 1917 Weizmann's material situation as well as his social and professional standing gave him new confidence in his future independence as a political leader and agent. He no longer served in the Ministry of Munitions, but he still had his Admiralty laboratory work and was to get a lump sum in compensation for his patented processes exploited by the government. Between this anticipated capital, the regular support of friends for his research and political work, and the income to be expected from other countries that were beginning to apply his discoveries, he could hope to maintain himself and his family in the style required by his growing prominence. They had moved to London in 1916; with his wife's ready and effective aid, he could now return the hospitality of the Rothschilds, Astors, and others who had made him something of a social lion in their homes.

Acceptance by the English ruling elite strengthened Weizmann's claim to leadership among Zionists; it bolstered his decision to base Zionist strategy on a clear-cut British orientation; and it emboldened him to advocate a particular policy for Britain—namely, exclusive control of Palestine as a British, pro-Zionist protectorate—instead of waiting for the government's decision before defining his own position. Yet it was only when Sykes and other second-rank officers tried to involve him in current operations that Weizmann could really hope to influence policy decisions at critical moments.

Sykes from the beginning thought direct control of the Palestine area essential in a British strategy.[52] But before the war the British had recognized a special French interest in the Levant. Lord Kitchener shared the vision of a wide British zone from the Mediterranean to the Persian Gulf but, as secretary for war, his priority was the battle of the Western Front; he had to give first consideration to relations with France. Under such constraints, the Bunsen Committee was able to suggest only modest revisions of the privileged positions granted to France in the prewar agreements. The provisions in case of an Ottoman partition (as later extended and elaborated in the Sykes-Picot treaty) divided the Syria-Palestine area into a French zone in the north; an internationally administered Jerusalem zone, extending from the Jordan River to the Mediterranean below Jaffa and above Acre; and a British enclave from Haifa to Acre, with right of way for transit from Haifa to Mesopotamia and the Persian Gulf.

During the Sykes-Picot negotiations, the Cabinet was beginning to note its difficulties with Jewish public opinion and to consider the possible impact of a gesture of sympathy for Zionist hopes in Palestine.[53] Sykes had already consulted on this topic with Samuel before leaving for Russia, where in March 1916 specific formulas were cabled to him for consideration with the Russians and the French. On returning to London, he asked Samuel to serve as his bridge to the Zionists. Samuel began by explaining to Gaster, Sokolow, and Weizmann the new approach being mooted in government circles—essentially, O'Beirne's formula: an international regime confined to Jerusalem and the Holy Places; an area for Zionist colonization in the rest of Palestine, under British (or, as some preferred, American) protection; and the whole included in a confederation under the suzerainty of an Arab prince. Samuel also asked Gaster to meet Sykes, together with Sokolow and Weizmann. Gaster preferred to act alone and met Sykes for several talks in the summer of 1916, reporting and consulting with Sokolow, but not with Weizmann. This may have reflected, apart from the relative warmth of Gaster's personal relations, the relative coolness shown by Weizmann toward the plans Samuel reported, which had, on the other hand, aroused Gaster to enthusiasm. In any case the first meetings with Sykes ended after a while with no concrete results.

Half a year later, Sykes became assistant secretary to the Lloyd George War Cabinet. In the interim he had met Aaron Aaronsohn in London and Cairo and conducted another tour of reconnaissance in the field. His perception of the Jews as a significant piece in his strategy had sharpened, and he had fleshed out his conception of a postwar partition of the Ottoman provinces on national lines—now including Jews together with Arabs and Armenians. He expected to return to the East as political officer with the troops invading Palestine (to balance Picot, whom the French sent to protect their interests), and he felt he needed to meet the effective Zionist leaders in London and come to an understanding with them before taking this task in hand. For this purpose he took advantage of the good offices of James Malcolm, local agent for the Armenian nationalists.

After initial contacts in January 1917 (and some maneuvering for position by Gaster and Weizmann), a representative group met Sykes in Gaster's home on February 7.[54] Besides Gaster, Weizmann, and Sokolow, it included James de Rothschild and his cousin, Lionel Walter, the second Lord Rothschild; Herbert Samuel; Harry Sacher, proposed by Weizmann; and the veteran leaders, Joseph Cowen and Herbert Bentwich, invited by Gaster. The Zionists at once impressed upon Sykes their opposition to the (vaguely rumored) possibility of a Franco-British condominium in Palestine and stressed that a protectorate by England alone was vital to the success of their plans; Sykes, of course, personally favored exclusive British control and understood the connection of such an arrangement with the chances for active Zionist pro-Allied propaganda in America and among Russian Jews. But he was also bound by his recently concluded agreement with Picot. Any revision of that agreement would pose the delicate problem of gaining French (and Italian) acquiescence to possible infringements of claims that they had just established or believed to be theirs by right. Sykes' talks with the Zionists had to skirt these still-secret matters while seeking expedients to avoid, or overcome, objections such as those the French had already voiced after the Petrograd negotiations. He accomplished this in a masterly fashion by simply delegating to the Zionists themselves the task of dealing with the French and Italians—without telling them what agreements had been reached with the Allies in the year past.

After this meeting the Zionists entered into an entirely new relationship with the government. Since it was a primary element in the new understanding that the Zionists would seek the adherence of their American and Russian comrades to their approach, special facilities for communicating with foreign countries were arranged for them. In this way the Zionists were tacitly recognized as an Allied entity; but it also gave the British full prior knowledge of the correspondence between Zionists. Sokolow, too, achieved a new recognition, as he was given the role of direct liaison with Sykes (over Gaster's objections). On March 31 he set out for Paris and Rome to gain the approval of those Allies for including the Jews among the claimants to be considered in their arrangements for a postwar settlement. Sykes, who was to leave for his post in Egypt soon after, promised to smooth Sokolow's way in the French and Italian capitals, which he would visit on his way to Cairo; and in Paris, Sokolow was accompanied (at the specific request of Sykes and Picot) by James Malcolm, who occupied a similar position to Sokolow's in Sykes' train. Another new role was also contemplated for Weizmann. Sykes asked for a Zionist representative to go with him as liaison with the Palestinian Jewish community and with other local elements who had to be prepared for the Zionist presence in the area—particularly the Arabs. Eventually, Weizmann undertook to fulfill this role himself, and he prepared to follow Sykes at a suitable moment.

The new situation confronted Weizmann with a rapid succession of adjustments that he had to improvise in his dealings with the British and with his Zionist cohorts. Sykes' attitude was sufficiently enigmatic. He clearly encouraged the Zionists to push for their preferred option, a British protectorate, but his commitment to the secret agreement with the French made him warn Weizmann from time to time against occasional excesses of Zionist enthusiasts in his circle. Weizmann was compelled to rein in his Manchester friends when their journal, *Palestine,* published plainspoken demands for a British-protected Jewish state or dominion, at a time when Sykes wanted to soothe French suspicions. On the other hand, Weizmann himself took a guarded view of Sykes' maneuvering. He complained to Scott that Sykes seemed to regard the Zionist connection as a secondary appendage to his plans for the Arabs; this no doubt reflected awareness of the proposal, conveyed by Samuel in 1916, to make Palestine an autonomous province in a confederation under a suzerain Arab prince. In this mood Weizmann became increasingly suspicious that, acting under Sykes' guidance, the diplomatic Sokolow might be conceding too much to the French insistence on a shared international administration in Palestine.[55]

Meanwhile, the revolution in Russia in March and the American entry into the war in April introduced new, incalculable elements of uncertainty. Also the British invasion of Palestine was checked at the border, and the question of abandoning or renewing the offensive arose for decision. An agitated Sykes advised his superiors that, if the conquest of Palestine were to be abandoned, it was essential to drop the developing connection with the Zionists before incurring commitments that could not then be honored. But the decision was to renew the British advance under a new field commander, General Sir Edmund Allenby, who was transferred from France to Egypt in June.

Before this decisive step, both Sykes and Weizmann had to suffer unexpected shocks that threw their plans (for a time) into a limbo of suspension—until reassurance was given and they were able to go forward with redoubled confidence. For Weizmann the first such shock was to learn through Scott in April of the existence and nature of the Sykes-Picot agreement; then followed assurances that the agreement was no longer considered a fixed policy now that the invasion of Palestine by British forces had begun and that the Russian Revolution as well as events in America were rapidly changing the political scene. (Indeed, before Sykes departed for his new assignment in Cairo in early April, he was instructed by the prime minister to see that the prospects of Zionist development under British patronage were not prejudiced and, if possible, to arrange for Palestine to be added to the British sphere.)[56] Soon after, however, Weizmann suffered a second alarming shock when he learned in June of an effort to drop the idea of a postwar partition of Palestine entirely in order to get Turkey out of the war by arranging a separate peace with her.

The Russian Revolution left that country's future policy uncertain, including its commitment to the plans for Turkey; the Americans went to war with the Central Powers in Europe but decided to remain neutral vis-à-vis the Ottomans; and although the British offensive brought pressure on the Turks, the stalled attack on Gaza gave both combatants a chance to reconsider their next move. All these factors combined to encourage those who still believed in retaining the Ottoman Empire intact, in its classic role as a buffer between rival powers, and there was pressure for a separate peace with Turkey.[57] Malcolm came to Weizmann with rumors of such a move among British Turcophiles. At the same time an American initiative to accomplish the same end was launched by Henry Morgenthau, who had retired from his ambassadorship in Constantinople in order to take part in Wilson's 1916 election campaign. Morgenthau's offer to undertake the peace mission himself—through his Turkish contacts—was taken up by the State Department and by Wilson's advisor, Colonel House—and the British (and French) were asked to cooperate. Men who had pinned their hopes on a partition of the Ottoman lands had reason to be alarmed; Sykes saw the incident as an intrigue against himself. Weizmann and Malcolm came to the Foreign Office; there Weizmann found himself unexpectedly involved with the Morgenthau mission, in which he ultimately took part as a representative of the British government.

On this occasion Weizmann forced the government's hand by stating his conditions for joining the Morgenthau mission. He had been uneasy for some time about joining Sykes in the East without British acceptance of the policy he intended to follow. He had outlined his policy to Scott at an early stage: Britain to assume the protectorate of Palestine, with the "entire burden of organization" and development to fall on the Jews under Zionist leadership. His constant advisor, Scott, strongly supported Weizmann's reluctance to take on the new task without such a clear understanding on policy (and he also urged him to wait for the question of his compensation to be settled). To send Weizmann on his own terms to represent England on Morgenthau's mission, as the Foreign Office then did, was not only an implicit promise for the future of Zionism, it virtually instructed him to block the attempt at a separate peace.

This was an assignment that Weizmann successfully accomplished with the help of an American member of the mission, Felix Frankfurter. The meeting with Frankfurter was Weizmann's first direct contact with one of the leading American Zionists closely tied to Brandeis. Close contact with them was increasingly crucial for the success of Weizmann's plans, and it now became a major concern to consolidate this new relationship.

The political perspective of the American Zionists before April 1917 was determined by the fact of American neutrality; thus it differed sharply from that of Zionists in Britain. Under American conditions Zionists found it easy and appropriate both to conform to the neutrality proclaimed by the WZO at an early stage of the war and to cooperate with the central headquarters in Berlin and its liaison offices in The Hague and in Copenhagen. The major wartime contributions of American Zionism, financial support of the Zionist institutions and relief activities in Palestine and other war-affected areas, were made possible by the neutrality it observed. On one hand, the contacts of the American Embassy in Constantinople with its German counterpart helped to spare Palestinian Jewry many threatened hardships at the hands of the Turkish regime; on the other hand, British agreement to pass shipments through their blockade allowed refugees from Palestine to be sheltered in Egypt and supplies to be sent to relieve the hungry and the sick in Palestine.

Official Zionist neutrality did not mean, of course, that Zionists individually were impartial in their feelings toward the belligerents. The Allies were

severely handicapped, both by the sympathy of the leading American Jews
for Germany, where many were born, and by the bitter animosity of Russian-
Jewish immigrants toward czarist Russia. The war heightened these sentiments, as Russian troops expelled and maltreated Jews in frontier areas and
the advancing Germans were hailed as rescuers and liberators. The Germans
made effective use of these advantages, and their agent, Dr. Isaac Straus,
working with the ambassador, was notably successful with broad sectors of
American Jewry. Jacob Schiff, with family connections to the Hamburg banking house of Warburg, was written down by the Allies as irreparably pro-German. The Yiddish press and labor movement opposed the war as imperialist
and hoped for a social revolution, particularly one in Russia. The one Yiddish paper that looked favorably on the Allies, *Di Varheit,* suffered a cata-
strophic loss of readership; and when Nachman Syrkin came out as a supporter of the Allied cause, deviating from the party line, he had to leave the
Central Committee of the Poalei Zion.[58]

The exceptional few who took an opposing stand were often found among
those in the professional and academic communities, who were acculturated
to the prevailing sympathies of the East Coast American elite. Among men
of native, Anglo-Saxon stock, ties to England—the old country of their proud
ancestry—outweighed motives for neutrality. Pro-Allied sentiments dominated the leading East Coast newspapers and Ivy League colleges, and Jewish
professionals and academics who had access to those circles were inclined to
share Anglophile, pro-Allied leanings. Professor Richard Gottheil was particularly outspoken in supporting the Allied cause; Brandeis had to find a way
to restrain his partisanship, at least when shown in a Zionist context, and yet
soothe his ruffled feelings when other Zionists (such as the emphatically anti-
war Magnes) tried to administer an official rebuke. In Brandeis' own close
circle, some of the most prominent figures—Frankfurter, de Haas, and Horace Kallen—had strong pro-Allied sympathies and maintained collaborative
relations with English friends active in America.[59]

Brandeis himself, for many reasons, left his personal views fairly obscure.
He was, in any case, less inclined than many progressives to involve himself
in issues of foreign policy. He had for some years been growing cooler to the
German associations of his family background and was more drawn to the
English left-liberalism of the Fabian socialists. But among such Englishmen,
some of the most prominent hoped for a negotiated end to the war and shared
Brandeis' profound distaste for the Russian autocracy. With such attitudes it
was easy for Brandeis to fall in line with the neutrality adopted by the WZO
leadership. In addition, the confidence reposed in him by the new progressive
Democratic administration placed Brandeis under an obligation of personally
observing formal neutrality, which Wilson had adopted as national policy.

Not only Brandeis, but a number of leading Zionists besides, had useful
relations with the Democratic administration. Stephen Wise had actively
assisted the Wilson campaign in 1912 and de Haas had also participated on
Wilson's behalf in New England. Both Wise and de Haas reported that they
had received assurances that their candidate favored the Zionist cause and
would take appropriate action if elected. Moreover, Henry Morgenthau, who

had been a major financial supporter of the campaign and was appointed ambassador to Turkey, was a leading member of Rabbi Stephen Wise's Free Synagogue and, during his tenure in Constantinople, was unfailingly helpful to the Zionists in their humanitarian labors. These were political connections rivaling those of any other American Jewish organization at the time and far more impressive than those available in England to the Zionists at the beginning of the war. But given the neutrality of the United States, close ties to the government could inhibit as much as facilitate independent political action by American Zionists.

Zionist political action early in the war followed much the same course, in certain respects, as in England. There was an initial flurry of contacts with ambassadors of the warring nations in Washington, in which Brandeis, Richard Gottheil, and others presented not only the case of Zionism, but general Jewish claims to equal rights and fair treatment in countries like Russia. Horace Kallen's academic contacts in Wisconsin, where Alfred Zimmern was a visiting professor in 1915, enabled him to forward Zionist proposals to the Foreign Office in London. The British Embassy was sufficiently conscious of the pro-Allied attitudes of some Zionists to try to use them on one occasion to induce the Americans to assume a protectorate in Palestine: Gottheil was approached for this purpose, without result, in July 1915. But direct attempts to influence policy were not seriously pressed in the early years, and the American Zionists, like their English counterparts at the time, mainly sought to build up a favorable public and government attitude for the future. They concentrated on strengthening their position in the Jewish community: indirectly, through their popular relief campaigns and the battle for an American Jewish congress; directly, by expanding the Zionist base of "Men! Money! Discipline!" In these efforts they relied on their leaders' contacts in the circles of government, and, by the same efforts, they tightened and extended such contacts.

The lesson Zionists seemed to have learned from their work in 1915 was that their best hope for the Jewish future—in Palestine and elsewhere—lay precisely in America's neutrality, which might lend it decisive influence on the shape of a negotiated peace settlement. With the approach of the 1916 electoral season, they began to consider how to gain a public commitment from the president on the lines of the private pledges some had received. In April Nathan Straus sent Brandeis a pamphlet he had reprinted containing the Blackstone memorial, an appeal to secure the return of Jews to Palestine which was sent to President Benjamin Harrison in 1891 over the signatures of a large collection of eminent Americans. The Zionists now proposed to renew this petition, and Reverend William Blackstone in May secured the approval and support of the Presbyterian General Assembly to this end. But the Zionists had to content themselves with new private assurances from Wilson at that time while planning to present the Blackstone memorial in order to secure the desired public response later.[60]

During Wilson's first term in office, the Zionists not only enjoyed unprecedented access to the administration, but felt they had the general sympathy of its supporters, undisturbed by opposing interests such as later appeared among groups close to the president. Wilson came into office after a long period of Republican dominance. This left the president many responsible positions to fill but few men with both the needed experience and compatible views to draw on—a situation further aggravated by growing involvement in foreign affairs remote from former American concerns. The sudden need to recruit loyal Democrats for high office produced a flood of applicants and severe pressure from the varied elements of the coalition Wilson had put together in his 1912 campaign.

In coping with these problems, the president relied heavily on the advice of Colonel Edward House, a man who had played a prominent part in Wilson's campaigns for nomination and election and whose ambition was precisely to serve as confidential guide to the president of the United States.[61] Acting in a private, unofficial capacity, he hoped to be all the more powerful by appearing to be disinterested. House, a seasoned political campaigner, gave due attention to placing his own associates—Southern progressive Democrats and old cronies—in positions of power, but his primary object was to consolidate the president's coalition. It was he who had brought about the conciliation of William Jennings Bryan that had gained Wilson the Democratic nomination and led to Bryan's becoming secretary of state in Wilson's Cabinet. But lack of confidence in Bryan was a contributing factor (along with the slight expertise of departmental staff in many areas involved in a world war) for Wilson's tendency to bypass the bureaucracy and handle foreign affairs personally. House became his primary agent for dealing with the issues of global war and peace. During 1915 while Bryan was secretary of state, House was active in Europe on the president's behalf, seeking a negotiated peace to end the conflict. When Bryan retired from office and was succeeded by Robert Lansing, Wilson kept foreign policy control in his own hands, with no greater reliance on the advice of the department. House came back from Europe to serve even more effectively as the president's man, and even better placed for his personal aim: to influence, without offending, the president in defining and carrying out his foreign policy.

In their wartime relief activities, Zionists found it vital to be on friendly terms with the bureaucracy. When issues of wartime and peace policy came into focus, it was necessary to keep an open door to Colonel House. In both cases the Zionists had fair success—more, perhaps because of respect for the place their leaders held in Wilson's political combine than because of any profound sympathy or understanding for the Zionist cause.

Another set of pressures that could affect policy over the whole range of Zionist activity came from Protestant philanthropists, missionaries, and progressives.[62] The president's early background as a "son of the manse" gave him a peculiar affinity with the values such men defended. Old and cherished friends, like his schoolmate at Princeton, Cleveland Dodge, sustained the Congregationalist and Presbyterian foreign missions that brought Western education and medical services to places like China and Turkey. Representing some of the first, and still among the most substantial American interests established in the Near and Far East, they felt obliged to monitor closely the policy and the personnel choices of the State Department in the areas of their operations. Sponsors of the Protestant missions not only founded the American Near East Relief during the war, but were prominent in the reorganized American Red Cross. Their influence covered a broad range of overseas relief and rehabilitation projects as well as associated foreign policy decisions.

Charles Crane, who was one of their circle, extended the range even more broadly, and with specific, personal concern.[63] He was heir to an industrial fortune, but he inclined more to public activity, especially in regard to distant countries like China and Russia, with which he became familiar in his travels. He was a leading backer of Western progressivism and one of the sponsors of LaFollette's presidential candidacy; thus he became a friend and collaborator of Brandeis'—an ally on whom the lawyer could rely for support in a common interest, like financing a journal for Norman Hapgood to edit. Crane had a brief, abortive diplomatic career as minister to China in 1909, which left his colleagues in Washington in some doubt of his capacity for such work. Having been a leading backer of the Wilson campaign, he was considered (but passed over) for a post in Washington, and he himself decided to decline the ambassadorial post offered him. Yet, by financing the careers of others (directing their studies to the fields of his own interest) and through his wide personal acquaintance with the new governing elite, Crane had a major impact on the development of American expertise in foreign affairs.

Crane was largely instrumental in creating a tradition of Slavic studies at the University of Chicago. He supported the career of Samuel N. Harper, son of the university's president, who became the Russian expert largely relied on by the State Department during the war and immediately thereafter. His ties to Washington bureaucrats were strengthened by the appointment of Crane's son Richard as personal secretary to the secretary of state when Robert Lansin assumed that position. Through his special interest in Russian affairs as well as the Protestant missions in Turkey and Syria, Charles Crane and his protégés were concerned with the very areas of foreign policy that affected Jewish interests.

There were for a time many points of convergence between the Zionists' and the Protestant missionaries' foreign affairs objectives. Their common concern for relief and protection of Ottoman minorities—the missionaries for the Armenians, Nestorians, and the Evangelical and Orthodox Arabs; the Jews for their coreligionists—made them press similar measures on the State Department and other government agencies. The Presbyterians who supported Blackstone's pro-Zionist petition as well as other Protestants feared Turkish reprisals against their institutions and their client community, as did the Jews, and they were no less persistent—and even more effective—in seeking to shape American policy toward Turkey accordingly. Under these circumstances, the roster of Jewish ambassadors in Constantinople—Oscar Straus, Henry Morgenthau, and (in 1916) Abram Elkus—took care to work in close harmony with the Protestant foreign missions. Morgenthau changed his travel plans on first taking up his post in the Turkish capital and sailed on the same boat with leading missionary personnel in order to have the benefit of their briefing and gain their confidence and cooperation. He was eminently successful in this effort and remained on terms of close mutual trust ever afterward. His recommendation of Abram Elkus to succeed him in Constantinople (Elkus, like himself having been a leading member of Rabbi Wise's Free Synagogue) was checked and approved by James L. Barton, the director of American relief for Armenia and Syria and a staff expert for the commissioners of the Congregationalist missions in the Near East.[64]

In the years of American neutrality, a common concern—to protect client communities against the savagery already visited upon the Armenians and to save them from hunger and disease—led American Jews and Christian philanthropists, jointly and in parallel efforts, to seek the aid of American diplomacy and naval supply vessels. But this cooperation in matters of common concern did not arise out of a mutual sympathy free from prejudicial feelings and potential conflict. There were, in fact, divergent views and interests that eventually emerged into public conflict as the American era of neutrality ended and the issues of a postwar settlement came into focus.

As noted earlier, Cleveland Dodge—and with more caution, Colonel House—had advised against Brandeis' appointment to the Wilson Cabinet in 1913 in barely veiled revulsion against a Jewish lawyer's elevation to office in the Justice Department. Charles Crane, even though he was a close collaborator of Brandeis', showed a strongly colored, midwestern-Populist vein of antisemitism in his suspicion of Jewish international bankers—represented in America by the figure of Jacob Schiff. (His bond with Brandeis—a fellow progressive of Midwestern coloration himself—was built in part on the lawyer's own distaste for the Wall Street Jews; this was highlighted in the Zionist clashes with the American Jewish Committee.)

Antipathy to Jews surfaced again when America entered the war, impelling all those with a special interest in foreign affairs to respond to opportunities and dangers perceived in the new situation. Jews were particularly concerned with Russian affairs, made salient by the revolution as well as America's joining in the war; when it was proposed to send a mission to Russia, the Jews expected to be represented. Brandeis was prominent among those mentioned for the assignment. But Crane as well as Samuel Harper and other official advisors on Russian affairs, sharing the bias of some of their British counterparts, considered that Jews needlessly involved the country in their special grievances against Russia, spread exaggerated reports of Russian oppression, and were leagued with their German coreligionists. The opposition of such men led to the selection of a Russian mission without a leading Jewish member (but including Crane) and headed by Elihu Root, a man with no particular sense for the Russian situation. In another context House, too, showed his irritation at the pressure of Jews to be considered in certain areas of foreign policy. When he was asked by Wilson to set up study groups to prepare American positions in the eventual peace settlement (after Frankfurter reported parallel preparation by the European Allies on his return from the Morgenthau mission), he found that Jewish applicants and delegations began to visit him with annoying frequency. Nevertheless, the prominent role of the *New Republic* staff in the inquiry that House set up, especially Walter Lippmann's appointment as its secretary, gave Brandeis assurance that Zionist views would be heard in American planning.[65]

Palestine and the surrounding areas of Zionist interest were destined to be a zone of contention with the missionary philanthropists. At first, American involvement in the war left the Protestant leaders and their diplomatic friends in a state of uncertainty and divided counsels. They feared that association with Turkey's enemies, the Allies, would turn Ottoman fury against themselves and their exposed clientele. They took a leading part in urging that Wilson not include Turkey in his declaration of war, which was provoked by the German renewal of unrestricted submarine warfare. Ambassador Elkus, who continued on the scene until the Turks broke off relations, joined in assuring Wilson that, in spite of German pressure, the Ottomans had no wish to close all doors to America. Wilson (who took pains to limit his commitment in many respects to the Allies, whom he preferred to call *Associates*) fell in with the counsels of restraint and kept America out of the war with Turkey, in spite of the break in diplomatic relations.

The first fears of Turkish reprisals against American interests having been quieted, the Protestant leaders concentrated their attention on postwar issues and on the conditions desirable for renewing their work in the Near East on a new basis. Here, too, they left open widely divergent options, best illustrated in the alternatives considered by their most active leader, James L. Barton. At first—perhaps still ruled by the revulsion inspired by the Armenian massacres—he favored an aggressive American policy: a landing of armed forces on the Eastern Mediterranean coast in order to knock Turkey out of the war or at least to protect American institutions and their clients and an American protectorate over Armenia, Constantinople, and the Straits at the war's end. Later, he was won over by advocates of another line of policy altogether: retaining an integral Ottoman realm in existence with provincial autonomy for its Armenian and Arab regions. This approach, too, was thought likely to assure the Protestant missions of the local goodwill essential to their future success.[66]

While others concerned with American policy toward the Ottoman realm were slow to take definite positions, the American Zionists by May 1917 had sharply altered their previous guardedly neutral stand.[67] At a meeting of the PZEC on May 9, the American Zionists approved a policy closely related to that of the British Zionists. They adopted a position favoring a British postwar protectorate in Palestine as the most desirable sponsor of the Jewish national home. Although assuring their British comrades of support for this aim, they made no public statement, confining their efforts to more private channels. This was a consequence of the understanding Brandeis thought he had just reached with Wilson at a time when America was still defining the extent, or the limits, of its new role in the global war.

After Wilson's reelection, sanguine Zionists had pressed ahead with their plan to submit the Blackstone memorial to the administration for approval. Stephen Wise discussed the matter with House, who was courteously encouraging, and de Haas prepared a memorandum for the Colonel in anticipation of further talks in Washington with Brandeis. But now events followed in rapid order, making old approaches irrelevant and opening up unknown new possibilities. America came into the war—but not with Turkey. From England came reports of the new Zionist contacts with Mark Sykes and the Lloyd George government, followed by alarmed reactions (from Weizmann and others in London) to Sokolow's Sykes-sponsored diplomacy in Paris and Rome, culminating in appeals from Weizmann and James de Rothschild to help head off demands for an internationally administered Franco-British Palestine and to secure an exclusively British protectorate as the best guarantee of Zionist aspirations. Soon Allied missions also began to appear in Washington—Britons, Frenchmen, and the emissaries of the new democratic Russia. The occasion was too pregnant with risk and promise for Brandeis to allow other Zionists a free hand. He discouraged proposals for them to deal with the French mission; and after some preliminary, initially social, conversation with Arthur Balfour (heading the British mission), Justice Brandeis himself took up the questions of interest to Jews in a lengthy private discussion with President Wilson. They met for three quarters of an hour on May 6, 1917. Thereafter, the PZEC adopted its position in favor of a British protectorate for the Jewish national home, which Brandeis cabled to the London Zionists together with his personal commitment.

It seems clear that in his May 6 talk with Wilson, Brandeis satisfied himself fully that he could take certain definite positions on currently discussed options regarding a policy on Palestine and rely on the acquiescence and ultimate support of the president. One possibility, which enjoyed tentative support in many circles and that was being advanced by Britons like Lord James Bryce and Balfour himself, was for the responsibility of a protectorate (for the Armenians in Constantinople or on behalf of the Zionists in Palestine) to be assumed by America, by itself or jointly with Britain. An article by Norman Hapgood proposing an American-protected Jewish state alarmed the British Zionist leaders: they feared that it would touch off a tempest of competing claims by France and others not helpful to the Zionist aims and might end in some form of joint administration in Palestine, which they dreaded as inherently inefficient. After conferring with the president, Brandeis not only secured PZEC approval of a British-protected Jewish national home in Palestine, but also firmly and consistently rejected the suggestion of an *American* protectorate in his concurrent talks with Balfour—this in the face of the continuing appeal of such an idea to sources close to the State Department, particularly among the leaders and patrons of the Protestant Near East missions.[68]

It seems clear that Brandeis believed that America was unlikely to extend its overseas responsibilities to the area of the Near East. He must have concluded from his talk with Wilson that the president rejected the suggestions of an American protectorate as a ploy intended to involve the United States in supporting British interests in the Near East and make him a party to the secret agreements between the Allies. Accordingly, Brandeis could hold to the Zionist preference for a *British* protectorate, confident that his stand was not in conflict with possible American claims. But he also was clearly bound by another aspect of Wilson's policy: the president's wish to go to the peace conference as a free agent—in a position to stand on principles rather than self-aggrandizing interests—and to be the impartial judge of the conflicting interests of the other participants. For this reason Brandeis could neither press the president immediately for a public commitment to clearly defined Zionist aims in Palestine nor even publicize his own preferred solution, a British protectorate. Together with the other leading American Zionists, he continued to rely on the president's pledge to take appropriate action in response to a Zionist request tendered at the appropriate time—after the end of hostilities. Until then he proposed to continue building Zionist strength and carry on its limited wartime program of "practical" work while directly advancing the ultimate political aim only by relatively discreet private lobbying and generally phrased public advocacy as the occasions arose.

The war, accordingly, produced a decisive shift in the policy of American Zionists toward the British Zionist stand—but this change was made evident only in the correspondence between Zionists in the two countries and, of course, in their privileged communications with the British and American governments. In deference to Wilson's plans, the fact that American Zionists now counted on a Turkish defeat and the partition of Ottoman territory did not lead them to agitate for an American break with Turkey. Indeed, when the government was induced to experiment with Morgenthau's attempt to bring about a separate peace for Turkey (which would have ended, if successful, any prospect for the British-protected Jewish Palestine the PZEC had endorsed as its aim), Brandeis and his coadjutants not only refrained from opposing this venture, they agreed to provide cover for it by allowing the mission to be presented as an extension of their humanitarian work in aid of Palestine Jewry.

At the same time, in this, as in other developments of the time, Brandeis and his aides necessarily discerned the gap that began to open between them and others closer to the president than themselves. The division grew slowly, so that cooperation continued to be sustained, but with increasing caution and difficulty. Thus, Brandeis had to explain to his circle that while Charles Crane was among those who expressed opposition to a Jew on the mission to Russia, his friend and Progressive ally had not been a prime mover but rather one who concurred with the anti-Jewish stand. So, too, the Zionists felt compelled to cooperate with the government's wish to let Morgenthau try his hand at dealing with the Turks. However, they called attention to Morgenthau's already demonstrated thoughtlessness, shown in his reckless remarks of the previous summer about buying Palestine from Turkey for the Jews. This reminder coupled with the wariness of government circles themselves led to including Frankfurter on the mission for America and Weizmann for the British—both expected to protect their governments, not only Zionist interests, from any untoward effects of Morgenthau's entrepreneurial enthusiasm.[69]

Shortly before going off to meet Morgenthau in Gibraltar, Weizmann, accompanied by Lord Lionel Walter Rothschild, had met Balfour and been asked to submit a draft statement of sympathy with Zionist aims for the government to consider. To reach this point, the Zionists had compiled reports (from the German press and the Zionist office in Copenhagen) of enemy attempts to win over Jewish opinion by supporting Jewish aspirations in Palestine. The sense of being threatened by an enemy maneuver proved as effective in precipitating a long-considered action on the Jewish front as had been the case earlier on the Arab side. Other elements in the situation that British policyshapers had to consider also fell into place at that time.

In May Weizmann had become sufficiently confident of his position to announce publicly that Zionist aims enjoyed government support. He was emboldened to take this step not only by his own conversations in England, but by the developments in America during Balfour's visit there over the past month. At that very time *The Times* (London) was about to publish letters from David Alexander and Claude Montefiore, the anti-Zionist cochairmen of the Conjoint Foreign Committee, vehemently objecting to the Zionist proposals. This touched off a furious debate in the press and in Jewish communal institutions that led to resignations from the Conjoint Foreign Committee and a revolt in its major constituent, the Board of Deputies of British Jewry. The old, anti-Zionist leadership was deposed—a development that removed one of Balfour's doubts about positive action in favor of Zionism. Another, his concern about antagonizing the French, was allayed when Sokolow, just back from Paris, was able to show his letter of June 4 from the French Foreign Ministry, assuring him [Sokolow] of sympathy for "your cause, the triumph of which is bound up with that of the Allies." Given these conditions and the encouragement of his recent visit to America, Balfour was ready to favor a British declaration that would counter the one expected from Germany and (without raising the issue implied in the reference in the French letter to a protectorate by "the Allied Powers" in Palestine) parallel the statement Sokolow had secured in Paris. He, accordingly, asked for a Zionist draft to be submitted by Lord Rothschild, who would also forward the Foreign Office response—thus avoiding any direct official communication to the Zionists that non-Zionist Jewish bodies might resent as an implied slight.[70]

With Weizmann absent with the Morgenthau mission in Gibraltar and Paris, the form of a draft was debated by Sokolow and others of the Political Committee set up by the leaders. A division sprang up at once between the Manchester militants, represented by Harry Sacher, and the moderate Sokolow. Sacher's draft, drawn up at Weizmann's request, respected his instructions (reflecting Balfour's conditions) not to refer to the suzerainty to be established in Palestine. However, Sacher insisted on including a statement that "the reconstitution of Palestine as a Jewish State" was "one of [the British] essential war aims," and he specified other details such as the powers to be granted Zionists under a charter. Sokolow, who was in touch with Foreign Office quarters, noted that the draft would have to be acceptable to Lord Rothschild, who would transmit it, and to the foreign secretary. His contacts in the Foreign Office, he reported, wanted a concise and general statement—something like the French declaration of moral support he had just brought back from Paris. Sokolow's own substitute statement was a brief draft of three sentence-paragraphs: it committed England, in principle, to recognize both Palestine as the Jewish national home and the right of the Jewish people "to build up its national life [there] under a protection to be established at the conclusion of peace"; it defined the essentials for realizing the stated principle—internal autonomy, free immigration, and a chartered corporation to develop the land; and it undertook to work out a detailed program of implementation in consultation with the Zionist Organization. This also proved too specific for the officials he dealt with. In the end Lord Rothschild sent Balfour, on July 18, 1917, a draft reduced to a Zionist version of the bare guidelines given Sokolow by the British themselves:

> 1. His Majesty's Government accepts the principle that Palestine should be reconstituted as the national home of the Jewish people.
>
> 2. His Majesty's Government will use its best endeavours to secure the achievement of this object and will discuss the necessary methods and means with the Zionist Organization.[71]

In acknowledging Rothschild's letter, Balfour noted that a matter of such high importance would, of course, have to be referred to the Cabinet, and he could not respond as swiftly as he would like. The draft then underwent successive revisions during the summer, tending to reduce the extent and specificity of the government's commitment.[72] Balfour himself compressed it to a single sentence and left the proposed discussion of "methods and means" for the Zionists to initiate, retaining freedom of action for the government. Lord Milner found in Herzl's Basle Program a more elastic Zionist formula than Rothschild's. In place of "Palestine . . . reconstituted as the national home," he proposed to substitute a statement that "every opportunity should be afforded for the establishment of a home for the Jewish people in Palestine"—a formula that might be interpreted as echoing O'Beirne's plan to permit Jews to develop areas within Palestine without constructing a political order for the whole country in line with the Zionist aim. This, like the Foreign Office revision, was worked out within the confines of government bureaus while the Zionists continued to await word of developments.

Weizmann came back late in July to find matters well advanced but still hanging suspended in a bureaucratic limbo. Other circumstances contributed to a tense, uneasy summer. His work at the Admiralty was about to end (but was renewed until June 1918), and the compensation promised by the government still had not been determined. Under these private pressures, he also faced a storm over the revived issue of the Jewish legion, with his discreet efforts in support now coming under public scrutiny.

The question of the Jewish legion had arisen for the government after the decision of March 30 to continue the advance on Jerusalem.[73] At a breakfast meeting Scott arranged with Lloyd George on April 2, Weizmann found an occasion in the course of a general discussion to raise the issue of the Gallipoli veterans, who were again about to be sent to France. Lloyd George was easily persuaded that such men were best used in the projected Palestine campaign, and he then brought up the question of the Jewish regiment at the Cabinet meeting on April 5. Pressed for action, the War Office restudied the matter and found no enthusiasm for enlistment among Russian immigrants—in spite of the changed attitude to Russia after the Revolution—and encountered strong opposition among English Jews to a segregated unit called a Jewish regiment and marked by the Jewish symbol of the Star of David. The matter rested there for months, while debate continued, until ratification of a treaty with Russia for the conscription of Russians in England, either into the British or Russian forces, brought it to a head. As a conscription bill was being passed through Parliament, the War Office issued a circular on July 10 announcing that formation of a Jewish regiment and calling for Yiddish-speaking officers in existing units who might be detached for service with the Russian-Jewish draftees.

Weizmann's ambiguous position in the face of these measures brought him into sharp conflict with other Zionists, especially his own group of young associates. They reacted against his alliance with Jabotinsky in much the same way as Zionists had rebelled against Cowen's position of a year earlier. In his own defense, Weizmann claimed that he had always made it clear that his sympathy for Jabotinsky's project was not an official position of the Zionist organization. This claim gained some support from the attitude of the government especially the Foreign Office and Herbert Samuel's Home Office, who did, indeed, treat Jabotinsky's project as primarily related to the issue of conscription, separate from the political questions raised by Zionism. Nevertheless, the War Office was not alone in its sensitivity to the obvious political implications; and what Weizmann sometimes excused as purely personal advocacy obviously went very far into political concerns. In his talks with Frankfurter in Gibraltar and Paris, he discussed the chances of bringing American forces into the Turkish campaign, at least through the medium of recruiting for the Jewish legion. To bring such a thing off, forming American ties with British interests—much desired by men like Balfour—would, of course, have raised Zionist prestige immensely.[74]

Weizmann resented as intrusions on his privacy attacks by his Zionist associates that focused on such matters as the hospitality extended to Jabotinsky in his home. He also took personally the attitude of Sokolow, who had had a hand in some offenses charged against Weizmann, but now managed to stay clear of the conflict and avoid being attacked. But it was a more serious danger when his critics proposed to take him at his word and adopt a formal resolution detaching the Zionist organization from the project of the Jewish legion. Weizmann was forced to parry this maneuver by announcing that he had built upon the prospect of a Jewish force, recruited in America as well as England, in his negotiations with the government. Although he had made clear that the Zionist organization was not officially involved, he formally warned the EZF Executive Committee that a resolution explicitly disowning the legion would undermine his standing as a Zionist spokesman.

The friction over this issue, together with other frustrations, brought Weizmann to the point of offering to resign, which he did in August and again on September 5. On the latter occasion, Weizmann received a response from Ahad Ha'am, which deserves being quoted at some length for its illumination of the position Weizmann had attained as well as the relations between the two men:

> I permit myself—for the first time in all the years of our friendship—to speak to you not simply as a friend . . . but as a collaborator . . . who was on the battlefield while you were still sitting on the school bench, and one who almost certainly had a certain influence, direct or indirect, on the development of your Jewish *Weltanschauung.*
>
> . . . what you are about to do is . . . a stab in the back for the whole cause of Zionism. . . . You are too wise not to understand that the consequence of your "resignation" will be a loss in the prestige of Zionist leaders in the eyes of those on whom the fate of our cause depends. . . . And not because you're the only one who can do the work. . . . There is no man who is absolutely irreplaceable. And if you left the work for some reason beyond your control, . . . it could be continued by other hands. . . . Nor, if at the very beginning you had presented yourself . . . as one elected . . . by the Zionist Organization . . . would your "resignation" cause such confusion. . . . But your situation is an exceptional one. You began your work here . . . as a private Zionist. Your personal qualities and favorable conditions brought it about that in a short time you became practically the symbol of Zionism for many men of influence. And now suddenly, one fine day, you announce you no longer concern yourself with the matter, you have resigned! . . . Who chose you and is now entitled to accept your resignation? You were chosen by objective conditions and objective conditions will dismiss you . . . when complete success or complete failure will make your further work no longer necessary. But until then you cannot leave your place without evoking attitudes very damaging to the Zionists . . . and no other persons could carry on the work that you began.

In closing, Ahad Ha'am sent Weizmann the text of a letter he intended to offer for official communication to his young friend, calling his proposed resignation an act of "treason." But it ended with a statement that "we are confident you are not capable of such an act."[75]

Following this exchange, Weizmann withdrew his resignation. The Executive Committee, for its part, did not pass the contemplated resolution. In the meantime, on September 3, two days before Weizmann's resignation and Ahad Ha'am's response, the British Cabinet finally took up the matter of the draft declaration in favor of Zionism. Thus, at a critical moment in the relations with the government, Weizmann had to fight off an implied reprimand from his own constituency. He could do so successfully because it was so evident to leading Zionists that he had become not only personally acceptable but virtually the chosen instrument of the British government for securing the support of world Jewry. Whether he could, indeed, carry out that assignment was now to be put to the test.

The September 3 session of the War Cabinet took place in the absence of both the prime minister and Foreign Secretary Balfour, who were still on vacation.[76] Attending however, was the secretary of state for India, Herbert Samuel's cousin Edwin Montagu, who had circulated a strongly worded memorandum opposing the pro-Zionist measures that were to be discussed.

The first item taken up was the matter of the Jewish regiment. Lord Derby, now secretary of war, reported that influential Jewish leaders—including Rufus Isaacs, Lord Reading, the chief justice—had objected vehemently against a "Jewish" regiment. It was decided that, for the time being, the units would be assigned numbers in the normal way rather than given a distinctive name and Jewish insignia. However, in view of the developing commitment to Zionism, the questions of a name and badge and the commitment of the troops to the Palestine front could be decided in the future. It was anticipated that recruiting of Jews abroad, especially in the United States, could raise the contingent to some four battalions.

The meeting then considered three documents bearing on the proposed statement for the Zionists: the drafts by Balfour and Milner and the memorandum in opposition by the secretary of state for India, Edwin Montagu. Montagu repeated his objection that proclaiming Palestine "the home of the Jewish people" would prejudice the rights of Jews everywhere. Defenders of the Balfour-Milner proposals used the response already made by Lord Rothschild in reply to the Alexander-Montefiore letter in *The Times* (London) months before. Rothschild had said (in a text submitted for editorial comment to Weizmann), "We Zionists cannot see how the establishment of an autonomous Jewish State under . . . protection of one of the Allied Powers can be considered . . . subversive to the position or loyalty of the very large part of the Jewish people who have identified themselves thoroughly with the citizenship of the countries in which they live." From another quarter it was objected that the Allies, especially the Americans, ought to be consulted on so important a matter. Sir Robert Cecil replied on behalf of the Foreign Office that there had already been pressure for months to act on the matter. The Cabinet decided that the views of President Wilson should be obtained. Cecil was instructed "to inform the Government of the United States that His Majesty's Government were being pressed to make a declaration of sympathy with the Zionist movement," and "to ascertain their views as to the advisability of such a declaration being made." A message in these terms was cabled to Colonel House for the president's attention.[77]

House sent the request on to the president, and a few days later, on September 7, sent a reminder, in which he added his opinion that the British ought to be "chary about going too definitely into that question," as there were "many dangers lurking in it." On the following weekend the president was House's guest at his summer home in Magnolia, on the Massachusetts North Shore, and they had occasion to discuss the matter further. On September 10 House then cabled Cecil that Wilson felt "the time is not opportune for any definite statement further, perhaps, than one of sympathy, provided it can be made without conveying any real commitment. Things are in such a state of flux at the moment that he does not consider it advisable to go further."[78]

This was not exactly the response the Foreign Office had wanted. On the day of its receipt, September 11, another wire had been prepared asking for an early reply, as Weizmann had just reminded them that September 17 would be Rosh Hashanah, when a declaration of sympathy would be especially effective. Also, having learned that the Americans were being consulted, Weizmann and his Political Committee had decided to wire Brandeis about the "opposition from assimilationist quarters" and seek his and the President's support of the draft declaration, already (as they believed) approved by the foreign secretary and the prime minister: that is, the July 18 formula submitted by Lord Rothschild, which was to be sent with their wire. But the receipt of House's reply on September 11 changed all these plans. The Foreign Office did not send its reminder to House and Weizmann's cable to Brandeis was held back. Instead of the New Year's message he had suggested, Weizmann received word on September 18, the second day of the High Holidays, that Wilson had purportedly vetoed immediate action. He met Balfour on the following day and got a further discouraging report of Cabinet proceedings—together with assurances of continuing sympathy. Upon the prime minister's return to work, Scott arranged another meeting for Weizmann with him—and Lloyd George had the question of the proposed declaration returned to the Cabinet agenda for new consideration.[79]

With the vacations over and the prime minister (who had been ill) back in control, Weizmann's friends—Philip Kerr, Sir Ronald Graham, and other supporters in the government—energetically pressed his cause. He himself stressed that swift government action would bolster his position and his ability to gain support for the Allies, noting his difficulties with his own followers (which he suggested were like those of the Russian government with the irresponsible Soviet and called for the same remedy—a firm hand at the center). On September 19, the day of Weizmann's talk with Balfour, his cable to Brandeis was finally forwarded; thus his appeal to another presumable constituency, American Jewish leadership, was sent on its way.[80]

The September 19 cable's urgent tone—the warning of the threat from the "assimilationists" and the unexpected reference to Wilson as an obstacle—stirred Brandeis to a burst of activity. He now had the specific text of a possible British declaration, and he at once arranged a meeting for himself and Wise with Colonel House on September 28.[81] Brandeis' reply to Weizmann was agreed on at the meeting—if House's self-congratulatory diary account is to be believed, was dictated by House himself. Brandeis must have checked with House his own recollection of his May meeting with the president against the negative impression of Wilson's response conveyed by Weizmann's cable and so learned of the terms and circumstances of the September 10 reply to the Foreign Office. According to House's record of his discussion with the Zionists:

> I confessed the President was willing to go further than I thought advisable; and that I had warned him against a more definite statement than the one I had cabled Cecil.

If, then, the conferees compared the formula now sent by Weizmann with the specifications House had indicated on September 10, they could well have concluded that the declaration the British were considering was essentially the kind of indefinite, noncommittal gesture of sympathy House had suggested to Cecil—House's diary calls it "practically identical." Accordingly, Brandeis was able to wire to London, in his own name and that of Wilson's "closest advisers," the assurance of the president's "entire sympathy" with the proposed statement, together with his own approval of the draft.

However, Brandeis' long talk with the president and other Zionist contacts of the past years gave him no grounds to differ with other conditions House required. House's diary states:

> I cautioned against pressing the President for any public statement. I suggested they bring the French, Italian, and Russian Governments as near the attitude of Great Britain and the United States as possible and then leave the matter there.

The Zionists had already concluded in June not to press their effort to get a public statement from Wilson by submitting the Blackstone memorial. As for securing parallel positions from the other Allies, Brandeis cabled London the suggestion that House proposed; he also gave House documentation of the results Zionists had already achieved on these lines. (Even more: the Zionists had to give their tacit support to House's continuing interest in exploring the chance of a separate peace with Turkey—pursued in October with the aid of former Ambassador Elkus, who had to suppress for this purpose his intended public commitment to Zionism.)[82]

Thus, when the proposed draft declaration was placed on the Cabinet agenda for the meeting of October 4, Brandeis' assurance of Wilson's sympathy was in hand as well as the French statement Sokolow had obtained. The pressure for the declaration was reinforced by the reports indicating that the Germans were preparing their own gesture of sympathy, which made preemptive action imperative. At this meeting the pro-Zionists in the Cabinet were represented in full strength, and the discussion was based on a text specially edited, by Leopold Amery, to forestall common anti-Zionist objections. The draft by Milner was used as a base (rather than the more sweeping version by Balfour) and Amery added two provisos intended to pacify (rather than yield substantively to) Jewish and Arab opposition. He drew on Lord Rothschild's letter to *The Times* (London) for the assurance that a Jewish national home in Palestine would not endanger Jewish rights in the Diaspora and on Weizmann's published statements that Arab legitimate rights would not be prejudiced. On the other hand, there was determined opposition from Edwin Montagu, who was again present and offered impassioned resistance.

Once more the draft declaration was not immediately approved, but two preliminary measures were adopted by the Cabinet. It was decided to ask President Wilson directly whether the time was not now opportune for a declaration, and (incidentally honoring the pledge to Lucien Wolf that British Jewish notables would be informed and consulted) representative Zionists and non-Zionist Jews were sent the draft for comment. This delay alarmed and irritated Weizmann and threw him into a frenzy of activity. The communal turmoil stirred up by the Alexander-Montefiore letter in May had already induced second thoughts about past neglect to organize greater and more visible support in the Jewish community and had also revived talk of an Anglo-Jewish congress. Now that the government was putting the issue of a declaration of sympathy to leading Jewish figures, the aroused Zionists stimulated local societies to send in hundreds of resolutions in favor. At the same time, Weizmann sent appeals to Russia, France, and America for similar personal and popular statements of support for the declaration in order to counteract the "assimilationists" and give him backing when, as he expected, he would appear before the War Cabinet at its next meeting in defence of the Zionist case. Together with his appeal he sent the text of the Milner-Amery draft then being considered, which with minor revisions became the Balfour Declaration.[83]

In Washington Brandeis received Weizmann's appeal on October 14 and at once asked de Haas and Wise to see Colonel House. By that time House had not only received copies of the Weizmann-Brandeis messages but had direct communications from the Foreign Office for the president. After the meeting of October 4, Balfour had seen to it that the consultation with the Americans be framed in such a way as to elicit the desired response. Both British intelligence liaison with House in New York and the American Embassy in London were used to send the president the new draft together with the significant advice that the "German Government are making great efforts to capture" Zionist support. It appears that House took up the British cables with the president in the course of a meeting at the White House on October 13—but probably in a perfunctory way without pressing for an immediate response. On October 16 House's morning mail in New York brought a note from President Wilson instructing House to advise London that the president "concurred in the formula suggested." House informed British intelligence, who cabled London on that day:

> Colonel House put formula before President, who approves of it but asks that no mention of his approval shall be made when His Majesty's Government makes formula public, as he had arranged that American Jews shall then ask him for his approval, which he will give publicly here.

On the same day the Zionists alerted by Brandeis came to urge the president, through House, to approve the proposed draft (with slight modifications), only to find that this had already been done. They left elated; but de Haas, at least, understood that the British Zionists in their embattled position needed some open manifestation of support from America. His report to Brandeis raised the question whether Weizmann's request for some public demonstrations by Zionists to help his cause should not be met. Brandeis vetoed the suggestion, preferring to rely on the president and leave him a free hand to act at the time he chose.[84]

With its consultations completed, the War Cabinet should have been ready to act on the proposed declaration. A Foreign Office memorandum was submitted to Balfour on October 24—to help bolster his case—in which it was urged that three months had passed since Lord Rothschild's letter was received and that the Germans were about to preempt the issue by a (rumored) statement of their own. The matter was pressing also because of the unstable situation in Russia, whose effectiveness—or simply persistence—in the Entente was at stake. Russian Jews, it was believed, were almost all Zionists, and the influence of the Jewish community was very substantial in the new Russia. But the meeting for which these arguments were prepared was again postponed, as Lord Curzon was composing a memorandum of his own for circulation. When it appeared a few days later, it was an incisive critique of the proposed statement, in the same skeptical spirit as his comments on earlier British proclamations of sympathy for the Arab national cause: essentially, Curzon warned against encouraging hopes that Britain would not, in the event, be able to make good. Finally, when the War Cabinet did act on the declaration, at its meeting of October 31, Curzon waived his objections in deference to the propaganda value of the declaration and contented himself with warnings against too firm or far-reaching commitments to Jewish nationalism.

When the last act of the struggle was performed at the October 31 meeting, neither Weizmann nor Montagu was present or took part. Montagu had left for India, already despairing of the result of his anti-Zionist crusade. Weizmann did not argue his case before the Cabinet, as he had anticipated, but (according to his memoirs) was "waiting outside, this time within call." Sir Mark Sykes, in a rather generous acknowledgment of Weizmann's claim to paternity, is said to have announced the outcome to him "with the exclamation: 'Dr. Weizmann, it's a boy!'"[85]

4

Encounter and Clash

The Zionist Commission

The Balfour Declaration was not the first statement of international sympathy Zionists had won during the war. Verbal assurances had been given Tschlenow in Russia, Sokolow in the Vatican, and to American leaders by Wilson; the French Foreign Ministry's letter to Sokolow and Wilson's cabled approval precipitated the British action; and even the tiny socialist-Zionist faction had won a supporting statement from the British Labor party before the declaration was finally approved. But when it came, it was recognized as an act of a quite different order of significance from earlier pro-Zionist gestures. It clearly demanded reciprocal action greater than anything Zionists were used to in the past.

Some British officers, not without antisemitic prejudice, had pressed for a declaration, expecting exaggerated, or simply fantastic, advantages for the Allies: for example, the collapse of the Young Turks, supposedly dependent on crypto-Jewish support. Some Zionists vainly imagined that their influence might counterbalance sentiment for a separate peace among Jews in Russia or persuade the Americans to become involved in the war with Turkey. Short of such goals, they felt committed to conduct effective propaganda among Russian and American Jews in response to the declaration. The immediate enthusiasm shown everywhere around the world seems to have satisfied Lloyd George (in retrospect) that their commitment was fulfilled. But British Zionists were aware that their triumph was flawed; neither in Russia nor in America did the Zionist leaders adopt a policy that was quite what Weizmann and his English colleagues had hoped.[1]

Of the Russian leaders, Ussishkin, in Weizmann's opinion, was deluded by the belief that Germany was bound to win the war. Tschlenow, moving between Russia and the neutral and Allied countries as a detached member of the Smaller Action Committee, was intent on maintaining the integrity of the world organization and the authority of its elected executive; this led him to greet the Balfour Declaration with notable caution and reserve.

The Americans, unlike the Russians, had approved the policy of a British protectorate in Palestine; but since their country was not a belligerent on the Turkish front, Brandeis vetoed any active propaganda for the Weizmann line. Local Zionists lent discreet support to recruitment for the Jewish legion in the United States and Canada. When the British Zionists called for a fund of two hundred thousand pounds sterling for activities entailed by the declaration, the Americans not only responded promptly to this appeal, they proclaimed their own hundred-million-dollar "Preparation Fund" for the work in Palestine. Yet their contributions to the immediate tasks soon to be faced by Weizmann in Palestine were hampered by the same considerations of American foreign policy that restricted their support for the Jewish legion.

In addition to such handicaps abroad, Weizmann faced complicated issues in the Zionist community in England. Despite the immensely enhanced prestige he gained from the declaration, the internal frictions of the past months still remained to be resolved.

After Weizmann's elevation to the presidency of British Zionism and the crucial meeting with Sykes at Gaster's home, there were sporadic efforts to form a proper organization of Zionist forces to support his leadership. The EZF was brought under some control by the appointment of his associates to its executive councils; later, the Order of Ancient Maccabeans chose Harry Sacher as its president to succeed Herbert Bentwich. The supervision Weizmann exercised over his own following was fairly minimal (in sharp contrast to the tight hold Brandeis easily managed in America); beyond these bounds, it required continual watchful maneuvers to pursue his chosen course among the shoals and eddies of independent Jewish and Zionist initiatives. A rough and ready combine of the several leading Zionist officials had been set up in 1915, and it was substantially supplemented by those selected to meet with Sykes in February, 1917; but this assemblage did not work regularly as a committee afterward. The main tasks agreed on with Sykes were taken over by Sokolow and Weizmann, who called on others to help at their own discretion. Gaster, Lord Rothschild, James de Rothschild, and even Harry Sacher had their means and channels of political action, and each occasionally worked at cross-purposes with Weizmann and Sokolow—who, for that matter, had their own differences.

Pressure for a more orderly, organized system of policy management came mainly from Weizmann's young associates.[2] They had been largely responsible for producing materials—ranging from books and Zionist journals to occasional articles, pamphlets, and memoranda—to bolster the lobbying of the leaders. The Manchester brothers-in-law, Sacher, Israel Sieff and Simon Marks, had strong connections with the provincial communal leadership most apt to challenge the dominant London Jewish establishment. They were effectively behind the attempted rapprochement with non-Zionists that began in 1915; later, in 1917, they undertook to line up synagogues and Jewish soci-

eties across the country as a pro-Zionist force and organized local endorse-
ments of Zionism in response to the Montefiore-Alexander letter in *The
Times* (London). They thoroughly disliked the informal, disorderly arrangements that allowed their leaders to select their consultants on an ad hoc basis
(reducing aides like themselves to subordination without authorized status);
they particularly abhorred the arbitrary use of privileged information, the
failure to record activities, and the absence of a proper staff of technical advisors and secretarial assistants inherent in the system. They pressed for inclusion as a group in a formally constituted Political Committee, entitled to full
information and authorized to advise on policy; they proposed to set up a
proper Zionist office to coordinate and carry out the required work. These
suggestions were heard without enthusiasm by the leaders, who were not
eager to let wider circles into the secrets of their confidential talks with the
government and, particularly, wished to avoid such prickly associates as Gaster on such a body. After many months of delay (excused by the assignments
of Sokolow and Weizmann abroad), the Political Committee and a formally
organized Zionist office were finally installed in the crucial months before the
declaration.

On receiving the declaration, the Political Committee met to consider its
next steps. Tschlenow, who had come on tour, reported that the Smaller
Action Committee, meeting in Copenhagen, had reaffirmed absolute Zionist
neutrality (in order to prevent injury to the Palestine Jewish settlement) until
it, as the constitutional authority, should sanction a change in policy. This
pronouncement (greeted, according to the privately kept minutes, with total
silence) could effectually veto the entire program of immediate action contemplated by the British Zionists. Convening the Zionists in Allied countries
to approve the policy of a British-protected Jewish Palestine, establishing an
official Zionist liaison (but not an official Zionist sponsorship) for the Jewish
legion—all such positive measures of identification with the declaration
would have to await approval by the German-led world movement. Weizmann's impassioned, tearful reply made it plain that, if persisted in, Tschlenow's position meant his own withdrawal and the end of Zionist access to
the British government. Sokolow and Ahad Ha'am rushed in to smooth over
the threatening rift, and a pragmatic agreement was reached. The British
Zionists, and such others as agreed with them, could pursue their policy, set
up a liaison with the Jewish legion campaign, and promote a British protectorate; Zionists in other countries would welcome the British declaration,
seek similar support from their government—but abstain from partisan positions they did not share.[3]

Another immediate task that awaited the Political Committee was the creation of a commission to serve in Palestine. Sykes had strongly pressed for
such a Zionist liaison with the army many months before. After rejecting others proposed for the task, Weizmann undertook to perform this function himself—a decision that entailed finally giving up his faculty appointment in
Manchester. But, in full agreement with his advisers and supporters, he had

deferred action until he could be assured of his right to work for an independent Zionist policy, tactitly favored if not officially adopted by the government.

Some parts of the broad program Sykes had in mind were taken up in Weizmann's absence by other Zionists who were in Egypt in early 1917.[4] Given the uncertain status of such surrogates and the halting British advance into Palestine, their role was restricted to the short-range needs of the military command. Thus, Aaron Aaronsohn's intimate knowledge of local conditions and the espionage network he led in Palestine made him an invaluable intelligence resource but could not easily yield direct political gains. Political implications in his work made British officers react with a bureaucratic defensiveness that he believed hampered and even endangered his men in the field. He also fought with other Jewish leaders in Egypt over the prerogative of channeling relief funds to the afflicted Palestine community. Aaronsohn argued that sending in gold shipments with his agents would earn his underground network the trust and support essential to its success. But his open contempt for leaders of the community expelled to Egypt from Palestine and the general fear of his adventurist activity strengthened the hand of rivals.

In June 1917 when Sykes returned to London to face Morgenthau's mysterious project of a separate peace with Turkey, another problem was to overcome the difficulties in setting up a proper Jewish liaison. Sykes had to contend with supporters of Morgenthau's initiative in British official circles who opposed his plans for a postwar partition of Turkey-in-Asia. It also seemed to be part of a larger Jewish pro-German trend, currently strengthened in Russia by support for a separate peace with Germany. It became urgent to activate the Zionists by sending someone like Sokolow to Russia to bolster pro-Allied sentiment there (a plan that was not carried out) and by reinforcing the Jewish liaison in Palestine so that it could effectively negotiate an understanding with Britain's Arab clients. Faced with such assignments, the Zionist leaders could more cogently press for a firmer, public commitment to their Jewish objectives in order to give them greater credence in the community. On both sides there was revived concern for a better form of Jewish liaison. The Balfour Declaration brought this issue to a head.[5]

Conditions had changed sharply since the matter was first broached early in the year. The war remained undecided, and hostilities continued for a year more, but attention was beginning to focus on the shape of an ultimate peace settlement. The Bolsheviks, who began peace negotiations with Germany soon after seizing power, denounced the Allies' secret agreements and demanded anti-imperialist goals for a world at peace. President Wilson promptly took up the challenge with his Fourteen Points. By the end of 1917, then, new plans had to be framed in terms of the situation Zionists might face at the end of hostilities and yet be acceptable to a military command still preoccupied with the uncertainties of a continuing war.

Tschlenow's analysis assumed that after the Bolsheviks' and Wilson's pronouncements, the postwar settlement would have to envisage the ultimate national independence of colonial and subjugated territories. Ahad Ha'am agreed with this premise and drew the conclusion that Zionists must lower their sights and demand no more initially than could be reconciled with claims of the current Arab majority in Palestine, which the British would probably respect. But Tschlenow (taking a view that was to be echoed repeatedly by the critics of the line Weizmann chose to follow) argued that precisely because of the new situation, it was essential to secure maximum commitments at the outset; for the administration set up by the military in occupying Palestine would necessarily define whose independent country Britain intended Palestine to become—Arab or Jewish—and would predetermine the outcome. Accordingly, Zionist proposals must project a provisional government for the whole country that symbolically recognized its Jewish national character in clear terms. The Armenians, he noted, had already demanded just such an assurance from the French—for no more than half a million residents—in a region where they were a distinct minority. Jews could resort to this precedent not only on the grounds of comparable historic suffering, but they could also claim self-determination for a dispersed, wandering people awaiting "repatriation" to Palestine in numbers that would make them a clear majority upon their resettlement.[6]

Zionists in London had begun their plans for Palestine's future in 1916 with a set of "demands" drawn from Herzlian blueprints for a chartered company in a colonial situation. The meetings with Sykes and Picot in 1917 posed the immediate task of designing a Zionist commision for liaison with the military government in Palestine. (Picot, expecting to share in a joint administration of Palestine as French high commissioner, urged this on the Zionists, in order—like the Syrians and Armenians he sponsored—to establish "facts.") Adapting their plans to a new framework, meant for international trusteeships in prospective independent areas, led the London subcommittee to conclusions similar to Tschlenow's. Their draft presented to the Political Committee in November 1917 included the following: a Jew to head the administration with the powers of a high commissioner; a police force initially recruited from existing Jewish security forces; and restoring war damages inflicted by Turkish policy through the repatriation of refugees and reorganization of Jewish arbitration courts, banking services, and other agencies.

Such a comprehensive plan, giving a Zionist stamp to what amounted to a provisional government for the whole country, was rejected by Sokolow and Sacher as going beyond the limits a military government would accept. Sokolow said the projected Zionist commission should confine itself to administering Jewish communal matters under the aegis of the occupation force. Although the plans were then recast under these instructions, the final product contained some provisions (with Weizmann's approval) that had in mind more than the transient needs of a military occupation. Weizmann was fully aware that the final disposition of Palestine at the peace conference would not assure Zionist aims unless the Jewish position in Palestine itself were swiftly reinforced.[7]

The guidelines eventually approved for the Zionist Commission included the original functions contemplated by Sykes: to help form the proposed

Arab-Armenian-Jewish coalition; to aid the occupation authority in dealing with the Jewish community (including repatriation of refugees, control of relief, and restoration of institutions). In addition, the Zionists' long-range objectives were given token recognition in a provision for studies of the potential for future development of the Jewish community in the light of the Balfour Declaration. Beyond this, immediate proposals of long-range significance included the following: a freeze on land transactions (to prevent speculative price inflation); reopening the Zionist financial institutions in Palestine and official use of their facilities; formal inauguration of the Hebrew University in Jerusalem; and such action as seemed appropriate for the local expansion and employment of the Jewish legion, with the concurrence of the British political officer assigned to the commission.[8]

Sykes' original proposal for a Jewish liaison had its own far-reaching political implications, being connected with his strategy of an Arab-Armenian-Jewish pro-Allied coalition; but the Jewish liaison officers appointed were to be subject to the authority of the Egyptian expeditionary force and its immediate staff decisions. If Weizmann had come to Egypt at Sykes' initial request, his role might have been a broader one than was played by Aaronsohn, but he, too, would have been subordinate to Sykes and other officers. He now could come as the chairman of a more or less independent commission, with a British political officer assigned to assist rather than command. His commission was to be an international one, that is, symbolically tied to the Allies generally, not solely to England, and deriving its legitimacy from the support of Jews everywhere, formally expressed in Allied countries. The latter condition (which would achieve immediate aims of British strategy, going beyond the specific needs of the Palestine front to the vital relationships with Russia and America) was an assumption posed by the British—a challenge Weizmann and his friends were hard put to meet.

Weizmann's delicate political assignment was to promote an exclusively British protectorate for the Jewish homeland while heading an international commission that did not openly flout the Sykes-Picot agreement; the British thereby escaped responsibility for voiding their commitment to France while Zionists worked to that very end for them. The point was underlined by the nomination of a token French member (chosen by Baron de Rothschild) and an eventual Italian representation on the Zionist Commission, with British Jews assisting Weizmann in the most critical positions. The main object, to obtain American and Russian participation, was not achieved at once. Russian Jews could not join Weizmann under the chaotic conditions of 1918 in their country. American official Zionist representation was vetoed by Washington while fighting continued with Turkey; a loose connection was maintained informally by an American secretary and by Aaronsohn, who returned from a brief mission to America for the British to serve as a technical aide on the commission.

Weizmann arrived in Palestine in April 1918 and stayed as head of the Zionist Commission until October. During that time he dealt for the first time directly with local factors on the issues precipitated by the Zionist victory in London: with the Arabs, the British administration on the scene, and the Palestine Jewish community. His irruption into their affairs radically altered the basic situation, and his policies posed new problems and patterns for dealing with them that would continue to dominate Zionist concerns for many years.

By 1918 a growing split between France and Britain in their common project of an Arab-Armenian-Jewish coalition was as clear as their diverging positions toward the Sykes-Picot treaty. The Armenians, because of their geographical distribution, fell naturally into the position of French (or potentially Russian) clients; the Jews, after the Balfour Declaration, were viewed as committed to England; and there was an undercover struggle for the political conquest of the Arabs—British sponsorship of the Beduin-based Arab revolt was contested by French-supported Syrian nationalists. Under the circumstances, Weizmann's role was not simply to supply a Jewish partner for Armenian and Arab nationalists. To secure further British interest in Zionism, he was required to bolster their position by making Zionism palatable to Arab leaders.

Weizmann discovered that, while London had urged wide publicity for the Balfour Declaration across the Diaspora countries, military headquarters in the Mediterranean had suppressed its publication locally for fear of adverse Arab reactions. His visit was hardly welcome, but he was able, with his usual application to such tasks, to establish more or less cordial relations with Allenby and other British officers important for his work. One of the first assignments he undertook, with their assistance, was to meet Arab leaders in order to reassure them about Zionist intentions. The Jews, he informed them, did not seek to dominate government in Palestine from the outset (a position he could reasonably support because of the changed formulation of immediate Zionist "demands" that he and Sokolow had secured in London from the Political Committee), nor did they aim to disturb the religious rights of non-Jews or displace them from economic positions. Zionist development work would necessarily proceed gradually, precluding any such danger.

The meetings with local Arabs, in Egypt and later in Palestine, were welcomed by English officers and rated as gratifyingly successful. Weizmann himself came away with less satisfaction: he judged Syrian leaders, Christian Arab landowners, and local Palestinian notables to be hostile and responsive to French-instigated propaganda. On the other hand, he took a sanguine view of the contacts he established with the Hejazi Beduin leadership. Weizmann came away from the meeting the British arranged for him in June with Prince Faisal, the leader of the Arab revolt, believing he had found the proper channel for an Arab-Zionist entente. He thought an understanding could be reached, based on Arab acceptance of a Jewish national position in Palestine and Zionist political and technical support for Arab nationalism elsewhere: an approach that matured at the peace conference and was to recur in later years. The unspoken premise of this conclusion (valid enough in the particular case) was that British policy firmly supported the arrangement; for Weizmann's final judgment was that only a clear and steady British pro-Zionist policy (already becoming questionable in other respects) could assure a proper Jewish-Arab relationship, given the multiple disparities between the parties in their strengths and weaknesses and in their outlook. In short, while the British were expecting the Zionists to placate the Arabs in the interest of British policy, the Zionists relied on the British to bring about Arab acquiescence by firmly pronouncing and consistently applying support of Zionism.[9]

Weizmann's mission to care for the immediate needs of the Palestine Jewish community was another matter that had concerned the British military earlier. The contentions between Aaronsohn and his rivals over control of aid distribution in Palestine—largely rendered moot by Allenby's occupation of Jerusalem—were now completely set aside when the Zionist Commission became the main channel for Jewish relief funds. The power this lent him, added to the general assumption in the Jewish community that the Zionists were about to share directly in the Palestine government, seemed to give Weizmann a chance for radical reform of local institutions. Building on beginnings made shortly before his arrival, Weizmann proposed to bring the separate Sephardi and Ashkenazi rabbinates into a single (dual) hierarchical authority within the broader Jewish communal structure; to introduce a minimum of secular instruction into the Talmudic academies; and to require orderly and efficient procedures to be followed by the traditionalist educational, judicial, and welfare institutions. He was unable to achieve his aims before he left, but his forceful intervention started a process that transformed the traditionalist community in Palestine; it brought some into a new, more integral relationship with the developing secular institutions of Palestine Jewry and provoked others to resort to new forms of political and extremist opposition.[10]

In these efforts Weizmann worked in support of local Zionists, who had initiated a reorganization of the community as soon as the Turks abandoned part of it to the advancing Britons. But the major impact of the commission's incursion into local affairs was to supplant the newly hatched communal representation as the authorized body to deal with the military governors. Recognizing this, the local provisional council sought to be represented on the Zionist Commission, but to no avail. The commission and Weizmann personally became deeply involved in the prickly issues that arose between the military government and the Jewish community.

In London, preparing for the commission's departure, Weizmann was able to find considerable support for expanding Jewish activities to serve current needs of the occupation authorities. The Jewish Colonial Trust and the bank it had founded in Palestine in 1909 (the Anglo-Palestine Bank) had to apply to him for help in reorganizing and raising adequate capital for the new tasks that awaited—a turn of events that hugely gratified Weizmann, who recalled earlier fruitless efforts of his group of "practical" Zionists to bring the financial institutions under greater control. He not only got the American Zionists to help refinance the bank and use it for transmitting relief funds, but also induced the British to use it for financial transactions involved in the invasion and occupation of Palestine. Agronomists available to the commission drew up plans for leasing state lands and cultivating large areas by dry farming methods in order to supply Allenby's forces. Having gained tacit approval for encouraging (without committing the Zionist organization) recruitment for the Jewish battalions—now possible in Palestine as well as America—Weizmann entered into delicate dealings with the military over the way this politically sensitive issue was handled.[11]

All such matters became difficult and complicated when the commission reached Palestine, especially when Weizmann tried to push his openings to the point where political implications became blatant. His suggestion to allow the Anglo-Palestine Bank to serve as a bank of issue and use its bills as Palestinian currency was rejected; the proposal to let the Zionists put large areas under cultivation to supply the army was ruled a political matter and referred by the local staff to London, where it died; and such matters as the use of Jewish battalions and even the idea of a symbolic inauguration of the Hebrew University, which had been warmly received in London and Washington, were treated with cautious or suspicious reserve, and it needed patient, persistent efforts to bring them to a conclusion.

In part the problem stemmed from the legal conditions under which the occupation operated, especially as interpreted where the Zionists were concerned. Under the Hague Convention, the occupying power was required to maintain the laws and conditions previously prevailing, pending a peace settlement and transfer of sovereignty. Allenby took a rigid position from the start in applying the convention, resisting French pressure to introduce civil administration, in which they could claim a share under the terms of the Sykes-Picot agreement. To be less rigid toward Zionist suggestions—for instance, to use Hebrew on official signs and stamps, or grant municipal rights to Jewish settlement councils and official jurisdiction to Jewish arbitration courts—would be inconsistent and could serve the French as evidence that the Britons planned to do them out of their treaty rights in Palestine. But the effect of freezing the status quo was to extend the existing Arab preponderance in Palestine by generalization: in Jerusalem, where Jews were the majority, the mayor appointed was an Arab, following precedent; and when police were recruited or civilian offices filled, the local personnel chosen to aid British officials were rarely Jews.

Weizmann soon came to believe, as did most observers, that there was more to this trend of events than the mere logic of a temporary legal situation. He early realized that British administrators drawn from the Egyptian or Indian colonial service were temperamentally disposed to find other "native" populations, like the Palestinian Arabs, easier to deal with than European Jews, especially Jewish nationalist politicos and radical, intellectual proletarians. Antisemitic bias was also evident: military convenience might account for the suppression of the Balfour Declaration in Egypt and Palestine, but not the widespread circulation among British officers of the *Protocols of the Elders of Zion,* fresh from its Russian sources. Weizmann began to press for clear pro-Zionist instructions to the local staff from London. In parallel, he constantly urged the English and American Zionists to send him men to serve in Palestine who were better suited to deal with English officials and with issues demanding professional expertise than were the Russian-Jewish enthusiasts and amateurs on the scene. Such pleas were sent with special urgency to America, whose share in the work of the commission was a sore disappointment.[12]

The American Zionists, especially such veterans as Jacob de Haas and Stephen Wise, were more than willing to share the responsibilities flowing from the Balfour Declaration, including the work of the Zionist Commission. Barred from official representation by the Wilson administration's policy, they hoped to maintain contact by sending Eugene Meyer's brother Walter as a volunteer secretary on Weizmann's staff and getting reports from Aaron Aaronsohn. In addition, they were eager to assume responsibility for the medical and sanitary services essential for rehabilitating the Palestine community and laying a sound foundation for constructive urban and rural development in the future. Nathan Straus' medical philanthropy and the visiting nurses' program financed by Hadassah in the prewar years gave them a claim to take on this task; initial efforts to renew these activities, interrupted by the Turks, had begun as early as 1916. Now they hoped to contribute this service at least in British-occupied Palestine.

But here again they encountered unlooked-for obstacles in the attitudes of American officials and other concerned organizations.[13] Not only the State Department, but the American Red Cross looked askance at the proposed medical mission of American Jews to their coreligionists in the Holy Land. The Jews' tradition of themselves providing necessary relief to their own coreligionists (in order to protect them from pressures to convert if they became dependent on Gentile charity), although frequently praised, was not met with universal sympathy—even apart from the missionary background and associations of so many leaders of American philanthropy. Red Cross and other American relief officials (in postwar Poland as well as in the case of Palestine) disliked efforts to aid particular parts of a needy population; they would have liked all American charity to be generally distributed and controlled by themselves. Thus, the American Zionist medical mission encountered official delays, whereas a Red Cross mission to Palestine arrived early. The Zionist mission arrived, in fact, at a time when Weizmann was at last leaving for England after his repeatedly extended and increasingly burdensome stay as the commission chairman.

Much as Weizmann valued the opportunity to head the Zionist Commission and enter the inner chambers of local Palestinian affairs, he remained nervously aware of the hazards of leaving the London center of Zionist politics to the care of others. He had pleaded with friends to keep him in close touch with developments, but their assurances failed to still his apprehensions about what line his colleagues might take in his absence. After two months in Palestine, he concluded that major difficulties faced by the commission in Palestine—the rigid application of the status quo ante by the occupation authorities; the hostile, sometimes antisemitic, attitudes of some British officials and the suppression of public notice of the Balfour Declaration; and, on the Jewish side, insufficient timely support for the commission's efforts—could only be dealt with abroad; and probably only by himself. His hope in June, as he wrote in a long letter to Balfour, was to leave the commission to the care of others, while he took up again pressing matters in England and America: securing clear policy instructions for the Palestine administration from London; rousing the Americans (and English Jews) to greater efforts; and preparing for a congress of Jewish communities in the Allied countries to be held in Palestine in anticipation of a peace conference.[14]

But months passed and Weizmann continued to be detained in Palestine, immersed in the mounting difficulties of the commission's work. The funds available to him dwindled and were not adequately replenished. The loans sought to finance the Anglo-Palestine Bank's branches, and to enable them in turn, to fund renewed work in long-neglected citrus groves and vineyards were slow in coming. Even the ceremonial inauguration of the Hebrew University on its recently acquired Mount Scopus site failed, in Weizmann's view, to be given the support and attention it deserved by Zionist leaders abroad. Most troubling of all was the failure of qualified, technically and administratively competent English and American Zionists to arrive. As his stay stretched out into the summer, his personal, domestic, and Zionist position seemed increasingly precarious. In September he finally left for England, arriving in October.[15]

The Peace Conference

In mid-September 1918 when Weizmann left Palestine, he still considered the Zionist Commission's work vital to bolster the Zionist position at an eventual peace conference. After visiting England and touring the United States, he expected to convene leaders from the Allied countries in Palestine and formulate the final Jewish proposals. But when he arrived in London, it was evident that no time remained for long-range preparatory measures. He was en route when Turkish resistance in Palestine was broken at Megiddo; as he arrived in England, word came that Damascus was occupied by the Arab Legion and, soon after, that French naval units had taken Beirut. On September 30 Bulgaria signed an armistice, and a week later the war with Turkey was over, too. Allied offensives forced Austria and Germany to appeal for an armistice on October 4; continued Allied pressure brought about internal collapse in both countries, and the November 11 armistice followed. By January 18, 1919 the peace conference had formally begun.

Spokesmen of all the nationalities who sought independence in the collapse of the German, Russian, Austrian, and Ottoman empires converged on Paris. Jews, a people thinly dispersed across the globe, were multiply represented: by delegates from Jewish national councils recently formed in Poland, the Ukraine, Palestine, and elsewhere on an assertedly democratic basis; by

the American Jewish Congress delegation and an AJC dual representation—
as part of the congress and also separately; by the nationalist WZO and its
non-Zionist opposition, the traditional establishment in France and England.
Instead of seeking unity at a deliberate pace as Weizmann had hoped, Zionist
delegates appeared in Paris and London to treat simultaneously with the
peace conferees, with non-Zionists, and with one another.

Jewish dispersion posed another problem for nationalists, one shared only
(to a degree) with the Armenians: how to claim self-determination while lacking its usual prerequisite, a majority of the population in any sizable territory.
Non-Zionists relied on the precedents of earlier international treaties that
provided for the individual enfranchisement of the Jews in certain countries;
their position implicitly ruled out claims for Jews collectively. It was urgently
necessary to find a way to avoid open conflict between the opposing positions
of Jewish advocates. The problem posed itself in two issues: What status
should be sought for Diaspora Jews in the newly independent states? What
status should be sought for Jews in Palestine?

In both cases the nationalist argument had to be made by an unusual
application of the doctrine of exterritorial rights.[16] The socialist theoreticians
who invented the concept had proposed that national minorities who were a
majority in some appropriate region of Austria-Hungary should be served by
autonomous institutions, even outside their region. A claim to personal, cultural autonomy by Jews, lacking the precondition of a regional majority, was
an extension of the concept not accepted by its authors. So, too, the Zionist
claim to Palestine, as a matter of historic justice and international equity,
implied an unusual, exterritorial principle of self-determination: one based
on the rights of those Jews *entitled* to settle there, not only those currently
settled. If the national home were to be in truth open to Jews as a matter of
right, then potential settlers (those Jews who could not, or would not, be
absorbed by assimilation in the Diaspora) would have legitimate interests
that must be respected in the governance of Palestine. This was a principle
that was to produce intricate disputes among the Zionists themselves and
sharp dissent from the non-Zionist opposition. But years of experience had
already yielded a tradition of workable compromise, and recent events
encouraged broader agreement.

Jewish anti-Zionist activism was diminished wherever the Balfour Declaration won government approval. In America the AJC publicly endorsed
the Balfour statement, though of course in its own, muted accentuation; only
a small collection of radical anti-Zionists organized in open opposition.

Whatever differences existed among Zionists in their commitment to
Diaspora nationalism, they were overborne at the peace conference by the
common determination that they, not the antinationalists, should control the
presentation of the Jewish case. French Jews and like-minded British Jews,
first on the scene, seemed about to prejudice the outcome by taking the initiative. The Zionist delegation led by Sokolow, already active in Paris, was
able to hold off this pressure until those directly concerned, the Jewish communities in the new, successor states (who wanted national minority rights)

were represented. The American Jewish Congress' delegation was committed by prior understanding to secure "group rights" for Jewish communities that demanded them in countries where other national minorities were recognized; in Paris the AJC leader, Louis Marshall, loyally helped win the inclusion of these demands in the treaties with the successor states. The European Jewish delegations, with the financial support of the WZO and under the leadership of Zionists like Motzkin, set up their Comité des délégations juives and played a major part in uniting other minorities interested in securing group rights in the treaties with the new states.[17]

Despite his sympathy for the cause of Hebrew culture in the Diaspora, Weizmann's interest in all this (unlike Sokolow's, who became more fully involved) was largely limited to the aim of blocking antinationalist domination. But this was enough to entail organizational commitments that later complicated his disputes with Brandeis over differences more immediately connected with the work in Palestine. The 1917 rebellion against old-line leaders in England was not as clear a Zionist victory as in America. A Joint Foreign Committee was reestablished by the West End notables and the new chiefs of the Board of Deputies without significant Zionist participation, and the League of British Jews, a more effective anti-Zionist force than its American counterpart, was organized. But other prominent figures, like Sir Alfred Mond of Imperial Chemical Industries and Sir Robert Waley Cohen of Shell Oil, were moved by the Balfour Declaration to support constructive Zionist projects. In France, as the postwar rivalry with England emerged, the Jewish establishment was backed by the government, if not led, in continued opposition to the nationalists.[18]

Both Weizmann and Brandeis shared the concern of other Zionists to secure Jewish rights in East-Central Europe, not to speak of physical security in the turbulent postwar days; both, too, preferred to confine themselves and their organization to the Palestine project, leaving Diaspora issues to other Zionist-led or non-Zionist bodies. On their primary concern, the desired political status in Palestine, Sokolow and Weizmann in Europe and Brandeis in America—in spite of episodic differences among them—in general found themselves together and often at odds with other Zionists during the peace conference. Also, the irresistible impulse to respond to pogroms in Poland and elsewhere led all of them to take action—sometimes moved as well by the political gain that might accrue to an organization that effectively urged governments to aid Jews in an emergency.

The approaching peace conference confronted Weizmann with a personal problem that had been looming larger over the past two years. The Balfour Declaration and his role as head of the Zionist Commission in Palestine had projected his image as the presumptive leader of world Zionism and the authentic voice of Jewish popular opinion across the globe; but this reputation rested, after all, chiefly on the confidence placed in him by Britons. This, in turn, depended on his ability to demonstrate that he could indeed evoke desired responses from Zionists and other Jews everywhere, especially in

Russia and America. It was a test he faced under the handicap of a very insecure personal position in the Zionist hierarchy and of resistance by other Jewish leaders, Zionist as well as non-Zionist, to actions that they neither controlled nor duly authorized.

Weizmann's achievement during the war years was made possible in good
part by the disorganization of world Zionism, and the leeway this afforded to
free-lance activists to take advantage of local opportunities. Nevertheless,
from the beginning, Weizmann shunned any blatant separation such as Jabotinsky deliberately adopted from the expressed consensus of fellow Zionists.
The early negotiations with Lucien Wolf apparently occasioned Tschlenow's
sanction for Weizmann's top-level lobbying. Later, Weizmann felt hampered
by his role as an officially subordinate, but in practice independent (if not
dominant), associate of Sokolow. Sokolow shared with Weizmann a pro-
Allied Zionist policy but seemed less committed to an exclusive orientation
toward Britain; Tschlenow once chided Weizmann for acting like a British
agent rather than a disciplined Zionist.[19]

As chairman of the Zionist Commission, Weizmann headed an international body purporting to represent world Jewry; he remained chairman in
absentia on returning to London, while a series of acting heads conducted the
work in Palestine. The new position simply intensified the discomfort of his
ill-defined status. Weizmann's claim to leadership was threatened by every
failure to respond to his pleas for action, let alone their rejection, whether by
organized Zionists or communal agencies in the Diaspora. During his service
in Palestine, Weizmann grew acutely sensitive to his dependence on cooperation from London and New York. Returning to London he found that it was
there, and in Paris, that his energies were required; but his uncertain status
was even more burdensome in the new setting.

The developing situation was making Zionist reorganization urgent. Since
Allenby's offensive began in late 1917, Sokolow and Weizmann's London
operation had been increasingly involved in administering relief and other
work in Palestine. The office set up to work with the leaders assumed responsibility for transfering funds on a growing scale, and development planning
for the future now had to go beyond generalities into specific, technical detail.
The makeshift staff, including part-time, volunteer workers, was hardly adequate; files were in a state that exasperated visiting Americans and local activists. Weizmann sought to remedy the situation by securing Julius Simon's
transfer from the Zionist office in The Hague to London; Simon arrived in
late 1918. When successive armistices sealed the Allied victory, further transfers of Zionist functionaries to London were indicated; they awaited only
British permission for travel by foreign nationals.[20]

Meanwhile, support for official recognition of Weizmann's leadership
gained new allies. As America had shifted from neutrality to association with
the Allies, the British appreciation of Weizmann gave him increased credi-
bility among American Zionists. In joining the Morgenthau mission, Weizmann met Frankfurter, the American most apt to share his unqualifiedly pro-
British orientation—and the one closest to Brandeis. Then Aaronsohn—
another in whom Brandeis placed great trust—became the accepted liaison

between the Zionists in London and Washington. Aaronsohn saw in Sokolow his particular adversary; reports came to London that he urged the Americans to accept Weizmann as the sole leader in London. Given the tight control and undivided authority by which Brandeis ran his organization, it was natural for the Americans to regard a similar presidential style in London as more efficient than the loose, indefinite arrangements that were in effect.

Action tending to satisfy Weizmann's claim for formal authority in the WZO structure was precipitated by members of the Smaller Action Committee located in Copenhagen and Berlin. In November 1918 Sokolow and Weizmann had asked Victor Jacobson, a member of the Smaller Action Committee and head of the Copenhagen office, to join them in London and to secure the consent of the Berlin chiefs to the transfer of authority. Soon after, the war ended. The German Zionists accepted the new situation swiftly and generously. Meeting in Copenhagen from November 29 to December 1 1918, they proposed a Zionist reorganization: As there were two executive seats vacant (one, because of Tschlenow's death in London earlier in the year), Weizmann and Julius Simon should be co-opted to the Smaller Action Committee; America should have a member to represent it; the headquarters should be moved to London. If the two members in Berlin, who were Germans, could not be permitted to join the others in London (the British indeed refused permission for their travel or even for communication with them), they offered to resign and make their positions available to others.[21]

Sokolow, with support from other veteran Zionists, met all such suggestions with firm opposition. He said that Weizmann already enjoyed sufficient authority to carry out his work under existing arrangements. He contended that the attempts to reorganize were illegal under the rules of the WZO. He complained about Weizmann's prolonged absence from Paris, where Sokolow was dealing with the impending peace conference; meanwhile Sokolow, in turn, deliberately avoided the meetings in London where reorganization was being considered. After a series of meetings in Paris and London, Weizmann was co-opted to the Smaller Action Committee in Tschlenow's place, in a procedure whose legality under WZO rules remained questionable. The larger matter of Zionist reorganization was set aside for later consideration while the meetings concerned themselves with pressing issues of framing the Zionist presentations to the peace conference, already beginning its sessions.[22]

All these matters were considered in late 1918 and early 1919 with the participation of a scattering of Zionist delegates from America, Russia, Palestine, and other centers. For Weizmann this meant the additional, quasiparliamentary burden of explaining his position and justifying his procedures before a new forum of critical outsiders. He had to introduce them to considerations (especially, of British policy and internal pressures) that they had not fully appreciated—and did not welcome. He also had to accommodate himself to their views, sometimes against his better judgment.

The proposals drafted for the peace conference were shaped by a bewildering variety of rather unrelated elements. There was first the tradition of Herzl's drafts for a charter, derived from the models of colonial practice. Even before issues of self-determination arose, Zionists realized that old, annexationist conceptions no longer appealed to all Englishmen. A new formula had to be framed on principles other than colonial precedent: not territorial aggrandizement for Britain, as the victor's right, but a trusteeship for internationally approved ends in Palestine; for the Jews, not a chartered company bearing the familiar white man's burden in a backward area, but an agency accredited under the trust document to represent the dispersed Jewish people and by the close settlement in their national home of the uprooted or insecure in the Diaspora making good their right to self-determination.

So much, in broad lines, was common ground for all Zionists and their sponsors and friends in the British government. There was a wide variation in the application of the agreed principle, leading to complex discussions among those involved in converting the Balfour Declaration into the Palestine Mandate.

The lines of division had begun to appear in the immediate response to the Balfour Declaration and in formulating terms of reference for the Zionist Commission. Weizmann was able, after acrimonious argument, to obtain agreement from other Zionists (to what they viewed as very modest powers for the commission) by stressing that these were provisional rules, limited to the period of military occupation in Palestine. The British authorities would grant no more; only by seizing the immediate opportunity could Zionists advance toward their ultimate goal. He then proceeded to prove his point by energetic, imaginative extension of the commission's work in Palestine, creating "facts" on the ground that advanced the broader aims his Zionist critics wished to spell out in advance. But in this very effort Weizmann became seriously concerned about the resistance to Zionism among British officers in Palestine. He came back intent on securing clear instructions from London for the military governors, only to find that attention had shifted to the proper legal forms for a civilian trusteeship.

Weizmann's years of close contact with British policymakers left him no illusions about the extent to which even the most sympathetic of responsible leaders could accommodate the fondest Zionist hopes. They made it clear to him that their commitment was limited not only by the rules of a military occupation, but by more permanent considerations. They did, indeed, acknowledge the strategic advantage the Zionist connection gave them in getting exclusive control of Palestine without the French condominium contemplated in the Sykes-Picot agreement. But they would not press this issue directly themselves; Zionists were expected to lobby independently without open British sponsorship, for this departure from the Allied wartime agreements. Furthermore, no responsible British leader was prepared to treat his commitment to Zionism as simply a matter of respect for the right of Jews to self-determination. (Jan Christiaan Smuts is a possible exception; Balfour saw the pledge to Zionism as flatly incompatible with self-determination, though, in his view, it was an act of historic justice outweighing that abstract principle.) The military governors in Palestine generally considered self-determination (if at all) only as ruling out Zionist claims, which were in any case a prime administrative nuisance. Friendly Brtitish officers, like Ormsby-

Gore, the commission's political officer, accepted Zionist claims as justifying *deferment* of the test of self-determination until the Zionists had a reasonable opportunity, under British protection, to resettle the country with a Jewish majority. This was the most Weizmann could expect, and it determined his approach in framing Zionist proposals.[23]

He encountered Jewish opposition, in the first instance, from those who were anti-Zionists on principle; but now, in strange alliance, they were joined by an old friend, Baron Edmond de Rothschild, who was annoyed by various aspects of Weizmann's rise to leadership. On personal grounds (which might have explained adequately a reserved and withdrawn attitude, but hardly active, if indirect, opposition) the Baron resented what he saw as Weizmann's presumption and the disregard shown for his own son James, who was relegated to the minor task of recruiting for the Jewish Legion in Palestine and Egypt. Not only private pique, but irritation at the difficulties Weizmann's pro-British policy was causing in France led the Baron to encourage opposing views. Sokolow's tendency to back off in the face of such opposition often worried Weizmann. The most threatening expression of Rothschild's displeasure was the activity of Sylvain Levi, whom the Baron had placed on the Zionist Commission. He went to the United States to seek support for the Baron's views on the future of Palestine resettlement at the very time when Weizmann returned to London in 1918; later, when the Jews presented their views to the Principal Allied Powers on February 23, 1919, he delivered an attack on the Zionist proposals in what his colleagues considered an act of unforgivable treachery.[24]

While resisting pressures from this side, Weizmann came under other pressures from Zionist delegations who came to London without previous exposure to the complexities of British policy formation.[25] Even those in England who had yielded earlier to the argument that political demands could not be written into their contract with a military government expected more extensive and definite guarantees for the Zionist program in a peace settlement. Others, coming with elaborate programs thrashed out at home, were sharply disappointed with the initial formulas adopted in London before their arrival.

During the last months of 1918, Herbert Samuel resumed an active role in Zionist affairs as head of a broad-based political advisory group. The Zionist "demands" were redrafted in a way calculated to be acceptable in government circles. Explicit commitments expected from Britain were stated in general, indefinite terms: Zionists would have to rely on subsequent understandings with the government for more specific needs, a situation disturbingly reminiscent of their current uncertain status under the military occupation. In government circles, on the other hand, even the revised draft gave pause to some friends and evoked open opposition in other quarters. Some flatly opposed Britain's taking on the mandate. Others rejected Zionist drafts that were explicitly committed to the ultimate achievement of a Jewish commonwealth or that proposed specific, extensive borders for Palestine for consideration by the peace conference.

Zionist critics took quite a different line. A manifesto issued by the Copenhagen office called not only for national minority rights in the Diaspora and the designation of Palestine as the Jewish national home, but also called for admitting the dispersed Jewish people to membership in the future league of free nations. The Palestinian Jews adopted an elaborate program based on international recognition of the land as the Jewish national home. Their program affirmed the right of the worldwide Jewish people to a decisive voice in the Palestine government, including particularly control of Jewish immigration and settlement as well as preference in taking up railroad and power concessions and developing uncultivated areas and wastelands. The WZO, representing world Jewry, would appoint a member of the government empowered to name the members of the governing council (subject to the trustee government's veto), except the minister for Arab affairs. The country's name *(Eretz Israel)*, flag, and official languages (Hebrew, Arabic—and English only if the trustee government demanded it) would symbolize its role as the Jewish national home.[26]

The Americans, too, had their program for Palestine's future development. Although defining broadly stated ideals rather than specific powers, it clearly implied a radical structural transformation in the Zionist interest: national ownership (gradually acquired) of land, natural resources, and public utilities; economic organization ("as far as feasible") to be small-scale and cooperative; free public education at all levels, with Hebrew as the language of instruction. Even though these provisions were meant to apply to the prospective autonomous Jewish settlement (not necessarily imposed by government on the whole country), the American delegates left no doubt that they contemplated a scale of immigration that would yield a Jewish majority in Palestine. Moreover, leading the delegation were old Herzlian political Zionists, Stephen Wise and Jacob de Haas, who were disposed to view with suspicion the policies of Herzl's erstwhile opponents, Weizmann and Sokolow. (Wise came in the midst of Weizmann's struggle with Sokolow for a recognized leadership status and returned to America with a devastating critique of Weizmann's pretentions and abilities; he himself left a singularly unfavorable personal impression on his London Zionist hosts.) It was easy for them to conclude that Weizmann's anxiety to retain the British government's favor had made him a poor bargainer for Zionism and his draft proposal too moderate in its claims.[27]

Such a combination of critics compelled Weizmann to accept extensive changes. A revised draft provided for Jewish appointments in the Palestine government; Hebrew as an official language; the Jewish Sabbath and holidays made official; broad powers of local self-government for the Jewish community; preferential rights of land acquisition (including undeveloped lands to be taken by eminent domain from large landowners) and contracting for public works; autonomous Jewish schools; and the convocation of a Jewish congress in Jerusalem to create a Jewish Council to carry out the Zionist development program. This draft was presented to the British in January 1919 for comment. The reply came in terms of utmost severity: Britain would not accept a mandate for Palestine framed in accordance with such proposals. As a result, after consultation, Weizmann obtained approval of a new draft that omitted specific obligations calculated to create the future Jewish Commonwealth. Eliminating the operative details made the precise wording of broader principles all the more important. A redrawn formula, mutually approved by the Zionists and the Foreign Office, recognized "the right of the Jews to reconstitute in Palestine their National Home"; it also included a reference to "the historic title" (subsequently, "right") of the Jewish people in Palestine. Weizmann and Ahad Ha'am, who was greatly concerned with this formulation, gained some satisfaction from the use of "reconstitute" and "historic right"; but by reinstating the more reserved phrasing of the Balfour Declaration (not "Palestine as the Jewish national home" but a national home "in Palestine") it left vague in what form and within what territorial bounds a Jewish polity was to be restored. All this was to depend on the (written or unwritten) understanding between the Jews and the future mandatory power.[28]

British approval of the new draft signified only that they withdrew the threat not to take up the mandate for Palestine. They still intended to avoid appearing as sponsors of the Zionist proposals, though everyone knew of their patron-to-client relationship. The Zionists themselves would have to call for an exclusively British mandate for Palestine; they were also expected to coordinate their activities with the pressure on France from another British-oriented quarter, the Arab delegation headed by Prince Faisal of the Hejaz. In return they might hope that in a future civilian mandate administration they would get sympathetic consideration for those rights and claims that the British would not allow them to present to the peace conference. Self-determination for world Jewry by resettlement in Palestine would not be insured by a share in the government from the start, but (in Weizmann's conception) it would grow gradually out of a friendly working relationship between a Zionist-led Jewish Council and the future British "mandatary." (Brandeis thought in terms of a supplementary treaty between the two parties.)

This was an arrangement whose attractiveness depended entirely on confidence that the Jewish leadership could sustain sufficiently good relations with the British government to achieve national self-determination in Palestine on the basis of a predominantly Jewish population on the ground. Such confidence involved several complex prerequisites on both the Jewish and the British side: first, breaking out of the frozen status quo by replacing the military occupation with a civil administration; second, ensuring that the cold hostility to Zionism of many military governors would not continue into the civil regime, preferably by replacing them with new men more supportive of a British pro-Zionist policy; finally, and most fundamental condition of all, an enduring commitment on both sides to a compact of friendship going beyond what was spelled out in contractual, legal, documented form.

The first condition, moving from a military to a civil government, was long in coming, since the conclusion of a peace treaty with Turkey was delayed. In the meantime Arab hostility to Zionism mounted and became violent; this embittered the relations between the Jews and British officers in Palestine, with effects lasting beyond the term of the military occupation.

This also led to harsh attacks on Weizmann's policy by Zionists who neither shared his considered line of trusting the British nor enjoyed his access to the shapers of British decisions. Those in whom he found the most effective and consistent support in the long, many-sided struggle to build the Balfour Declaration into the peace settlement for Palestine were the Americans who joined him in London during those arduous and agonizing days.

The first Americans who came were among those who compelled Weizmann to revise Herbert Samuel's prudent draft of Zionist proposals. But abrupt rejection by the British negotiators in Paris was enough to convince leading Americans (though not some other Zionists) to follow the line of Weizmann, Sokolow, and Samuel; they, too, in dealing with government in Washington and New York, had learned to bend with the wind of official preferences. Moreover, some Americans began to arrive—Frankfurter; the young lawyer, Benjamin V. Cohen; and Brandeis' Louisville friend, Bernard Flexner—who were not only constitutionally disposed to share Weizmann's policy, but particularly well suited to aid in carrying it out. They were lawyers and so inclined to negotiated settlement; they had experience in communal and political work that taught them how to affect policy within the limits of applied technical expertise. It was a set of qualifications that precisely met the needs of the policy line Weizmann and Sokolow were following. And in the long, tortuous negotiations with the Foreign Office over the next years to reach agreement on a text for the Palestine mandate, American expertise and political connections were immensely valuable to the Zionists.[29]

The draft prepared for the British in February 1919 was not acted on by the peace conference. The Zionists, like other ethnic spokesmen, were granted a hearing by the Council of Ten, made up of the five leading Allies. Their appearance produced the most public intramural challenge to Zionism since the May 1917 exchange of letters in *The Times* (London), and it was hailed as a victory when Weizmann responded to Sylvain Levi's attack in a highly acclaimed exposition of Zionist aims. But, as the Allies took no action on the Zionist proposals, Weizmann's perceived triumph was a momentary one, a check to opposing currents that were felt to be mounting. The Americans in London were prevented from sharing in that historic confrontation by the French conference hosts' abrupt scheduling of the Zionist presentation; but they played a major role in the other political skirmishes over issues involved in the conference. Among these, the tenuous tie with Arab spokesmen developed under British patronage required continual attention.

Sykes' project of an Arab-Armenian-Jewish pro-Allied coalition reached its climax, not during the war, but at the peace conference (which he did not attend owing to his sudden death). By then, the project had been transformed from a general Allied war measure to an issue between France and Britain, which was conducted on Britain's behalf by Arab and Jewish proxies, joined in alliance by British mentors—but each acting in his own interest. The Arab-Zionist entente (opposed by Jewish anti-Zionists and Syrian Arabs under the French aegis) had been initiated by Weizmann's meeting with the leader of the Arab revolt, Emir Faisal in June 1918; it was confirmed, under T. E. Lawrence's guiding hand, in the written agreement the two signed in London on January 3, 1919, with a reservation writted by Faisal (in Arabic) conditioning his commitment on the satisfaction of demands he then addressed to the Foreign Office. Later, in an interview published in the Parisian *Le Matin,* Faisal startled the Zionists with expressions of an ominously different character. It was through Frankfurter's efforts—and, no doubt, the respect his American prestige generated—that the situation was restored in March by a letter from Faisal explaining away the interview in *Le Matin.*

The Paris proceedings also brought into sharp focus the political stresses the American Zionists were beginning to feel in dealing with their own government.[30] One of the effects of the war's end was to make moot the reservations imposed by American neutrality in regard to Turkey. The American Jewish Congress, delayed until then, was brought into session under Zionist leadership and adopted a resolution calling for the restoration of a Jewish commonwealth in Palestine. Zionist confidence was buoyed by the New Year's message Wilson was prevailed on to send the Jewish people on August 31, 1918—through the offices of Rabbi Stephen Wise: the Balfour Declaration was at last endorsed publicly and the work of the Zionist Commission in Palestine was hailed, particularly the initiation of the Hebrew University in Jerusalem. But this presidential act, like the original private approval of the Balfour Declaration, was disliked by the State Department and treated as a nonbinding effusion; Secretary Lansing's expressed opposition included an unabashed reference to the revulsion Christians would feel against handing over the Holy Land to the deicide Jews. Although official communications on this matter were not public (and a leader like Stephen Wise, blissfully unaware of them, persisted in thinking of Lansing and House as firmly pro-Zionist), the American movement sensed the growing antagonism among influential Christian circles, particularly missionaries.

The Morgenthau mission of 1917, undertaking to seek a separate peace with Turkey, necessarily raised doubts about the administration's commitment to the Zionist line Brandeis cleared with President Wilson in their lengthy private discussion on May 6. Nevertheless, Brandeis advised his Zionist subordinates and friends not to be unduly suspicious and to rely on the president's friendship. Later, when Colonel House proposed to renew the attempt at a separate Turkish peace—with the assistance of Ambassador Elkus—Brandeis instructed his Zionist friends not to pursue their recruitment of Elkus to the Zionist movement in deference to House's plans. American Zionists' plans had a similar ambiguous relation to the inquiry (the postwar planning project) House had set up for the president.[31]

Reports written for the inquiry on Zionism and Palestine generally assumed that the country would be designated an area for Jewish resettlement, with provisions for international protection of Christian religious interests and the welfare of the non-Jewish population. Boundaries proposed for the future Palestine accordingly took into account the claims formulated by Zionists, though not accepting them in full or giving clear support to the prospect of a Jewish state. The final report of the inquiry, submitted early in 1919 for the guidance of the American peace conference delegation, was still more positively favorable to Zionism on both these points. At the same time other trends, more ominous for Zionist hopes, were evidenced. Sidney Mezes, House's brother-in-law and both president of New York University and head of the inquiry, strongly favored a proposal floated by Henry Morgenthau: to keep the Ottoman Empire intact after the war and provide for the rights of its subject nations by granting autonomy in a federal structure. After some consideration, James Barton, the missionary strategist on Near Eastern matters, energetically supported Morgenthau's federation plan in submissions to the inquiry, though he continued to lobby for an independent Armenia through other channels. The advantages of a federated Near East from the missionary viewpoint were great: it fell in with the general American partiality for federalism; responded to fears of a Balkanized, economically weak and politically unstable environment resulting from partition; and it gave the missionary establishment in Beirut and Constantinople access to the heart of the Christian Holy Lands unhampered by intervening borders. After the Turkish surrender killed any prospect of an undivided Ottoman realm, the weight of the missionary interest swung behind a federated Arab state based on a Greater Syria, preferably under American or British mandate. Inherently opposed to Zionist designs and drawing strength from the American drive to scrap the Allied secret treaties in favor of local self-determination, the missionary pressure became a major matter of concern for Frankfurter, who represented American Zionists at the peace conference.[32]

A sense of the Protestant opposition grew slowly among American Zionist leaders. Evangelical Protestants had been early supporters of Zionism and had recently sponsored the revived Blackstone memorial. Also, Protestant liberalism, propagated by the American Social Gospel theorists, influenced the policies of the educational and welfare missions overseas, as well as men like Crane, Brandeis' friend and associate in domestic politics. But in the course of the war, particularly at its close, Zionists—and in certain ways, other Jewish activists—grew increasingly aware of opposition arising from divergent Christian and Jewish perspectives in matters of common interest such as administering relief and rehabilitation. Christian charity, rooted in a conversionist impulse, sought to be universal in its coverage; Jewish philanthropy (as it was called euphemistically) was an intracommunal enterprise, a policy of ethnic self-support and self-maintenance, whose aim was often to protect needy Jews from conversionist pressures. The quasi-political quality of such an intra-Jewish welfare policy, barely suppressed from consciousness by other leaders, was explicit and called for appropriate changes in practice among Zionists. Hence, when a JDC leader like Felix Warburg (who once proposed a merger of the Jewish Theological Seminary and the nearby [Presbyterian] Union Theological Seminary) had to defend his organization against demands to sink its funds and personnel in general American relief supplied to all in the war zones, he negotiated compromise arrangements that avoided a clash between the Christian and Jewish approach. The JDC not only dealt with this issue in Europe, but helped finance and took part in the

American Red Cross mission to Palestine in 1918. So, too, when Morgenthau went on a mission to Poland after the war, he managed to deal with pogroms and harassment of Jews in a way that enraged the Jewish public abroad but raised no hackles among American diplomats anxious to preserve the good image of liberated Poland. Zionists reacted strongly against both the Polish events and the preference granted the missionary-dominated Red Cross over the American Zionist Medical Unit in going to Palestine.[33]

Friction over these issues made it hard to ignore that the Protestant missionary lobby had become a prime antagonist, especially when Henry Morgenthau, closely involved with them, mounted a vigorous public campaign against Zionism. When Barton adopted the Morgenthau federation plan, which would have precluded the Zionist design for Palestine, awareness of the threat became acute. Stephen Wise could no longer content himself with the president's Rosh Hashanah message. He secured further oral assurances on January 1, 1919, before the president left for Paris; later, after Wilson's brief return, Wise and Louis Marshall were able to report his approval of the proposal that the American Jewish Congress delegation was about to submit in Paris: to make Palestine a "Jewish commonwealth." Lansing and others in Paris, alarmed at the report, asked Wilson if he had been correctly quoted; he confirmed the substance but said his words were not directly quoted and that a "Jewish commonwealth" was more than he had intended. From the other side, an agitated Frankfurter, bemused by the shifting trend of American policy, also asked Wilson for clarification and was told that Wilson could not see why his commitment to the Zionists should be doubted.[34]

The test of the issue so blandly dismissed came with the King-Crane Commission, sent by the Americans to investigate the Near Eastern situation.[35] Pressure for such a commission had come since early in 1919 from the headquarters and field staff of the Protestant missions—originally as a proposal for a private commission headed by Barton—to visit Syria on behalf of the Near East relief group. This developed into a more far-reaching project for a study of Syrian opinion by an international commission that would report officially to the peace conference; to the dismay of Zionists, the suggestion was then adopted by the American delegation and by Wilson and came under serious discussion by the conferees.

The area to be studied was redefined, because of French objections, to include the whole Ottoman Empire. The situation on the ground at the time was one of a military occupation under the overall command of General Allenby but dominated locally by different forces: British in Palestine and Mesopotamia; Arab, backed by British support, in the Syrian interior; French in the Levant coastal area—but only after an Arab attempt to take over had been overruled by Allenby owing to the vehement protests of the French; and in the lands of Asia Minor, Anatolia, Turkey in Europe, and the eastern border provinces a confusion of conflicting Allied and indigenous claimants and their armed elements. The French were unwilling to submit their claim to Syria to an inquiry into local preferences held under the gun of claimants other than themselves. They preferred that any revision of previous agreements be made in Paris; but if local populations were to be consulted, in deference to Wilson, they wanted others to be at risk as well as themselves. In the end the French refused to join the commission while Syria remained under Anglo-Arab occupation; the British withdrew their own members; and the commission went out as a purely American venture assigned to collect evidence for Wilson's consideration in framing his policy.

During the months while the issue of the inquiry commission was debated in Paris, Zionists actively sought to secure their own interests. A proposal to add Frankfurter to the American staff was pursued for a time, but to no effect; Frankfurter insistently urged Brandeis to hasten his long-delayed and still-tentative trip to Palestine in order to be able to influence the commission's findings. On the English side, during the time that British participation remained a possibility, Weizmann, Frankfurter, and the others kept in close touch with D. G. Hogarth and Arnold Toynbee, prospective nominees. When the commission finally went out at the end of May, led by men whom they could only regard with suspicion, the Zionists had to content themselves with soothing assurances. In addition to the statements extracted from Wilson, they had House's word that the Balfour Declaration still enjoyed American support.[36]

The American commissioners, Charles R. Crane, Brandeis' old Progressive party colleague, and Dr. Henry Churchill King, president of Oberlin College (who happened to be traveling in Europe), were chosen ostensibly as persons likely to be impartial because they had no previous connection with the area of study. In fact, both had close ties with the Protestant missionary establishment that initiated their venture; they relied on the aid and advice of those old Near East hands, and shared their perceptual biases. Their assignment was nominally to study social and economic conditions and popular political opinion throughout the Ottoman realm, but certain limiting conditions were indicated from the start. The English had already conducted a plebiscite in Mesopotamia, which they occupied, indicating support for themselves as mandatory power; on the strength of this, the commission omitted Mesopotamia from its itinerary. They were also told that Palestine had been virtually assigned by general consent to Britain with a mandate to provide for a Jewish national home; but this was the first scene they visited. They ignored, or dismissed as erroneous, the views of experts assigned by the technical staff of the Paris delegation, reflecting the guidelines of earlier American policy planning. One expert, Dr. George C. Montgomery, a strong advocate of the Armenian cause, posed questions showing a rare grasp of the argument for territorial claims of exterritorial, dispersed and decimated peoples; the other, Captain William Yale, whose special concern was to safeguard American interest in the region's oil resources, saw the concessions to Zionism as part of a delicate package deal on which the peace settlement depended. Disregarding both, the commission chiefs (holding to conclusions voiced within days of their arrival) proposed a drastic reduction of Zionist claims. So too, they proposed to eliminate the French entirely as a mandatory power in the area. America, they found, was by far the most popular choice for that role.

But since they intended to nominate America for the mandate over the entire northern half of the Ottoman Empire, with three subordinate divisions in Constantinople, Anatolia, and Armenia, they allocated everything to the south, short of the Arabian Peninsula, to a Syrian state ruled by Prince Faisal under a British mandate.

This was, of course, not only offensive to the French, but a sharp rebuff to both Armenian and Jewish nationalism. Yet the trends of political opinion at the time (which in the final balance made the commission report utterly irrelevant) offered some considerable support for the latter, if not the former, set of conclusions. The military advisers in the field, both in Constantinople and in Jerusalem, sent strong warnings about the hostility of local majorities against Zionist claims in Palestine, against Armenian claims in Anatolia and Asia Minor, and against suggestions of colonizing India's surplus population in Mesopotamia. Support of such pretensions, they said, was stirring up violent reactions that threatened Jews and Armenians and that would compel their would-be protectors to maintain large garrisons at great expense in order to keep the peace. Pressures of this sort (together with a simple, unqualified perception of self-determination as the right of local, resident majorities) were leading to softer support in the American peace delegation for Armenian and Jewish national aspirations; autonomy within a federal structure rather than independence might be all these clients of American benevolence could expect. On the British side, too, the Zionists came under growing pressure from the men in the field to accept a definition of their claims that ruled out any pretension to a "Jewish commonwealth"—not only as an immediate demand, but as an ultimate goal as well. The King-Crane findings reflected the direct and indirect impact of such opinions among British officials in Palestine.[37]

What doomed the King-Crane report to irrelevancy was its proposal that America assume the mandate for Turkey, the Straits, and Armenia. The possibility of an American mandate for Armenia held up the conclusion of a peace with Turkey long after the Versailles Treaty with Germany was settled in June. King and Crane returned to Paris as the American delegation was winding up its work; their report reached Washington as Wilson was about to return in collapse from his futile tour of the country in an effort to rally support for the League of Nations. Under the circumstances, there could be no hope for an American mandate in the Near East and the King-Crane report was pigeonholed.

Moreover, while the King-Crane commission was pursuing its studies in the Near East, negotiations between the parties at the peace conference were preempting decisions on issues the American investigators took to be open. Lloyd George and Georges Clemenceau, as early as February 1919, had agreed on leaving Palestine ("from Dan to Beersheba") for Britain alone to administer, scrapping the Sykes-Picot provision for an international regime there. By September, as the King-Crane proposals for a British-mandated integral Syria were ready for submission, the French and British had reached agreement on a reshuffling of the military provisional administration of the occupied area that robbed other ideas of any meaning. Unwilling to bear the strain of protracted military occupation over lands it did not expect to hold, Britain agreed to end Allenby's control of the zones entrusted to France (the Levantine coast) and to Faisal (the Syrian interior) by November. This left Faisal bereft of the British support he had relied on in his resistance to French pretensions under the Sykes-Picot agreement. It marked the end of his interest in the British-mediated Zionist connection that he had been able to play off against the French earlier, and it signaled the beginning of a clash with France that ended in his expulsion from Damascus.

During the same time the Zionists suffered the strains of uncertain, ambiguous relations with their own avowed sponsors. The British officers in the field continually lapsed into hostility, rating Arab sensitivity more important than Jewish claims; only repeated Zionist recourse to support in London restored the situation—to the satisfaction of Weizmann and of Brandeis' cohorts, if not their disgruntled colleagues in Palestine. In Paris and London English negotiators used the Zionist connection to justify retention of Palestine in violation of the Sykes-Picot terms and Zionist requirements for land and water served as an argument for extending Palestine's boundaries northward into areas France claimed. These were factors the Zionists thought they could rely on in negotiating with England the terms of the mandate to be submitted to the League of Nations. The boundaries they secured for Palestine were not in the end nearly what they had hoped, but they were able to negotiate (provisionally) a draft mandate that granted the legal facilities that might enable them, with luck and immense effort, to gain their end, a Jewish commonwealth in Palestine. In all these labors, the Americans despatched by Brandeis, and Brandeis himself, were a major source of strength. It was the highwater mark in their relations with Weizmann and Weizmann's with them.

London, 1919

Brandeis had intended to defer his visit to Palestine until all political issues were resolved so that he could concentrate on a design for social and economic development.[38] Frankfurter's urgent appeal to deal with the King-Crane commission precipitated his voyage in the summer of 1919, and he met the American commissioners briefly in Palestine, to little effect. Observing the difficulties of Zionists (including Americans now active on the Zionist Commission) under the military government, he noted that obstruction by hostile personnel, not simply the status quo policy of an occupation regime, was hampering their work. Brandeis' critical report, like Weizmann and Sokolow's earlier complaints, led the London authorities to restate their pro-Zionist policy and order certain personnel shifts. But, as before, the improvement was only temporary, and the position remained unsettled throughout the period of military government in Palestine.

A more lasting effect of Brandeis' trip was the powerful emotional attraction he experienced to the land and the people he met there, though not without ambivalence in some respects. Also, the visit occasioned his formulation of certain conclusions that could only provoke resistance among many other Zionists.

The end of the war, with Britain in control of Palestine, raised hopes for a swift return to the homeland among all sorts of Zionists. The practical Zionist school, who had continued settlement in the absence of suitable political conditions, were under pressure to accommodate victims of the postwar disorders, in a land now recognized as a haven for Jews. Political Zionists were predisposed by Herzl's visionary analysis to expect a mass transfer to Palestine as soon as the necessary political conditions had been won. When de Haas reached London among the early American delegates after the war, he surveyed the potential immigration to Palestine and reached an estimate of fifty thousand immediately available; he had not shared the experience that made the Zionist Commission seek to freeze land transfers and postpone new immigration. After a brief stay in Palestine, Brandeis dealt a body blow to such hopes. The poverty and disease he found in Jerusalem as well as the fact that some British officials questioned the wisdom of immigration at a time of unemployment convinced him that the immediate need was to provide for those already there rather than bringing new Jews to Palestine. Another conclusion, that further settlement should await a massive project of sanitation to clear malarial swamps, went beyond the caution for which the Zionist Commission was criticized.

Other drastic conclusions amounted to a direct attack on policies for which Weizmann shared responsibility. Weizmann had pleaded for American or English aides better able to deal with British officials than the Zionists on the scene; Brandeis proposed simply to abolish the commission Weizmann had set up as an intermediary with the Palestine government. He also backed the American resistance to demands that the medical unit they sent to Palestine come under regulation by the Zionist Commission and join the campaign to revive Hebrew by conducting its correspondence in that language. This was part of a general pragmatic distrust that Brandeis showed to the cultural programs of the WZO. He was a firm supporter of the proposed Hebrew University (not surprisingly, in view of his appreciation of professionalism and advanced training), but mainly of vocationally useful faculties that such a school should, in his opinion, stress initially. He strongly opposed, on the other hand, the WZO's assumption of responsibility for the full range of schooling it thought Palestine Jewry required. This, he argued, was a function that should be left to the local community and the Palestine government. If that meant a more rudimentary level of schooling than the veteran cultural Zionists thought appropriate for the Jewish national home, he cited the example of the Pilgrims, who contented themselves with the bare minimum that pioneers could afford. He was even more hostile to the WZO commitments to support Diaspora nationalism given to the Jewish national councils at the peace conference.

In these matters Brandeis extended to the WZO principles he had adopted in reorganizing the American movement in 1918; thereby, the clash was precipitated.

The early years of Brandeis' active Zionist leadership brought new strength and prestige that fully satisfied the hopes of those who had recruited him. They also engendered some problems, which grew more acute after Brandeis joined the Supreme Court and had to control Zionist affairs through his proxies. The FAZ was turned into a subordinate instrument of policies that Brandeis determined through the PZEC, which was increasingly dominated by "associate" members co-opted from his own circle. This naturally caused grumbling, which became more vocal when Brandeis' directives were handed down by deputies who did not enjoy the same acceptance as their principal. Among them, Jacob de Haas, in whom Brandeis reposed the fullest trust (well merited if personal devotion was the test), was particularly apt to irritate fellow Zionists, including among others the Chief's close associates. When issues of principle began to divide American Zionists in 1920, there was already an aggrieved opposition group to take up the quarrel.

Another problem united rather than divided the leadership. In seeking to expand the constituency he spoke for, Brandeis adopted expedients similar to the Zion associations and other special-purpose societies long familiar in the movement. College men were urged to join a newly organized University Zionist Society; obviously, they could not be expected to share the company and customary activities of veteran Zionists who were largely of unassimilated, immigrant background. One of the effects of this approach, however, was to make FAZ no more than a loose cover for largely autonomous member societies. The veteran leadership, while accepting the need for diversified organization, continually sought ways to bring the movement under greater control and discipline; "discipline," of course, was also one of Brandeis' constant rallying cries.

The problem of discipline was not urgent so long as the continuing war justified the existence of the PZEC as an emergency measure. Policy could then be determined by the PZEC chairman and his aides while the membership organizations had merely to carry out their decisions. But after Brandeis' withdrawal and with the approach of peace, the old question of efficient central control of Zionist affairs arose again; it was complicated by sharpening conflicts between the FAZ and PZEC leaders, on one side, and the two ideologically separated bodies, the religious Mizrachi and the socialist Poalei Zion, on the other. Unlike Mizrachi, which was felt to be drawing on the same potential membership as the FAZ, the socialist-Zionists might be considered useful in reaching out to circles the FAZ could not easily reach; Brandeis' circle not only supported them in this effort—notably, in the battles over the American Jewish Congress—but hoped to attract into their own ranks activists who had begun as labor Zionists. But with America's entry into the war, the strong neutralist stand of the majority of the leftists became an embarrassment; their determined resistance to the final compromises between Brandeis' group and the AJC on the Jewish congress issue made them a positive menace. By 1917 both Mizrachi and the Poalei Zion had broken their

ties to the PZEC. Zionist reorganization plans that began to be floated provided for eliminating the independence of both ideologically separated Zionist parties.

By June 1918 the plans of Brandeis and the FAZ bureaucrats had matured
and were presented to the FAZ Convention. In spite of some opposition from
veteran downtown Zionists, the reorganization plan was adopted; what a man
like Lipsky had sought in vain many times before was now obtained through
the influence of Justice Brandeis and his cohorts from the sometimes-reluc-
tant Zionists. Members of all the component societies—Hadassah, the youth
groups, and the fraternal societies—were registered individually in the new
Zionist Organization of America (ZOA) rather than in bulk by the constituent
units. The new ZOA was a centralized body with its membership organized
not only in special interest groups, but geographically for administrative convenience in districts and regions under the central control group. Those who
had led the PZEC now took personal charge of the ZOA; Judge Mack became
president, with Brandeis as honorary president; Stephen Wise, vice president;
and de Haas, executive secretary with general responsibilities. Louis Lipsky,
formerly chairman of the FAZ Executive Council, stepped down to a more
limited role as secretary for organization, one of several departments in the
new structure. He devoted himself (with little personal assistance from those
who had joined Brandeis in the intense barnstorming of 1914–15) to the task
that, next to a major fund-raising effort, brought the reorganized Zionists
their most impressive immediate success: registering individually the loosely
attached, or potential, members attracted to the cause by the activity of the
recent past.[39]

The top leaders, working with Brandeis, pursued recruitment in another
quarter, among the non-Zionist leaders of the communal establishment.
Brandeis' old strategy of capturing them by encirclement had to be modified
during the final phase of the Jewish congress conflict. His original idea, of
achieving an overwhelming consensus that would effectively isolate the AJC,
did not fully succeed; his opponents retained enough allies, at the point when
a settlement had to be concluded, to make concessions necessary in order to
break the stalemate. Under the changed conditions, with the establishment
having yielded to pressure for democratic participation in communal affairs
(at least, for the time of the peace conference), Brandeis adopted the policy
once urged by Magnes. The Zionists henceforth would leave other Jewish
concerns to general Jewish organizations in order to devote themselves exclusively to the cause of the Jewish national home in Palestine. In that cause
(where the ZOA claimed paramount, if not exclusive, authority on behalf of
the Jewish people) the aim of securing the adherence of the whole community
persisted; the method of achieving this was simply to enroll all Jews, in principle, as members of the ZOA. The effort to accomplish this began with an
abortive effort to recruit Jacob Schiff in 1917 and was renewed after the ZOA
was founded.

When Brandeis returned to London from his Palestine trip in 1919, he found
himself in the middle of a meeting of the Zionist representatives who had

come in connection with the peace settlement.[40] He plunged directly into the
complex internal issues of the world movement and the continuing debates
about the future development of Palestine. Weizmann was absent from the
early sessions of the conference in February 1919, as he was engaged abroad
in talks with German Zionist leaders who were still barred from admission
to England. When he returned, the conference took up the question of the
Jewish Council, proposed in the Zionist memorandum to the Paris peace conference, and precipitated a head-on collision between plans Brandeis and
Weizmann had been separately preparing.

It was generally assumed in the Zionist movement that, although the
WZO had acted legitimately in the name of the whole Jewish people as a
matter of political urgency in the past, a broader base of representation was
now required to ratify Zionist political gains and to build a solid structure
upon them. The advisory committee of Zionist and non-Zionist, Jewish and
non-Jewish consultants that Weizmann and Sokolow set up immediately
after the Balfour Declaration was revived on the eve of the peace conference
not only for legal and political advice, but for support in the enormous tasks
of social and economic engineering involved in building the Jewish national
home.[41] Weizmann was anxious to extend the same principle internationally:
to demonstrate that the Zionist project was, indeed, backed by a general
worldwide Jewish consensus and to secure the effective aid of those financially and professionally most competent to carry the project to success. In
this connection he thought primarily of the Rothschilds and other established
philanthropists and agencies who might be attracted.

Conscious as Weizmann was of the critical need for the financial resources
and expert counsel that such men could supply, it was no less obvious to him
that ultimate control must remain in Zionist hands; this concern was largely
responsible for the support he lent the Diaspora nationalists in organizing the
Comité des délégations juives. Now, too, the bankers and technicians of the
Jewish national enterprise must submit to the popular will, of which Zionist
leaders were the authentic exponents. Making this unduly obvious to Baron
Edmond and James de Rothschild had been one reason for the abrupt chilling
of their relationship with Weizmann in 1918. One of his major objectives
now was to repair that rift, and he was ready to grant far-reaching executive
authority to the Rothschild heir (as to other essential outsiders, like Alfred
Mond) in the planning and management of the national home's economic
development. This may have seemed more acceptable, since the Zionist
movement's enhanced prestige made many powerful supporters potentially
available; Rothschild's former unchallenged dominance might be balanced
by other men of stature. Moreover, qualified men of requisite power and
competence might now be found among Zionists in America, as in Russia
and Germany; but here, too, one had to be wary. Weizmann was already concerned that the Brandeis-recruited contingent did not have what he would
regard as a true Jewish national consciousness. Their Zionism, in his opinion,
resembled the combination of political with philanthropic activism—without
profound meaning for themselves—that had been encountered, and over-

come, in German Zionism. Thus, a critical element in Weizmann's plan was to balance the pressures of new men in Europe and America by winning the confidence of veteran Zionists in Europe and Palestine.[42]

The Palestinian and East-Central European communities were represented in Paris and London by delegations from the recently formed Jewish national councils. The Palestinians came with grievances about their failure to be represented on the Zionist Commission or have their Zionist-maximalist program properly reflected in the Weizmann-Sokolow submissions to the peace conference. The primary concern of the delegates from Europe was to achieve broad national minority rights for their several communities; here, too, Weizmann offered less than enthusiastic support. But Weizmann found common ground with his nationalist critics on a design for the projected Jewish Council that gave a significant role to the Palestinian and European Jewish national representative bodies. The statement presented to the peace conference in February proposed that, "A Jewish Council for Palestine shall be elected by a Jewish Congress representative of the Jews of Palestine and of the world." Pending the convocation of the congress, "A Provisional Jewish Council of representatives of the Zionist Organisation, of the Jewish population in Palestine, and of such other Jewish organisations as are willing to co-operate in the development of a Jewish Palestine shall be formed forthwith by the Zionist Organisation." The men entrusted with executive responsibility at both stages might (if Weizmann had his way) be chosen for competence, whether or not they had Zionist credentials in the past; but they would be answerable to the representative council that chose them. More demanding decisions in the same spirit were adopted by the London conferees in March: the Zionist Commission was to be immediately strengthened by adding representatives of the Palestine community and of the Poalei Zion and Mizrachi parties. In choosing the Provisional Jewish Council members, those invited should be Jewish organizations active on behalf of Palestine projects in the past, those representing the Jews of each country, and others whose participation was likely to be particularly helpful.[43]

The February proposal to the peace conference was approved and signed, among others, by the seven-member American delegation, including Judge Mack, Rabbi Stephen Wise, and Jacob de Haas. But a tripartite council, representing the WZO, Palestine Jewry, and other Jewish organizations, stood in sharp opposition to the design favored by Brandeis. In August 1919 when he came to London after his Palestine trip, he presented the assembled conferees with his own conception, confronting Weizmann with a challenge impossible to ignore but dangerously costly to repel.

Brandeis' design for the reorganization of the world Zionist movement was a direct outgrowth of the redeployment he and his associates were carrying out in America. The structure he imposed on the local Zionists, involving the exclusion of the socialist and Orthodox religious Zionists (unless they gave up the constitutional autonomy granted those ideological parties by the WZO), was a pattern he wanted followed in the world movement as well.

Weizmann's gestures of acquiescence to the religious and socialist factions' demands for representation on the Zionist Commission and the projected Jewish Council (concessions that were never truly consummated) were observed with irritation by the American leaders.

They also differed on the proper method of attracting support from previously non–Zionist Jewish sources, though in full agreement on the need to draw in men of means and appropriate experience. The Brandeis approach—framed in the course of settling the American Jewish Congress dispute and fleshed out in creating the ZOA—claimed a predominant role for the Zionists in building the Jewish national home while renouncing any part in Diaspora affairs. Other Jewish organizations, active in the Diaspora, would be welcomed if they wished to support the Zionist effort financially or to undertake specific auxiliary tasks (as the religious and labor Zionists might also do if they persisted in separatist independence); but if their leaders were to be entrusted with centrally important tasks, they must become regularly enrolled members of the Zionist organization. If this conception were to be extended to the world movement, it meant scrapping the arrangement for a Jewish Council that had recently been agreed to by the American delegates. Brandeis appeared on the scene in August, determined to do just that.

His position was quite clearly hardened in response to the views expressed in Paris and London by East European nationalists; assumptions implicit in the settlement of his dispute with American non-Zionists were now more explicitly formulated in response to Zionists. With the Balfour Declaration about to be embodied in the Palestine Mandate, he held that Zionism should retire from ideological controversy. Once the political point was foreclosed by (international and general Jewish) consensus, all reasonable Jews could be expected to join a single, disciplined, and efficient united organization for the remaining practical Zionist work in Palestine. A coalition arrangement like the projected Jewish Council would introduce irrelevant ideological issues. He had preferred to dispense with the accession to Zionism of so notable a force as Jacob Shiff when the banker wished to stipulate a religious definition of Zionism as his condition for joining; he had fought the claims of the Poalei Zion and Mizrachi to continue as autonomous, ideological factions within the movement. So, too, the ideology of a World Jewish Congress or Jewish Council with substantial representation of the new Jewish national councils from East-Central Europe having the power to control the development of the Jewish national home was one he could not stomach. He had no patience with abstract discussion or management by political maneuver (though he excelled in maneuver before reaching an agreed settlement, or in its absence); he had no confidence in the management skills or reliability of the veteran Zionists or of East European Jews as a general rule; and he saw the whole proposal as undercutting his own plans for the reorganization of the movement and development of the Jewish national home.

Weizmann shared, to a significant degree, some of Brandeis' perceptions. He regarded the Diaspora nationalist leanings of some of his friends as naively optimistic and as a distraction from the task that should command the full attention of the movement—the practical work in Palestine; he had written to Tschlenow at one point of the excessive "Helsingforsism" of the Russian Zionists. He continually complained of the slack and inefficient performance of their Zionist duties by his fellow Easterners. But, unlike Brandeis (and in the same terms as were argued at the August conference by his old associate, Victor Jacobson), he envisaged the immense labors to which the Zionists summoned the Jewish people as a work of national awakening, an enthusiasm of the masses: rings torn from their ears and fingers would be contributed by women in Poland; young laborers would press forward to emigrate; professionals (like himself) would cast aside former careers to dedicate their lives, without reservation, to the cause. Thus the whole effort would be guided by the full and free expression of the national, popular will in common assembly—but carried out by efficient executive agencies. He had gained his political triumphs by persuading the British that he could evoke such a response, and his position now depended critically on making good the promise.[44]

But neither the World Jewish Congress nor the project of a Jewish Council for the Palestine enterprise was within reach at the time, and there was pressing work to be done. Weizmann, therefore, was ready to revise the policy and have the WZO itself assume the functions of the proposed Jewish Council as an immediate measure, setting aside reorganization on a broader basis until a later date. This was a delaying action by which he hoped to parry the criticism that he had undermined the Zionist position by conceding too much to the non-Zionists. But the effect was to precipitate a new quarrel in which Weizmann found himself opposed to Brandeis and aligned in basic sympathy with the European veterans, who opposed the strategic and tactical line that, in good part, he shared with the Americans.[45]

Julius Simon, who had directed the London Zionist office since the beginning of the year, tried to mediate an agreed position between Weizmann and the Americans. The effort collapsed when Weizmann's version was rejected by the American leader and Simon presented a resolution that came down on Brandeis' side: the WZO (as both versions agreed) would assume at once the functions proposed for the Provisional Jewish Council in the February proposals and also propose within two years a program to secure the cooperation of a broad range of concerned Jews. But while Weizmann wanted to retain the earlier language ("all Jews and Jewish organisations willing to assist"), Simon yielded to Brandeis' insistence on eliminating "Jewish organisations." Simon thereby incurred his old friend Weizmann's bitter resentment and opened the way for his own later close ties to the Brandeis group.

Weizmann made his irritation with the Americans clear in angry statements that put the issue in far-reaching ideological terms that went beyond the concrete questions of effective organization to personal attitudes and commitments:

> You have built a Monroe Doctrine around American Zionism. I consider it my duty to break through this Monroe Doctrine with full force.... If you

suffer discomfort because of the creation of a general Jewish organization, you will have a choice between remaining American or joining the general Jewish organization. For such a choice may still be open to you in the next twenty-five years. . . . We, ghetto Jews, have nothing but the Jewish home, which we must have. Therefore we will give up anything in order to build it. If the Council is needed for it, we will create it. . . . You still have another home. Since the Jewish national home only hovers in the distant horizon of your vision, you are not prepared to imperil your [present] home. I respect this position but I cannot give it my assent . . . if you cannot on any account accept the Council, I shall yield to you, for I do not want to break the Organization, but I will look to the day when I shall be able to work against you with all my power; that is how we brought the German Zionists into the Zionist Organization.

In spite of the pathos of his appeal, Weizmann made clear that his differences with the Americans were not as great as those of some others. No more than Brandeis did he wish to commit the Zionist movement to direct involvement in national minority politics in the Diaspora; but with single-minded concentration on the task of building the Jewish national home, he wanted the backing of all organized Jewish forces, including especially those of Diaspora nationalists. The difference, Weizmann implied, was that he felt himself at one with the people who persisted as a national entity in the Diaspora while building the national home in Palestine, whereas Brandeis and the other Americans did not. His Palestine-directed Zionism (like that of Jabotinsky or Ussishkin) now expressed itself in a full-time, professional commitment to movement work and to living in Palestine; the Americans were willing to devote no more than short-term service to the cause and would not reroot themselves in the national home.

Concluding his speech, Weizmann directly challenged the Americans to respond to the issues he had raised:

I do not intend to bring my proposal to a vote. But for me this issue represents a moral cleavage. Now I call upon the American gentlemen to give a clear answer to the basic question: If they reject the Council because of technical problems, let us unite on a common position. But if there are moral reasons at play here, say it plainly. All of us who take a different view will abstain from presenting our proposal and you shall know with certainty that in this act we have opened a great moral breach.[46]

Brandeis took up the challenge on behalf of the Americans, objecting to Weizmann's plan mainly on tactical or technical grounds, but also on principle.[47] He, too, welcomed cooperation from other organizations, but not in a joint body. Other than the ICA, he saw no such organizations and felt no need to create them. The main instrument was the WZO, which must change to suit its new functions and be open to everyone who wished to work for the national home. If a World Jewish Congress would help to achieve the goal, it should be convened and constituted by the Zionists themselves, not by a loose collection of organizations with diverse, extraneous concerns:

We must unite for the work in Palestine in a single organization. The Zionist organization must be that organization—and for practical reasons; it exists, it is recognized, it is disciplined, and it is trusted.

There was also the question of Diaspora nationalism, taken by Brandeis to be objectionable in principle for "Americans, Canadians and others" (he did not distinguish between Zionists and non-Zionists in this connection). The principle involved was presented, in good pragmatist style, as embedded in historical conditions. The day might come, Brandeis readily conceded, when the proposal to organize on the "principle of Jewish unity in all matters, including non-Palestinian matters" would be generally acceptable—"perhaps in fifty years." But "that is not the case today. . . . The conditions that created the differences in views are real and present."

Brandeis then imposed his views, with little regard for injured feelings or traditional Zionist procedures. The American delegation, which bulked large among the scattering represented in London, had no status under the authority of the last Zionist Congress in 1913. The controversial decision was reached (with many of those present, including the most clearly authorized, abstaining in order to avoid offending the Americans) when Brandeis, as chairman, held up the vote until de Haas could be summoned to break a tie.

The London Conference, 1920

After the August meeting, an uneasy balance prevailed in the conduct of Zionist affairs; the two leaders seemed each to have secured the minimum requirements for playing their respective roles in the movement. Weizmann, raised to the position of a co-opted member of the Smaller Action Committee in the January duel with Sokolow, was able to work relatively smoothly with Sokolow thereafter. Following Brandeis' August victory, Weizmann renewed his effort to enlist non-Zionist support on terms that did not at first seem to clash with the American conceptions. But rapidly changing conditions outside and the recrudescence of factions within the movement over whom neither rival leader exercised direct influence put new pressure on both.

European Zionism had an explosive resurgence in the postwar years and faced critical problems far removed from those that divided Weizmann and Brandeis in August 1919. After the collapse of the Central Powers, revolution and counterrevolution in Russia, Germany, and Hungary and the battles of Poles and Ukrainian nationalists with the Soviets kept all Eastern, Southern, and Central Europe in constant turmoil. The Zionists of those areas, reinforced and radicalized by young recruits, were inflamed by desperate urgencies and messianic hopes. They demanded immediate, extreme measures that clashed with the tempered policies of Western Jews, Zionist and non-Zionist alike.

Civil disorder and anti-Jewish violence together with the miraculous promise of the Balfour Declaration impelled considerable numbers of young people to seek immediate entry into Palestine. They had been recruited for farm and construction labor and defense in Jewish settlements by Trumpeldor and others all through Eastern and Central Europe, and by David Ben-Gurion and Yitzhak Ben-Zvi in America. Among the Russians were war-hardened Red Army men; others were fired in the crucible of their service in Jewish self-defense groups during pogroms. Disregarding both British regulations and official Zionist policy, they began to move to Constantinople and other ports, and then to flow into Palestine. Additional pressure came from those who enlisted in the Jewish Legion in Palestine as well as in America. They demanded more militancy from the leaders in pressing for their employment in action: at the front, during the hostilities; domestically, as a garrison force; and finally, for their settlement on the land. Rallied by Jabotinsky and by the new labor party, Ahdut Avoda (a coalition negotiated in their encampments), they exerted a new force in the internal reorganization of Palestine Jewry and thus in the affairs of the WZO.[48]

The British Palestine administration and overall policy in London were meanwhile going through successive transformations. Shortly after the August 1919 Zionist conference ended, the government decided to withdraw British supervision from that part of the occupied Ottoman area not likely to fall under a British mandate. This meant that the Arabs in Damascus were left to dispute control of the Syrian-Lebanese territory with the French in Beirut without the intervening authority of the British command; also, the boundary between British-administered Palestine and the area still in dispute between French and Arab claimants remained to be settled and was open to the spillover of violence from their quarrel.[49]

The abandonment of overall British control of the occupied Ottoman areas spelled the demise of Sir Mark Sykes' plan for an Arab-Armenian-Jewish combine allied to Britain as well as the compact between Faisal and the Zionists that arose from it. The loss of the British backing that Faisal counted on made the always-questionable Zionist connection quite worthless for him; the Syrian nationalists to whom he committed himself had already adopted an anti-Zionist position and, in anticipation of the King-Crane Commission, laid claim to Palestine. On the British side, too, when a choice had to be made, the Palestine administrators leaned heavily toward conciliating the Arab majority while in London the Zionists encountered divided councils in the government, the press, and public opinion.

Weizmann in those days divided his efforts between Palestine, where he served for three extended periods as head of the Zionist Commission; Paris, where he shared in the continuing negotiation of terms for the mandate Britain was to assume; and London, where he took part in planning and preparing for the future work in the mandate territory. The strain of constant travel and frustrating uncertainty in his public role was compounded by the continuing unsettlement of his private affairs: a family separated for months at a time, without a fixed residence—and still no decision from the British government on the award to be granted to him in compensation for his war services. His letters to friends tell a tale of continual bodily woes, added to the trials and tensions of the highly volatile political situation.[50]

Weizmann came to Palestine in October 1919 fortified by the administrative changes introduced under his own and Brandeis' combined pressure. The new political officer, Colonel Richard Meinertzhagen, was a staunch pro-Zionist, and Lord Curzon had sent orders to instruct the staff (but not the public) that the question of Zionism was to be considered *"chose jugée"*—a strong hint to refrain from obstructionist tactics. Also, there was general agreement that the rigid application of a status quo policy was no longer appropriate after so long a period of military occupation. But Weizmann's hopes were soon disappointed. The new economic initiatives of the military government—reopening registration of land titles, proposals to supply credit to cultivators—seemed to the Zionists to favor Arab large landowners in Beirut and Jerusalem as well as bankers in Egypt at the expense of both the Arab cultivators and the Zionists. Thus landownership would be further concentrated in the hands of a few speculators and Zionist settlers would be compelled to pay inflated prices for land. Even more ominous was the rapid relapse of the local administration into a posture of hostility; Meinertzhagen was soon brought to the point of resigning his appointment.

The hiatus in authority after the British gave up responsibility for Syria and Lebanon led to irregular warfare that endangered Jewish settlements in the undefined northern border area. Trumpeldor, who had gone to organize the defense in one such village, Tel Hai, was slain together with several comrades by a Druze band in February 1920. For months Arab demonstrations in Jerusalem and elsewhere had raised tension, and the intelligence the Zionist Commission received led them to warn of violent disturbances that were being prepared (as Weizmann regularly stressed) against the government policy as well as the Jews. The commission supported rudimentary self-defense preparations, led by Jabotinsky and Rutenberg (who had come to Palestine after the Bolsheviks overthrew the Petrograd local military government that he headed). Jabotinsky trained his volunteers openly as a demonstration intended to impress the British with the preparedness of the Jews to serve as official guardians of the peace; he did not believe (after his experience with Jewish self-defense in Russia in 1903–5) that they could protect the community effectively without official approval. It was also assumed that the British would never permit Jerusalem, particularly the holy sites of the walled Old City, to be desecrated by mob violence. Thus, no Jewish defense was in place in the Old City where, in fact, the three days of riots and looting in April 1920 were concentrated. Moreover, an attempt by Jewish defenders to enter the Old City was barred by British troops, and some British-recruited Arab police were seen to take part actively in the assault. In the aftermath Jabotinsky and several other Jews were arrested along with Arabs apprehended for participating in the outbreak.[51]

Weizmann, generally given to sharp changes of mood, reacted to these events with extreme bitterness. He had been uneasy for months about the changing position, especially in regard to his contacts with middle-range British officials. Even in London, Balfour's absence in Paris and his replacement by Curzon as acting chief of the Foreign Office had worried him, and the departure to other service of old friends at lower levels made him venture to suggest that persons familiar with, and sympathetic to, Zionism be appointed to provide necessary liaison. Anxiety on this score was redoubled when it came to the personnel in Palestine; Weizmann (powerfully backed by Brandeis) not only urged the appointment of Meinertzhagen as political officer, but tried to have a friend, Sir Wyndham Deedes, succeed the retiring military governor of Palestine. He also pressed for the appointment of Jews to the Palestine administration and police, which he feared were being filled with Syrian officials and local Arabs at the lower levels and hostile British colonial administrators at the top. The role played by the police and administration in the April riots made him and other Jewish observers shudder with the sense that they were seeing a replica of Russian pogroms in Palestine under the British flag.[52]

At the time of the riots, the San Remo conference of the Allied powers was convening to settle the disposition of mandates for the occupied Ottoman lands in anticipation of a Turkish peace treaty. The outbreak in Jerusalem seemed calculated to upset the hopes Zionists pinned on the conference. Weizmann left Palestine for San Remo in great agitation about the outcome. In the event, the Allies agreed to assign the Palestine mandate to Britain and to provide for the inclusion of the Balfour promise to the Jews in the Turkish peace treaty. Moreover, at San Remo Weizmann learned that the military occupation would soon be replaced by a civil administration in Palestine, to be headed by none other than Herbert Samuel (who now became Sir Herbert), the man who had been his main support in his political struggles during the war and the political and economic planning that followed and whom he had tried for months to bring into the policy-making councils of the Palestine administration.[53]

San Remo was a sudden change in Zionist fortunes that lifted Weizmann out of boundless embitterment and depression into a state of euphoria. He expected an agreement with the new civil administration that would realize all the immediate goals the Zionists could not secure at the peace conference: a favorable decision on Palestine's frontiers; an internal security force manned by Jews; access to state and wastelands; industrial development concessions for the Zionists; and close cooperation with the government in facilitating the immigration and settlement of Jews in their homeland. He now was dismayed at the continuing, mounting hostility between the military government, in its last months in Palestine, and the local Jewish community. The crux of antagonism became the issue of Jabotinsky's incarceration: infuriated Zionist militants, who threatened to break the Jewish prisoners loose by force, vented their anger in denunciation of the London leaders' slackness in defense of Jewish honor and interests. Weizmann, for his part, fumed and fulminated against the Palestine Jews' "hysteria," which he feared would destroy the brief, golden moment of opportunity he had won for his people.[54]

He returned to London in May 1920 eager to launch the practical labors needed to make a reality of the political triumph that (as he felt in common with Brandeis and others) had been all but guaranteed at San Remo. Hoping to enlist the skills and wealth of Western Jewry, he offered men like James de Rothschild, Alfred Mond, and Robert Waley Cohen an extended term on a reconstituted Zionist Executive, with far-reaching discretionary powers in matters of economic investment and development. In this way he largely accommodated his plans to the ruling conception of Brandeis and the Americans, whose financial support and expertise were essential. Nevertheless, he made it clear enough to those whom he courted that still-pending matters might involve anyone named to the Zionist Executive in polical negotiations vis-à-vis the British government—a prospect that led Waley Cohen to decline the invitation. Weizmann, in other words, acted on his final warning at the August 1919 meeting: although he submitted to the decision to make the WZO solely and directly responsible for the Palestine work, he remained opposed to it, and he took any occasion to point out its difficulties and (implicitly) the advantages of the alternative, a Jewish council or agency constituted by the WZO and other concerned and representative Jewish organizations.[55]

The American leaders during this period were satisfied that they had overcome Weizmann's opposition. The impromptu, unrepresentative character of the 1919 meetings required another conference—convened on a more regular, more legitimate basis to ratify and flesh out the decisions. The Americans prepared for that session with much confidence in their success but with growing indications of trouble in their own home base.

Brandeis' insistence on having his own way in reorganizating the WZO stemmed in good part from his difficulties in carrying out a similar plan in America. With the issuance and general endorsement of the Balfour Declaration, now followed by the Zionist political victory at San Remo, he felt that all Jews could be expected to enlist as members of a reorganized Zionist movement, one committed to the remaining practical tasks of development and resettlement, in which they could participate with no ideological qualms. His efforts in 1917 to recruit Schiff and his following had, however, run into difficulties; when he renewed them in 1919, the problems remained. Schiff may perhaps have raised the demand of a religious test for an acceptable Zionism as a pretext for backing out at the last moment in 1917; but it was clear from other participants in the discussions, like Louis Marshall, that there was another obstacle. American non-Zionists (like the French Baron Rothschild) preferred to remain a separate and equal entity in their collaboration with the Zionist project. Their recalcitrance would certainly have been strengthened by Weizmann's plan, allowing non-Zionists to share in the Palestine work without joining the WZO. But if Brandeis succeeded in imposing his view on the WZO and recruited British non-Zionists to a reconstructed Zionist leadership, it might be effective in winning over the American notables as well.[56]

Brandeis' experience in Palestine and Europe in 1919 strengthened another motive for insisting on his design. His arguments for the inherent compatibility of Zionism and Americanism were primarily useful in polemics against anti-Zionist Jewish opponents, but they also had some effect among those whom Brandeis particularly wanted to recruit as Zionist activists. This aspect was increasingly stressed when America entered the war and suspicion of alien influences sharply rose; afterward, the postwar wave of anti-Bolshevik sensitivity, interlaced with antisemitic militancy, kept alive the sense that Zionists had best guard themselves against imputations of disloyalty. Those most likely to feel exposed to pressure on this score were the acculturated, socially and professionally advancing young Jews whom Brandeis was especially anxious to attract.

He hoped that in the new era of Zionism such recruits could find in practical work opportunities to combine their professional competence with an elevating idealism. What the medical unit meant for Hadassah and for a group of dedicated doctors and nurses, similarly constructed special agencies that addressed the technical problems of development in Palestine would come to mean for young American Jewish fiscal experts, engineers, lawyers, and accountants: types more likely to be found among second- or third-generation, college-trained new recruits than among the immigrants who were the mainstay of the FAZ and other prewar Zionist societies.[57]

The Brandeis regime's disdain for the old-style Zionists, implicit in the methods of administration applied in America, became explicit in the proposals the Chief brought with him to London. His earlier visit to Europe and Palestine had given his preference for a tight, trimmed-down controlling apparatus an additional sharpness of edge. His own experience and the reports of Americans who worked with the Zionist Commission in Palestine or visited the London bureau confirmed the impression that few, if any, of the old-time activists were suitable for executive responsibilities in the new era of Zionism. The political struggle was all but over, and the need for propagandists had gone by. The time had come to confide Zionist executive functions to a small, workmanlike group of technical experts and managers. The veterans (all but Weizmann and Sokolow, who had special qualifications) should retire voluntarily or be retired with pensions.

Finally, the encounter with the heightened nationalist visions of East-Central European Zionism, in Palestine as well as in London and Paris, made Brandeis (and others in the American delegation) more acutely aware of the conflict between their own requirements and the European perspectives. They were quite willing—and had pressed the non-Zionist AJC to the same conclusion—to back the Eastern nationalists in their demand for national minority rights in the new, postwar states, but only the immigrant ideologues wanted remotely similar arrangements in America. Weizmann's willingness to work for an eventual World Jewish Congress—largely representing the European Jewish national councils—and to yield ultimate control of the Palestine enterprise to officers elected by them threatened Brandeis' plans fundamentally. It could frighten off non-Zionist notables and repel expert administrators who would not accept ideological supervision; it was hardly less repugnant to Brandeis' own close circle of Zionist aides.

The American leaders had to prepare themselves for another battle over these issues in the near future. The initial victory in August 1919 was encouraging, but not conclusive, since the ad hoc meeting in London was not competent to make constitutional changes in the Zionist structure. Plans to hold a more representative annual conference presented a more serious challenge for the Americans. They needed to bolster their position by demonstrating greater strength, both in registered membership and in funds collected. But just at that time their situation at home took an ominously downward turn. The near-one-hundred-fifty-thousand total registered members reported to the ZOA convention in December 1919 was not retained the following year, when little more than a third of that number could be reported. The major efforts of the ZOA, whether in seeking signatures for a mass petition in favor of Zionist aims or contributions of funds (at a previously unimaginable level needed for the new reponsibilities in Palestine), fell sharply below their goals. Not only had the intense commitment of the war emergency flagged, both among the activists and the community at large, but disillusionment with President Wilson's peace conference role, a decline in popular support for progressivism, and a postwar recession in economic activity were part of the background of the Zionist leaders' increasingly sober mood. In addition to the other elements that motivated their plans for the ZOA and WZO, Brandeis and his circle were now disposed to view with more caution and moderation the goals Zionism could set for itself in the immediate future.[58]

Brandeis' leadership in many ways ran against the grain for the veteran, rank-and-file Zionists. And as the new registrants attracted by the movement's wartime work and the Balfour Declaration began to fall away, the mood of the core constituency became a factor of increasing importance in matters of organization. The compromises that ended the battle with the AJC had been imposed against the will of many, including Brandeis' close associates Horace Kallen and even, for a time, Stephen Wise. The arrangement by which Brandeis channeled his directives to other Zionists through de Haas caused continual irritation in many circles; old-time Zionists who had been consigned to a subordinate role in the days of PZEC now demanded that, with the end of the emergency, the regularly elected executive committee of the new ZOA, not the personal associates of Justice Brandeis, should determine policies. And there was growing uneasiness at the way the leaders around Brandeis were moving the ZOA away from the familiar activities and style of the older societies toward those that had once been designed to attract prominent and influential, but peripheral, supporters to the Zion Association and similar auxiliary organizations.[59]

A disgruntled opposition began to be heard, but no clear omens of division were at first visible. The incumbent administration suffered a defeat at the 1919 ZOA convention when it offered a resolution to divest the Mizrachi and Poalei Zion parties of the recognition they enjoyed as autonomous Zionist units with direct access to WZO headquarters. The rank-and-file delegates saw this as part of the tendency to submerge typically East European, immigrant expressions of Zionism, which they had feared when the centralized, American-style ZOA was formed a year earlier. The incumbent administration had to conciliate the opposition with a gesture of recognition of the prerogatives of the elected executive committee; but in practice the smaller group of Brandeis' confidantes continued to control policies for the succeeding term. In other respects the Brandeis administration still enjoyed the backing of a solid consensus. American Zionists were united in seeking greater recognition from the world movement for their new leading role; they shared the impression—confirmed by reports from men like Stephen Wise and Jacob de Haas of the fiscal and managerial disorder in the London office and the Palestine operation of the WZO—that only their own new leaders could bring the needed efficiency to the tasks confronting the world movement. Brandeis was thus able to go to the London conference during the 1920 summer recess of the Supreme Court at the head of a large, united American delegation.

The 1920 London conference brought together leading Zionists from all the scattered countries that had been divided by the war for so many years. The plenary sessions lasted from July 7 to July 22, and there were preliminary and subsequent meetings that extended the discussions over a period of two months. This was a major conclave, with hundreds of delegates and additional visitors; the Americans brought over forty participants, including twenty-nine official delegates. The conference was authorized under the WZO constitution to legislate for the movement and choose its leaders, and it took up the whole range of issues arising from the old commitments and new tasks of the movement. But the impression left on those who attended was that of a failed occasion, leaving behind the seeds of division and conflict in spite of the gains in organization and legitimated leadership that were achieved.

One reason for the discordant atmosphere of the meeting has been noted in all accounts: the American impatience with the European-style parliamentary proceedings of the Zionist assemblies. The presentation of lengthy reports and theses, followed by an unfocused "general debate," was particularly offensive to Brandeis, a man who hoarded his time and energy. But when he presided over meetings and tried to impose the same businesslike, tightly controlled guidance of the discussion that he exercised in the American movement, he irritated the delegates—and failed to accomplish his aim. Weizmann suffered his own discomfort at the sessions; his administration of affairs came under heavy attack, particularly from the Palestinian delegates. But in the matter of the order of discussions, particularly the "general debate," he stood with the European veterans.[60]

The formal sessions of the conference were for the leading Americans a pointless distraction; they concentrated their efforts, instead, on private negotiations concerning the future organization and leadership of the movement. Before arriving, the Americans had talked with Lord Reading—who came on a British financial mission to America—and with Julius Simon—who hoped to patch up the rifts between the London and New York Zionist offices. There seemed to be sufficient convergence to justify the hope that the American and the London-based leaders might work out a common basis for reorganizing the movement.

Meanwhile, Weizmann and Sokolow went far along the road favored by Brandeis in offering Mond, Anthony de Rothschild, and Waley Cohen leading posts in executive organs of the Zionist movement. The candidates proved reluctant to take up the offers for various reasons: Mond's stake in his political future as a current member of the British government; Rothschild's feeling that more influential local figures would have to be on the Political Committee before he could agree to head it; persisting ideological qualms in the case of Waley Cohen. Weizmann fell back in his talks with Mond on an alternative suggestion, less clearly political: a role as Herbert Samuel's successor on the economic advisory council, to be integrated eventually in the prospective Jewish Council or Jewish Agency that would be constituted by a coalition of Zionist and other representative Jewish organizations. Mond took exception to so large a body as Weizmann contemplated as the controlling center for economic policy; he suggested a small executive group, to work in cooperation with the WZO, but independently.[61]

With Brandeis' arrival, the discussions took another turn.[62] He developed his plan, taking over the initiative, in consultation with Lord Reading, a man with whom the London leaders had only slight contact in spite of his prominence in English public life. Brandeis proposed, in view of the reluctance of the non-Zionist notables to stand for election by the Zionist constituency, that a small Executive be elected with power to co-opt others for essential roles—a method similar to his practice in shaping the PZEC in America. Also, at the instance of Lord Reading, he stipulated that the new Executive, with its elected and co-opted members, be given a three-year term in order to build a solid foundation for the Jewish national home in Palestine. Having framed his program in private conversations with the consent of Sokolow and the seeming tacit submission of Weizmann, Brandeis had to present it for formal approval to the conference delegates, most of whom had no inkling of what was being planned.

Brandeis approached this task by submitting the plan first to the caucus of the American delegates, whom he expected to bind in support of the project. Like others unaware of the radical new turn that was being planned, the American delegates were taken aback by the seeming surrender of Zionist prerogatives to non-Zionists and of democratic rights to an oligarchy. But what concerned them most was Brandeis' own role; they were willing to go along with him if they were assured of his direct, personal commitment to take an active part in the Zionist leadership. The most that Brandeis could promise was to accept a role as honorary president of the WZO, with others assuming the responsibility for active, current leadership of the movement. His specific plan proposed the election of Weizmann as acting president, Sokolow as chairman of the executive committee, and Bernard Flexner (a close friend and neighbor of the Brandeis clan in Louisville, whom Justice

Brandeis had recently co-opted to Zionist activity) as the fourth Zionist member of that committee. Those four elected leaders would have power to co-opt to the Executive, for its three-year term, notable and expert managers who would not stand for election by the movement; Lord Reading, Sir Alfred Mond, and James de Rothschild were those intended to serve as the management group in London for three years.

The plan met with stiff opposition in the American caucus, and the demand was raised that Brandeis resign from the Supreme Court and become the active president of the WZO; nevertheless, the line was held and Brandeis retained the bloc vote of the American delegation. He then took the proposal to a closed session of the conference's steering committee, the so-called Senioren Convent; there he was supported by Sokolow, subjected to critical comments by Weizmann, and coldly received by many other veteran leaders. Thereupon further specifications were added, making clear that the co-opted as well as elected members of the Executive would report regularly to the constituted movement control group, the Actions Comité. But at that point Weizmann delivered a coup de grace to the whole proposal in a late-night meeting with Mond and James de Rothschild, the details of which remain obscure (Weizmann himself left no clear report; Mond wrote only a brief response to charges that were made; and the main accounts are those of Brandeis partisans, who were not present at the meeting). In any case there is agreement that the candidates for co-optation—at least Sir Alfred Mond, among the most prominent—preferred to cooperate in the work outside the Zionist framework.[63]

De Haas, Frankfurter, and others of Brandeis' aides tried in vain to patch up the split in the Zionist leadership by inducing Weizmann to conciliate Brandeis; before their effort could bring the two together, Brandeis had already appeared before the Senioren Convent in the early morning and announced that he had been betrayed by Weizmann and could no longer work with him. Anguished pleas from the American and European leaders alike swayed him only to the extent of agreeing to serve as honorary president, but he was adamant in forbidding the election of any American to the executive committee of an administration actively led by Weizmann. The personal taboo he imposed on Weizmann was rigidly maintained for years afterward; so, too, the American movement in the remaining period of Brandeis' domination drew increasingly apart, and followed a course increasing distinct, from the reorganized WZO.

Weizmann's autobiography repeats a commonly accepted explanation of the break that occurred at the 1920 London conference:

> The Brandeis group envisaged the Zionist Organization as henceforth a purely economic body. Since, in their view, it had lost its political character by fulfilling its political function, there was no longer any reason why non-Zionists . . . should refuse to become members. But our reason for wishing to keep the Zionist Organization in being as a separate body was precisely the conviction that the political work was far from finished.

The difference cited here was certainly one that was stressed in the polemics that developed in the subsequent years, but it hardly was decisive in the Brandeis-Weizmann clash of July 1920. Weizmann was as sanguine as Brandeis after the San Remo decision in the belief that the main political struggle was all but over; henceforth the Zionists could proceed on the basis of a practical understanding to be worked out with Britain. Both leaders, too, believed that the impression of American support for Zionism had been a decisive factor in gaining the Balfour Declaration and in sustaining the Zionist cause at the peace conference—and Brandeis continued to underscore the role of American pro-Zionist pressure tied to the strength of the American movement in ensuring that Britain would faithfully perform its duties under the mandate. One can hardly imagine that Weizmann defeated Brandeis' project for fear that undue concentration on economic tasks would hamper the WZO in dealing with its pressing political problems.[64]

If there was a possible political issue between the two, it was a certain latent, unexpressed difference over the proper Zionist relationship with the mandatory power. Weizmann was well enough acquainted with the ruling circles in London and Jerusalem not to rely on them for a positive policy of government action aiming to achieve the Zionist goal in Palestine; from the beginning, he found it persuasive in approaching them to stress that it was up to the Jewish people and the Zionists themselves to make a reality of the aim that the Balfour Declaration and the mandate would merely hold open as a legitimate aspiration. Brandeis, leaning toward the neo-Herzlian positions of men like de Haas and Wise in his circle, expected that with a properly executed mandate text (and under international—especially American—scrutiny) the British Palestine administration together with the local Jewish community could adequately provide for many functions that Weizmann and other veteran Zionists believed required the resources and political weight of the WZO and the prospective council or agency of world Jewry.

This difference expressed itself, certainly, in the August 1919 conflict between Brandeis and Weizmann over the Jewish Council and the participation in it of other than Zionist organizations or simply of all concerned Jewish persons. Nevertheless, less than a year later in 1920 Weizmann was evidently willing to meet Brandeis' requirements at least halfway. His preference for a coalition with other Jewish organizations was, in good part, based on the wish to conciliate the Rothschilds. But he now found that another, vitally important associate, Sir Alfred Mond, preferred a small board of qualified persons rather than a consortium of organizations to direct the work in Palestine; complying with Mond's preference (within the restricted sphere of economic activity in Palestine) brought Weizmann closer to Brandeis' specifications.

What undoubtedly made Weizmann's recalcitrance unavoidable at the last moment were the specific details of the proposal finally submitted by Brandeis. The scheme called for three English non-Zionists to be co-opted to the Zionist Executive by four elected members, nominally assuring Zionist dominance. Those elected would be the veteran pair, Weizmann and Sokolow, together with Brandeis as honorary president and Bernard Flexner,

Brandeis' man in the active, routinely functioning administration. One could easily imagine that given the array of voting members of the Executive, Weizmann's active presidency of the WZO might amount to little more in practice than Lipsky's role in the American movement under Brandeis' ascendancy. Weizmann could draw little assurance from the nominal majority of Zionists on the Executive. His doubts about Brandeis' Zionist instincts (not to speak of Flexner's) were heightened by the confidence reposed in an unknown quantity like Lord Reading. For all his distrust of the nationalist "hysteria" sometimes seen in his European and Palestinian veteran colleagues, Weizmann was at one with them in experiencing Zionism as a movement of national awakening, extending to Jews in every corner of their dispersion. He did not trust an executive committee constituted as Brandeis planned and dependent on the absentee honorary president's casting vote in case of ties to keep the Palestine project from declining into the limited, philanthropic dimensions non-Zionists tended to favor. For Brandeis, on the other hand, the arrangement he proposed was necessary in order to make his own contribution to the work feasible without retiring from his responsibilities as a Supreme Court justice; his hopes of bringing the leading American non-Zionists into the fold also seemed to him to depend on it.

A remarkable, puzzling consequence was the extreme animus that Brandeis showed thereafter toward Weizmann (and subsequently against Lipsky and his "ilk," virtually the code name by which Brandeis partisans, echoing the Chief, referred to their opponents in the ZOA after 1921). In a somewhat parallel case noted earlier, Brandeis' tactic of deliberately ignoring Magnes after the Congress issue led to their break was explained as a matter of political expediency. It implied no detraction of Magnes' moral stature, but quite the opposite: concern that exposure to his impressive influence might lead Zionists astray from the proper direction of wise policy. One may detect some of the same motivation in Brandeis' long-sustained ostracism of Weizmann (and, later, even in his cold disdain for Lipsky, the leader of his American opposition). He took a grim satisfaction in the snubs he administered to Weizmann in the years that followed, reporting them to his associates with a clear intimation that thereby he was denying to a dangerously able antagonist the advantage of appearing to accept his right to lead. This, of course, meant acknowledging that Weizmann was dangerous precisely because he possessed qualities of leadership. But in this case Brandeis conceded to his opponent only the brains needed for leadership; in moral qualities (which he had acknowledged in Magnes' case) he found Weizmann specifically disqualified—untruthful, unreliable, and disloyal. Later, he was to extend the condemnation in similar terms not only to Lipsky and his "ilk," but to the fiscal irresponsibility and moral laxity that he tended to find generally prevalent among the Zionists of East European cast, in spite of the often truly admirable qualities they showed in other respects.

It would be consistent with Brandeis' style in action if he had hammered away at Weizmann's perceived flaws of character in a continuing battle to reassert leadership. But he made no serious attempt to oust his opponent from the WZO presidency; indeed, his reluctant consent to his own honorary presidency was a tacit endorsement of a kind. He recognized that Weizmann's role as the man most acceptable to the British, who after all were to rule as the mandatory power in Palestine, was indispensable for success of the movement. But if he then persisted in morally disqualifying his rival without trying to displace him—a procedure totally at odds with his ordinary cool and rational practice—he was clearly responding in an emotional, passionate way, not by calculation alone.

Early in his career Brandeis had been advised by Professor Nathaniel Shaler, a good friend and patron at Harvard, that he was too sensitive to be a successful rough-and-tumble lawyer. The extraordinary success he achieved, particularly in the lists of public controversy and unbridled polemic, was won by dint of stern control of impulsive and emotional responses. He was ruthless and expert in the use of cutting and hurtful attack, but always up to, and never beyond, the extent of the damage needed to gain his immediate end. As for invective and slander against his own person, he schooled himself to ignore whatever did not need to be immediately refuted in order to gain a particular objective. Bearing a grudge was not his practice, since it represented a wasteful use of energy. The inveterate, cold hostility to Weizmann, after defeat at his hands, was thus an exceptional reaction for Brandeis and calls for specific explanation.

Brandeis' facade of indifference to insult covered his sensitive nature well enough when he knew he was falsely accused. All observers have noted, on the other hand, that he was unusually given to candid, unembarrassed reversals of his position if convinced by the arguments of opponents; sensitivity of a high order combined with a strongly rooted self-assurance produced his extraordinary intellectual courage and open-mindedness. What is noteworthy in his expressions at the London conference, on the other hand, is the overtone of defensiveness and barely hidden embarrassment in the explanation he gave his followers at that time. The occasion for his lengthy apologia was the blunt demand made in the American caucus meeting that he resign his Supreme Court post and take over personally the presidency of the WZO. The reasons he gave for being unable to do so—his age, his significant role as champion of progressivism on the Court—could have been stated briefly and bluntly as considerations that simply outweighed for him any duty he might have had toward the Zionist cause or the Jewish people; very few of the American Zionist delegation would have felt shocked or reacted in any other way in his circumstances. But his apologia was neither brief nor blunt, nor was it confined to these obvious points. He explained at length, in addition, that retiring from the Court might undermine his argument that Zionist and American loyalties were compatible and claimed, rather weakly, that he could be more helpful to the Zionist cause by staying where he was. It was, of course, a line of argument that implied that one's duties as a Jew and a Zionist were—or should be—no less compelling than those as an American.[65]

There is reason to think that this was not merely an implication appropriate to leave on a Zionist audience, but one felt sincerely—and not without some pain. Brandeis had occasion to be chagrined more than once at the reluctance of his Zionist circle, heavily committed to various public functions at home, to free themselves for necessary Zionist service. The men he had been able to send to the Zionist Commission in Palestine, for example, were able to remain only for brief periods, never long enough to leave a lasting impression. Weizmann and other Europeans, on the other hand, showed a kind of personal Zionist commitment that (in other cases, then and later) Brandeis unfeignedly and warmly admired. A man who took his personal obligations seriously, Brandeis could not but know that his own response to Zionist challenges set a standard for his followers, close and far. The direct challenge flung by Lipsky and others at the American caucus and the indirect one constantly presented by the example of a man like Weizmann undoubtedly contributed to the irritated tone of Brandeis' expressions in the wake of the London conference.[66]

The WZO Annual Conference ended with Weizmann's election as president and Sokolow as chairman of the Executive, with additional (Zionist) members to be selected by them as heads of functional departments. Brandeis agreed to be an honorary president but would allow no American to serve actively on the Executive. An era of conflict loomed ahead.

Attack and Counterattack

The London conferences evoked a sharper definition of differences, particularly marked on the American side after the defeat in 1920. There was a certain asymmetry in the relative attitudes of the main protagonists. Weizmann's distrust of Brandeis rested on a general reservation conditioning his admiration for Western Jews, more than on disagreement with particular policies. For Brandeis, who had his own reservations about Eastern habits of work, what chiefly mattered were the policies in dispute. The issue that forced their conflict into public view—the question of the form in which Jews previously outside the Zionist organization would be brought into the Palestine project—posed alternatives that precluded one or the other from functioning effectively in his chosen role, so that the prospect of defeat (for Weizmann in 1919 as for Brandeis in 1920) led them to a more drastic, intransigent formulation of positions. Partisan opposition grew sharper in two respects: opposing policies were more unconditionally defended and were justified on grounds of mutually offensive, categorical antipathies. "West" was arrayed against "East" over a broad range of disputed details of the movement's aims and methods.

Differences of approach had long been evident, especially after the Americans began in 1919 to work directly in Palestine, but they had usually been adjusted or overlooked. The American medical unit quickly came into conflict with Ussishkin (newly installed as acting head of the Zionist Commission) over his demand that they use the Hebrew language in their correspondence. But during the April 1920 Arab attacks, the work of Hadassah in

Jerusalem won warm praise from Weizmann and others. Brandeis' brusque demand at the 1919 meeting to halt agricultural settlement until malaria could be effectively controlled was similarly smoothed over by Dr. Harry Friedenwald's assurance that the proposal was merely a suggestion of priorities that were necessitated by the temporarily tight fiscal situation of the movement. So, too, the program adopted by the ZOA at its founding convention to nationalize all land and natural resources in Palestine was rejected by European Zionists as being excessively doctrinaire; they were planning to attract private capital (especially funds salvaged by emigrants fleeing the Bolshevik Revolution) for land acquisition through the Zionist land office, Palestine Land Development Company. American submission to such pressure was easy to come by since American cooperative land-purchase syndicates, reorganized during the war as the American Zion Commonwealth, also relied on private investment.

Thus, prior to the stunning collapse of Brandeis' agenda at the 1920 conference, the American leaders readily came to terms with critics of overrigid formulations of their demands, especially as the opponents made more far-reaching concessions to American positions. But after the 1920 defeat (in keen resentment of Weizmann's tactics, just as Weizmann had resented Brandeis' parliamentary maneuvers in 1919), Brandeis turned to a new line of sharp and lasting opposition to the elected WZO administration, which was dominated by his successful rival.

For years thereafter Brandeis remained coldly aloof from the elected leadership of the world Zionist movement while continuing to lead a group of Zionists loyal to himself. Immediately after the 1920 conference, the group attached to him included the official American federation, the ZOA. He allowed no American to become a member of the WZO Executive for fear that such representation might be taken to mean that his honorary presidency implied accepting responsibility for the policies of its active leaders. However, he did leave Bernard Flexner behind for a while after he left London, for contact with the new administration; in addition, Ben Cohen remained to work on the still-unsettled draft mandate for Palestine. Also, enough direct connection was retained with some of the London staff, like the new secretary, Julius Simon, and the Dutch Zionist, Nehemiah de Lieme, so that coordination remained possible.[67]

Relations with the new Executive in fiscal matters now changed from a chronic irritation to an acute issue, increasingly seen as one of principle.[68] During the war the Americans had readily supplied funds for WZO activities conducted on traditional lines or dictated by the emergency—in any case without a significant share in determining policies. After the war they were less inclined to defer to others; they felt entitled, by their special competence and predominant share in contributed funds, to assume the leading role. Moreover, their hopes for attracting massive support in America rested on the appeal that humanitarian and constructive projects in Palestine might have for donors disinclined to support other Zionist activities (considered ideological and controversial) or the organizational expenses they entailed.

They wanted such donors to be able to earmark their contributions, which should not be diverted to a general administrative budget; accordingly, they also demanded considerable autonomy for the American and other territorial federations in the projects they would sponsor in Palestine.

In the 1920 meeting the Americans ran head on into a conception of Zionist budgeting and administration diametrically opposed to their own. Weizmann confronted them at an early meeting with the demand that each one should pledge a tenth of his property (not simply his income) for the reconstruction of the Jewish national home. This might have been acceptable as a symbolic gesture expressing Zionist commitment by a group of leaders, but it soon became clear that it was a seriously meant claim (proposed by some Russian leaders) for a form of self-taxation to be demanded of all Jews under moral pressure of the common national interest. They planned in this way to obtain within one year pledges of twenty-five million pounds (one hundred twenty-five million dollars), the initial amount required to build the Jewish national home in all its cardinal aspects. This was, of course, an approach totally opposed to the American project of attracting donors by restricting the use of their contributions to purposes they specifically approved and exempting them from traditional Zionist commitments.

The issue was made even sharper by the administrative setup entailed by the European, as contrasted to the American, concept. Brandeis' idea of the WZO as a kind of international conglomerate, a combine of territorial federations, each with its chosen, limited project in Palestine, envisaged the Action Committee as a corporate board of directors. It would meet to hear reports and give approval to the discretionary decisions of the operating managers taken over a considerable period; the main control would be a fixed budget. The European conception tended to see the WZO in the light of a government. The Action Committee would represent Zionist parties with different socioeconomic programs and ideologies and would thus exert much specific control over activities; the project managers would function as, or under, the department heads of an Executive as constituted by the dominant factions of the latest congress; and all the revenue of the WZO from its donated funds would be at the disposal of the congress and the Executive for budgeted or contingency expenditures according to the changing requirements of a political movement. Such a structure not only ruled out Zionist membership for those willing to contribute solely to earmarked funds (they could cooperate through separate organizations in the projected Jewish Agency instead), it also obliged the WZO's territorial federations to respect the congress' discipline and share in activities directed by the Executive rather than concentrating on autonomous projects of their own, as Brandeis seemed to intend.

Such issues that concerned the organization and fiscal controls of the WZO itself were now added to the earlier split over the proper mode for associating all Jews with the work in Palestine; these issues became, indeed, the chief bone of contention. Old complaints and irritations—formerly raised and glossed over as unrelated, disparate matters—were now elevated into

questions of principle, as Brandeis launched a systematic attack on the methods of the veteran, newly reinstalled, administration of Zionist affairs. The
creation of a Foundation Fund, the Keren Hayesod, for the self-taxation of
Jews on behalf of the Palestine work afforded a major target for Brandeis'
fundamental critique. The veteran Russian Zionists chosen to head the Keren
Hayesod and Weizmann's choice of Ussishkin (and later of Jabotinsky) to
join him and Sokolow in the leadership of the new Executive made the critique more heated and acrimonious.[69]

Brandeis was appalled by the pretentious demand of the old/new leaders
that world Jewry tax itself for the amount thought necessary for the work they
planned in Palestine. Most of this sum, he knew, would have to be contributed by American Jews, and recent experience had shown severely disappointing results in raising much smaller sums for previously budgeted activities. Brandeis therefore proposed to limit closely the sums that the ZOA
would forward to the London office for the Executive and to husband the
resources of the American movement for its own chosen projects in Palestine
such as the medical unit. He was no less displeased with the reckless enthusiasm or fanciful propaganda about the spontaneous outpouring of sacrificial
offerings by housewives, householders, workers, and bankers that would flow
from world Jewry aroused by an army of nationalist agitators. He saw this
not only as the perfervid nationalism (including the specter of worldwide
Diaspora nationalism) that immediately threatened his hopes to bring all
American Jewry into the fold of the ZOA, but also it impressed him as part
of the general irresponsibility that he more and more felt to be characteristic
of European Zionists, particularly in their fiscal management. This led him
to concentrate his fire on the proposed management and functioning of the
Keren Hayesod.

The Keren Hayesod was envisaged by its advocates as the main source of
funds for all three types of financing generally accepted as necessary and distinct: donations to be invested without expecting any return, *"à fonds perdu";*
quasi investments in productive facilities, with relatively minor expectation
of returns (described by Brandeis as share capital); and ordinary investments
(e.g., in fixed-interest bonds). It is clear that Brandeis had practical objections
to such an approach; it meant allocating funds under the political pressure of
rival parties in the WZO and could alienate potential supporters whom he
hoped to recruit to the ZOA. But in the heat of argument, he turned the quarrel into an issue of principle. He resorted to an absolutist moralism, attacking
the "commingling of funds" involved in combining donations with investments in the same fund as if it were a case of fraud. The point, to be sure,
begs the real question involved: if the Keren Hayesod had, indeed, come into
being as a substantial treasury based on "taxation," there could hardly be any
moral objections (though, no doubt, understandable political ones) to drawing on it for productive, self-liquidating, as well as nonremunerative investment. Brandeis' attack on "commingling of funds" implicitly assumes that
the Zionists would receive donations according to his own plan: donors
controlling the use of their funds that were given only for previously

stipulated, narrowly restricted purposes. His attack accordingly took on the indignant tone of a judgment against trustees accused of malfeasance in office.[70]

Brandeis' critique was also sharpened by extending the negative impression of the veteran Zionists that he had entertained in a mild form long since. During his visit to Palestine in 1919, he had concluded that men like Ussishkin should be retired—if necessary, on pensions. Like Weizmann, he attributed the friction between the Zionist Commission and the British military to the fractious and rude manners of Russian Zionists as well as the anti-Jewish prejudice of British officials. But he parted with Weizmann in finding that the extensive functions taken on by the commission (seen by the British as a state within the state) exacerbated the difficulties. Weizmann considered such independent initiative of world Jewry (initially shown in rallying wartime support) to be part of the compact he had struck with Britain, who would be expected only to facilitate the Zionist work, not bear the direct burden. After the 1920 meeting, Brandeis' harsh comments on Weizmann's character lumped him implicitly with unreliable East Europeans like Ussishkin. Subsequent disputes confirmed Weizmann in his own alignment with the Easterners and hardened the East-West split.

In the developing conflict, Weizmann's old friend, Julius Simon, and other fiscal conservatives among veteran Zionists held an intermediate position and tried in vain to bridge the threatening cleavage. Weizmann was anything but eager to break with the Americans, and Brandeis always recognized that Weizmann was indispensable in the WZO leadership. Nevertheless, hopes of restoring a working relationship between Brandeis and Weizmann were doomed to failure; Simon and his fellows were themselves involved in the critical disputes that forced Weizmann to choose between them and their old-line opponents.

An immediate issue arose when the initiators of the Keren Hayesod, the Russian émigré industrialists, Isaac Naiditsch and Hillel Zlatopolsky, demanded authority in expending funds as well as raising them—a status somewhat like that which Brandeis and Weizmann had planned to concede to non-Zionist financiers before the 1920 negotiations collapsed. Julius Simon, on the other hand, insisted that the elected Executive must retain control of investment policy and personnel selection; those chosen to head a short-term fund-raising effort could not expect authority over long-term projects that the Executive should properly supervise. This dispute evoked memories of the old differences between Zionist political leaders and financial managers, going back to Herzl's attempts to keep the main Zionist fiscal agency, the Jewish Colonial Trust, under his control. Weizmann, who had long criticized the trust's detachment from WZO policy, was consistent in supporting Simon in this matter. Also, he was still trying to set up non-Zionist cooperation in an economic council and to achieve reconciliation with the Americans. These were further reasons for a compromise that gave Julius Simon, representing the Executive, a seat with veto power on the Keren Hayesod Board.[71]

In the same early period of the Brandeis-Weizmann split, a Reorganization Commission was set up to deal with the problem-beset Zionist Commission. The new body was composed of Julius Simon and Nehemiah de Lieme, chosen at the 1920 London Conference, and they co-opted Robert Szold as the third member—altogether a group congenial to Brandeis' spirit and approach. As a condition for Szold's participation as American representative, Weizmann agreed to grant the commission plenary powers: understood by Simon and the Americans as the right to impose, not simply propose, reforms in the Zionist apparatus and activities in Palestine. The commissioners then produced a barrage of harsh criticisms of past performance and drastic proposals for change, largely echoing those made earlier by Brandeis and other Americans. Not only should the Zionist Commission be scrapped, the Executive, in absorbing its functions, should not stand in the same way between the local Jewish community and the Palestine government. The commission adopted a position in some ways resembling that advocated by Jabotinsky (and other politically oriented Zionists): the mandate government—with a suitable infusion of Jewish and sympathetic officers—should become the primary agent of Zionist policy. In another way, however, they stood with Weizmann, relying on tact and diplomacy rather than forceful political pressure to ensure good-faith performance of its Zionist duties by Britain as well as peaceful acquiescence by the Arabs. Making the local Jewish community rather than the WZO responsible for relations with the Palestine administration also had financial implications. The major burden of maintaining the entire Jewish school system, which the WZO had assumed, would gradually become the responsibility of the government and the local community; if fund-raising abroad were necessary to sustain it at the desired level, sources other than the Zionist organization—as in the case of other welfare functions—would have to be tapped. The WZO would confine itself to projects of economic development alone.[72]

The attack on the veteran leadership of the Zionist Commission and the proposal to divest the WZO of its prized cultural and educational functions produced a storm of protest; a dispute over economic development policy brought it to a head. The Zionist Commission, led by Ussishkin and acting on the advice of the veteran Ruppin, had been negotiating the purchase of the Emek Jezreel lands held in absentee ownership by the Sursook family of Beirut. This was land requiring much swamp drainage but suitable for intensive cultivation. Preparatory work could speedily absorb laborers, now coming in rising number with the permission of the new civil administration, and the land would eventually support a fairly dense population; but there were insufficient budgeted funds available for the purchase, let alone the subsequent investment. The Reorganization Commission favored an alternative proposal. During Allenby's advance into Palestine, Aaronsohn (since deceased—in an airplane crash over the English Channel) and the agronomist, Isaac Wilkansky, had proposed to cultivate large areas of semiarid southern Palestine by dry farming methods in order to supply the troops. Wilkansky now favored the same approach: the acquisition of broad stretches, available for sale in the south relatively cheaply, for extensive cultivation and gradual resettlement. The Reorganization Commission recommended Wilkansky's plan and also favored buying land in the cities as a reserve against future growth. Ussishkin and Ruppin, however, were confronted with the pressure from unemployed immigrants and persisted in the Emek Jezreel purchase, over the protest of de Lieme, then one of the heads of the Jewish National Fund.[73]

During the Reorganization Commission tour of Palestine Jabotinsky had come to a new understanding with Weizmann. He was co-opted to the board of the Keren Hayesod and expected a place on the WZO Executive under conditions leaked to the press—evidently by Jabotinsky himself. They included an expanded Executive with major representation of the Palestine community; pressure for reconstituting the Jewish Legion as a garrison force in Palestine; and repudiation of the Reorganization Commission's critique. On the return of Simon to London (and during Weizmann's absence from the scene), there was added to the Emek Jezreel affair an open conflict in the Keren Hayesod Board, which had adopted decisions in Jabotinsky's spirit in defiance of Simon's veto power—in one instance, claiming that Weizmann had agreed while acting in Simon's place earlier. In January 1921 Simon and de Lieme submitted their resignation (to take effect on March 1) from the Executive and, in Simon's case, from the Keren Hayesod Board.[74]

Since the encounter at the 1919 conference, Weizmann had come to see the American leaders as lacking a true nationalist conviction, much like his earlier West European political Zionist adversaries.[75] Yet he was drawn into the current intra-Zionist conflicts, for which he at bottom blamed them, against his better judgment. He certainly viewed with sour dislike the basic attitudes implied in the postures of American Zionist leaders, but on many specific issues he largely shared their views. Although avoiding open partisanship in an effort to foster a consensus in the movement, he backed Simon on the point of the Executive's control of the Keren Hayesod; he felt that the Zionist Commission was being conducted in his absence in a way gratuitously irritating to the British; and he had his own doubts about the wisdom of the Emek Jezreel purchase, and avoided any decisive involvement in the question.

In the period after the 1920 conference, following a vacation on the Continent, Weizmann immersed himself in two primary problems. There was, first of all, the continuing tortuous negotiation of outstanding political issues; this was made particularly tense by the fact that Lord Curzon was now foreign secretary. The delay in reaching agreement among the Allies about a Turkish treaty—and then the nullification of the treaty signed with the Sultan owing to the nationalist uprising led by Kemal Ataturk—allowed many gains the Zionists thought secure to come into question again. The Zionist claims for adequate boundaries in the north and the east were, in the end, settled in a form severely disappointing to them. It took long, arduous efforts to restore to the draft mandate some provisions thought to be accepted in 1920 but then brought under cold scrutiny by the new men in the Foreign Office.

While absorbed in these critical discussions, Weizmann was also greatly preoccupied in talks with non-Zionists who might be drawn into the work in Palestine; this matter involved decisions bearing directly on the internal organizational issues that divided the Zionists themselves. With Samuel's assumption of office in Palestine, the bars were lifted and a sudden rush of immigrants sought employment; it became possible to buy lands for settlement; and substantial loans were needed by both the Palestine government and Zionist-inspired projects. Even the Reorganization Commission (which concluded that immigration should be suspended and development of new land acquisitions proceed only after careful experimentation) issued appeals for emergency transfusions of funds to Palestine to ease the existing pressures and hardships. Weizmann approached the Rothschilds, Mond, and Waley Cohen to help in raising capital for immediately urgent projects, like Rutenberg's plan to develop hydroelectric power for industry and agriculture. He came with plans for cooperation based on previous designs for a Jewish Council for Palestine, after adjustment to the latest revisions of the draft mandate and the decisions of the 1920 London conference.

At first Weizmann and Sokolow thought of a twofold approach to Anglo-Jewry: a broadly based conference to rally the whole community and a small Economic Council of experienced and influential men of affairs. Only the latter idea was long pursued, and it, too, soon encountered serious obstacles. Eventually an arrangement seemed possible, committing to the prospective Economic Council that part of the Keren Hayesod income that was budgeted for investment as loan and share capital in development projects (the remainder of the contributed funds having been allocated in fixed proportions to the Jewish National Fund for land purchase and to the WZO for its departments of health and education and for other current functions). The Economic Council or its leaders, for their part, were to endorse the Keren Hayesod publicly. Close relations between the two agencies would be secured through a "reasonable" Zionist representation on the council and equal representation of both parties on a Keren Hayesod management board supervising all the transactions and accounts of the Foundation Fund. Mond, concerned that British commitment to the Palestine project could be undermined by intra-Jewish squabbles, was ready to accept this scheme in late November 1920; other non-Zionist notables raised difficulties. Some opposed working together with Zionists outright. Waley Cohen, considering such responses, decided that he could only mobilize support for joint work in his circle if the Zionists would, in effect, yield all control of economic activity in Palestine to the council. James de Rothschild's recalcitrance took the form of a brief, rather vague, suggestion of willingness to replace Weizmann as head of the WZO, for which, in a visit to America in January 1921, he found some readiness for an affirmative response. In the end Weizmann was able to enlist only Mond and Lord Lionel Walter Rothschild, James' English cousin, as original sponsors of the finally proclaimed Keren Hayesod campaign. Waley Cohen and James de Rothschild agreed to continue on the Economic Council and also aided the Palestine economy through their independent channels, but they would not endorse the Keren Hayesod. The Zionists, for their part, withdrew the agreement to give the council the previously contemplated authority to supervise the work of the Keren Hayesod.

Weizmann conducted this struggle of half a year following the July conference under conditions of incessant strain. The hope that flared up at San Remo and flamed on the installation of Sir Herbert Samuel had to be sustained in the face of ominous reverses on all sides. The Foreign Office under Lord Curzon was not the same friendly place, and a war-weary British public and press showed dwindling enthusiasm for such burdens as a Zionist mandate. Impatient Zionists in Europe and Palestine kept up a drumfire of criticism of Weizmann's restrained policy, while others, including the American leaders, carped at his excessive deference to the Zionist radicals.

In January 1921 Weizmann accompanied his most valuable ally, Sir Alfred Mond, on a reconnaissance tour of Palestine that sealed the latter's commitment to Jewish and Zionist work. When he returned in mid-February, Weizmann found the movement at a critical juncture that required decisive action. Simon and de Lieme's resignations, announced in his absence, would take effect at the beginning of March. This was also the month that Weizmann made known as the time for his long-anticipated trip to America to deal with a major obstacle to the friction-free functioning that was vital, as all agreed, for the success of the Zionist enterprise. He speedily set in place a provisional reorganization of the Zionist Executive, subject to approval at the first opportunity by, at least, the Greater Action Committee. His choice of new men, including Jabotinsky, plainly aimed to satisfy his radical Zionist critics in Palestine and Europe; but, as he certainly realized, it could only alienate the leaders of the American Zionist movement just as he was about to visit them in their own stronghold.

What undoubtedly contributed largely to Weizmann's new policy line was the fact that he had abandoned temporarily the attempt to bring non-Zionists into a formal partnership with the WZO and Keren Hayesod. This left him with the Zionist project of a national Jewish treasury, raised by self-taxation and available for all the politically necessary tasks of the movement, as the main fiscal agency of the WZO. He now had to find support in America for the Keren Hayesod in the face of Brandeis' foreseeable opposition. He fortified himself by securing the participation of Albert Einstein (recently named Nobel laureate) in his party for the American trip. He could also count on concrete support from the opposition forces that had been building up in the American movement. Nevertheless, the Weizmann who set out, challenging conflict, remained the same man, temperamentally drawn to consensus politics rather than thirsting for battle.[76]

After the American delegation returned from the London conference in the summer of 1920, a split opened and speedily developed in the ZOA. Long-suppressed dissatisfaction was heightened by the unpalatable choice Brandeis forced on his followers at the conference: to give up their hopes of active leadership in the WZO or break with Brandeis' leadership at home. Both the budding opposition and Brandeis' close associates in the ZOA had come to the London conference with the aim of installing their chief in active control of world Zionism. De Haas shared the sanguine hope of Julius Simon that Brandeis might resign from the U.S. Supreme Court to guide the Palestine project personally. When the American delegation met to consider the drastic proposals Brandeis was to lay before the London conferees, not only luke-warm associates like Lipsky, but those unconditionally loyal to him, pleaded that he commit himself fully to Zionist leadership; only on that condition could they have confidence in the deal he was proposing to close with non-Zionist notables. When he chose to continue as the voice of progressivism on the Supreme Court and serve the WZO as an absent leader (arguing that this course was in the best interests of Zionism and American Jewry), only his own circle accepted the decision without question. Other American Zionists began to murmur and find fault more audibly, and in public.[77]

The grounds for complaint were tied to new grievances by the policy the Brandeis group now followed in administering the ZOA. The setback in London provoked them to impose on the ZOA as rigid principles policy lines they had previously urged on the WZO with some moderation. They determined that the American Zionist organization must devote itself entirely to promoting the economic development of Palestine and strip itself of functions not directly connected with that goal—first, the ZOA education department. This meant giving up not only propaganda and publications that had absorbed a good part of the professional staff of the ZOA, but its active commitment to Hebrew (and Yiddish) culture. (Brandeis insisted that, if needed, such activities should be funded and conducted by a special agency outside the ZOA; he was prepared to contribute a significant sum personally to that end.) Lipsky, returning from London before the others, tried to accommodate the financial strictures the movement was subject to by cutting the education department himself and by trying to absorb some of its functions, which were otherwise doomed to suppression, into his own department of organization. But this maneuver was foreseen by Judge Mack, the ZOA president, and Jacob de Haas; taking matters into their own hands, they not only abolished the education department, but ordered severe cuts in Lipsky's apparatus. The animosity aroused by these measures stirred up a festering opposition in the ranks of Zionist officials and activists that spilled over into vehement criticism in the Yiddish press of the Brandeis regime and of the absentee leadership of Brandeis himself.[78]

The position of the leaders in regard to the Keren Hayesod and their relation to the WZO authority structure—still subjects of suspicion rather than of clear knowledge—raised the personal issues into a broader range of general policy. The insistence on dividing donation funds from investment projects—not only in expenditure budgets but in Zionist revenue raising—was interpreted by suspicious opponents as a sign that the ZOA leaders were bent on blocking the Keren Hayesod appeal in America. Those more closely concerned sensed that the Americans were likely to confine their efforts to the special projects they selected for their own and, moreover, would most probably refuse to submit them to the policy line of the WZO and the authorized Zionist agencies in Palestine. Opposition to the Brandeis group was therefore inflated, beyond the aggravated local issues, into a defense of the integrity of the world movement itself. Concerns like these were, of course, shared by the WZO London office and by Weizmann. Ties with the American opposition, initiated at the London conference in the summer, were growing into an effective alliance of forces. But at the annual ZOA convention, held in Buffalo in November 1920, the opposition was still weak and ill organized. The Brandeis faction won a decisive victory; a resolution barring the "commingling of funds" was passed, auguring ill for the prospects of the Keren Hayesod in America.[79]

News of the Buffalo decision reached Weizmann in the midst of disheartening struggles on other fronts. From Frankfurter he heard that it would be best not to come on his long-intended American tour unless he could present detailed plans—for example, specific plans for the development of state lands with a documented concession in hand; this, he replied, depended on the prior settlement of the issue of Palestine's frontiers. From others he heard that the economic slump then under way in America made his trip inadvisable in any case. But what most concerned him was the Buffalo decision, with its reference to the "commingling of funds" that suggested that there would be little or no American cooperation with the Keren Hayesod. His letter to Frankfurter on December 1, 1920, complained in bitter tones of Stephen Wise's "defeatist" speech at the ZOA convention; of the abandonment of a generation of Zionist pioneers in Palestine by the Brandeis plan, which (according to Weizmann) proposed to surrender all the Zionists had done to the tender mercies of non-Zionist experts; and of the apparent intent of the ZOA leaders to work solely on their own projects without reference to the policy or authority of the WZO.[80]

Shortly afterward, Weizmann clearly decided that he had to take firm measures to save the deteriorating situation, which was becoming the subject of remark in friendly as well as hostile British quarters. The arrangement finally achieved for the Economic Council was far from the full involvement of wealthy non-Zionists originally planned; it also implied much greater reliance on the efforts of the Zionists themselves and therefore depended on Zionist unity and morale. In this respect the Executive that was jerry-built after the 1920 conference—by co-opting Ussishkin, on the one hand, and de Lieme and Simon, on the other—was proving a sore disappointment; the strife engendered by the Reorganization Commission now severely compounded the mischief. For all these developments, and for the "defeatist" mood that consequently had spread throughout the movement, he blamed the oppositionist (and, as he increasingly felt, obstructionist) attitude of the American leaders. All these conclusions—together with a clear threat that the Americans must either see him resign and themselves take on the burden of

WZO leadership or submit to the line of the majority—he sent to Judge Mack in January 1921 in a long letter explaining his decision to convene the Greater Action Committee in February to resolve existing differences and reorganize for effective work.

This challenging missive was sent from Paris in the course of a swift tour of European Zionist centers Weizmann carried out together with Jabotinsky. The trip was a bracing experience for him. He felt he had succeeded in dispelling the defeatist miasma he found on arrival and had aroused enthusiasm that belied opposing leaders' gloomy predictions that little in the way of financial support could be expected from Dutch and Belgian Jewry. This was followed by his trip to Palestine in the company of Sir Alfred Mond, which raised his morale and self-confidence still further. When he returned in February, the plan to convene the Greater Action Committee was dropped and Weizmann carried out his own reorganization of the WZO apparatus, pending approval by the next Zionist Congress. He then also undertook his long-delayed trip to America—under different circumstances and for a different specific purpose than originally planned. On April 2, 1921, he and his entourage arrived in New York for the openly proclaimed purpose of launching a Keren Hayesod campaign in the United States and Canada.[81]

The American Zionist scene had been radically transformed since the ZOA's November convention in Buffalo, especially after Weizmann's letter to Mack reacting to it. The opposition encountered in Buffalo, even though in the end ineffective, was enough to make Brandeis and his associates unwilling to put up any longer with resistance in their own administration. Lipsky and others still retained in staff positions found themselves under tightening pressure; their oppositionist animus was not thereby moderated. They saw the Brandeis policy, as Weizmann did, as an assault on the unity and authority of the movement. They blamed their ineffectiveness at Buffalo on the fact that they were fighting Weizmann's battle in his absence without clear instructions from him, and they were disposed to continue their struggle if those conditions should change.

Weizmann's letter to Mack in January touched off an immediate reaction in the circle of Brandeis adherents. Brandeis himself was among the most decisive in his antagonism. He took the view that Weizmann's challenge had ended any possibility of half measures and compromises, and could only be answered by actions, not talk. The specific action required at once was to refuse to attend the meeting of the Greater Action Committee announced by Weizmann as a forum for settling differences. That meeting, of course, never took place; instead Weizmann proposed to come and launch the Keren Hayesod in America. The American leaders prepared a detailed position paper setting out their own views in preparation for the encounter with Weizmann that seemed inevitable. Their "Summary of the Position of the Zionist Organization of America in Conference with Dr. Weizmann and Associates" was presented to the ZOA National Executive on March 19–20. In a meeting attended by less than half of the Executive Committee, fifteen Brandeis adherents adopted the statement on behalf of the ZOA. The nine opponents in attendance protested the preparation and presentation of a policy paper that ended any doubt about the Brandeis group's intentions: it seemed to propose a reorganization of the movement that could only be dealt with by a Zionist Congress and suggested, if not outright secession, as the critics said, then far-reaching isolation of the ZOA from the policies and authority of the WZO.[82]

Shortly afterward, the victors published the resolution approving their statement as ZOA policy. The opponents then made public their scathing criticism of the policy and the manner of its adoption, thereby emerging as open, formal antagonists of the Brandeis administration. Word of these developments reached Weizmann aboard ship on his way to America together with conflicting proposals from the two sides regarding the program he should follow on arrival. Judge Mack urged private meetings with the ZOA administration; Shmarya Levin—sent on to America earlier—and Emanuel Neumann—the young former head of the disbanded ZOA education department now engaged in preparatory work for the Keren Hayesod—proposed a plan of mass meetings and public appearances. Weizmann's choice was to ask that the latter course be avoided so that his visit not be marred by controversial incidents at its very start.

Both suggestions were, in fact, realized more or less simultaneously. Weizmann's delegation was greeted by a tumultuous mass reception at the dock and a noisy motorcade accompanied him to his hotel. For the first time he received the kind of public adulation that had been accorded Herzl in his time. Two days later he plunged into difficult discussions with the Brandeis team; their differences were laid out in harsh terms and the slender prospects of compromise and agreement were considered.

The Americans began by proposing their statement, with its comprehensive roster of disputed issues, as the basis of negotiations. Weizmann flatly dismissed this suggestion: his mission was limited to setting up the Keren Hayesod on the basis of the unanimously adopted decision of the 1920 London conference, not that of the ZOA in Buffalo. The Brandeis team tacitly accepted Weizmann's restriction of the agenda, and at a meeting of the ZOA National Executive on April 9–10, Frankfurter offered a compromise solution of the main issue. The language of the London resolution provided that the Keren Hayesod was to be established in each country according to local conditions. For America he proposed that it be set up as a "donation fund" by the ZOA president "in agreement with Dr. Weizmann . . . on the basis of the Buffalo resolution," which corresponded to American local conditions. Further, the American receipts were to be "applied exclusively in Palestine"— that is, not spent in the Diaspora on *Gegenwartsarbeit*— and through "instrumentalities" and procedures agreed on by the two presidents. The Frankfurter proposal was passed by the majority of the ZOA National Executive Committee over the objection of the opposition. At the same time the executive committee decided that it would respond to an invitation from Weizmann to appoint two or more members to the WZO Executive, which would have ended the Brandeis-imposed boycott of that body.[83]

If this was meant as an overture to the Weizmann delegation, surrounding circumstances did little to advance the purpose. The ZOA executive committee did not take its new position privately to Weizmann for discussion but gave him his notice of it by publication; the ZOA opposition responded with its own publicity. Weizmann's immediate response—automatic, in view of these circumstances—was to reiterate publicly that he was acting on the basis of the London decision to establish the Keren Hayesod and rejected the ZOA resolution as a basis for negotiations. However, among his close counselors were moderate men like Leon Stein, his secretary in the delegation, and Abraham Tulin and Bernard Rosenblatt, who belonged at the time to the ZOA opposition but dreaded a split in the movement. They represented him in drafting sessions of a group of lawyers from both sides that worked for days to bridge the differences. On the other side, Weizmann was under constant pressure from radical ZOA insurgents and from Ussishkin and Shmarya Levin of his own delegation; at a mass meeting in which both sides were to participate, Ussishkin launched a vehement attack on the Americans, upon which Mack and Stephen Wise left the hall without delivering their addresses. Moreover, the middle ground the moderates were able to find after nearly a week of labor was based on temporary acceptance of the American proposal until the next Zionist Congress decided the issue. Buffalo rather than London would lay down the rules for the time being; but the ultimate authority of the Zionist Congress would be acknowledged and certain provisions for regular support of the WZO Palestine budget would be included.[84]

How Weizmann himself felt about these suggestions is a much beclouded question. He apparently was prepared at first to accede to the latest compromise draft, but when presented on the next morning with a more detailed version prepared overnight, he rejected it and told Mack, who also received the draft, that he would now announce the establishment of the Keren Hayesod in America as an act of the WZO. Brandeis took this as further evidence that Weizmann's words were deceitful; others in the wider Brandeis circle (soon augmented by men like Julius Simon and Abraham Tulin) remarked on a weakness they claimed to perceive in Weizmann's character, which led him to back out under pressure when he had brought negotiations to the point of a satisfactory understanding. His critics published a report that on this occasion Weizmann had at first leaned toward accepting the final draft given him on April 17 in the morning, but the threats of his militant European and American allies broke down his resolve. In any case, the Brandeis partisans were not dismayed; some were even relieved by Weizmann's decision. Many thought their own concessions—offering to join the WZO Executive and submit to a decision of the next congress—departed too far from Brandeis' blueprint. When Mack got word of Weizmann's final decision, he at once published a statement blaming the WZO's president for breaking up the talks. Weizmann then followed with a public announcement of the establishment in America of the Keren Hayesod on the basis of the London resolution.

On the following day Weizmann went to Washington, where Brandeis had been keeping a close watch on developments. He visited the justice in a meeting that Brandeis conducted, with cool politeness, in a deliberately humiliating fashion. He heard out Weizmann's report on Palestinian matters, confining himself to questions, but when the current quarrel was raised at the very end of the time allotted, Brandeis coldly turned aside hints that one could still find ways to avoid the unfortunate impending confrontation. He speeded his parting guest with remarks about the weather; then he wrote to his friends with barely disguised enjoyment of the manner in which he had dealt with Weizmann. They did not meet soon again.[85]

From that point on, there was open warfare. The two sides descended on the clubs and affiliates of the ZOA with speakers and rival publications, each setting forth its version of recent events and of the iniquities of the other. Lipsky resigned his ZOA post to join the battle. Judge Mack announced that the next annual convention of the ZOA would begin in Cleveland on June 5, thus setting a date for the confrontation. There were, of course, many who tried at the last minute to patch up the differences, but the antagonists were too far committed to listen.

It rapidly became clear that the ZOA opposition would have the upper hand at the convention. Brandeis and his friends prepared their response in advance for the event of defeat. The convention was marked by a succession of votes that went against the administration. The final blow came in a vote of nonconfidence in the administration. When this passed, Mack rose and announced the resignation of thirty-five leading Zionists, beginning with Brandeis and himself, from all their offices in the ZOA and WZO.

The break had come. Thereafter, both sides in the quarrel continued their Zionist work, but they worked for the most part independently of each other and in an atmosphere of mutual antipathy and suspicion.

5

Epilogue and Conclusions

The Men

From the London conferences of 1919–20 to the 1921 ZOA convention in Cleveland, the point at issue between Brandeis and Weizmann shifted from the Jewish Council (or Agency) to the Keren Hayesod. But neither body became what either man wished to make it; the controversies that arose in later years were not those debated by Brandeis and Weizmann. The polemics of the Brandeis-Weizmann clash, which became the source for accepted accounts of the events in later literature, presented the specific issues as sharply defined alternatives that cleanly divided the antagonists and were embedded in deeper divergences between Jewish communities. On this assumption, our two heroes emerged as the initiators, or at least the focusing medium, of historic effects; their exemplary achievements purportedly shaped the attitudes and self-image of Jewish communities long after. But the record hardly bears out such assumptions.

The two men could easily have found common ground on most of the specific issues if they had not been deeply and personally involved; it was not ideological dogmatism, nor was it petty pride, but indispensable conditions for each one's service in the leadership that divided them. Their quarrel, to be sure, brought to the surface basic differences in Jewish attitudes, rooted in their personal backgrounds; but neither could these in themselves have necessitated their clash nor did they produce a continuing tradition of cleavage in Jewish history.

Thus, a cardinal issue, equally stressed in the polemics on both sides, was whether the political era of Zionism had ended. Brandeis stalwarts staunchly upheld this contention, and the Weizmann camp loudly denied it. But the positive tone adopted by both was not matched by equal consistency in theory or conviction in practice.

One might claim to be a Herzlian Zionist, as the Brandeis partisans did, and argue that with the Balfour Declaration-San Remo decisions Herzl's political precondition, the charter, had been secured; it now remained for his projected Jewish Company to carry out the social engineering required to resettle masses of Jewish emigrants in the Jewish homeland. However, Herzl's conception of the powers granted to such a Jewish Company, conceived on the lines of a colonial land grant, included direct administration of Palestine. After the 1908 Young Turk Revolution and again a decade later, professed Herzlians understood that old colonial precedents no longer applied and the WZO could not be granted government power in Palestine. It could, however, expect preferential rights and concessions in the economic development of the country under the public law status conferred on a Jewish agency in the mandate.

With this basic legal standing secured, the Brandeis group insisted that all other political relations with the Palestine administration should be left to the community in Palestine. This demand logically followed, no doubt, from this premise, but actually it flowed more effectively from another source. Brandeis might claim preferential status under the public law of Palestine for the WZO (as Jewish Agency) in implicit recognition of the national rights of a dispersed people, but only for a sphere of competency limited to professedly nonpolitical, economic-developmental functions. It was not that his trust in Britain, however confident, was total. With the League of Nations' approval of the mandate and the demarcation of Palestine's borders still pending, no one could doubt the need for continued political activity by the WZO London Bureau; Brandeis further pointed out the importance of a strong Zionist movement in America to keep continued pressure on the mandatory to fulfill its obligations. But a political role in Palestine for the WZO, representing Jews the world over—particularly when justified by East European theories about political rights to be exercised by an exterritorial nationality—could cripple his hopes to unite American Jewry and rally its men of wealth behind the reconstruction work for the Jewish national home.

In many respects Weizmann shared Brandeis' views and did not share in principle those of his veteran Zionist allies. He differed with Brandeis in practice primarily because he relied on a massive popular response, stimulated and led by the example of prominent and wealthy men, to carry the Palestine project to success. That globally manifested commitment was also the source from which he expected to draw the necessary funding. Brandeis' critique of the veteran Zionists' reliance on public funds and their emotional methods in collecting and spending revenue led him to urge strongly the value of private funding based on rational business principles. But he was no less responsive than any other Zionist to the idealism manifested in the movement; his partiality for social experimentation and cooperative organization certainly equalled that of Weizmann or other typical East-Central European Zionists. In his later years the radical left-wing communes of the Zionist youth movement, Hashomer Hatzair, were one of his favorite projects and objects of his benevolent concern.

There was also much exaggeration in the charge made against Brandeis that his intention was to secede from the world movement and challenge its authority with a schismatic, rival organization. The fear expressed in this accusation was a real one, and there were considerable grounds for it in the program Brandeis espoused in 1919–21. The autonomy he proposed for the Zionist constituent territorial federations together with other elements of his program left few significant functions for the world organization to perform. Considering the resistance of the American leaders to the WZO's main fund-raising agency, the Keren Hayesod, and the ZOA policy of limiting the funds it was prepared to channel through WZO control, (and directly funding its own special projects in Palestine), opponents could easily form the impression that there was a concerted effort to undermine the authority of the world organization and its elected executive committee. In fact, the Brandeis group had much more moderate designs.

Following their Cleveland defeat, they confined themselves to a few select projects that in no way challenged the WZO on its own grounds as the organ of the Jewish nationalist movement and recognized as such by the mandate government. Neither did they renounce their Zionist commitment or individual membership nor announce an ideology opposed to standard Zionist theories: they confined their opposition to questions of method and tactics. In spite of unbridled attacks on the character and morals of their opponents, which suggested a total rejection of their proximate aims and methods, the ultimate grounds on which the ZOA leaders based their case were decidedly narrow. At bottom, they argued for the right of the American Zionist movement to be treated as a special case. Brandeis himself had opposed European Diaspora nationalism at the 1919 London conference in this way. Although rejecting WZO espousal of Helsingfors-style activities as unacceptable under American conditions, he freely conceded that under other conditions they might some day come to seem appropriate in America, too—and in the battle over the American Jewish Congress, Brandeis-led Zionists had, of course, successfully defended the claim of national minority rights for Jews in Europe. In 1921 the ZOA's last-ditch defense against the Keren Hayesod's incursion into the American scene was based on the London conference resolution calling for the adjustment of Keren Hayesod methods to "local conditions."

Another underlying difference between the Brandeis and Weizmann approach did not figure as prominently in their polemics but was perhaps much more significant. Weizmann's adherents in 1921, like Brandeis' cohorts in the battle over the American Jewish Congress, spoke as the champions of democracy in Jewish communal life; but neither leader was himself much inclined to submit to a regime of participatory democracy in conducting the movement's affairs. Both were felt by their critics to have autocratic tendencies, acting without adequate consultation with colleagues or respect for the views of the rank and file. But they differed in the way each dealt personally with the apparent disjunction between a commitment to democracy (in both cases, quite sincere and deep-rooted) and an unqualified preference for one-man control in carrying out executive functions. With Weizmann, a man who gave free play to his emotions, the resolution of the problem was easy—he relied on intuitive judgments; Brandeis, a man of cool intellect and enormous emotional control, acted on principles he had explicitly formulated in other cases.

The difference in temperament expressed itself in sharply different styles of approach, whether to government officials and leaders or to the mass support of their own political leadership. Both excelled in face-to-face negotiations with men of power and influence at the highest levels; but where Weizmann gained his point by his sensitive perception of the other side's possible interests and presented his case in that light, Brandeis trusted in facts and logic to persuade, if not compel, others to see things as he saw them. Brandeis, unlike Weizmann, regularly relied on mass organization and the power of public opinion in order to impress his views on policymakers. But it was Weizmann rather than Brandeis who had effective rapport (based, to be sure, on sentimental affection, not respect) with the common folk he aspired to lead.

Brandeis held the proper role of the masses in a political democracy to be to elect its chosen leaders and then leave them free to employ their expert skills in government so long as the results justified the confidence reposed in them. The uninstructed, impulsive, and unstable mood-ridden masses could not be trusted to influence continuously the formation of rational policy decisions. He favored small managerial bodies, commission government, and expert, professional administration—always, of course, over operations small enough in scale to be controlled efficiently by one man or a small executive group. Holding these opinions, he had to take a different view of the proper functions of Zionist membership after the presumed victory of San Remo from that he held before it. To gain the victory it had been necessary to mobilize and deploy the united force of a mass membership: the intended effect was statistical, cumulative, an impact of uniformity and numbers depending on the discipline Brandeis incessantly urged. After the essential political goal had been won and the task of economic and social reconstruction became urgent, a different schema of Zionist organization was necessary.

The new tasks, by their essential nature, required the energy and judgment of diverse managers and workers applying their strength and practical intelligence to specific undertakings small enough to be handled efficiently by individuals or by groups capable of working closely together. Larger, centralized managerial instruments of the movement—apart from whatever political work remained—should define and supervise general policy. The movement should also supply elements of infrastructure, like land and capital (through banks adapted to various special needs) and make limited initial contributions to essential cultural and welfare institutions, which were needed in the early stage of reconstruction and could then be funded by the Palestine government or the local Jewish community. The latter, economic, social, and cultural functions should devolve as soon as possible to the control of those immediately concerned and not be administered centrally by the WZO Executive.

Within this concept the Brandeis group (defending itself against charges that it was undermining the movement's popular, democratic base) claimed that it provided for more active, closer personal involvement of Zionist members than did its WZO rivals. As stockholders of new Palestinian institutions or volunteer leaders of support groups for Palestinian medical, welfare, educational, or agrotechnical institutions, Diaspora Zionists could become involved in the work of reconstruction more fully than by simply contributing to the Keren Hayesod or voting in occasional Zionist elections.

What is also clear is that such an organizational scheme provided the only basis on which Brandeis, while continuing to serve on the Supreme Court, could lead the WZO in the same way as he had the wartime PZEC and the ZOA thereafter. He felt confident of his ability to supervise and coordinate the manifold efforts of the projected Zionist enterprises on the basis of regular reports submitted to him in Washington and supplemented by more direct contact with the other leaders during the summer recess of the Court. All this depended on certain strict conditions: the reports to him had to be detailed, frequent, and standardized; those who reported and directly managed the several activities had to be lieutenants personally trusted by Brandeis; and, above all, while serving on the Supreme Court, he could not risk being exposed to the controversy and public scandal that might be inevitable if the other leaders of the Zionist enterprise represented independent bodies (whether non-Zionist or opposing Zionist factions or federations). Such possibilities, implicit in the alternative arrangements Weizmann preferred and ultimately secured at the London conference in 1920, made it impossible for Brandeis to accept an active role in the WZO structure. After Cleveland in 1921 he could not work in the only way acceptable to him in the ZOA either.

Considerations of the same order were decisive for Weizmann as well. He had no occasion to work out an explicit doctrine harmonizing his democratic sentiments with his strong preference for one-man control of executive functions: his political career had not combined the role of administrative consultant with that of lobbyist as extensively as had that of Brandeis. He accepted his need to work within an organizational consensus, yet to operate independently, without seeking a rationale for his political instincts. Moreover, much as there was in common in the relation of the two leaders to their constituents, Weizmann differed radically from Brandeis in his specific methods.

Many have noted the striking lack of close ties between Weizmann and the Zionist public. For all his skill in addressing audiences in their own Yiddish manner, his mastery of anecdote and his ready native wit—a man as able to ingratiate as to cut deep—Weizmann was a remote and aloof figure. He did not live among his people nor in their style. From his beginnings as a youth leader in the Democratic Faction, his associates were an elite group of Zionists who never became the core of an integrated popular party.

But Weizmann, as he himself explained, could not stand alone against the stream of the movement that filled his life and bear, like Jabotinsky, the reproaches heaped on obdurate dissidents. Nor, like Buber, was he truly content to work with the Democratic Faction as no more than academic study and consulting unit. In a long memorandum to Herzl on May 6, 1903, Weizmann set forth a strategic analysis of the Zionist situation that made the organization's future hinge on the ability of his group, properly supported by a revised WZO policy, to win over Western Jewries. Since oppressive conditions (in his opinion) left little hope for a healthy movement (or for the Jewish community) in Russia and there were impassable barriers to political or economic work in Palestine, the immediate task was to imbue Western youth and intellectuals with the profound national feeling and secular Jewish culture of the East. Only in this way could the movement be saved from sliding into the narrow confines of a Jewishness limited to the synagogue and a merely philanthropic relation to coreligionists—a danger to which Weizman felt that Herzl's purely political Zionism was all too much exposed.

As for his own role, Weizmann alternately dreamed of serving as a scientist in the agroindustrial development of Palestine or of leading the national movement in the style of Herzl. The latter image required a people stirred to heroic ardor by a leader acclaimed in the way Herzl had been and who was even more successful in reaching the seats of power with the movement's message. In the radically changed circumstances of the postwar period, Weizmann's vision of himself as popular leader was no longer merely the subjective ambition of earlier years; it amounted to an obligation to the British government, a tacit condition of an understanding with them on which the upbuilding of the Jewish national home depended.

A major element of Weizmann's successful lobbying during the war had been his professed ability to rally worldwide Jewish support for the Allies; from the peace conference to San Remo, his ability to demonstrate a massive Jewish demand for Great Britain as the Palestine mandatory was equally important. In the period that followed, Zionists were confronted with growing resistance in England to burdensome military and fiscal responsibilities abroad; the rising wave of violent Arab opposition evoked dangerous criticism of the Zionist project in the press and the House of Lords and, after Curzon succeeded Balfour in the Foreign Office, in government circles as well. Weizmann's chief defense against the onslaught that threatened was the firm base of agreement he had established with powerful men in the ruling circle, and this depended on his effective control of the WZO and of the Jewish public.

Supporters like Lloyd George, Balfour, and (with growing discomfort after he became Colonial Secretary) Winston Churchill made quite clear what they expected of Weizmann: he was to relieve the British taxpayer of expenses for building the Jewish national home by raising the necessary funds in his own worldwide community; he was to restrain the Jewish national movement's activities and expressions within limits that would provoke the least possible irritation among Arabs and so lighten the task of the Palestine administration. To meet such obligations, Weizmann needed unequivocal acceptance by his constituency as the responsible Zionist leader and the spokesman for Jews at large in regard to Palestine. He often reminded his English friends of that fact when arguing with them against measures that could undermine his leadership by injuring Zionist prospects; his ability to do so effectively was a well-understood asset of the Zionist movement since his early success during the war.

If the position Weizmann had arduously won for himself and for the movement were to be preserved, it was obvious that he could not accept the plan Reading and Brandeis worked out for Zionist reorganization. He had concluded from the struggle to form an Economic Council earlier that only by relying primarily on veteran Zionists could he cooperate with non-Zionist friends without surrendering the future of Jewish settlement in Palestine entirely to their control. The "Reading plan" Brandeis put forward at the conference (with an Executive of three enrolled Zionists and three English notables not previously affiliated, led by Brandeis himself with a casting vote) could not be seen by Weizmann as an adequate safeguard for the kind of national awakening he needed. The dominant coalition in such an executive committee might well take a line not unlike that of the Western Jewish philanthropists active in Palestine. As for his own position, it would be reduced to one of the many lieutenancies required for Brandeis' effective functioning. None of this accorded with Weizmann's vision of a massive popular response, led by himself, to which he was committed vis-à-vis the British government; nor could it, in his judgment, shape in Palestine the kind of Jewish revival his school of Zionists hoped for.

When first confronted with the outlines of Brandeis' plan in 1920, Weizmann responded with the same critical but passive acquiescence he had adopted after his defeat at the 1919 session. The hope for a workable consensus was strong in him, and he expressed dissent by abstaining but not voting against the American proposals. Such apparent submission, continuing the line of conduct he had followed in the past year, evidently misled the Brandeis group into the belief that they had effectively harnessed Weizmann to their program. They were struck with consternation when he then laid out for Mond and James de Rothschild the varied functions Zionist veterans and the rank and file would expect members of their executive committee to perform—a prospect that made it quite clear that such men, the most well disposed of non-Zionists, would much prefer to cooperate with the Zionists outside their framework in a bilateral council or agency, as Weizmann proposed, than to join the Zionist Executive on Brandeis' broadly sketched terms for reorganizing the movement's program. Brandeis viewed Weizmann's action as a weak submission to pressure from old Zionist cronies, but more than that, an act of disloyalty and betrayal to himself. Events in the following year confirmed him in the fixed resolve to have no further dealings with Weizmann and to hold his entourage to a similar policy of personal boycott.

This attitude, which persisted for many years, calls for further explanation. There were other reasonable options open to a leader of American Zionism. He could do as Weizmann had done when the case was reversed: continue to work as a loyal dissenter in the leadership of a regime he opposed while awaiting his chance to replace its policies with his own. But such a course was simply not possible for Brandeis. His position in American public life ruled out any Zionist role for him but that of private leadership, universally acknowledged and uncontested; further involvement in partisan wrangles and controversies could end in the same way as the Hotel Astor incident in July 1916.

Moreover, Brandeis was fully aware of weaknesses in his position in the Zionist movement and the corresponding strengths in Weizmann's, which made him unwilling to seek his rival's removal from office. He understood fully that Weizmann's special relationship with the top British leaders was indispensable for the Zionist cause. Although his faction stressed continually in debate that the political phase of Zionism was over and that one could now simply rely on Britain's legal commitment, Brandeis was well aware that the satisfactory performance of mandate obligations would not be automatic. Britain's bona fides could probably be relied on, but it was not certain. Indeed, Brandeis emphasized the continuing importance of a strong *American* Zionist movement as a necessary measure of insurance to secure it. At the same time he was in no doubt that the essential, primary point of contact remained in London, and there Weizmann was the indispensable man. After the break he opposed pressures in his own group to join battle with Weizmann once more for control of the WZO.

Another reasonable option conceivably open might have been to drop out of Zionist affairs entirely. Brandeis could then, perhaps, work through an independent agency in Palestine, as Rothschild and Waley Cohen did, under an arms'-length, but cooperative rather than adversarial, relationship with the WZO-Keren Hayesod apparatus. But this, too, was not possible for Brandeis. His situation was radically different from Rothschild's or Waley Cohen's. The former inherited a professionally staffed organization in charge of the family-supported Jewish settlement project in Palestine, which he reorganized and led personally. Waley Cohen organized a new group, the Palestine Corporation, but needed only the financial participation of a few wealthy friends and a small staff to direct its investments. When Brandeis left the leadership of the ZOA, he was accompanied by a major fraction of the top and middle lay and professional leadership of the organization. These were not men who could be kept permanently out of contention for control of the movement to which they had given much of their lives. Brandeis could only hold them to the line of isolation from ZOA and WZO activity that he laid down by offering an alternative program of independent Zionist action with the prospect that, in the foreseeable collapse of the Weizmann policy, it would be a base for their return to lead the American and world movement. This meant that their relation to their Zionist rivals had to be adversarial, not cooperative from the start.

So much can be understood simply from the logic of Brandeis' situation.

Even the extreme moral disapprobation that he applied against Weizmann and Lipsky and their "ilk" could be explained as a tactical measure—something like his attempt to ostracize Magnes after the Hotel Astor affair in order to nullify the effect of the man's charisma. But in the case of Weizmann and Lipsky, Brandeis showed none of the detachment that a purely tactical depreciation of his rivals might suggest. In fact, he seemed to find pleasure in humiliating his opponent if one may judge from the strangely smug descriptions he sent his associates of certain encounters between them. When Weizmann visited the justice in Washington after the last attempts to patch up a compromise broke down in 1921, Brandeis gave him no opportunity to bring up their differences in the hope that there might still be found an opening for reconciliation and cooperation. When Weizman finally delicately raised the matter shortly before the end of the time allowed for their interview, his host reportedly turned away to a window and made some remarks about the weather. Brandeis reported this and similar meetings with the other side with dry, unconcealed relish in round-robin notes sent to his leading associates.

That more was involved here than a deliberate tactic against an adversary—and Brandeis in an adversarial role had always been quite ruthless—is especially clear if one compares Weizmann's reception at his hands with that of other spokesmen of the official WZO policy who visited the justice in December 1921. Sokolow and Otto Warburg, then touring the United States on fund-raising missions, took the occasion to try to ease Brandeis' obdurate opposition in successive visits. Brandeis reported to his aides—in one of his round-robin memos on December 14—that "[Sokolow] and daughter called, stayed about 40 minutes." After some general discussion, evidently in a friendly atmosphere, Sokolow "spoke of his desire to get something from the American Administration (Dept. of State)" to help deal with difficulties in obtaining League of Nations' approval of the Palestine Mandate that was being obstructed by the French and other interested parties:

> Just as he was leaving he dropped a gentle hint about my help—I didn't pick it up. I talked then of [unrelated matters]. Escorted S. and daughter to the elevator.
>
> And lo and behold—all was over. A joyous interview and no harm done.[1]

Brandeis' tactics in his case were the same as with Weizmann earlier, but the atmosphere was apparently significantly warmer; Sokolow, it may be worth noting, was much more cordial than Weizmann in the manner of his response to Brandeis' plan in 1920 and had no hand directly in its abrupt rejection. On December 23 Brandeis notified his lieutenants of another visit: "Prof O[tto] Warburg was in yesterday 1-1/4 hours." Warburg clearly had none of the hesitation of the justice's earlier visitors and forced the issue. After "fully 3/4 hours" on topics of common, practical interest, like the Hebrew University and the agricultural experiment stations, Warburg "came out flatfooted, saying he had not come officially but he wanted to know whether some treaty of peace could not be negotiated etc. . . ." In this case Brandeis did not turn his back and talk about the weather:

> I could not avoid the question and concluded that it would be [in]advisable to refuse to talk to him. So I told him of the moral problems involved, honest finance etc. . . .; discussed Ussishkin's failings and our attempt to keep him from the position of infinite harmfulness . . . that he has occupied. . . . Of our attempt in 1919 to put Bob Szold, the ideal man, in charge and that if those in power had feared half as much British and Arab, as they did U[ssishkin], it would have been done. . . . I endeavored otherwise to make him understand our position, that we had done and would do nothing to prevent their success and that we, on the other hand, were trying to do what little we could to help in the cause. But we could not take the responsibilities incident to a position which would involve in effect our recommending people to put their money into the hands of those whose administration we could not trust. . . . He answered that our failure to approve the K[eren]. H[ayesod]. was hindering them and pleaded that we should, at least, [give *pro forma* approval]. I indicated rather than said we could not. All very friendly. But I gave him no encouragement.[2]

Several points strike the reader of these lines. Brandeis not only talked— and at length—to Warburg, but tried "to make him understand our position." The implication is that at least the moral defects attributed to Weizmann, Ussishkin, and the new WZO-ZOA administration as a body did not apply to him. To try to make him "understand," as Brandeis did, implies that Warburg was not totally underserving of trust, like Weizmann and others whom Brandeis did not think worthy of the effort of reasonable persuasion; he deserved at least the minimal trust inherent in frank communication between reasonable men.

But if condoning "Ussishkin's failings" or tolerating morally questionable, if not dishonest, financial practice (a description of the transactions in question that reflected Brandeis' puritanical habits of bookkeeping rather than judicial balance) were reason enough for the deliberate snubs administered to Weizmann over the years, why did Warburg deserve better treatment? Few actions committed by Ussishkin were more irritating to the Brandeis group than the purchase from the Sursook family of the Jezreel Valley, contracted before there was any assurance of funds to cover it; it was a cardinal point in the Reorganization Commission's critique of the Zionist Commission and contributed significantly to the resignation of de Lieme and Simon from the WZO Executive. But Otto Warburg, cochairman of the Jewish National Fund, approved of the purchase from the start and thereby blocked his fellow chairman, de Lieme, from exercising the right to veto it. Weizmann, on the other hand, doubted the advisability of the Jezreel acquisition and only acquiesced when a majority of the Jewish National Fund Board voted in favor of it.

If one were not dealing with a man like Brandeis, there are several obvious differences between Warburg and Weizmann that might seem to point to an explanation. Warburg was not an excitable East European like Weizmann, but the scion of a wealthy German banking family, and one might imagine that the greater respect accorded him was a matter of commonplace intra-communal prejudice; or one might suppose that his brusque, forthright approach was more effective than Weizmann's (or Sokolow's) subtlety in dealing with Brandeis' cold hostility. Such a social or psychological explanation hardly seems adequate in the light of Brandeis' long-sustained disdain for the German-Jewish banking elite or for the deference owed to men of power whom he had occasion to confront as an adversary.

But another difference seems more pertinent. Brandeis never had reason to presume that he could count on Warburg's support in the issues currently in dispute in the WZO; up to the last minute in the 1920 London conference, he counted on Weizmann's tacit, if not enthusiastic, support. After Weizmann upset his applecart, Brandeis' references to his opponent continually harped on the deceitfulness and moral cowardice that (in his opinion) made it impossible to rely on Weizmann's word. This was the justification he regularly used for his sustained boycott of the WZO leader.

Another way of putting the point would be to say that Weizmann was disloyal. That would make his offense appear to be the injury done to Brandeis' pride—and Brandeis was, of course, too proud a man to justify a public policy on personal grounds. Even if unspoken or suppressed from consciousness, wounded pride may well have had a part in the extraordinary harshness of Brandeis' conduct toward Weizmann and Lipsky. His peculiar way of praising clients as "loyal" has been noted previously, and he himself was outstandingly loyal; an act of disloyalty by a friend or subordinate, especially one ending in a humiliating defeat for a man in his highly exposed position, could easily lead him to reject any further relations with the offender. On the other hand, Brandeis bore the scars of many battles in which opponents had sought every means to humiliate him, including such as were calculated to touch him most personally. In the past he had shown unusual ability to rise above provocations and treat the occasion with a cool appreciation of the balance of gains and losses that might result from his choice of a suitable response. His express explanation of the policy of treating Weizmann like a pariah generally was based on such tactical grounds, but it also constantly cited basic moral concerns said to be involved.

One may surmise that besides personal pride another, possibly still more powerful motivation, was a suppressed element in Brandeis' extreme reaction. What Weizmann and Lipsky did in London and Cleveland was not only a political defeat, it was a challenge to the moral basis of Brandeis' Zionist leadership. Lipsky was not the only American delegate in London who asked Brandeis to give up his Supreme Court seat in order to take command of the WZO. Some of the most eager to press this request were men of Brandeis' inner circle, like de Haas, and firm supporters, like Julius Simon. But Lipsky demanded such a commitment by Brandeis as his condition for going along with a policy he did not accept on its merits. In emerging as the leader of an

American opposition after the London meeting, he made Brandeis' refusal to place his Zionist duty above his role in the judiciary seem like a fundamental character deficiency in one who presumed to lead the movement. Weizmann, for his part, left a similar implication in the wake of his repeated challenge to his American antagonists to take over full, direct responsibility for the movement if they refused to accept its duly adopted decisions and cooperate with the Keren Hayesod—which had been approved by the London conference with the full assent of their delegation.

What must have rankled most sorely was that Brandeis was far from immune to the implied challenge: he and his followers were acutely aware that they were neither ready nor able to take up the gauntlet that Weizmann from time to time threw down to taunt them. Whatever one might say about Weizmann, he had given up his professorial post to devote himself full-time to Zionist work; there could be no doubt that he and many other veteran Zionists of his kind planned their future with serious consideration of their chance to settle in Palestine. It was a reproach that Brandeis could not ignore, and one he frequently voiced himself, that it was so hard to find Zionist activists in America for service in Palestine and that those who did serve so often limited their stay to such brief terms.

Objectively speaking, Brandeis was among those least open to criticism on such grounds. A man approaching the normal age of retirement and older by nearly a generation than Weizmann and other antagonists, his years alone could have excused him from so radical a midcareer shift as was suggested. Indeed, one consultant, Bernard Rosenblatt, (tactfully omitting to mention the justice's senior status) flatly told him that getting into the trenches of Palestinian, Zionist politics would wear him down—by implication, both physically and politically. Brandeis, as frank as he was proud, mentioned his advanced age in passing when justifying his decision before the American delegation in London; but he then went on to a lengthy list of other considerations, protesting altogether too much. His retirement from the bench, he pleaded, would be harmful to the Zionist cause (he did not touch on the possibility that it might in other respects be helpful) because of the impact on American opinion: it would undermine his argument that multiple (Jewish and American) loyalties were compatible. Another argument, that American progressivism would lose a major support with hs departure from the Supreme Court, was undoubtedly true and sincerely felt. But it is hard to believe that citing the advantage to Zionism of *not* taking up its leadership was anything but a tortuous excuse; giving up the WZO presidency-in-action rather than the Supreme Court—even though it might avoid anti-Zionist reactions—was just as clear a disproof of the compatibility of Zionist and American loyalties as the other option.

If an excuse, Brandeis' rationalization was one more apt to put his own mind to rest than to persuade his constituents. The overelaborate reasons he gave them for not making himself available for active leadership of the WZO look very much like an implicit plea in mitigation of a harsh verdict he might otherwise have pronounced against himself.

Brandeis, it will be recalled, was led by his involvement in national Progressive party politics into a more comprehensive, partisan commitment than he had formerly preferred. Zionism was another cause that seduced him into identifying with a broad, ideological program and a partisan grouping in the community—and in this case because the transition was relatively so abrupt, it clashed more obviously with his natural inclination to be a detached "counsel for the situation," standing above the narrow self-interest of any particular party.

There was also a noticeable difference between his role in progressive politics and in Zionism that was reflected in his relations with fellow progressives and fellow Zionists. As a progressive, he continued to serve as an expert consultant, a legal draftsman and economic-administrative advisor. He found close friends among progressives, men who were his own peers or chosen leaders: the former were social and professional intimates whom he addressed by their first names in correspondence; the latter, men to whom he was unreservedly loyal.

A different relationship developed between him and other Zionists, including those within the small circle of his personal aides. Much against his own inclination, perhaps, he became the chosen leader of a partisan, ideological movement in the American (later, the world) Jewish community. Coming as a leader from the outside and one appealed to under the stress of an acute emergency, he fell into a paternalistic relation with the Zionists—a large extension of the role he had played earlier as mediator and arbitrator for the Jewish immigrant workers and employers of the garment industry. As before, he was charmed and impressed by these new associates of his own people, but also found them trying in their irresponsible and sometimes extremist impulsiveness. His inclination to take charge of situations grew under these conditions into a plainly paternalistic attitude toward his nominal constituents. Given the emergency, Brandeis was enabled to conduct Zionist affairs in America unrestrained by the movement he led and aided by a corps of adjutants largely recruited by him personally, outside the ranks of the regularly enrolled long-time Zionists. For these assistants he was the revered Chief: not only their commander in action, but a father figure in whose image they formed their Zionist identification.

These were roles that placed somewhat different demands on Brandeis from those he was used to in his public life previously; they resembled most nearly those that were implied in his relations to his children, to relatives whom he undertook to guide and support in their careers, and to some of the junior lawyers in his firm. He was expected not only to guide the Zionist thinking and direct the activities of his co-workers and disciples, but to serve them as a model in his personal and political conduct. The loyalty he so much prized in his clients could not be won simply by his superior command of facts and rational analysis of situations. Since it meant something approaching reverence for his total persona, it demanded a standard of integrity on his part that deserved the unlimited devotion of his following.

Brandeis cannot have been unaware of the significance of his example for those who held him their Chief. When therefore his Zionist commitment was rudely called into question by Lipsky's open challenge and Weizmann's emphatic example, he had to be aware what vital and sensitive centers of his moral position were being attacked. Hence, the defensive elaboration of reasons for a decision (which could have been simply justified) not to give up the Supreme Court for the WZO presidency: a man so constant in urging others to commit themselves fully to the Zionist work could not lightly make peace with the (quite compelling) reasons for his inability to set the example his role in the movement required. (It is noteworthy that Brandeis devoted a surprisingly thorough period of discussion to this question, whose final determination was a foregone conclusion; in later years his interest in Americans who served or resettled in Palestine was warm and intense, and his aid was generous and unfailing.)

The moral pressure Brandeis was under vented itself in a curious, circuitous way. It found an outlet in overreacting to the political victories his antagonists scored against him and in overstated assaults on their moral integrity.

The Movement

The Brandeis-Weizmann dispute was argued by both parties as a clash between two versions of Zionism, exemplified by the rival leaders and inherently related to the distinct life experiences of Western and Eastern Jewries. This, too, is the generally accepted account in later literature. To check it, a brief sketch of developments after the critical encounters of 1919–21 is needed together with a summary analysis of the history already examined.

It is immediately clear, before details are studied, that neither case conforms to the most ambitious model of a charismatic hero. The Zionist movement did, indeed, effect a radical break with the Jewish past by introducing the previously unarticulated idea of secular-national Jewishness. This new self-identification was the positive response Zionism offered to those East Europeans who were caught up in transition from Jewish-traditional to cosmopolitan-European culture and whose faith in Russian liberalism was shattered by the pogroms of 1881–82. But there was no one leader whose biography generated the symbols that expressed their common trauma and presented new, liberating values to them. A number of contemporaries, like M. L. Lilienblum in his autobiographical and publicistic writings and Leo Pinsker in his brochure *Autoemanzipation,* formulated the symbolic values and laid the foundations of the new movement. Those primary functions had been performed before Weizmann or Brandeis became active. The role left for them was to shape a secondary phase of development, to implement rather than generate fundamental change.[3]

Even at such an intermediate stage of historic change, there may still be charismatic heroes, exemplary leaders amid the traumas and confusion of their own generation. Zionist history is rich in such cases; the very time of the Brandeis-Weizmann encounter saw the birth of the pioneer *(halutz)* youth movements in Austro-Poland and Russia, with their intimate collective solidarity and identification between leaders and comrades. However, those organizations began as small cells within a broader Zionist movement, already too large for the close personal contacts such leadership requires. A leader of masses like Herzl—or Brandeis or Weizmann—had to possess a different kind of charisma: one derived not from the perception that he shared his followers' problematic situation and offered a heroic example for imitation, but from an opposite perception. All three men were essentially "leaders from the periphery": they possessed their charisma because they had escaped in one way or another from the traps that still held their followers, and they were thought to have power, accordingly, to release those left behind. Their hold over the mass of members was partly a return of love for their loyalty to the people and partly adulation that grew with their triumphs and was able to survive setbacks.[4]

A leader of masses cannot rely on charisma alone, especially when it depends so much on their faith in his future triumphs. Such a leader, in any reasonably large and complex organization, must necessarily go beyond the constituency that may share his personal background and values. The Zionist movement that Herzl, Weizmann, and Brandeis each encountered at the outset of their leadership had already been riven by inner dissension; it could be controlled only by forming a coalition, by bargaining, and by compromise. Each man had—and still has—his circle of devotees, personally dedicated to the leader in his lifetime and zealous in his cause and memory after death: followers who revered him as a personal ideal, a light for their life. But precisely the values they prized in the hero could alienate others whose support was essential; hence, uncongenial compromises were often required by the logic of the situation.

Both Brandeis and Weizmann clearly commanded (in different ways and at different stages of their Zionist leadership) the devotion of followers who took them as exemplary models. As leaders of masses, they could conceivably have historic impact in another way: by forming lasting coalitions or shifting alliances that entrenched their major policies in the institutional character of the movement through compromises on other matters. A further possibility exists (exemplified, among others, by the case of Jabotinsky): to reject compromise and fail to compose a ruling coalition, but set up a standard of opposition for future triumphs.

There are, thus, three models that may be employed in considering Brandeis and Weizmann's relation to the history of American and world Zionism: cult hero, coalition leader, or rebel chief.

Following the 1921 Cleveland convention, Brandeis and Weizmann set out on separate ways to consolidate the organization each needed to carry out his policy. The difficulties they encountered owing to personal situations and the changing fortunes of the Zionist movement brought them into recurrent collision, or guarded collaboration, for the rest of their days.

The Brandeis group immediately formed an instrument for practical work in Palestine based on their earlier plans for the ZOA and WZO. They set up a Palestine Development Council to collect funds and distribute them (at the option of the donors) as contributions to a Palestine Endowment Fund or as investments in projects still to be approved by the leaders. Brandeis emerged from seclusion in Washington to take part in the initial meeting; afterward he allowed others to develop what he had begun while making himself available for direct and written consultation.

Other concerns preoccupied him at the time, including his wife's nervous disorder and an indeterminate stage in the life and career of various family members. In his public life he was faced with the political ebb tide in America. Rather than advising President Wilson on current legislation, Brandeis now aided the ex-president in composing sweeping programs for some future Democratic reform administration; later, he followed with sympathy an even less promising prospect, LaFollette's campaign as a third-party candidate for the presidency. He also took a very active interest in publicizing progressive views, particularly through a stream of suggestions to Felix Frankfurter, his contact with the *New Republic* editorial board, for articles and editorials, and suitable authors. He did not confine himself to specific, current suggestions but outlined what amounted to an alternative social philosophy, opposed to both laissez-faire and monopoly capitalism, to socialism, communism, and guild socialism (though here the difference is unclear): an experimental approach based, he said, on democracy and cooperation. Finally, in his main active role, as a justice of the Supreme Court, he entered on the highroad of his historic career as the voice of progressive American dissent.[5]

Brandeis' role after 1920 was one of leading or keeping alive a dormant opposition in American public life. The same description quite clearly would apply to his position in Zionist affairs at the time. In both cases there were strong considerations that inhibited him from full and free commitment to rebel leadership: the appearance of judicial restraint that had to be preserved by avoiding controversial, activist politics; his habitual preference to serve as "counsel for the situation" and propound solutions commending themselves to all right-thinking parties in contention. As he was no longer in control of policy, Brandeis' activity became critical, even academic, rather than executive in tone. This mismatch between his situation and his inclination for action brought about a certain disorientation in Jewish matters, in which he found no clear new role like that enshrined in his dissenting judicial opinions.

Weizmann found himself in a quite different situation. His victory in Cleveland in June was followed in September 1921 by his election to the presidency of the WZO by the Zionist Congress in Carlsbad. The formal confirmation of his no-longer questioned leadership placed on Weizmann the onus of taking decisive action to meet the movement's pressing, even threatening, problems. While he was engaged in the struggle with Brandeis in America, Arab attacks on Jewish settlements all over Palestine had been touched off by a clash between rival Jewish May Day demonstrations in Tel-Aviv. This upheaval—coming after occasions usually marked by Arab protests had passed peacefully in the first year of Sir Herbert Samuel's administration—

destroyed the high commissioner's optimism and changed his policy in a way that acutely alarmed the Zionists. In London, moreover, Palestine affairs were being transferred from the Foreign Office to the Colonial Office, where Winston Churchill, not yet deeply involved in the problems of Palestine, allowed Samuel to take the lead. All this, added to the still unsettled question of League of Nations' approval of the Palestine Mandate, thrust Weizmann into a crisis atmosphere from the day he returned from America.[6]

One issue that arose immediately and cropped up repeatedly in the history of the Palestine Mandate was that of interpreting the understanding between Britain and the Zionists implied in the arduously worked out mandate text. The Zionists, led at first by Herbert Samuel, thought that the wording of crucial provisions gave them the right to expect conditions in Palestine permitting them, for an undefined period, to work toward the goal of a Jewish majority and Jewish commonwealth in Palestine. To accomplish this aim, they understood, was their task, not Britain's; but they expected Britain to hold the door open and thus facilitate their success. They—that is, Weizmann and those who followed his lead—further realized that they were expected to make the British task easier by assurances that they had no pretensions to rule *immediately* in Palestine. Such assurances and not simply tacit acceptance of the fact should be publicly offered in order to gain Arab acquiescence to a British regime under which the small Jewish minority could grow gradually into something much larger. This was the conception not only of the Zionists, but of leading British statesmen who supported them in London. It was Samuel's conception of his task as well when he arrived in Jerusalem as high commissioner.

The 1921 outbreak caused Samuel to abandon his previous hopes.[7] He concluded that England could not afford to keep to the terms of the contract he had helped to devise. The mandate—certainly, the unwritten Anglo-Zionist understanding—had to be changed by expressly ruling out any prospect that a Jewish state or commonwealth would ever be erected in Palestine. This must not only be made explicit in British policy, but the Zionists must be required to accept it openly, to endorse publicly this change in their expectations.

Samuel's about-face was too sharp a reversal for men like Lloyd George and Balfour, who understood their commitment to the Zionists in the same sense as Weizmann did. The Zionist leader was able to limit the damage by securing a meeting with them and with an uneasy Churchill, who was not happy with the burden of Palestine but not ready to support fully Samuel's radical departure. The terms of the mandate, with its opening for indefinite Zionist development, remained essentially unchanged. But Samuel's views did not change either, and he not only controlled the Palestine administration, but strongly influenced Churchill's decisions on Palestine in London. In principle, Samuel's proposed interpretation, that a Jewish commonwealth was specifically ruled out, became the view taken by anti-Zionists among administrators in Palestine thereafter. In practice, Samuel's own readiness to facilitate limited Zionist development—given the goodwill he made evident—allowed Zionists enough scope to work up to the limits of their practical capacity in his time.[8]

Official British policy was defined in the Churchill White Paper of 1922, issued after a long series of discussions with an Arab delegation in London. It rejected the Arab demand to scrap the mandate with its implicit opening for the ultimate Zionist aims. The extent of the British commitment to Zionism was restricted by closing the area east of the Jordan River to Jewish development and setting up Abdullah, son of the King of Hejaz, to rule there under the Palestine high commissioner. Jews were to be admitted to the rest of the mandate area "as of right, not on sufferance," but subject to a criterion of "economic absorptive capacity." (Samuel, who was largely responsible for this provision, undoubtedly meant to limit Jewish immigration by the current state of the dominantly Arab economy; such an approach was in conformity with his intention to preserve the relative position of the native population against the emergence of a Jewish majority. But if an ultimate Jewish majority were not to be ruled out in advance, as Churchill agreed, then the "economic absorptive capacity" in question would have to mean that created by the Jews themselves through their investments. This was, in any event, the interpretation accepted by the Permanent Mandates Commission of the League of Nations.)[9]

The Churchill White Paper was rejected flatly by the Arab delegation. The fact that it, nevertheless, served as the basis of British policy in the following years meant that the violence of the past two years had not fundamentally altered British policy, and this may help to explain the relative quiescence of Palestine over the next six or seven years. On the Jewish side the new policy presented itself as an alternative to revisions of the mandate such as Samuel proposed, if not its simple abandonment under the pressure of criticism the British government was sustaining from a growing pro-Arab faction and a public impatient with foreign burdens. The government demanded that the Zionists formally accept Churchill's policy, including the closure of Transjordan and the economic limits applied to Jewish immigration. The London WZO Executive—including Jabotinsky, immediately upon his return from an American mission—bowed to necessity and endorsed the White Paper. Half a year later, in the aftermath of this and other developments, Jabotinsky resigned from the Executive, eventually forming his Zionist Revisionist organization. Weizmann, on the other hand, was constrained by the same circumstances to crystallize and define his gradualist approach more specifically within the terms of the latest official British policy.[10]

Samuel's attitude, largely though by no means fully reflected in the White Paper, found expression in other acts of the Palestine administration of particular concern to Jabotinsky. On the installation of a civil administration, the military command centered in Egypt gave up control of Palestine security, and for a while it seemed possible that Jewish Legion veterans might serve in a Jewish unit of a new Palestine gendarmerie. The May 1921 fighting ended all such possibilities: the Palestine police were allowed to remain nominally Palestinian but, in effect, they were Arab. Samuel's newly defined approach—

to care for the native population's welfare as if there were no Jewish claims in Palestine—became the precise inverse of Jabotinsky's demand that the mandate government give full, active support to the Zionist project, necessarily setting aside incompatible Arab claims. Samuel, to be sure, recognized the Jewish national interest in Palestine in the same way that Jabotinsky recognized that of the Arabs: Jews had the right to promote their interest, but the government had no obligation to do so beyond what clearly served the general interest. In the matter of security, the Jewish settlements were allowed after the May events to stock arms for their own defense, as it had been demonstrated that Arab policemen could not be relied on for this purpose and other troops were being withdrawn. Weizmann, in common with labor elements and others in the Palestinian Jewish community, was able to accept such an arrangement; for Jabotinsky, it was a symbolic crux.

Distrust of the British, in Jabotinsky's case, caused him to prescribe open political protests as the appropriate Zionist tactic. He argued that British interests were at stake in keeping the Zionist connection so that a firm and frank Jewish protest would compel them to change their policy and give Zionism active government support. Accordingly, Jews must insist that defense of the Zionist project was a government obligation and that the Jewish military force needed to effect this must be an arm of the government. The same distrust, shared by many who had followed Jabotinsky into the Jewish Legion and particularly by labor elements, led others to opposite conclusions. They reorganized Jewish defense units, like those Jabotinsky and Rutenberg had drilled with studied openness, and turned them into a semisecret operation. The permission given to store weapons for local defense was welcomed but not seen as the permissible limit of their activity (conducted in good part without the benefit, or restriction, of government license)—somewhat in the spirit of the underground self-defense such people had organized in Europe against pogroms.

The autonomist leanings shown in this matter extended to the whole range of Zionist activity; it made these men particularly apt to serve Weizmann's strategic aim: to build the Jewish national home autonomously from the outset as the organic outgrowth of small beginnings in every field. The natural alliance between Weizmann and the labor Zionists was inhibited at first by the unbridged gap between their distrust and his strategic reliance on the British; when the alliance finally became firm, it represented the full fruition of the characteristic Weizmannist approach.[11]

The Brandeis partisans, on the other hand, shared the view of Jabotinsky and other neo-Herzlian political Zionists that the WZO should retire from the political field after achieving a mandate instrument embodying the Balfour Declaration and that the Palestine administration itself together with the Palestine Jewish community should henceforth bear the political responsibility for carrying out its terms. But in this case, too, an alliance otherwise natural was blocked by mutually opposed positions in regard to relations with the British. The radical opposition between Jabotinsky and Brandeis—the former flatly assuming British ill will but relying on their self-interest, the latter prepared to press the British on particular issues but confident that Britons would honor their pledged word—was apparently made bluntly obvious at their first meeting. Jabotinsky became, together with Ussishkin, the cardinal example for the Brandeis circle of the kind of overheated East European political amateur who should not be permitted to deal with British officials.[12]

Bringing Jabotinsky into the leadership in London had been one of the critical decisions that helped precipitate the break between Brandeis and Weizmann. But the alliance between Weizmann and Jabotinsky was itself doomed as soon as the WZO Executive had to bow to Churchill's redefinition of British policy in Palestine. Weizmann thereafter pursued a more closely defined version of his gradualist synthetic Zionism, continuing to rely on his understanding with Britain; Jabotinsky went into opposition.

Having accepted the Churchill White Paper, followed by approval of a revised mandate, including its provision regarding Transjordan, Weizmann now had to work on the assumption of a stable political situation in Palestine. His political aim thenceforth had to be to preserve the status quo from further attrition and to press forward within its terms with the autonomous social-economic development of the Jewish settlement in Palestine—a resumption of the practical Zionist emphasis of his prewar version of synthetic Zionism. This meant that economic growth was a primary concern and that success in securing adequate capital investment became critically important. Given the Bolshevik regime in Russia, rampant inflation in Germany, and social and political turmoil throughout East-Central Europe, Weizmann had to seek his vital requirements primarily in America. He relied on Sokolow, Jabotinsky, and the new ZOA administration that had succeeded the Brandeis regime during the political uncertainty of 1922. In 1923 he returned in the first of a recurrent series of visits.

Weizmann came back to America in a stronger position, politically and personally. The fruits of his wartime chemical contributions were ripe for gathering. The government's award for his invention for the manufacture of acetone at last had been granted and his patents were released for commercial exploitation; he was soon able to devote himself to political leadership from a base of financial independence. Both new acceptance by his constituents and relative peace and prosperity in Palestine created favorable conditions for Weizmann's work. The American situation, too, was better than before; yet vital improvements were urgently required and this determined the main thrust of his efforts.

After the shocks and tremors of the immediate postwar years, the American Zionist movement, disjointed and weakened, settled into a new pattern.[13] Much of the energy and creativity of the period was diverted into channels detached from the main effort Weizmann hoped to strengthen. The two ideological parties, Mizrachi and the labor Zionists, devoted themselves to special concerns of their own. Mizrachi worked for modern Orthodox education and cultural institutions in Palestine, and its adherents played a prominent part in similar projects such as the Yeshiva University in America. The labor Zionists were affected by the enthusiasm for the Russian Revolution that swept the entire international socialist movement and met with widespread sympathy among Jews. Those Poalei Zion who did not split off into the Communist or Communist-leaning camp eventually coalesced with the Zeirei Zion, a group of Zionist youth drawn to East European populist socialism. The two sides were able to unite on a common ideology that regarded the cooperative network being built by their sister parties in Palestine (with the support of a WZO apparatus committed to Weizmannist gradualism) as the nucleus of an organically developing socialist, or cooperativist, Jewish commonwelath. In America, they fostered secular Jewish schools and culture in Yiddish and Hebrew and sporadically took part in political action initiated by other socialists and progressives. Like Mizrachi, they concentrated their main fund-raising effort on getting support for special—in this case, labor-initiated—projects in Palestine; for this and for political support, they were able to draw on sympathy generated beyond the Zionist or the Jewish circle owing to their ties with trade unions and progressives in the general community. But—again, like Mizrachi—they were a quite negligible factor in raising funds for the Keren Hayesod or other major projects contemplated in Weizmann's blueprints for Palestine.

Among Zionists, Weizmann could rely chiefly on those he had helped to take control of the ZOA in 1921. A major part of the new leadership, and certainly its most articulate part, were Lipsky's close allies, the downtown Yiddish journalists. Their support in arousing popular opposition to the Brandeis regime had been a prime factor in the Weizmann-Lipsky victory; now, they were compensated for the slights endured in past years by securing prominent roles in the new leadership.

In addition, there were other new elements whose position in the 1921 conflict had been less clear. These were immigrants who had attained wealth and prominence over the years, particularly during the war: manufacturers, merchants, and real estate developers. Their guides in communal matters included such men as the leading Jewish educator, Dr. Samson Benderly, who had been Magnes' right-hand man in the New York Kehillah, and the young rabbi, Mordecai M. Kaplan. Those two intellectual leaders, operating in a milieu already more integrated in America-at-large than were the Yiddish journalists, were strongly attracted to social and economic activity beyond the academic limits of their profession: Benderly responded to the challenge of the Balfour Declaration by organizing a group of congenial businessmen as an investment consortium interested in economic development in Palestine; Kaplan was beginning his illustrious career as a communal ideologist and organizer. At the height of the Brandeis-Weizmann clash in 1921, such groups had been primarily concerned to prevent the splitting of the movement. Afterward, in spite of their strong attraction to the methods and persons of the Brandeis group, they drifted back into the fold of the ZOA and became influential leaders of what was, after all, the Zionist milieu closest to their own primary community.[14]

The prominence in the ZOA of Yiddish journalists and immigrant businessmen who were influenced by rabbis and Hebrew educators gave it a superficial resemblance to the dominant contemporary trend in European Zionism: a commitment to preserve Jewish (secular or traditional) culture in the Diaspora had seemingly won over the plan to pare down Zionism to a core program of social-economic development in Palestine. In one respect the ZOA's relatively stronger affinity for Zionist intellectuals did, in fact, give it a substantial advantage over the Brandeis group. During the 1921 struggle, the Lipsky-Weizmann camp conducted a far more active and effective campaign in the press and on speakers' platforms than their opponents were willing or able to do; in later years, Brandeis—who was always able to mobilize outstanding intellectual and journalistic support in his other endeavors—had reason to complain that his group was not able to match ZOA propaganda at a comparable level of competence. But beyond this, the ZOA demonstrated no significant commitment to cultural or intellectual labors: such work by their adherents was done outside the frame of ZOA activity. The main activity of ZOA members became their participation in the Keren Hayesod and other Zionist fund-raising campaigns. Thus they were the main reliable base from which to work for Weizmann's primary objective: to find the funds essential for meeting the urgent needs in Palestine.

In his 1921 visit Weizmann had learned some lessons about the extent and limits of his potential success in American fund-raising. He says in his memoirs that he had told Brandeis at the 1920 London conference that unless the ZOA could promise more adequate support for the WZO Executive's budget, he would come to America himself to do the job—a threat to which he attributes the animosity that the justice thereafter showed toward him. After his first visit, he felt he had proved that American Jewry, properly approached, responded more generously than his opponents had forecast. The ZOA, like other downtown Zionists, had always been able to turn out a larger popular response—to door-to-door solicitation, protest meetings, and periodical Zionist elections—than could be anticipated in the light of their small regularly organized membership. After the Brandeis-Lipsky split, it was shown again that the downtown method of propagandistic consciousness raising, which the post-1921 ZOA administration used (known then as creating *Stimmung*), had greater success in raising funds than did the quiet, business-oriented Brandeis approach to socially conscious investors.[15]

But this comparison, however useful for intra-Zionist polemics, was irrelevant to the main test Weizmann faced. What he raised in pledges in 1921, a half million dollars or so, fell ludicrously short of the American share of over a hundred million dollars that was felt to be needed for the initial five years of planned development. More modest goals could not be set below the minimum required in 1923 to meet currently urgent tasks, and this, too, exceeded what he could expect American Zionists to raise on their own. Although the ZOA achieved significant results and reached out widely in the community on behalf of the Keren Hayesod, a much more limited circle committed to the JDC collected far larger amounts for non-Zionist Jewish philanthropy overseas. If the Zionists hoped to avoid damaging setbacks, non-Zionist support had to be enlisted.

In 1921 Weizmann and his friends, aided by Louis Marshall, had secured some cooperation from non-Zionists in setting up the Keren Hayesod, as they had done in England with the help of Sir Alfred Mond. The main work was done by the ZOA membership, and Emanuel Neumann served as the executive in charge. But Marshall's law partner, Samuel Untermyer, lent his prestige as president of the Foundation Fund; it was presented to the contributing public as a nonpartisan instrument of the community at large for the work in Palestine. Since Keren Hayesod receipts, nevertheless, failed to meet the anticipated requirements in Palestine, Weizmann began in 1923 to seek further aid in non-Zionist circles. The plans he proposed to Marshall called for non-Zionist help in raising investment funds for projected Palestine banks, power plants, and other essential economic development; they also revived the old issue of non-Zionist participation in a representative body that would take over from the WZO the powers granted in the Palestine Mandate to the Jewish Agency.[16]

Weizmann had to negotiate for six years before he could bring the non-Zionists into the Jewish Agency in 1929. During that period he encountered new opposition in the Zionist movement specifically aimed against his compromises with the American non-Zionists. Strong factions in Poland and Palestine pressed for a Jewish agency constituted at a world Jewish congress and based on democratically elected national councils in every country of the Jewish world. Jabotinsky founded the Zionist Revisionist party in 1925 primarily in opposition to what he considered a weakly submissive policy toward England; he joined in the attack on Weizmann's plans for the Jewish Agency as another surrender of national interests and Zionist principle. Similar criticisms had been voiced by Brandeis earlier against Weizmann's concept of a Jewish council; but now the Brandeis group did not take a prominent part in opposing the developing Weizmann-Marshall project. In part this resulted from divided councils in their camp; in part, it reflected their withdrawal to limited functions of economic support for the constructive work in Palestine.

The independent course that the Brandeis adherents should take was an issue from the beginning. Some, like de Haas, wanted to keep up pressure on the ZOA and WZO and build an organization ready to resume control at the first opportunity. For this purpose he pushed for the recruitment of Palestine Development Leagues across the country in which small investors would pool resources to be committed to projects approved by the Palestine Development Council; in this way the Brandeis group would secure a base of popular support for the recapture of Zionist leadership. Mack and others heartily disliked this approach; they preferred to rely on a smaller base of major contributors and investors who could offer solid support for economic projects.[17]

Brandeis' own preference was somewhat complex. He counseled strict abstention from anything like open contention for Zionist control. The Weiz-mann-Lipsky policy, he predicted, would fall of its own weight, doomed by the irrationality of its dishonest policy. The efforts of his own group until then should demonstrate the efficacy of a proper policy, single-mindedly dedicated to economic development. Their return to power would follow in time, but it should not be won by political exertions and thin margins. As for the Pal-estine Development Leagues that de Haas was working so hard to create, they should be given their chance if only because a loyal comrade devoted such selfless effort to them, but Brandeis did not see them as levers for displacing Lipsky and Weizmann from leadership. Yet this restrained policy did not mean total abstention from internecine Zionist politics; within carefully guarded limits, Brandeis himself played a part in the continuing battle.

The Brandeis faction did not participate in the 1921 Carlsbad Zionist Congress but they were represented there by Julius Simon, who then came to join the group. Inadequate access to the Yiddish press hampered them in voicing publicly the criticism of Zionist affairs that continued in their private correspondence, but occasional opportunities to do so were seized on. Bran-deis' instructions in such cases were to avoid attacking Weizmann and the WZO and concentrate fire on "Lipsky and his ilk." Open battle was success-fully conducted by one group closely tied to Brandeis and his methods, the women's Zionist organization, Hadassah. Hadassah not only was conquered by a leadership that hewed to the Brandeis line, but became by far the most successful Zionist membership organization. When the JDC gave up its share in the American Zionist medical unit, this project became Hadassah's full and exclusive responsibility; the organization succeeded after a struggle in having all funds its members raised—apart from dues, out of which all orga-nizational expenses were met—expended for medical work by its own appa-ratus in Palestine. The women also won a battle with Lipsky over the right to full autonomy for themselves together with representation in the ZOA gov-erning councils. In such battles, Brandeis' support and counsel were freely given; in some, especially when Hadassah's decision might determine the future shape of the ZOA, he privately—and very discreetly—underwrote the organization's expenses.[18]

However, political activism of this sort was not a significant part of the Brandeis group's program until the late 1920s. Its members, most of whom were leaders in their own right, had to content themselves with the scope for action that their limited economic agenda provided—a prospect that grew steadily less attractive for many. The field that the Brandeis cohort could cul-tivate successfully proved narrower than one might have hoped. Brandeis could not have expected that his personal appeal—even backed by his own contribution as a matching or contingent grant (as was often his practice)—would be effective among Jewish notables of much greater wealth who had little liking for him and whom he liked equally little. Judge Mack, who enjoyed better relations with men like Julius Rosenwald, found them either antagonistic to Zionism or more ready to respond to Weizmann and the WZO than to a Zionist splinter group. The Brandeis group had to fall back on the newly rich immigrant donors and investors and to organize small investment clubs prepared to pool funds for investment in Palestine projects; but here, too, the ZOA's modest success with the Keren Hayesod and the American Zion Commonwealth outdid their own. The core group of Brandeis partisans, nevertheless, persisted with their scrupulously managed undertaking—though even among them some could not resist the drift back to active leadership in other settings: the renewed American Jewish Congress, the Keren Hayesod, or the ZOA itself.[19]

Given the weakness of both American Zionist leadership groups, the non-Zionist AJC had a clear road to resume its dominance in the community. Weizmann and the Brandeis group alike found it necessary to seek aid from Louis Marshall and the JDC leader, Felix Warburg, in funding their Palestine projects. The AJC notables were concerned for the success of the work in Palestine because, having been accorded presidential and congressional approval, it became a test involving Jewish prestige. Moreover, with the clear prospect that immigration restrictions would soon shut American doors to Jews in flight from Europe, another haven was badly needed. The AJC notables not only were ready to rally support in non-Zionist circles, but felt obliged to press for more unity in the ranks of the Zionists themselves. Thus, in seeking AJC aid in their respective projects, the Zionist rivals were edged into resuming contact with each other.

The JDC continued to work directly in Palestine after leaving the medical field to Hadassah. Their Palestine Committee, entrusted with the remaining JDC relief and social work, was headed by Bernard Flexner, one of Brandeis' close circle and most trusted associates; his interest, like that of Marshall, was not limited to charitable services, but extended to the entire social-economic activity involved in the resettlement of Palestine. A parallel contact on the other side was signalized by Untermyer's role as lay head of the Keren Hayesod; it had a more substantial base in the personal contacts that Weizmann cultivated with Marshall and Felix Warburg. In this way the AJC-JDC directorate was in a position to mediate between opposing Zionist factions with double effect: by offering a bridge that could join them and by applying incentives and pressures to compose their differences.

A first attempt to bridge the Brandeis-Weizmann split by joint practical activity occurred during the Jabotinsky-Sokolow mission to America in 1921–22. Rutenberg had just been granted a concession for hydroelectric and other power plants in Palestine and was seeking financial support in France, England, and the United States. Jabotinsky's proposal that the newly formed Palestine Development Council together with the WZO's Jewish Colonial Trust invest in this project was beyond the financial capacity of the new Brandeis-led company, and it was unwelcome on other grounds as well. Cooperating with a body whose fiscal and moral reliability it openly doubted was not an appealing prospect; Brandeis partisans, moreover, suspected the European Zionists of favoring Anglo-German industrialists over an American firm— one like General Electric, for example, whose head was a Brandeis acquaintance, Gerard Swope. (Considerations like these were cited by Weizmann somewhat earlier as explaining the American Zionist opposition to his plans in 1919–21.) In the following year when Weizmann returned, he organized with Louis Marshall's help a "nonpartisan" conference that met in New York on February 17, 1924—representatives of the Brandeis circle were at first excluded from the discussions. However, in consequence of the nonpartisan conference, the Brandeis effort received significant reinforcement. A conference resolution had set up a committee to explore possible economic projects in Palestine, and Flexner used the occasion to propose cooperation between the JDC and the Palestine Development Council. Out of this grew in 1926 the Palestine Economic Corporation (PEC); building on assets created by the Brandeis group such as a mortgage credit bank and a bank for cooperative institutions, the PEC became a major factor in financing economic activity favored by the social policy of its joint sponsors.[20]

Another resolution of the nonpartisan conference, to study ways to bring non-Zionists into the Jewish Agency, did not come to fruition until 1929, nearly six years later. It was beset with difficulties in America at the very start owing to a complicated quarrel over fund-raising. In the wake of the conference, the JDC and Keren Hayesod agreed to conduct a united Jewish campaign, with Palestine to receive agreed parts of the proceeds. This was an understanding pressed by the leaders, Marshall and Weizmann, that swiftly came under opposing pressure from staff professionals and lay leaders on both sides. The JDC was engaged in a massive effort in cooperation with the Soviet government to resettle Russian Jews in the Crimea—a project vehemently attacked by Zionists as a diversion from the only real solution for displaced Jews. On the other side, the director of the JDC campaign, ignoring pleas from Marshall, deliberately suppressed Palestine-oriented campaign material as being offensive to major contributors. This, of course, was a procedure that could adversely affect the level of contributions earmarked for the Palestine budget, and it provoked furious protests. Marshall, who had tried in vain to restrain the militancy of the JDC staff, resented personal attacks vented on him by angry Zionists and demanded that Weizmann keep them in check. Weizmann did so and issued soothing statements on Zionist aims in Palestine similar to those pronounced earlier to pacify Arab unrest at the request of British officers. The incident helped delay progress on expanding the Jewish Agency, (which was in any case beset by other difficulties); the measures Weizmann felt forced to take in dealing with it divided the forces joined in the new ZOA administration. Men like Emanuel Neumann, whose major commitment was to the Keren Hayesod, were prompted to consider a change in alliances.[21]

Underlying the changes that eventually occurred was the unstable Zionist situation in Palestine. The improvement after Samuel's first years as high commissioner was heightened by a considerable rise in Jewish immigration and investment, impelled by monetary and social-economic policies of the Polish government that bore down hard on lower-middle-class Jewish traders and artisans. The boom years of 1924–25 were followed by a collapse of values that left many Jewish enterprises in Palestine in severe difficulties. Among them was the American Zion Commonwealth, with which the ZOA had intimate connections. The internal ZOA opposition, led by staff members smarting from the Weizmann-Lipsky pressures in the JDC-Crimea matter, was further inflamed by reports that Lipsky had used Keren Hayesod receipts to help the American Zion Commonwealth out of its difficulties. A panel of judges examined the issues and concluded that the ZOA administration had been lax and morally, but not legally, culpable in its management of funds, and should be replaced. The Brandeis group now responded conditionally to appeals to return and repair the damages suffered by the organization. They demanded a clean sweep of the old administration, and a special campaign to retire the large accumulated deficit, before they would assume responsibility.[22]

In the maneuvering that followed, the Brandeis faction had a powerful ally in the leadership of Hadassah. That organization joined other Zionist fund-raising bodies in setting up a United Palestine Appeal (UPA) in 1925 in the wake of the dispute over the JDC-Crimea project. But with the onset of economic difficulties in Palestine soon after, the chronic financial embarrassment of Zionist budgets sharply worsened and the UPA had to resort to loans to meet its current obligations, among them the regular budget of Hadassah's medical work. Hadassah refused to be responsible for the new UPA borrowing and, instead, opened an independent campaign to supplement its UPA receipts; at the same time the leaders determined that they must be represented adequately not only at ZOA conventions and WZO congresses, but in the executive bodies that controlled day-to-day administration.

They pursued this aim in common with like-minded Brandeis partisans for three years before gaining a definitive victory. In 1927 they won a compromise agreement whereby Lipsky brought opposition figures into the administrative and financial committees; but this fell short of the conditions set by Brandeis, who speedily reopened the attack. In 1929, however, Lipsky's adroit maneuvers dealt the Hadassah-Brandeis opposition a resounding defeat at the ZOA convention. Later that year, the Zionist Congress agreed to the terms for non-Zionist participation in the Jewish Agency. At the next ZOA convention in 1930, non-Zionists interested in uniting the quarreling Zionists for effective cooperation helped restore the Brandeis group to power in the ZOA. In the following year the ZOA delegation to the Zionist Congress joined in voting the temporary dismissal of Weizmann from the presidency of the WZO.

The negotiations for including non-Zionists in the Jewish Agency entered their final phase with the appointment of a Joint Palestine Survey Commission in 1927. Weizmann still had to contend with persistent opposition in Zionist circles, but the Brandeis group could not unequivocally join the irreconcilable critics. Their own compact with the non-Zionists to set up the Palestine Economic Corporation logically precluded them from criticizing Weizmann's partnership offer to the same people: the PEC was no less clear a

departure from their original idea of absorbing Schiff, Marshall, and Warburg
in the Zionist organization. While some, like de Haas and Stephen Wise,
strongly inclined to the hard line of Polish Zionists who fought Weizmann's
Jewish Agency plans to the end, Brandeis, with some reluctance, took a more
moderate view and had a hand in the preliminary briefing of the Palestine
Survey Commission experts.

The expansion of the Jewish Agency in 1929 was followed by an outburst
of Arab attacks on the Palestine Jewish community, producing a flurry of
British inquiry commissions and expert reports that submitted previous policy to severely critical reappraisal. At the same time Louis Marshall died after
undergoing surgery, leaving non-Zionist leadership in the Jewish Agency in
the hands of Felix Warburg, chairman of that agency's Administrative Committee, and Cyrus Adler, who became the AJC president.

The influence of AJC leaders had for some time been a significant factor
in the inner-Zionist political struggle. In 1927 and 1928 Lipsky and Weizmann's courting of non-Zionist notables under the pressure of the desperate
financial situation had been seen by the ZOA opposition as an impending
betrayal of the UPA and Keren Hayesod to which they had committed themselves. Warburg had then, on the eve of approaching ZOA conventions, indicated confidence in Lipsky by appropriate public gestures.

The creation of the Jewish Agency and what followed produced a new
situation particularly disadvantageous to the ZOA. An emergency fund to restore the property and personal losses from the Arab violence was announced
by Warburg, who determined the expenditure of its receipts; the ZOA was
thereby displaced from its main function in American Jewry. Warburg also,
tutored by Cyrus Adler, claimed as chairman of the Administrative Committee (the body that occupied the same place in the agency structure as the
Action Committee in the WZO) to have authority over current policy
between sessions of the Agency Council (equivalent to the WZO Congress);
on these grounds the AJC leaders allowed themselves some political acts
viewed with alarm by Zionists. Weizmann had to curb Warburg's pretensions
in private communications, insisting that the London Executive had exclusive control of political matters. Lipsky took a more publicly antagonistic
line: the ZOA announced a campaign for a mass roll call in protest of the
Palestine developments, which Warburg considered a direct defiance of his
and the Jewish Agency's authority.

At the same time a meeting was arranged by Flexner between Brandeis
and Warburg at which the non-Zionist Maecenas expressed his readiness to
be guided—or even better, led officially—by the Zionist sage. Another nonpartisan conference was arranged, for which Brandeis emerged from seclusion
to participate publicly. An open rapprochement between the new non-Zionist
leaders and the Brandeis Zionists together with the opening breach between
the Lipsky administration and the non-Zionists in the Jewish Agency produced both dismay and new hope in Zionist ranks, particularly among the
financial backers prominent in the ZOA leadership. They brought intense
pressure to bear for new negotiations to heal the breach in Zionist ranks

before the next ZOA convention. The negotiations that began in February 1930 boiled down in the end to a deal over the distribution of offices in a reorganized ZOA. Brandeis' rigid insistence on a clean sweep of the old administration and an interim period of six months to two years during which the organization would be run under a receivership held up agreement until after the convention was in session. Only then did the justice yield to the entreaties of his friends and agree to compromise, whereupon a new administration headed by Robert Szold came into office.

No clean sweep of the old leaders was secured, and the ZOA under its new leader continued to be run more or less in the same way as before. The main concern of the ZOA was declared to be the economic upbuilding of Palestine—a Brandeisist position adopted long since by the Lipsky regime; Zionist education or propaganda on the same scale as before was now admitted to be essential even for the sake of raising the funds needed for Palestine development—a lesson learned from the experience of past years in both camps.[23]

The Brandeis victory of 1930 demonstrated, in effect, that the old issues of the debate in 1919–21 no longer meant anything to the movement's rank and file. In the years that followed, the movement was concerned with new issues that had been peripheral and hence indeterminate in the personal experiences that shaped Brandeis' or Weizmann's Zionist perspective. An assumption common to both leaders, reliance on the good faith of the British government, became increasingly unacceptable to the Jewish and Zionist public; neither Weizmann nor Brandeis in their separate ways could deal with this development in total harmony with preestablished patterns that continued to influence them. The pressure on this point was heightened critically by the rise of Hitler and also by the changing relationship of each man to the power structure with which he had to contend: the rise of Roosevelt once more gave Brandeis access to the seats of power, whereas in England Weizmann had to rely increasingly—against his ruling inclination—on opposition forces for political support. The result in each case was a marked instability in response and a growing drift toward a position detached from the current of opinion in the movement at large. In the overwhelming shadow of the new situation, the differences between the two heroes of ancient battles were overcast and blurred, but never effaced completely. The underlying opposition between the old rivals remained a factor of potential importance that continued to be taken into account by new antagonists in the disputes of the time.

Unstable lines of division and alliance made themselves evident in the very time of the Brandeis restoration and Weizmann's "demission"; they became apparent in the relations of the rivals to both the non-Zionists and the British authorities. In spite of Felix Warburg's professed eagerness to be guided by Brandeis in Palestine affairs, it soon turned out that he was open to influence from quite another quarter. Judah Magnes, having exposed himself and his patrons to unwelcome risks by his wartime pacifism, had gone to Europe and Palestine in search of a new mission and ended by becoming the chancellor of the newly founded Hebrew University in Jerusalem. After the

1929 Arab attacks, he began actively to seek a basis of Arab-Jewish understanding as part of a new group of Jewish intellectual and social leaders, Brith
Shalom; he also opened independent negotiations with St. John Philby, who
offered himself as a go-between with Saudi and other Arab leaders. Warburg,
who had a long-standing connection of close friendship and material patronage with Magnes, let himself be guided by Magnes' approach within fairly
broad limits.

This was not a development that either Weizmann or Brandeis welcomed;
but although both opposed Warburg's tie to Magnes, their own relative positions vis-à-vis the non-Zionists were subtly, but suddenly, reversed. Weizmann, required by his position to check Warburg's susceptibility to Magnes
more directly than was Brandeis, was also impelled to move noticeably closer
to the mitigated Zionism that Magnes and others thought likely to interest
putatively moderate Arab leaders. In the Brandeis circle, on the other hand,
the hard line of veteran antagonists of the AJC and strongly political nationalists prevailed and contributed to the revolt that deposed Weizmann from
the presidency at the 1931 Zionist Congress.

The switch was also related to the different premises from which Brandeis
and Weizmann had arrived at their common reliance on British good faith.
Brandeis had a general esteem for the Anglo-Saxon ethos and a lawyer's presumption, barring clear evidence to the contrary, that legal rights would be
respected. For Weizmann, reliance on British bona fides was the unspoken
moral and political foundation on which his own leadership was based; if it
failed, he could hardly know where to find firm footing elsewhere. When trust
in the British did, in fact, begin to fail, Brandeis could allow himself—or
understand in such friends as Stephen Wise—an uninhibited expression of
indignation and moral outrage; Americans could hope to find alternative
backing for Zionist claims in their own government, especially after the Brandeis circle's ties with Roosevelt grew stronger in FDR's second term. Weizmann could be effective in his sphere of operations only by continuing to play
on his old bonds of loyal association with Britain, by appeals to the British
public and its political and intellectual leaders. Thus, on the American side
the logic of the situation favored unbridled public protest against the
"betrayal" of Zionism; in England, protest, both public and private, had to
be accompanied by a display of understanding for the undoubted difficulties
in which the Zionist commitment had enmeshed the British government.

Given the special conditions of each man's leadership, one can understand the apparent role reversals that occurred in their relative positions on
Zionist political objectives. In 1918–19 when Brandeis' aides (particularly de
Haas, since Stephen Wise avoided the task) still hoped to attract non-Zionist
notables to the ZOA, they had to pitch their rhetoric at a soothing, nonrepel-
lent level. None other than the Herzlian devotee, de Haas, disputed Weizmann's (and Ahad Ha'am's) insistence on fighting for phraseology in the
mandate that specified a "Jewish Commonwealth" as an ultimate goal; he
also, of course, pressed for specific provisions—opposed by Weizmann—to
include Jewish personnel in the Palestine government immediately on the

assumption that it would commit itself positively to building up the Jewish national home. In his own dealings with non-Zionists, Brandeis at that time virtually denied Jewish statehood as a possible goal; he certainly gave Louis Marshall the impression that the Zionists had given it up in practice, whatever their formal professions of faith. Later, following the May 1921 disturbances in Palestine, Brandeis was inclined to credit British findings that held Zionist provocations to blame for Arab violence.[24]

The changes that occurred in the 1930s altered both leaders' perspective. Weizmann—who faced pressure in London from a government increasingly cool to Zionism and pinned his hopes for new support on the American non-Zionists—seemed to be moving toward a position closer to that of Judah Magnes, that is, one involving surrender of Zionist hopes. Now it was he rather than Brandeis who let it seem he was ready to see the goal of an ultimate Jewish state foreclosed; Brandeis allies in the ZOA delegation together with other Weizmann opponents seized on the occasion to bring about his defeat at the 1931 Zionist Congress. Men like Wise, de Haas, and Emanuel Neumann then showed strong affinities with the most consistent anti-Weizmannist line, that of Jabotinsky's Revisionism: for Wise, one of the characteristically transient phases of a temperament moved by impulse rather than calculation; for the other two, a more-lasting expression of their basic Zionist orientation.

But this was anti-Weizmannism of a sort that Brandeis could not share; his inclination was already taking a different turn when the hard-line Revisionist-leaning alternative was presented to him by some within his circle. Throughout the 1930s Brandeis cultivated a growing relationship with the Palestine Jewish labor movement. He grew particularly close to the student Zionists and American Jewish youth movements most intimately connected with the left-Zionist federations of communal settlements. To them he showed a fatherly warmth uncommon in one generally seen as cool and aloof; the "manly" dedication he saw in those young people—particularly those who came out of American colleges—brought out a strangely soft and human side in him not usually shown beyond the family. In the broader Palestinian labor movement, he found a political affinity with those who had recurrent differences with Weizmann. This relationship became significant in the closing years of the generation of Zionist political leaders to which Brandeis and Weizmann belonged.[25]

Events in the late 1930s—the world business depression and other portents of war, the rise of Hitler and formation of the Nazi-Fascist Axis, the flight of Jewish refugees from Germany and Central Europe as the reign of racist anti-Semitism spread, the Arab revolt of 1936–39 and the rule of an appeasement-minded government in London—made it constantly harder, eventually impossible, to hope that old rights and rules could stand by their own strength. But it was not easy for heroes of the old regime to cast aside their old weapons and rearm for impending new conflicts beyond their imagining.

Brandeis met the crisis in Europe and its outcrops in Palestine with all his

old militancy. Stephen Wise responded to the rise of Hitler to power by turning the American Jewish Congress (supplemented after 1936 by a newly
founded World Jewish Congress) once more into an instrument of mass
action. He ran protest rallies and, with some hesitation, committed his organization to the anti-Nazi boycott that was prosecuted in America until the
beginning of war. These measures were opposed by the AJC and by established communal leaders of German Jewry but won the full support of Brandeis. Wise and Brandeis also used their period of influence with Franklin
Roosevelt to obtain from the president ringing statements of moral condemnation against the Nazi oppression. Meanwhile, across the Atlantic, Weizmann added to his duties the task of relief for German Jewry, most directly
by seeking their removal to the Jewish national home in Palestine. It was an
approach wholeheartedly shared by Brandeis and his circle, among whom
men like Frankfurter and Ben Cohen in addition to Stephen Wise and the
justice himself enjoyed positions of trust and exceptional personal access to
the president.[26]

But just as the Jewish settlement in Palestine became more crucial than
ever as a haven for Jewish refugees, its own future faced critical threats. The
Royal Commission inquiry into the causes of the 1936 Arab revolt concluded
that the Palestine Mandate was unworkable and proposed a partition into
linked Jewish and Arab states as its preferred solution of the problem. Upon
consideration, the British government abandoned the idea of partition
(though it remained an option briefly entertained again in some government
quarters). It then adopted a policy conclusively dismissing the understanding
on which the Zionists, led by Weizmann, had worked: a top limit on Jewish
immigration and severe restrictions on further land sales to Jews were
announced, virtually guaranteeing that the mandate would end with the
establishment of Palestine as an Arab, not a Jewish, state. As a result the
doors of Palestine remained sealed, with fateful consequences for both British
and American policy toward the impending Holocaust. The Zionist movement, not yet confronted with the full horror that emerged, was immediately
faced with the question of new policies to deal with the new situation.[27]

The logic of the situation offered two straightforward choices for Zionist
strategists. The new British policy was not only treated as a betrayal by Jewish
opinion, it was declared to be a breach of the previously accepted interpretation of the Palestine Mandate by the Permanent Mandates Commission, to
whom holders of League of Nations' mandates regularly reported.[28] Relying
on this, one could argue that the new British regulations were illegal and
demand a return to the constitutional requirements of the mandate. Alternatively, one could conclude that British interests would override legalities
and that Zionist strategy must therefore be prepared to seek a new legal base
other than the mandate for the future. Such a base might possibly be found
in the partition proposal—though, obviously, after it had been officially dismissed by the British government, there were clearly tactical problems for any
Zionist strategy based on adopting that idea. Zionist leaders were attracted
by other aspects of the situation toward one or the other alternative or toward

various intermediate combinations devised to avoid the drawbacks of either choice.

What most clearly divided Weizmann and Brandeis was that one had his political base in Britain and the other was equally firmly based in America. Weizmann, even while rallying opposition forces in England against the new line of official policy, had to hope that if and when the mandate era ended, he could find a new basis of mutual support between the Jewish national home and the British Commonwealth; the partition idea, as sketched by the Royal Commission, might allow such an arrangement to develop after the war. If Weizmann entertained such hopes, as Emanuel Neumann claimed, he lived long enough to see them bitterly disappointed. The Jewish Commonwealth he dreamed of was won (by other men and by a different strategy) amid hateful and violent scenes of British repression and Jewish rebellion that carried over for years afterward in fixed habits of suspicion and hostility.[29]

Although Brandeis could hardly fail to see that there was little chance of continuing under the terms of the mandate as he understood them, he did not have Weizmann's reasons for looking to a new arrangement that would leave open a possibility for restoring the tie with Britain. The events of the 1930s meant for him that England had been false to her legal trust; he was not one to forgive easily the moral offense involved. If England broke her word, there was America to call on—and America, he and his lawyer friends argued, was entitled under its treaty rights in regard to the Palestine Mandate to pass judgment on significant departures from its terms such as the new British policies. But Brandeis, too, was destined to see his hopes disappointed and his assumptions proved false. He did not live to see the final abandonment of Jews to the Holocaust, but when he died in 1941, he knew that his reliance on American support, whether for the immediate relief of refugee needs or the basic issue of sustaining the Palestine Mandate as internationally binding, had been misplaced. In a somber interview with Eliezer Kaplan, treasurer of the Jewish Agency, he concluded that Zionists could do no more than educate a new generation of Jews who might take up the burden under better conditions in a future time.[30]

If an element of tragedy is inherent in the life story of anyone destined to be enshrined as a hero, it is one not lacking in the Zionist career of Brandeis or Weizmann. But another element, heroic stamina and persistence, is equally present in the closing chapter. Weizmann, half blind and grieving over the loss of his son at war, was still able by personal intercession and through the diplomatic staff who worked along his lines to prick the conscience of those who ruled London and gain some of the few diplomatic victories Zionism won in Washington. Brandeis and men who took his lead had a major share in the political awakening of American Jewry. The support he gave Wise in arousing America against Hitler's racism also went to Dr. Solomon Goldman, who first effectively deployed American Jewish mass pressure in protest against the 1939 British White Paper. What was only a trial run then assumed major proportions after Brandeis' death in the combined

work of Abba Hillel Silver and David Ben-Gurion, two men who, at different
times and in different ways, came into Brandeis' sphere of influence.[31]

But these were now men of the new time, addressing themselves to situations neither Brandeis nor Weizmann was fully prepared to face.

Conclusion

In a general, elementary way, Brandeis and Weizmann were undoubtedly typical of the conditions in which the Jewish identity of each was formed. Weizmann can readily be classified in terms native to the Eastern and Central
European milieu in which he was reared. Brandeis may be roughly described
as a typical Western Zionist, sharing traits common to certain emancipated
Jews in Europe and America.

Weizmann's abiding concern as a Jew was one as old as the Hebrew
enlightenment movement, the Haskalah. His constant aim, expressed in various different ways through the years, was to induct oppressed, tradition-rid-
den East European Jews into the free, secular, modern culture of the West.
As a Zionist, he held that this must be done in the true freedom of an autonomous Jewish settlement in Palestine. He despaired of Russia and tried to
pursue his Zionist goal in the West; but the constituency he saw as his own
remained East European, the immigrant Jewries of the West and the pioneer
settlers in Palestine.

What made Brandeis a Zionist was the typically Western pride of a truly
emancipated Jew; the same secure, unconditioned liberalism that moved not
only Herzl but men far removed from Jewish nationalism, like Adolphe Cre-
mieux and Gabriel Riesser, to bold assertions of their Jewish identity. As a
Zionist of this type, Brandeis saw true, political oppression as the Jewish
problem of Eastern Europe; he inclined to regard it as an intractable problem,
one to be solved only by the removal of Eastern Jews from the benighted,
reactionary areas they inhabited. In this respect, his Zionism, if it was not
merely philanthropic, mechanically political "projectmongering" as Weizmann charged, did have a decidedly patronizing, paternalistic quality. This
was not, however, the main meaning Zionism had (in Brandeis' view) for his
natural constituency: young, college-bred American Jews. Such men, even
when quite detached from the religious disputes that feed antisemitism,
found themselves impeached for their Jewishness. It was Brandeis' main
objective to teach them through Zionism how to bear the impeachment in a
"manly" manner and turn it into a positive source of pride; he was in this a
Zionist in the style of Max Nordau, the Zionist authority for many in the
Brandeis circle such as Horace Kallen.

It is hard to take this line of approach much further. Neither Brandeis nor
Weizmann led simply by voicing the consensus, or even the latent inclination, of the constituency they presumed to lead. Both, as noted earlier, were
leaders "from the periphery."

If Weizmann had a personal circle to which he was most indebted for the basic commitments of his mature identity, this was the Russian-Jewish student society he joined when he began his studies in Berlin. He formed his specific Zionist position largely in line with theirs; he sharpened his individual variant of the common attitude by his apprenticeship as an organizational leader in their company, in the give-and-take of comradeship and contention among intimate friends. After Weizmann left the Continent and settled in England, a type of Zionism most akin to his own came into power in the German movement; Weizmann could only cooperate with its congenial leaders as a distant ally. In his new Western milieu he neither found a congenial peer group like that he had in Berlin and Geneva nor did he share the life experience of the immigrant community, his natural constituency. The position he won in English society and among academics and political leaders was the true basis of his claim to leadership—a claim never unequivocally acknowledged during the years of his most dramatic success, even by some in his immediate circle of aides and disciples. He had to win recognition as the legitimate leader by arduous struggle and years of coalition building.

Only after this victory was won could one say that the Zionist movement entered a period dominated by Weizmannism. Weizmannism was a "synthetic Zionism" that considered political action and social-economic construction to be organically related aspects of a single endeavor, each aspect depending on success in the other. Under the British Mandate, the Weizmann approach based itself on a status (which had to be guarded) considered sufficient to permit the goal of a self-sustaining Jewish society and free Jewish Commonwealth to be attained gradually through steady, small advances in social and economic construction.

Put in such terms, Weizmann's approach was one Brandeis fully shared. Weizmannism was not the issue between them—nor was the issue any alternative Zionist doctrine to which Brandeis was fundamentally committed. The differences that precipitated their clash were of a specific, technical nature, to which, to be sure, far-reaching differences of personal and communal orientation were attached for polemical purposes.

Unlike Weizmann, Brandeis did not grow up a Zionist and define his particular Zionist position dialectically in the company of a like-minded peer group. But he did come into the movement under the impetus of his broadening progressivism and out of a series of earlier Jewish contacts that he found refreshingly congenial: with Jewish workers, civic-minded businessmen and professionals, college men and communal social workers. When he took up the challenge of Zionist and Jewish leadership at the urging of such men, he tried to recruit activists by personal persuasion primarily among those he liked and approved of most. One may say that in his case a cadre of Zionists was built up that reflected the leader's personal orientation and that expressed a certain idiosyncratic communal style: youthful, professional, striving for integration at elite levels in the American institutional structure—a second generation out of old-country stock, not part of the entrenched Jewish plutocratic establishment.

Weizmann, in his days as youth leader of the Democratic Faction and thereafter, liked to work with a similar cadre, *mutatis mutandis.* He, like Brandeis, also regarded the work of political negotiation as one best done alone, with a competent staff and without the distraction of committee or plebiscitary participation. Both men, nonetheless, understood the political utility and moral necessity of securing free and informed popular assent to their leadership. In a movement as diverse as the Zionist movement, one that aspired to activate the whole Jewish people, leadership based simply on the support of a committed cadre was obviously insufficient. The role to which such leaders pretended implied recourse at critical points to a wider consensus, seeking the broadest agreement to their policies that could be reached by their heterogeneous concerned public. Facing the same necessity, the two men were divided, beyond the special requirements of each one's personal situation, by subtle differences in their approach to the practice of leadership, differences of political style.

Both men knew themselves from early days to be destined for action and for leadership. They diverged in an early phase of growth in the style of leadership they chose to emulate. Only Weizmann committed himself to a public role of political party activism from his youth—always, to be sure, under the pressure of the need to be personally independent, a pressure that severely hampered and perplexed him at several points in his rather stormy, eventful career. Weizmann was also a chemist, a distinguished one in the field of applied, industrial science. The real dedication to research of a man who, like Weizmann, returned successfully to the laboratory at the age of fifty-eight, after ten years in unrelated work, cannot be doubted. But political leadership was always his primary commitment.

Brandeis always wanted to be a lawyer; no other vocation ever seemed higher to him. What he conceived a lawyer to be was, of course, a far from simple profession. It comprised teaching: his own career included teaching law at Harvard and the Massachusetts Institute of Technology, and he took great pains to encourage Frankfurter and others to devote a major part of their life to this mission. A lawyer should be an economist, a statistician, an accountant as well: he should understand the affairs of his clients better than they did themselves and guide them into courses that not merely served short term private interest, but allowed them to perform their true social function in the way most beneficial to all concerned. A lawyer, in fine, should be a public servant: his highest merit was in acting precisely as a public "counsel for the situation," a consultant for the general interest.

It is not very surprising that a man with such pretensions consistently avoided invitations to run for public office. The one occasion on which he fought for a position was the struggle over his appointment to the Supreme Court, and his participation, though active indeed, was strictly private. In Zionism Brandeis fought bitter battles for leadership—but never for his own candidacy. He fought against the plans and persons of others, usually though not always, behind the scenes; in none of these battles did he hold out the prospect that he would himself be available for active leadership if elected.

The reasons for this attitude, which goes far to explain his defeat on several occasions, have been discussed; in addition to the overriding consideration of his Supreme Court seat, other factors vary in importance from case to case. One element not used in explanation by him or others, nevertheless, seems to be everywhere apparent. Brandeis did not want to be a political leader if it meant continual maneuvering and negotiation to maintain that position. He was ready to govern by general consent when plenary powers were conceded to him, for example, in such a situation as the Zionist emergency of World War I. He was even prepared to carry out short, fierce political battles (once elevated to the Court, only behind the scenes), but not to be tied down in the unremitting struggle to survive at the top that political party leadership involved. Weizmann always understood and accepted this necessity. On top of other differences between them, this had much to do both with their clash and the outcome of its successive phases.

Notes

Introduction: Heroes and Their Public

1. Isaiah Berlin, *Chaim Weizmann* (New York, 1958), pp. 2–4.
2. Kurt Lewin, "The Problem of Minority Leadership," in Alvin Gouldner, ed., *Studies in Leadership* (New York, 1950), p. 193.
3. To pose such a problem involves sociological assumptions; cf. the appendix in Ben Halpern, *The Idea of the Jewish State* (Cambridge, Mass., 1961). Conceptions pertinent to the present study derive from Karl Mannheim's *Wissenssoziologie* and from Erik Erikson's psychohistorical work, which are freely adapted to suit the material analyzed here. Further discussion is found in Halpern, "Generational Models and Zionist History," in a forthcoming Festschrift for Shmuel Ettinger.

Weizmann

1. The comprehensive collection of Weizmann's correspondence, *The Letters and Papers of Chaim Weizmann,* 23 vols., ed. Meyer Weisgal et al. (London and Jerusalem, 1968–80), does not cover this period. Cited hereafter as *WL*. Weizmann's autobiography, *Trial and Error* (London, 1949), and his sister Haya Weizmann Lichtenstein's memoirs, *B'Tsel Koratenu* (Tel Aviv, 5713/1952–53) have been used, and I had the good fortune of seeing, in manuscript, chapters of Jehuda Reinharz's thorough study, *Chaim Weizmann: The Making of a Zionist Leader* (New York, 1985).
2. Weizmann, *Trial and Error,* pp. 21f.
3. Ibid. pp. 17, 22, 23.
4. Lichtenstein, *B'Tsel Koratenu,* pp. 13, 33, 71ff.; Weizmann, *Trial and Error,* p. 22.
5. Lichtenstein, *B'Tsel Koratenu,* pp. 44ff., 97ff.
6. Ibid. pp. 69f.
7. Weizmann to Ovsey Lurie, October 5, 1980, *WL* 1, pp. 40f.; Weizmann, *Trial and Error,* p. 25.

8. Sources for this period are *WL* 1 as well as Weizmann's memoirs. A full account may be found in Reinharz, *Chaim Weizmann,* chap. 3.

9. Israel Klausner, *HaT'nua l'Zion b'Russiya,* 3 vols. (Jerusalem, 1962, 1964–65) is a detailed descriptive history of this period. David Vital's projected three-volume study is an analytic history of which *The Origins of Zionism* (Oxford, 1974) and *Zionism: The Formative Years* (Oxford, 1982) have been published to date.

10. On the Bund see *Di Geshikhte fun Bund,* 2 vols. (New York, 1960, 1962) or Henry J. Tobias, *The Jewish Bund in Europe from Its Origins to 1905* (Stanford, Calif., 1972).

11. See Bein's biographical essay in Alex Bein, ed., *Sefer Motzkin* (Jerusalem, 1938).

12. A detailed, discursive account of Austrian Zionism is offered in vol. 1 of N. M. Gelber, *Toldot haT'nua haZionit b'Galitsia,* 2 vols. (Jerusalem, 1958); there is a concise survey in Adolf Böhm, *Die Zionistische Bewegung,* 2 vols. (Tel-Aviv, 1935), vol. 1, pp. 89–95, 135–41.

13. Richard Lichtheim, *Die Geschichte des deutschen Zionismus* (Jerusalem, 1954), pp. 99ff., 110ff.

14. Ibid., pp. 92ff., 112ff.

15. Halpern, *Idea of the Jewish State,* pp. 131–40.

16. See Jacques Kornberg, ed., *At the Crossroads: Essays on Ahad Ha-am* (Albany, 1983); Samuel Tschernowitz, *B'nei Moshe uT'kufatam* (Warsaw, 1914).

17. Weizmann, *Trial and Error,* p. 90.

18. Ibid., pp. 67f.; Lichtenstein, *B'Tsel Koratenu,* p. 98. The nature of Weizmann's discovery in 1897 is not known, but it is probably closely related to the subjects of his subsequent dissertation and later work in Geneva on dyestuffs chemistry. See Louis F. Fieser, "Investigations in Polycyclic Compounds," in Meyer W. Weisgal, ed., *Chaim Weizmann: Statesman, Scientist, Builder of the Jewish Commonwealth* (New York, 1944), pp. 271ff.

19. *The Complete Diaries of Theodor Herzl,* 5 vols. (New York, 1960). vol. 1, pp. 13–24, 407–12.

20. Böhm, *Zionistische Bewegung,* vol. 1, pp. 211–23.

21. Herzl, *Diaries,* vol. 2, p. 581.

22. Saul Raphael Landau, *Sturm und Drang im Zionismus* (Vienna, 1937), pp. 117–46.

23. See Israel Klausner, *Oppozitsia l'Herzl* (Jerusalem, 5720/1959–60).

24. Weizmann to Vera Khatzman, March 19, 1901, *WL* 1, p. 99; Weizmann to Motzkin, November 30, 1901, *WL* 1, p. 212.

25. Weizmann to Vera, July 17, 1901, and August 10, 1902, *WL* 1, pp. 154f., 355; Reinharz, *Chaim Weizmann,* pp. 65ff.

26. Weizmann to [Catherine] Dorfman, July 5, 1901, *WL* 1, pp. 149–52; cf. Reinharz, *Chaim Weizmann,* pp. 72–91.

27. A full account is found in Klausner, *Oppozitsia l'Herzl,* pp. 31ff., 115ff., 141ff.

28. Weizmann to Vera, June 28, 1902, *WL* 1, p. 272; Weizmann to Dorfman and [Anne] Koenigsberg, July 5, 1902, *WL* 1, pp. 282ff.

29. *WL* 2, p. 270–71, n. 10; Weizmann to Marmor, July 25, 1903, *WL* 2, p. 439.

30. Weizmann to Herzl, May 6, 1903, *WL* 2, pp. 301–22, p. 339, n. 3; Martin Buber, *Briefwechsel aus Sieben Jahrzehnten,* 3 vols. (Heidelberg, 1972–73), vol. 1, pp. 195–201; cf. Alex Bein, *Theodor Herzl* (Philadelphia, 1941), pp. 372–75, 405–10.

31. Weizmann to Dorfman, August 11, 1901, *WL* 1, p. 167; see Reinharz, *Chaim Weizmann,* pp. 101ff.

32. Gedalia Yogev, introduction to *WL* 3, p. xxv.

33. Vital, *Zionism: The Formative Years,* p. 305.

34. Weizmann to [Menahem] Ussishkin and others, October 28, 1903, *WL* 3, pp. 81f. The formulations in this letter reflect Ahad Ha'am's views in his famous essay "Slavery Within Freedom" and, more directly, another article originally sent to Buber in April 1902 for publication in a projected issue of *Der Jude* (which failed to appear) and later included by Ahad Ha'am in his collection *Al Parashat Drakhim,* 4 vols. (Berlin, 1921, 1930, vol. 3, pp. 190–93) under the title "Mizrah uMaarav" ("East and West"). The unmistakable literary influence does not, of course, prove any more than Weizmann's tactical use of Ahad Ha'am's formulas.

35. Reinharz, *Chaim Weizmann,* pp. 175–77; Buber, *Briefwechsel,* vol. 1, pp. 201f.; Weizmann to [Abraham] Idelson and [Michael] Kroll, September 6, and to Ussishkin, September 16, 1903, *WL* 3, pp. 1–3, 10–13.

36. Weizmann to Dorfman, October 16, 1903, *WL* 3, pp. 58f.

37. Weizmann to Dorfman, August 4, 1901, *WL* 1, p. 104.

38. Weizmann to Victor Jacobson, November 26, and to Ben Zion Mossinsohn, December 3, 1903, *WL* 3, pp. 140ff., 155; see also bridge note, p. 213.

39. Weizmann to Vera, July 30, and August 12, 1902, *WL* 1, pp. 331ff., 363, n. 1.

40. Weizmann to Gaster, March 22, to Jacobson, April 20, and to Ussishkin, June 21, 1904, *WL* 3, pp. 224, 250, 262.

41. Weizmann to Ussishkin, May 17, and to Buber, June 6, 1904, *WL* 3, pp. 259ff., 261.

42. Weizmann, *Trial and Error,* p. 123; Weizmann to Ussishkin, July 14, 17, and to Vera, July 9, 1904, *WL* 3, pp. 274ff., 280–83, 288–90.

43. See Böhm, *Zionistische Bewegung,* vol. 1, pp. 320ff., 350ff.; Jonathan Frankel, *Prophecy and Politics: Socialism, Nationalism, and the Russian Jews, 1862–1917* (Cambridge, 1981), pp. 134ff.; Vital, *Zionism: The Formative Years,* pp. 383ff.

44. See Elhanan Orren, *Hibbat-Zion biV'ritannia* (Tel-Aviv, 1974), and Stuart A. Cohen, *English Zionists and British Jews* (Princeton, 1982).

45. Weizmann to Ussishkin, July 17, 1904, *WL* 3, pp. 288–90; see Robert G. Weisbord, *African Zion: The Attempt to Establish a Jewish Colony in the East Africa Protectorate, 1903–1905* (Philadelphia, 1968).

46. Weizmann to Vera, July 18, and to Aberson and [Saul] Stupnitzky, July 20, 1904, *WL* 3, pp. 293ff., 296.

47. Weizmann to Ussishkin, November 9, 1904, and March 29, 1905, *WL* 3, p. 359, and *WL* 4, p. 64; Weizmann to Vera, May 18, 20, 1905, *WL* 4, pp. 91–94.

48. See Reinharz, *Chaim Weizmann,* pp. 215ff.

49. Böhm, *Zionistische Bewegung,* vol. 1, pp. 221ff., 307ff.

50. Vital, *Zionism: The Formative Years,* pp. 416ff.

51. Reinharz, *Chaim Weizmann,* pp. 351ff.

52. Weizmann to Ussishkin, July 14, 28, 1904, *WL* 3, pp. 282–85, 305ff.; Reinharz, *Chaim Weizmann,* pp. 239ff.; Ben Halpern, "The Disciple, Chaim Weizmann," in Jacques Kornberg, ed., *At the Crossroads: Essays on Ahad Ha-am* (Albany, 1983).

53. Reinharz, *Chaim Weizmann,* pp. 243ff., 270ff.; Cohen, *English Zionists,* pp. 105–23.

54. Weizmann to Vera, August 24, 1904, *WL* 3, p. 331; June 6, 1905, and April 24, 1906, *WL* 4, pp. 101, 270; Weizmann to Mossinsohn, May 25, 1905, *WL* 4, p. 98; Weizmann to Gaster, February 7, 1907, *WL* 5, p. 16.

55. See Reinharz, *Chaim Weizmann,* pp. 290ff., 319ff., 330ff.; Weizmann to Wolffsohn, February 9, 1909, *WL* 5, pp. 97f.

56. Louis Lipsky, *Memoirs in Profile* (Philadelphia, 1975), p. 103.

57. Reinharz, *Chaim Weizmann,* pp. 327ff, 334ff.; Halpern, *Idea of the Jewish State,* pp. 264ff.; Mordecai Eliav, *David Wolffsohn, ha'Ish uZ'mano* (Jerusalem, 1977), chaps. 7, 10.

58. Reinharz, *Chaim Weizmann,* pp. 327ff., 334ff.; cf. Eliav, *David Wolffsohn,* pp. 255ff., 260ff.; Weizmann to Wolffsohn, February 17, 1910, *WL* 5, pp. 181ff.

59. See Jehuda Reinharz, ed., *Dokumente zur Geschichte des deutschen Zionismus, 1882-1933* (Tübingen, 1981), pp. 87–96; and Weizmann to Elkan Adler, to Ussishkin, to Gaster, to Sokolow, February 20, 1910, *WL* 5, pp. 189–95; Buber, *Briefwechsel,* vol. 1, pp. 296f.

60. Reinharz, *Chaim Weizmann,* pp. 289ff., 305ff.

61. Cohen, *English Zionists,* pp. 105–23; Weizmann, *Trial and Error,* pp. 149ff., 169ff.

62. Weizmann to Otto Warburg, December 3, 1908, *WL* 5, pp. 91, 93; *WL* 5, pp. xviii, xxff.; cf. Reinharz, *Chaim Weizmann,* pp. 302f., 311ff.

63. This episode is fully discussed in Reinharz, *Chaim Weizmann,* chap. 15.

64. Weizmann to Vera, January 28, 29, 1913, *WL* 5, pp. 362, 366.

65. Weizmann to Sacher, January 9, 1913, *WL* 5, p. 342; Weizmann to Norah Schuster, March 3, 1913, *WL* 6, p. 5.

66. A full account in Reinharz, *Chaim Weizmann,* chap. 16; cf. Joseph Schechtman, *Rebel and Statesman: The Vladimir Jabotinsky Story* (New York, 1956), chap. 1.

67. Weizmann to Julius Becker, July 6, 1913, *WL* 6, p. 110.

68. Weizmann to Julius Simon, July 27, 1913, *WL* 6, pp. 121f.

69. See Moshe Rinott, "Histadrut haMorim, haT'nua haZionit, vehaMa'avak al haHegmoniya baHinukh b'Erets-Israel, (1903–1918)," in *HaZionut,* 4 (5736/1975–76), pp. 114–45.

70. Weizmann to Magnes, April 19, and August 4, 1913, *WL* 6, pp. 40ff., 128; Magnes to Weizmann, May 23, 1913, in Arthur Goren, ed., *Dissenter in Zion* (Cambridge, Mass., 1982), pp. 136–38.

71. Weizmann to Vera, January 3, 1914, *WL* 6, p. 193; Weizmann to Magnes, January 12, 1914, *WL* 6, pp. 197–202.

Brandeis

1. Of the early biographies, only Jacob de Haas, *Louis D. Brandeis, a Biographical Sketch with Special Reference to His Contributions to Jewish and Zionist History* (New York, 1929) treats extensively Brandeis' Jewish activities and includes full texts of Zionist statements from 1912 to 1924. Alfred Lief, *Brandeis: The Personal History of an American Ideal* (Harrisburg, 1936) has scattered references to Jewish matters, relying on de Haas' occasionally inaccurate recollection. Alpheus T. Mason's *Brandeis: A Free Man's Life* (New York, 1946), still the major full biography, devotes one chapter on Zionism (out of forty-five in his book) to Brandeis' Jewish concerns. Of the numerous Brandeis studies that have appeared recently, Allon Gal's *Brandeis of Boston* (Cambridge, Mass., 1980) is a major source for understanding Brandeis' Jewish contacts in the pre-Zionist years. On the family background the prime source is *Reminiscences of Frederika Dembitz Brandeis.* These letters written to Brandeis by his mother from December 1880 to December 1886 were translated by his wife, Alice Goldmark Brandeis in 1943 (after his death) and privately printed. Accounts of family history in

Josephine Goldmark, *Pilgrims of '48* (New Haven, 1930) rely on the same source and on other family correspondence and records, as does Mason's biography.

2. Gerschom Scholem, "A Sabbathaian Will from New York," in Jewish Historical Society of England, *Miscellanies,* Part 5 (1948), pp. 193–211; Goldmark, *Pilgrims,* pp. 191–94; Frederika Brandeis, *Reminiscences,* pp. 3ff.

3. Frederika Brandeis, *Reminiscences,* pp. 4, 9–12.

4. Ibid., pp. 22, 32–34.

5. Ibid., p. 47.

6. Ibid., p. 15; "Sabbathaian Will," *Miscellanies,* Part 5, pp. 200, 202.

7. Mason, *Brandeis,* pp. 23ff., 48ff.

8. See Stephen G. Mostov, "A 'Jerusalem' on the Ohio: The Social and Economic History of Cincinnati, 1840–1875," diss., Brandeis University, 1981.

9. Mason, *Brandeis,* pp. 18–28; Goldmark, *Pilgrims,* pp. 198–242.

10. See George R. Leighton, *Five Cities* (New York, 1939), chap. 2.

11. Ernest Poole, "Brandeis," foreword to Louis D. Brandeis, *Business—A Profession* (Boston, 1933), p. xi.

12. Quoted in Mason, *Brandeis,* p. 1.

13. Brandeis to Warren, May 30, 1879, quoted in Mason, *Brandeis,* p. 54ff. I am indebted to the library of Harvard Law School for access to the full correspondence in the Felix Frankfurter collection.

14. Accounts from different perspectives are Mason, *Brandeis,* pp. 33–47 (the most comprehensive); Allon Gal, *Brandeis of Boston,* pp. 5–11; Philippa Strum, *Louis D. Brandeis: Justice for the People* (Cambridge, Mass., 1984), pp. 15–23. I am indebted to Radcliffe College for access to the papers of Elizabeth Glendower Evans in the Arthur Schlesinger collection.

15. Gal, *Brandeis of Boston,* pp. 9, 13f. (on Brandeis' partners, Dunbar and Nutter), 17f., 21, 25, 91, 153f.

16. Ibid., pp. 11ff., 15–20.

17. Brandeis to [George W.] Anderson, March 6, 1916, in Melvin I. Urofsky and David W. Levy, eds., *Letters of Louis D. Brandeis,* 5 vols. (Albany, 1971–78), vol. 4, pp. 104ff. Cited hereafter as *BL.* Louis D. Brandeis, *Business—A Profession,* pp. 5ff., 9ff.

18. Mason, *Brandeis,* pp. 86ff.; see Samuel J. Kanofsky, *The Legacy of Holmes and Brandeis* (New York, 1956).

19. Gal, *Brandeis of Boston,* passim; Mason, *Brandeis,* pp. 99–106.

20. Lief, *Brandeis,* pp. 31ff.; Gal, *Brandeis of Boston,* chap. 2.

21. Claude M. Fuess, *Joseph B. Eastman, Servant of the People* (New York, 1952), chaps. 4, 5; Strum, *Brandeis,* pp. 396f.

22. See Alden L. Todd, *Justice on Trial: The Case of Louis D. Brandeis* (New York, 1964); Irving Katz, "Henry Lee Higginson vs. Louis Dembitz Brandeis: A Collision Between Tradition and Reform," *New England Quarterly,* 41 (1968), pp. 67–81.

23. Gal, *Brandeis of Boston,* pp. 198–201.

24. Brandeis to Alfred [Brandeis], August 19, 1909, *BL* vol. 2, p. 288; New York State, *4th Report of the Factory Investigating Commission, 1915* (Albany, 1915), vol. 5, pp. 2895–96. Brandeis' testimony at the New York hearings was brought to my attention by the late Andrew Reutlinger, whose tragic death in early youth cut off a life of high promise.

25. Mason, *Brandeis,* pp. 245–51.

26. See Benny Kraut, *From Reform Judaism to Ethical Culture: The Religious Evolution of Felix Adler* (Cincinnati, 1979).

27. A concise survey is found in Lloyd P. Gartner, "Immigration and the Formation of American Jewry, 1840–1925," in H. H. Ben-Sasson and S. Ettinger, eds., *Jewish Society Through the Ages* (New York, 1971), pp. 267–83.

28. Moshe Davis, "Jewish Religious Life and Institutions in America, . . . " in Louis Finkelstein, ed., *The Jews: Their History, Culture and Religion,* 2 vols. (Philadelphia, 1949), vol. 1, pp. 361–414; cf. Marshall Sklare, *Conservative Judaism: An American Religious Movement* (Glencoe, Ill., 1955); and Leon A. Jick, *The Americanization of the Synagogue, 1820–1870* (Hanover, N.H., 1976).

29. C. Bezalel Sherman, *The Jew Within American Society: A Study in Ethnic Individuality* (Detroit, 1961), chaps. 3, 4; Moses Rischin, *The Promised City: New York's Jews, 1870–1914* (Cambridge, Mass., 1967), pp. 51–75, 95ff.

30. Rischin, *Promised City,* pp. 103ff.; Judah J. Shapiro, *The Friendly Society: A History of the Workmen's Circle* (New York, 1970), pp. 11–59.

31. Rischin, *Promised City,* pp. 38–47; Ronald Sanders, *The Downtown Jews: Portrait of an Immigrant Generation* (New York, 1969), chaps. 4, 5.

32. Robert Morris and Michael Freund, eds., *Trends and Issues in Jewish Social Welfare in the United States, 1899–1958* (Philadelphia, 1968), pp. 113–29.

33. See Marnin Feinstein, *American Zionism, 1884–1904* (New York, 1965); and Julius Haber, *The Odyssey of an American Zionist* (New York, 1956).

34. Melvin I. Urofsky, *American Zionism from Herzl to the Holocaust* (New York, 1975), pp. 85–113; cf. Yonathan Shapiro, *Leadership of the American Zionist Organization, 1897–1930* (Urbana, 1971), chap. 2; and Evyatar Friesel, *HaT'nua haZionit b'Artsot-haBrit baShanim 1897–1914* (Tel-Aviv, 1970), pp. 49–51.

35. See David Polish, *Renew Our Days: The Zionist Issue in Reform Judaism* (Jerusalem, 1976); and Kraut, *From Reform Judaism to Ethical Culture,* pp. 135–68.

36. Friesel, *HaT'nua haZionit,* pp. 95–108.

37. Ibid., pp. 77–89; cf. Y. Shapiro, *Leadership,* pp. 37–46.

38. Friesel, *HaT'nua haZionit,* pp. 77–82, 84ff., 209f.

39. See the exchange between Friesel and Urofsky in *American Jewish History,* 75, 2 (December 1985), pp. 130–48, 159–64, 175–83.

40. Arthur A. Goren, *New York Jews and the Quest for Community: The Kehillah Experiment, 1908–1922* (New York, 1970).

41. Urofsky, *American Zionism,* pp. 87ff., 100ff., 105ff.

42. Agreement on this point among recent writers does not preclude opposing specific formulations: cf. Urofsky, *American Zionism* and *A Mind of One Piece: Brandeis and American Reform* (New York, 1971); Gal, *Brandeis of Boston;* and Strum, *Louis D. Brandeis.*

43. Mason, *Brandeis,* p. 32; see Louis Harap, *The Image of the Jew in American Literature* (Philadelphia, 1974); and Ronald Steel, *Walter Lippmann and the American Century* (Boston, 1980).

44. Brandeis to Alfred, July 28, 1904, *BL* 1, p. 262.

45. Brandeis to Adolph [Brandeis], November 29, 1905, *BL* 1, p. 386.

46. Gal, *Brandeis of Boston,* pp. 75–77; Brandeis to Adolph, July 11, 20, and August 29, 1905, *BL* 1, pp. 336, 338, 354f.

47. Gal, *Brandeis of Boston,* pp. 77–79, 85–95.

48. Mason, *Brandeis,* chap. 19; cf. Melech Epstein, *Jewish Labor in USA: An Industrial, Political and Cultural History of the Jewish Labor Movement,* 2 vols. (New York, 1950, 1953), vol. 1, chap. 22; vol. 2, chaps. 2, 3.

49. Mason, *Brandeis,* p. 308.

50. Gal, *Brandeis of Boston,* pp. 88, 119.

51. Ibid., pp. 128–38.

52. *Boston Post,* July 4, 1915, "Clippings 2," in the collection of Brandeis Papers at the University of Louisville, to whose law library I am indebted for access to this source.

53. Cyrus Adler to Herbert Friedenwald, April 7, 1911, Cyrus Adler Papers, American Jewish Committee Archives. I am indebted to Naomi W. Cohen and the AJC archivists for this reference.

54. See quotations and discussion in Gal, *Brandeis of Boston,* pp. 162–68.

55. Ibid., pp. 201–3.

56. Lief, *Brandeis,* p. 278; cf. Gal, *Brandeis of Boston,* pp. 178ff.

57. Gal, *Brandeis of Boston,* pp. 150–62.

58. The account in de Haas, *Louis D. Brandeis,* pp. 52–53, is critically examined in Gal, *Brandeis of Boston,* p. 257, n. 98.

59. Strum, *Louis D. Brandeis,* pp. 140, 145ff.; Brandeis to [Robert] LaFollette, July 29, 1911, and to [Woodrow] Wilson, September 12, 1912 ("Suggestions . . . "), *BL* 2, pp. 467–72, 688, 692ff.

60. Todd, *Justice on Trial;* cf. the provocative, if doctrinaire, analysis in Y. Shapiro, *Leadership,* pp. 61–68. I am indebted to the Sterling Library, Yale University, for quotations from the Colonel House Papers, including phrases elided in Charles Seymour, ed., *The Intimate Papers of Colonel House,* 4 vols. (Boston, 1926–28), vol. 1, p. 91.

61. Brandeis to Sokolow, August 1, 1913, and to [Israel] Friedlaender, June 25, 1915, *BL* 3, pp. 158ff., 541; Ahad Ha'am to Brandeis, October 3, 1917, *Igrot Ahad Ha'am* (Jerusalem and Berlin, 5684/1923–24), vol. 5, p. 317.

Wartime Leadership

1. Manifesto of August 31, 1914, *BL* 3, pp. 291ff.

2. Brandeis to Marshall, August 31, 1914, *BL* 3, pp. 293ff.

3. Leonard Stein, *The Balfour Declaration* (New York, 1961), chap. 4.

4. Cf. accounts of Urofsky, *American Zionism,* pp. 168–71 and Naomi W. Cohen, *Not Free to Desist: A History of the American Jewish Committee* (Philadelphia, 1971), pp. 85ff.; Y. Shapiro, *Leadership,* pp. 78–80; and de Haas, *Louis Dembitz Brandeis,* pp. 71–74.

5. Brandeis to [Judah] Magnes, September 14, to [Benjamin] Perlstein, September 18, to [Richard] Gottheil, October 5, 1914, and January 14, 1915, *BL* 3, pp. 296, 298, 312, 404. Cf. Mason, *Brandeis,* pp. 443–45; Strum, *Louis D. Brandeis,* pp. 248ff.; and Urofsky, *American Zionism,* p. 120f.

6. Brandeis to Lipsky, October 5, 1914, January 18, 1915; and to [Horace] Kallen, January 14, 25, and February 10, 23, 1915, *BL* 3, pp. 316ff., 405, 408ff., 415, 426ff., 441ff.

7. Brandeis to Nathan Kaplan, October 5, 1914, and to [Richard] Gottheil, June 22, July 28, 1915, *BL* 3, pp. 314, 538f., 555; Irma Lindheim, *Parallel Quest: In Search of a Person and a People* (New York, 1962), pp. 51–57, 73–76, 81–89.

8. Zosa Szajkowski, "Concord and Discord in American Jewish Overseas Relief, 1914–1924," *YIVO Annual of Jewish Social Science,* 14 (1969), pp. 99–158.

9. Jerome M. Kutnick, "Non-Zionist Leadership: Felix M. Warburg, 1929–1937," diss., Brandeis University 1983, chaps. 2, 3.

10. Brandeis to Otto Warburg, April 6, 1916, *BL* 4, pp. 154ff.

11. The fullest discussion, though from a particular vantage point, is Jonathan Frankel, "The Jewish Socialists and the American Jewish Congress Movement," *YIVO Annual,* 16 (1976), pp. 202–339. Cf. N. W. Cohen, *Not Free to Desist,* pp. 90–98; and Urofsky, *American Zionism,* chap. 5.

12. Deborah Lipstadt, "The Zionist Career of Louis Lipsky, 1900–1921," diss., Brandeis University, 1977, pp. 206–16.

13. Brandeis to Adler, July 27, and to [Adolf] Kraus, August 25, 1915, *BL* 3, pp. 551–54, 570ff.; Adler to Brandeis, August 3, 1915, *Cyrus Adler, Selected Letters,* 2 vols. (Philadelphia, 1985), vol. 1, pp. 276–84.

14. Frankel, "Jewish Socialists," *YIVO Annual,* 16, pp. 227ff., 240–44.

15. Adler to [Solomon] Schechter, October 11, 15, and to [Jacob] Schiff, November 19, 1915, *Cyrus Adler, Selected Letters,* vol. 1, 290ff., 296f.; Brandeis to B[ernard] G. Richards, November 16, 1915, *BL* 3, pp. 634ff.; Frankel, "Jewish Socialists," *YIVO Annual,* 16, pp. 247–54.

16. See the correspondence with [Edward] McClennen and other aides in the winter of 1916, *BL* 4, passim; Brandeis to [Gifford] Pinchot, June 27, to Chief Justice [Edward D.] White, June 29, and to [Jacob] de Haas, July 5, 1916, *BL* 4, pp. 239, 241ff., 244–47; Urofsky, *Mind of One Piece,* chap. 6.

17. Frankel, "Jewish Socialists," *YIVO Annual,* 16, pp. 263–66.

18. Ibid., pp. 269–71.

19. Ibid., pp. 274–78; cf. Urofsky, *American Zionism,* pp. 176–94; and Y. Shapiro, *Leadership,* pp. 80–98.

20. Frankel, "Jewish Socialists," *YIVO Annual,* 16, pp. 279–85.

21. Brandeis to Hugo Pam, July 21, and to Marshall, September 8, 1916, *BL* 4, pp. 250–62; Brandeis to [Julian] Mack, December 9, 1919, *BL* 4, pp. 442; Brandeis to Alice [Goldmark Brandeis], December 4, 1918, *BL* 4, p. 370.

22. Brandeis to Alfred [Brandeis], March 27, April 18, 1910, April 20, 1912, and October 21, 1914, *BL* 2, pp. 327, 333, 611; 3, p. 334; Brandeis to Charles Nagel, July 12, 1879, *BL* 1, p. 37.

23. Ahad Ha'am to Weizmann, November 15, 1914, *Igrot Ahad Ha'am,* 5, pp. 202ff.

24. S. Cohen, *English Zionists,* chaps. 2, 4, 6.

25. See note 23 above; Ronald Sanders, *The High Walls of Jerusalem: A History of the Balfour Declaration and the Birth of the British Mandate for Palestine* (New York, 1983), pp. 471–83.

26. Regarding Zangwill: Weizmann to Shmarya Levin, September 8, to Magnes, September 8, to Ahad Ha'am, September 14, 16, to Zangwill, October 19, to J. Cowen, November 10, to [David] Jochelman, November 15–16, to Zangwill, November 20, to [Harry] Sacher and Leon Simon, December 3, 4, 1914, *WL* 7, pp. 2–8, 25–28, 34, 39ff., 47ff., 67–70. Regarding Lucien Wolf: S. Cohen, *English Zionists,* pp. 223–30.

27. W. N. Medlicott, *Contemporary England, 1914–1964* (New York, 1967), pp. 11–36; Stein, *Balfour Declaration,* chap. 2; Elizabeth Monroe, *Britain's Moment in the Middle East* (Baltimore, 1963), pp. 23–37.

28. Charles K. Webster, *The Art of Diplomacy* (London, 1961), chap. 7.

29. Julia Namier, *Lewis Namier: A Biography* (London, 1971), pp. 204ff.

30. Regarding Rothschilds: Weizmann to Dorothy de Rothschild, November 22, 1914, *WL* 7, pp. 218ff.; regarding Milner et al.: Weizmann to [Alfred] Zimmern, July 4, 1915, *WL* 7, pp. 218ff. See John E. Kendle, *The Round Table Movement and Imperial Union* (Toronto, 1976); Sanders, *High Walls,* pp. 288ff., 375ff.

31. Sanders, *High Walls,* chap. 7.

32. Weizmann to Scott, February 16, 1915, and March 23, 1915, *WL* 7, pp. 153–55, 183–85.

33. Vladimir Jabotinsky, *The Story of the Jewish Legion* (New York, 1945), pp. 48–51.

34. Jehuda Reinharz, "Science in the Service of Politics: the Case of Chaim Weizmann During the First World War," *English Historical Review,* 100, 396 (July 1985), pp. 572–603.

35. Sanders, *High Walls,* pp. 192–96, 284–88, 291–92, 294–300.

36. Weizmann to Ahad Ha'am, September 28, and November 1, to Shlomo Ginzberg, December 17, 1914, *WL* 7, pp. 13, 31, 91; Jacob Yaari-Poleskin, *Pinhas Rutenberg, ha'Ish uFo'alo* (Tel-Aviv, 5699/1938–39).

37. Jabotinsky, *Jewish Legion,* pp. 29–45; Yigal Elam, *HaG'dudim ha'Ivri'im b'Milhemet ha'Olam haRishona* (Tel-Aviv, 1973), pp. 11–33; Isaiah Friedman, *The Question of Palestine, 1914–1918: British-Jewish-Arab Relations* (New York, 1973), chaps. 1, 2.

38. Jabotinsky, *Jewish Legion,* p. 60.

39. Yoram Efrati, ed., *Yoman Aaron Aaronsohn* (Tel-Aviv, 1970), pp. 101–113, 118–136. See Eliezer Livneh, *Aaron Aaronsohn: ha'Ish uZ'mano* (Jerusalem, 1969).

40. The extensive literature on the ensuing agreements is critically covered and largely superseded by Elie Kedourie, *In the Anglo-Arab Labyrinth: The McMahon-Husayn Correspondence and Its Interpretations, 1914–1939* (London, 1976).

41. Elie Kedourie, *The Chatham House Version and Other Middle-Eastern Studies* (London, 1970), p. 17; Kedourie, *Anglo-Arab Labyrinth,* pp. 23–31, 66–68, 91–97.

42. Elam, *HaG'dudim,* pp. 121ff.

43. Nahum Sokolow, *History of Zionism, 1600–1918,* 2 vols. in one (New York, 1969); Weizmann, *Trial and Error,* pp. 197ff., 223–28; Jabotinsky, *Jewish Legion,* pp. 46ff., 73ff.

44. Sanders, *High Walls,* pp. 333–336; Elam, *HaG'dudim,* chap. 13.

45. Stein, *Balfour Declaration,* pp. 200–205, 218ff.; Sanders, *High Walls,* pp. 325–331.

46. Friedman, *Question of Palestine,* p. 53ff.

47. Sanders, *High Walls,* p. 338.

48. Stein, *Balfour Declaration,* pp. 223ff.; Friedman, *Question of Palestine,* pp. 110–18.

49. Sanders, *High Walls,* pp. 429–33; Simon Schama, *Two Rothschilds and the Land of Israel* (New York, 1978), pp. 200–04; Weizmann to [Lucien] Wolf, September 3, to Dorothy de Rothschild, September 21, to James de Rothschild, October 15, 17, 30, and November 5, 1916, *WL* 7, pp. 291ff., 297ff., 303–12.

50. Elam, *HaG'dudim,* chaps. 13, 14.

51. Ibid., pp. 113 ff.

52. See Christopher Sykes, *Two Studies in Virtue* (New York, 1953), pp. 173ff., for an intimate sketch, which is occasionally inaccurate in detail.

53. Sanders, *High Walls,* chap. 25.

54. See Stein, *Balfour Declaration,* chap. 24.

55. Weizmann to Sykes, February 15, to Sokolow, February 16, 18, to [Samuel] Tolkowsky, February 28, to Scott, March 20, and to Sokolow, April 27, 1917, *WL* 7, pp. 329–31, 335, 343ff., 384f.

56. Sanders, *High Walls,* p. 497.

57. Ibid., pp. 551–56; for a parallel approach to the Germans reported to Weizmann at the time, see Samuel Tolkowsky, *Yoman Zioni M'dini, London, 1915–1919*

(Jerusalem, 1981), July 9, 1917 entry, pp. 103ff. Tolkowsky's journal contains the fullest available record of Zionist proceedings in London in the war years.

58. Zosa Szajkowski, *Jews, Wars, and Communism,* 2 vols. (New York, 1972, 1974), vol. 1, chaps. 2, 4, 12.

59. Brandeis to [Richard] Gottheil, October 27, 1914, and January 1, 1915, and to Stephen Wise, January 13, 1915, *BL* 3, pp. 339f., 400f., 403.

60. Brandeis to [Louis] Lipsky, April 26, 1916, microfilm copy of Zionist correspondence in Brandeis Papers (University of Louisville Law Library), deposited at Zionist Archives and Library, New York, and at Goldfarb Library, Brandeis University. Hereafter cited as *BPm.* Brandeis to Blackstone, May 22, 1916, *BL* 4, p. 196.

61. Seymour, *Intimate Papers of Colonel House,* vol. 1, pp. 25–28, 31, 40ff., et passim; cf. House's anonymously published novel, *Philip Dru, Administrator: A Story of Tomorrow, 1920–1935* (New York, 1911).

62. See Joseph L. Grabill, *Protestant Diplomacy and the Near East: Missionary Influence on American Policy, 1810–1927* (Minneapolis, 1971); also John A. DeNovo, *American Interests and Policies in the Middle East, 1900–1939* (Minneapolis, 1963), chaps. 1–5.

63. See Leo J. Bocage, "The Public Career of Charles R. Crane," diss., Fordham University, 1962; also Samuel N. Harper, *The Russia I Believe In: The Memoirs of Samuel N. Harper, 1902–1941* (Chicago, 1945), chaps. 1, 2.

64. Henry Morgenthau, *All in a Lifetime* (New York, 1922), pp. 175ff.; Grabill, *Protestant Diplomacy,* p. 74.

65. Szajkowski, *Jews, War,and Communism,* vol. 1, pp. 22–33, 258–82; Colonel House Papers: *Journals,* April 9, 14, 16, and 17, 1917; *Letters,* House to Wilson, October 3, 1917. See also Lawrence Gelfand, *The Inquiry: American Preparations for Peace, 1917–1919* (New Haven, 1963); Frank E. Manuel, *Realities of American-Palestine Relations* (Washington, D.C., 1949), 211–15.

66. Grabill, *Protestant Diplomacy,* pp. 89ff., 94ff., 99ff., 102ff.; James L. Barton, "The War and the Mohammedan World," *Biblical Review,* 4 (January 1919), pp. 28–46.

67. Ben Halpern, "Brandeis and the Origins of the Balfour Declaration," *Studies in Zionism,* 7 (Spring, 1983), pp. 71–100.

68. Memorandum by de Haas of Brandeis' report by telephone of his May 6, 1917, interview with Wilson, in the de Haas Papers; microfilm copy in Goldfarb Library, Brandeis University, courtesy of the Zionist Archives and Library, New York.

69. Brandeis to Alice [Goldmark Brandeis], June 5, and to de Haas, June 7, 1917, *BL* 4, pp. 295, 296f.

70. Stein, *Balfour Declaration,* pp. 394–465; cf. S. Cohen, *English Zionists,* pp. 231–76.

71. Stein, *Balfour Declaration,* pp. 464–72; cf. Tolkowsky, *Yoman Zioni M'dini,* pp. 111–34.

72. Sanders, *High Walls,* pp. 560–77.

73. Elam, *HaG'dudim,* pp. 127–35, 138–40.

74. Gibraltar Conference report, July 6, 1917; Weizmann to Vera, July 8,1917, *WL* 7, 465–70.

75. Ahad Ha'am to Weizmann, September 5, 1917, *Igrot Ahad Ha'am,* vol. 5, pp. 315–17.

76. Sanders, *High Walls,* pp. 573–77.

77. See Ben Halpern, "Drafting of Balfour Declaration," *Herzl Year Book,* 7, p. 273f.

78. Halpern, "Brandeis and Origins of Balfour Declaration," *Studies in Zionism,* 7, (Spring 1983), pp. 91f.

79. Sanders, *High Walls,* pp. 578–80; Weizmann to Sacher, September 18, to [Philip] Kerr, September 19, to Scott, September 20, to Tolkowsky, September 21, and to Sokolow, September 30, 1917, *WL* 7, pp. 513–20.

80. Weizmann to de Haas and [Elias W.] Lewin-Epstein, September 30, 1917, *WL* 7, pp. 516f.

81. Colonel House Papers, *Journals,* September 21, 23, 1917.

82. Halpern, "Brandeis and Origins of Balfour Declaration," *Studies in Zionism,* 7 (Spring 1983), pp. 95f.; Brandeis to Stephen Wise, October 6, 1917, *BL* 4, p. 313.

83. Weizmann to Brandeis, October 9, to Herbert Samuel, October 10, to Percy Marks, October 11, to [Maurice] Hankey, October 15, and to [Gaston] Wormser, October 16, 1917, *WL* 7, pp. 530–36.

84. Halpern, "Brandeis and Origins of Balfour Declaration," *Studies in Zionism,* 7 (Spring 1983), pp. 96–99.

85. Weizmann, *Trial and Error,* pp. 260–62.

Encounter and Clash

1. Stein, *Balfour Declaration,* chaps. 38, 39; Sokolow, *History of Zionism,* vol. 2, pp. 83–129.

2. Tolkowsky, *Yoman Zioni M'dini,* January 8, and June 4, 6, 1917, pp. 24, 101ff. et passim.

3. Ibid., November 2, 3, 6, 1917, pp. 193–210.

4. Eliezer Livneh, *Aaron Aaronsohn, ha'Ish uZ'mano,* pp. 230–49, 257–60, 274–84.

5. Doreen Ingrams, *Palestine Papers, 1917–1922: Seeds of Conflict* (New York, 1973), pp. 20–22; Tolkowsky, *Yoman Zioni M'dini,* August 26, 28, November 6, 1917, pp. 159–61, 210.

6. Tolkowsky, *Yoman Zioni M'dini,* November 16, 1917, pp. 216f.

7. Ibid., November 22, 26, 27, 1917, pp. 222, 227, 236ff.

8. Evyatar Friesel, *HaM'diniut haZionit l'ahar Hats'harat Balfour, 1917–1922* (Tel-Aviv, 1977), pp. 36–39, 419–23.

9. Ingrams, *Palestine Papers,* pp. 23–51; Friesel, *HaM'diniut haZionit,* pp. 45–56; Weizmann, *Trial and Error,* chap. 19.

10. Weizmann, *Trial and Error,* pp. 39–42, chap. 20. See Menachem Friedman, *Hevra v'Dat: ha'Orthodoxia haLo-Zionit b'Erets-Israel, 1918–1936* (Jerusalem, 5738/1977–78), chap. 1.

11. Weizmann to Brandeis, January 14, to Colonel [John] French, February 8, to [Nahŭm] Sokolow, April 18, and July 30, 1918, *WL* 8, pp. 51, 79–80, 141, 243–44.

12. Weizmann to Balfour, May 30, and July 17, to Brandeis, July 12, 17, to Sokolow, June 23, and July 29, 1918, *WL* 8, pp. 197–203, 214–15, 225, 230–32, 241.

13. See Weizmann to Vera, July 11, 1918, *WL* 8, pp. 222–24; cf. Manuel, *The Realities of American-Palestine Relations,* pp. 191ff.

14. Weizmann to Balfour, May 30, 1918, *WL* 8, p. 206.

15. Weizmann to Vera, August 24, 1918, *WL* 8, pp. 262–64.

16. Oscar L. Janowsky, *The Jews and Minority Rights, 1898–1919* (New York, 1933), chaps. 1, 2; cf. Jacob Stoyanovsky, *The Mandate for Palestine: A Contribution to the Theory and Practice of International Mandates* (London, 1928), chap. 1.

17. Urofsky, *American Zionism*, pp. 213–18; S. Cohen, *English Zionists*, pp. 243–60; Jukka Nevakivi, *Britain, France and the Arab Middle East, 1914–1920* (London, 1969), pp. 52ff.

18. Janowsky, *Minority Rights*, pt. 2; N. W. Cohen, *Not Free to Desist*, pp. 112–19; Tolkowsky, *Yoman Zioni M'dini*, February 11, 1919, pp. 410–12; Nathan Feinberg, *La Question des minorités à la conférence de la paix de 1919–1920 et l'action juive en faveur de la protection internationale des minorités* (Paris, 1929).

19. Tolkowsky, *Yoman Zioni M'dini*, November 2, 3, 6, 1917, pp. 195, 197f., 204, 207.

20. Friesel, *HaM'diniut haZionit*, p. 63f.; Weizmann to [William] Ormsby-Gore, November 15, 1918, *WL* 9, pp. 24f.

21. Friesel, *HaM'diniut haZionit*, pp. 64ff.

22. Ibid., pp. 65–67.

23. Ingrams, *Palestine Papers*, chaps. 3, 4.

24. Weizmann to Vera, March 27, April 24, and May 7, 1918, *WL* 8, pp. 112f., 155f., 179; Weizmann to [David] Eder, September 14, and October 3, 1918, *WL* 8, pp. 270–71, 275; Weizmann to Vera, February 28, 1919, *WL* 9, pp. 116–18.

25. Friesel, *HaM'diniut haZionit*, pp. 72–77; Esco Foundation for Palestine, *Palestine: A Study of Jewish, Arab, and British Policies*, 2 vols. (New Haven, 1947), vol. 1, pp. 151–59.

26. Janowsky, *Minority Rights*, pp. 272–73; Moshe Atias, ed., *Sefer haT'udot shel haVa'ad haL'umi l'Knesset Israel b'Erets-Israel, 1918–1948* (Jerusalem, 1963), pp. 7–11.

27. See de Haas, *Louis Dembitz Brandeis*, pp. 94–109, cf. Weizmann, *Trial and Error*, pp. 300–11.

28. Friesel, *HaM'diniut haZionit*, pp. 78–79, app. 2, pp. 424ff.

29. Esco, *Palestine*, vol. 1, pp. 164–77.

30. Urofsky, *American Zionism*, pp. 164–77.

31. Brandeis to Alice [Goldmark Brandeis], June 5, to de Haas, May 4, 8, June 13, 26, and October 17, 1917, *BL* 4, pp. 286, 290, 295, 301, 319.

32. Manuel, *Realities of American-Palestine Relations*, pp. 211–18; Grabill, *Protestant Diplomacy*, pp. 102–4 et passim.

33. Weizmann to Vera, July 11, 1918, *WL* 8, p. 223; Boris D. Bogen, *Born a Jew* (New York, 1930).

34. Urofsky, *American Zionism*, pp. 234–36; cf. Manuel, *Realities of American-Palestine Relations*, pp. 233–44.

35. See Harry N. Howard, *The King-Crane Commission* (Beirut, 1963).

36. Weizmann to [Sir Eric] Drummond, to House, April 14, to [Julius] Simon, March 27, May 5, 19, 23, 26, and June 2, 1919, *WL* 9, pp. 125, 136–37, 139, 144–46, 148f.

37. Howard, *King-Crane Commission*, chaps. 2–4, pp. 221ff., 256ff.

38. Brandeis to Frankfurter, June 5, 9, and to Alice [Goldmark Brandeis], August 1, 8, 15, 1919, *BL* 4, pp. 396, 397, 420–22.

39. Lipstadt, "Lipsky," pp. 260–63; cf. Shapiro, *Leadership*, chap. 5, and Urofsky, *American Zionism*, pp. 158–61.

40. The protocols of the meetings in London have been published in Hebrew translation (Menahem Dorman, tr.): Yehoshua Freundlich and Gedalia Yogev, eds., *HaProtocolim shel haVa'ad haPo'el haZioni, 1919–1929*, vol. 1, February 1919–January 1920 (Tel-Aviv, 1975). For an English edition covering the period 1903–5, with documents in the original languages, see *The Uganda Controversy*, ed. Michael Heymann (Jerusalem, 1970, 1977), vols. 1 and 2.

41. Nahum Gross, *Nisyonot l'Tikhnun Calcali Zioni: haV'ada haM'ya'etset shel 1919 b'Roshut Herbert Samuel* (discussion paper of the Maurice Falk Foundation for Economic Research in Israel [Jerusalem, 1976]).

42. See Weizmann to Bella Berligne, August 15, 17–19, and to Eder, August 17, 1919, *WL* 9, pp. 195–202.

43. Freundlich and Yogev, *HaProtocolim,* pp. 44, 294ff.

44. Weizmann to Tschlenow, September 1, 1917, *WL* 7, p. 498; Freundlich and Yogev, *HaProtocolim,* pp. 174–75 (on Jacobson); p. 177 (on Frankfurter).

45. Ibid., p. 173.

46. Ibid., pp. 178–81; see Friesel, *HaM'diniut haZionit,* pp. 89–96, and Julius Simon, *Certain Days: Zionist Memoirs and Selected Papers* (Jerusalem, 1971), pp. 93–95.

47. Freundlich and Yogev, *HaProtocolim,* pp. 181–83.

48. Alex Bein, *Return to the Soil* (Jerusalem, 1952), pp. 227–42; Moshe Braslawsky, *T'nuat haPo'alim haErets-Israelit,* 4 vols. (Tel-Aviv, 1966–), vol. 1, pp. 146–69.

49. See Nevakivi, *Britain, France and the Arab Middle East,* pp. 58f., 70–78, 190–95.

50. Weizmann to Bella Berligne, June 14, July 10, and September 10, 22, 1919, *WL* 9, pp. 155ff., 169ff., 212, 222ff.

51. Ben-Zion Dinur et al., eds., *Sefer Toldot haHagana,* (Tel-Aviv, 1964), vol. 1, pt. 2, chaps. 31, 33.

52. Weizmann to Balfour, April 9, July 23, September 26, to Frankfurter, July 10, 1919, to Vera, March 21, 29, April 19, 1920, *WL, 9,* pp. 128–32, 168ff., 188, 226f., 324ff., 330f., 336.

53. Weizmann to Sokolow, December 22, 1918, to Balfour, September 27, 1919, and to Vera, April 26, 1920, *WL* 9, pp. 82, 229f., 340f.

54. Weizmann to Zionist Commission, May 21, and June 6, to Ben-Gurion, June 6, to Sokolow, June 7, and to [David] Eder, June 8, 1919, *WL* 9, pp. 348ff., 352–60.

55. Friesel, *HaM'diniut haZionit,* pp. 140–43.

56. Brandeis to de Haas, November 22, 1917, to Alice, June 13, 1919, to Mack, December 2, 9, 1919, January 15, 1920, *BL* 4, pp. 322ff., 398ff., 439, 442–44; cf. Shapiro, *Leadership,* pp. 113–17, 129–32, Lipstadt, "Lipsky," pp. 271–75.

57. See, for example, Brandeis, "A Call to Educated Jews" and "Taking the Initiative in Palestine" in de Haas, *Louis Dembitz Brandeis,* pp. 190–200, 286ff., 290–92.

58. Brandeis to Mack et al., February 24, to de Haas and Lipsky, September 26, to Wise, November 10, and to de Haas, November 11, 1919, *BL* 4, pp. 381ff., 428, 436–37.

59. Y. Shapiro, *Leadership,* pp. 99–111, 117–28; cf. Lipstadt, "Lipsky," pp. 260–71.

60. There is no official protocol of the 1920 London Conference; see the report in the London *Jewish Chronicle,* July 9, 1920, p. 38; Bein, *Return to the Soil,* pp. 261–72.

61. Note 55 supra; cf. S. Cohen, *English Zionists,* pp. 281–82.

62. Brandeis, "Review of the London Conference," in de Haas, *Louis Dembitz Brandeis,* pp. 234–41.

63. Evyatar Friesel, "Leil haMashber bein Weizmann l'vein Brandeis," *HaZionut,* 4 (1975), pp. 146–64; cf. Y. Shapiro, *Leadership,* 145–50.

64. Weizmann, *Trial and Error,* p. 326f. In justifying his unwillingness to retire from the Supreme Court bench in order to lead the WZO, Brandeis argued that to do so could endanger "the support . . . of the American government without which we, in Palestine under the mandate, will not, in my opinion, be safe." Records of the Amer-

ican delegation to the London conference, July 14, 1920, *BPm,* reel 12, frames 547–80.

65. Ibid.

66. Brandeis' disparagement of Weizmann's character began before the 1920 clash during the earlier 1919 encounter, but then it was focused on Weizmann's perceived "weakness" under pressure from veteran European Zionists rather than the "deceitfulness" and "disloyalty" alleged after 1920. Brandeis to Alice [Goldmark Brandeis], August 15, 1919, and to Frankfurter, January 6, 1920, *BL* 4, pp. 423, 443f.

67. Julius Simon, *Certain Days,* pp. 86–107; Böhm, *Zionistische Bewegung,* vol. 2, pp. 108–31.

68. For a comprehensive, analytical account of the development of Zionist fiscal policy, see Jacob Metzer, *Hon L'umi l'Vayit L'umi, 1919–1921* (Jerusalem, 1979).

69. Friesel, *HaM'diniut haZionit,* pp. 155–58, 161ff.

70. Metzer, *Hon L'umi,* pp. 102–18. Metzer (see app. 6) notes correctly that these issues of principle were not raised emphatically at the 1920 annual conference or in Brandeis' "Zeeland Memorandum" (de Haas, *Louis Dembitz Brandeis,* pp. 260–72) but arose afterwards at the ZOA Buffalo Convention of November 1920.

71. Friesel, *HaM'diniut haZionit,* pp. 158–61; J. Simon to Feiwel, September 12, to J. Berger, October 1, 1920, in Simon, *Certain Days,* pp. 216–18; Metzer, *Hon L'umi,* pp. 118–24.

72. Simon, *Certain Days,* pp. 108–11; Friesel, *HaM'diniut haZionit,* pp. 176–80.

73. Bein, *Return to the Soil,* pp. 272–80; Böhm, *Zionistische Bewegung,* vol. 2, pp. 186–99.

74. Schechtman, *Rebel and Statesman,* pp. 358–74; Friesel, *HaM'diniut haZionit,* pp. 218–21.

75. Weizmann to [Bella] Berligne, August 7, to Herbert Samuel, August 8–10, to [Morris] Rothenberg, September 25, to J. Simon, September 28, and October 17, to Ruppin, September 29, and to Vera, December 31, 1920, and January 6, 1921, *WL* 10, pp. 6, 8–10, 45f., 49–51, 64f., 123, 126.

76. Friesel, *HaM'diniut haZionit,* pp. 180–85, chaps. 8, 9.

77. Lipstadt, "Lipsky," pp. 278–88; Weizmann to Sokolow, August 21, to [Louis] Robison, August 22, to [Abraham] Tulin, August 22–31, 1920, *WL* 10, pp. 22–35.

78. Lipstadt, "Lipsky," pp. 289–97.

79. Ibid., pp. 297–310; Friesel, *HaM'diniut haZionit,* pp. 167–76, 213f.

80. Weizmann to Frankfurter, December 1, 1920, *WL* 10, pp. 104–6.

81. Weizmann to Vera, December 31, 1920, and January 6, 1921, and to the ZOA Executive, January 6, 1921, *WL* 10, 122–25, 128–37.

82. Friesel, *HaM'diniut haZionit,* pp. 228–31, app. 3. On this and ensuing developments, cf. a different view in Urofsky, *American Zionism,* pp. 285–91.

83. Friesel, *HaM'diniut haZionit,* pp. 232–33, app. 4, documents 1, 2.

84. Ibid., pp. 233–35, app. 4, documents 3, 4, 5.

85. Ibid., pp. 235ff.

Epilogue and Conclusions

1. Brandeis to Mack, Wise, de Haas, December 14, 1921, *BL* 5, pp. 36f.

2. Brandeis to Mack, Wise, de Haas, December 23, 1921, *BL* 5, pp. 38f.

3. Halpern, *Idea of the Jewish State,* chap. 6; Vital, *Origins of Zionism.*

4. Walter Laqueur, *A History of Zionism* (New York, 1972), chaps. 3, 6, 7, 9.

5. Brandeis to Frankfurter, September 4, 6, 19, 24, 25, 1922, *BL* 5, pp. 59–71; Konefsky, *Legacy of Holmes and Brandeis.*

6. Elie Kedourie, "Sir Herbert Samuel and the Government of Palestine," *The Chatham House Version,* pp. 52–81; Friesel, *HaM'diniut haZionit,* pp. 251–58.

7. Friesel, *HaM'diniut haZionit,* pp. 258–68.

8. Ibid., pp. 268–76; Weizmann to Balfour, July 8, and to Shmarya Levin, July 15, 1921, *WL* 10, 213–17; bridge note, ibid., p. 227; Ingrams, *Palestine Papers,* chap. 12.

9. Aaron S. Klieman, *Foundations of British Policy in the Arab World: The Cairo Conference of 1921* (Baltimore, 1970); see Halpern, *Idea of the Jewish State,* pp. 312–29, 345–51.

10. Friesel, *HaM'diniut haZionit,* pp. 283ff., chap. 12; cf. Schechtman, *Rebel and Statesman,* pp. 419–24.

11. Ingrams, *Palestine Papers,* chap. 13.

12. Schechtman, *Rebel and Statesman,* pp. 320ff.

13. There is no satisfactory account of this period of American Zionist history. For special aspects, see Emanuel Neumann, *In the Arena: An Autobiographical Memoir* (New York, 1976), chaps. 7, 8; Urofsky, *American Zionism,* pp. 300–23; Donald H. Miller, "History of Hadassah, 1912–1935", diss., New York University, 1965, pp. 105–45; Gilbert Klapperman, *The Story of Yeshiva University* (London, 1969), pp. 141–45.

14. Weizmann to [Louis] Robison, August 20, and September 25, to [Samson] Benderly, September 25, 1920, *WL* 10, pp. 21, 47ff.; Brandeis to Mack et al., January 8, and February 6, to [Gedalia] Bubelik (Bublick), June 5, to Mack et al., December 23, 1921, *BL* 4, pp. 522ff., 532, 564; *BL* 5, p. 39.

15. Weizmann, *Trial and Error,* pp. 327f., 337–39.

16. Sam Y. Chinitz, "The Jewish Agency and the Jewish Community in the United States," master's thesis (undated), Columbia University, pp. 2–30.

17. Urofsky, *American Zionism,* pp. 335–41.

18. Brandeis to de Haas, June 5, 1927, and to Robert Szold, April 14, 1938, *BL* 5, pp. 291ff., 599; Carol Bosworth Kutscher, "The Role of Hadassah in the American Zionist Movement, 1912–1922," diss., Brandeis University, 1975, pp. 182ff.; Brandeis to Mack, April 2, 1929, *BPm,* reel 15, frames 46–47.

19. Urofsky, *American Zionism,* pp. 337–42, 345, 346f. et passim; cf. Shapiro, *Leadership,* pp. 183–86, 191–93.

20. Urofsky, *American Zionism,* pp. 311–20; cf. Shapiro, *Leadership,* pp. 193–95.

21. Neumann, *In the Arena,* pp. 83–88; Chinitz, "Jewish Agency," pp. 35–57.

22. Urofsky, *American Zionism,* pp. 346–63; cf. Shapiro, *Leadership,* chap. 8.

23. Jerome M. Kutnick, "Non-Zionist Leadership: Felix M. Warburg, 1929–1937," diss., Brandeis University, 1983, pp. 187–99, 203–28; Brandeis to Frankfurter, September 23, 1929, and to Mack, October 20, 1929, March 9, 16, and June 11, 1930, *BL* 5, pp. 389ff., 408, 420–22, 427.

24. Brandeis to Frankfurter, September 6, 1929, and to Mack, July 20, 1930, *BL* 5, pp. 383, 436.

25. Brandeis to Mack, July 20, 1930, to Robert Szold, January 18, to Warburg, July 11, 1931, and to Wise, March 19, 1935, *BL* 5, pp. 437, 472ff., 483, 551.

26. Brandeis to Wise, May 18, 1933, November 21, 1935, and March 27, 1939, *BL* 5, pp. 516, 562, 614ff.; Weizmann, *Trial and Error,* chap. 32.

27. Ibid., chaps. 36–38.

28. Halpern, *Idea of the Jewish State,* pp. 350ff.

29. Neumann, *In the Arena,* p. 265.

30. I am indebted to Dr. Zvi Ganin for Kaplan's report of this interview to the Central Committee of Mapai, August 22, 1940. See also Isaiah Berlin's memoir, "Shlihut l'New York," *Ha'Arets,* October 3, 1972.

31. Allon Gal, *David Ben-Gurion—likrat M'dina Yehudit* (S'deh Boker, 1985).

Index

American Jews (*continued*)
  societies of, to aid immigrant Jews, 84
  and trade union movement, 85
  value of Zionism for, 99, 105
American Near East Relief, 157
American Palestine Committee, 100
American Red Cross, 157, 180, 193
American Zion Commonwealth, 259
American Zionism, 185, 200–201, 252
  and aid to Palestine, 84, 86, 89, 161, 172,
    178, 219–21, 239, 260
  and Brandeis, 4, 8, 75, 82, 88, 94, 98–
    102, 104–8, 110–12, 161, 197–98,
    204, 209, 211–14, 217–19, 222, 227,
    234, 240, 243–44, 246, 247
  Bundists and, 91
  composition of members of, 86, 107, 110
  conflicts within, 93, 104, 107, 111, 115–
    26, 154–55, 198, 211, 214
  and cultural pluralism, 88
  growth of, 111, 113–15
  and Herzl, 87–88
  in the immigrant ghetto, 86
  and Israel, 4
  meaning of, for American Jews, 99, 104–
    6, 200–201, 203–4, 214, 224
  and the Paris Peace Conference, 182,
    183, 188, 190–94, 196
  a program for, 105–6
  role of, because of World War I, 110,
    115, 153, 155, 159, 161, 172, 176,
    179–81, 190, 192
  socialists, 91, 104–5, 110, 115–16
  societies of, 85, 86, 198
  and Weizmann, 180, 184, 188, 190, 200,
    203–4, 209, 211, 212, 214, 215, 222,
    228–31, 239, 253–54, 258, 259
  and WZO, 86, 89, 93, 110, 112, 114, 197,
    211–14, 216, 221, 222, 226–28, 230,
    234, 235, 240, 243, 244, 257
American Zionist Medical Unit, 193, 218,
  256
Americanization, of Jewish immigrants, 86
Amery, Leopold, 140, 148, 149, 168, 169
Anatolia, 193, 195
Anglo-Jewish Association, 129
Anglo-Palestine Bank, 178, 179, 181
Annen-Realschule, 70, 71
Antisemitism
  in Boston, 80
  causes of, 6–7, 84
  and connection with Zionism, 5–7, 9,
    130, 205–6, 246
  and Gentiles, 5, 17, 143
  in Germany, 16–17, 51, 65, 263

and Herzl, 16–17
and the Jewish exile, 5
Jewish views of, 5, 6
in Great Britain, 143, 144, 146, 171, 179,
  180, 207, 221
and pogroms of Russia, 5, 9, 16, 32, 33,
  39, 90, 91, 96, 208
rise of, in Central Europe, 6, 263
in the United States, 84, 158, 161, 191,
  210, 266
Arabian Peninsula, 142, 195
Arabs, 176, 177, 179, 188, 189, 193, 194,
  206
  anti-Jewish violence of, in Palestine, 207,
    208, 248, 260, 261, 263
  revolt of, against the Ottoman Empire,
    140–42, 177
  revolt of, in 1936–39, 263, 264
  and Zionism, 150–52, 169, 170, 174,
    175, 177, 178, 189, 190, 207, 218,
    223, 238, 248–51, 258, 262
Armenians, 150, 157–60, 175–77, 182, 190,
  191, 194, 195, 206
Asia, 127, 141, 150
Asia Minor, 193, 195
Asquith, Herbert, 127, 129, 132, 133
Assimilation by Jews, 4, 17, 19, 169, 182
Austria-Hungary, 31, 109, 126, 181, 182
Autoemancipation
  different interpretations of, 17, 39
  and the Jews, 5, 6, 14–17
Autoemancipation, 246
Autonomy, 50, 182, 195, 251, 252

Balfour, Arthur, 47, 131–33, 135, 148, 160,
  162, 166, 167, 169, 170, 181, 186,
  194, 208, 209, 215, 234, 238, 249
Balfour Declaration, and its consequences,
  169, 171, 172, 174, 176, 177, 180–
  82, 189–91, 200, 205, 211, 253
  transformation of, into the Palestine
    Mandate, 186, 202, 251
Ballinger case, 82, 97
Bambus, Willy, 16
Barondess, Joseph, 91, 116, 117
Barton, James L., 158, 159, 191, 193
Basch, Victor, 144
Basle, 22, 34
Basle program, 24, 29, 163
Bayard, Mabel, 80
Bayard, Thomas, 80
Bayer works, 26, 37
Beirut, 181, 192, 206, 223
Belgium, 109, 126, 229